FORENSIC ART ESSENTIALS

FORENSIC ART ESSENTIALS:
A MANUAL FOR LAW
ENFORCEMENT ARTISTS

LOIS GIBSON

AMSTERDAM • BOSTON • HEIDELBERG • LONDON
NEW YORK • OXFORD • PARIS • SAN DIEGO
SAN FRANCISCO • SINGAPORE • SYDNEY • TOKYO

Academic Press is an imprint of Elsevier

ELSEVIER

Acquisitions Editor:	Jennifer Soucy
Assoc. Developmental Editor:	Kelly Weaver
Project Manager:	Phil Bugeau
Publishing Services Manager:	Sarah Hajduk
Marketing Manager:	Diane Jones
Cover Designer:	Joanne Blank

Academic Press is an imprint of Elsevier
30 Corporate Drive, Suite 400, Burlington, MA 01803, USA
525 B Street, Suite 1900, San Diego, California 92101-4495, USA
84 Theobald's Road, London WC1X 8RR, UK

This book is printed on acid-free paper. ∞

All suspects pictured are innocent unless proven guilty in a court of law.

Library of Congress Cataloging-in-Publication Data
Gibson, Lois.
    Forensic art essentials : a manual for law enforcement artists / Lois Gibson. —1st ed.
        p. cm.
    Includes bibliographical references and index.
    ISBN 978-0-12-370898-4 (hard cover : alk. paper) 1. Police artists—Handbooks, manuals, etc.
2. Criminals—Identification—Handbooks, manuals, etc. 3. Drawing—Technique—Handbooks, manuals, etc. 4. Facial reconstruction (Anthropology)—Handbooks, manuals, etc. I. Title.
    HV8073.4.G54 2007
    363.25'8–dc22

                                                                                            2007035601

British Library Cataloguing-in-Publication Data
A catalogue record for this book is available from the British Library.

ISBN: 978-0-12-370898-4

For information on all Academic Press publications
visit our Web site at www.books.elsevier.com

Printed in the United States of America
07 08 09 10 9 8 7 6 5 4 3 2 1

Working together to grow
libraries in developing countries

www.elsevier.com | www.bookaid.org | www.sabre.org

ELSEVIER   BOOK AID International   Sabre Foundation

CONTENTS

ACKNOWLEDGMENTS

Tiffany Celeste Gibson provided technical support, photography, editorial advice, sculpting, transcribing, illustrating, proofreading, and much more the entire duration of this work.

The following individuals in some capacity facilitated the solutions of crimes described in this text.

Chief Harold Hurtt, Al Amato, Lori Roberts, Dennis Gafford, Robert Tonrey, Juan Gorge, Sheriff Tommy Thomas, Danny Billingsly, Deborah Goldman, Dr. Sheryl Green, Adonna Pennington, Captain Joseph Lampignano, Lt. Ron Walker, Charles McClelland, Sgt. Stephen Morrison, Ph.D., Sgt. J. "Billy" Belk, Sherric Anderson, Christina Espinoza, Sgt. Danny Silva, M. Zamora, Ph.D., Jeff Wagner, Heidi Ruiz, Kyle Evans, Rusty Gallier, Officer Paul Deason, Harry Fikaris, Boyd Smith, "Sonny" Wright, U. P. Hernandez, C. T. Mosqueda, L. W. Hoffmaster, H. G. Welch, C. P. Abbondandolo, T. R. Hernandez, P. J. Guerrero, D. D. Shirley, G. J. Novak, L. Webber, T. J. McCorvey, D. Shorten, C. B. Douglas, Charles Smith, Tracey Lynn Deel, Sgt. Scott Dudek, Dorothy Kerr, Ed Chicoine, Claire Freidlander, David Dellaria, David Bumgartner, Lieutenant Don McWilliams, Diane Denton, Captain Bobby Adams, Sergeant Douglas Osterberg, Chief Gerie Stewart, Lee P. Brown, Judge Sam Nuchia, Norman Giles, Christina Shiets, Captain Richard D. Williams, Thomas C. Jennings, Dr. Sharon Garner-Brown, Pam Holak, Lizzy Greene Hargrove, Skip Haynes, Liz Scardino, Christa Hardin, Lin Mills, Ken Homes, Gary Tindel, Darrell Harris, Chris Forsyth, Mark Griffin, Alison Galloway, June Frost, Ben Beall, T. Walton, Mike McKenna, Emma Rodriguez, Jeannine Maughmer Miller, Eugene Yanchak, Monica Gustafson, Pete Schnieder, Ralph Yarborough, and Danny Morgan.

CHAPTER 1

THE MOST UNIQUE
ART DISCIPLINE

No other art is like forensic art. Other professional artists try to create something that is either fresh, beautiful, moving, virtuous, or inspiring. Simply put, throughout history art needed to be desirable to survive. Forensic art is the only artistic profession where the image can be poorly done, sketchy, unfinished, and otherwise flawed yet become perfect if it generates a successful outcome. No matter how poorly a sketch from a witness comes out, if it helps identify the perpetrator depicted, it becomes a perfect work.

The highest degree of difficulty in forensic art is the elusive task of pulling a face from a witness's memory. However, this is the artistic duty most frequently needed by investigators of crimes against persons. In robberies, aggravated assaults, and homicides where someone lives through the scene who saw the face of the perpetrator, a sketch yielding a vision of the attacker's face from the witness's memory can enhance investigative efforts.

Many individuals find this work so difficult that, after sketching with a victim of crime once or twice, they never do it again. Others train in forensic art, but avoid sketching with witnesses if at all possible. Artists who become skillful and at ease working with witnesses find helping investigators capture violent offenders so gratifying, they rarely care for any other kind of work thereafter. My goal is to make sketching with witnesses not only doable, but also so comfortable for the artist that it becomes his or her life's work. Here you will find techniques and methods never before shared in print, which will allow an artist to truly master the art of sketching from someone's memory.

The suggestions in this book are a compilation of determinations made after comparing over 1,142 sketches done from witnesses' memories to the subjects they saw. After each comparison, when possible, it was determined what happened during the sketch interview to cause parts of the image to be dissimilar to the face of the person described. With each case comparison, there were lessons learned about how to avoid mistakes. Conversely, methods that worked were understood when sketches came out successfully. These comparisons constitute a valid scientific study of what can be drawn from a witness's memory of the face he or she has seen. The suggestions and techniques for successful sketching in

Figure 1.1

The sketch on the left was done from the memory of a 10-year-old girl who was sexually assaulted by the man on the right. When the man saw the sketch on television news, he called the authorities and turned himself in (courtesy of the Houston Police Department).

this situation were distilled from this large sampling. You may or may not use or agree with the methods presented, but my goal is to offer ways to avoid mistakes, and methods to gain a better likeness in your efforts to help identify sought-after criminals.

Figure 1.1 consists of an extremely flawed sketch next to a man who some might say looks similar. This sketch was done from a description given by a sexually assaulted 10-year-old girl of her attacker. After seeing the sketch on his television, this man called the police and *turned himself in*. The detective got a confession, the little girl picked the man out of a lineup, and ancillary evidence led to his conviction.[1] Therefore, this sketch helped solve this egregious crime.

Understanding how and why this defective sketch performed perfectly is one of the most important lessons in this book. The beginning forensic artist should understand that you can start working in this field with at least this caliber of drawing skill and be successful. The investigators can realize the sketch obviously does not need to be perfect to help them find the man for whom they search. It is a *forensic sketch*. This means it has a utilitarian purpose. Since this pitiful sketch fulfilled its purpose perfectly, the creator need not worry about the virtuosity of the artwork.

This book will not be a showcase of the most perfect sketches I've done. Instead, I provide imperfect sketches, in order to teach the most important lessons. Explanations of how the sketch was created, details of the interview, and what went wrong will be given in detail. An explanation of why mistakes were made will help illustrate how to avoid them. Most importantly, you will understand how those sketches with all those mistakes still represent successful work because they helped reveal the identity of the criminal to the investigator.

If you are someone who has delved into art in any capacity, you know it is unheard of for an artist *not* to aim to do the most virtuous work possible. In this line of work, if you can let your pride go and keep your head in the game—that *catching the criminal* is more important than work that *looks good*—you can be successful. For all of history, it has been the artist's goal to please people with the beauty of his or her creations. In the profession of forensic art, if the sketch helps identify the person being described, the artist is free to sketch in any manner. A very ugly sketch can be the one that helps the investigator solve the case, so that ugly sketch can be thoroughly fulfilling. This, in a manner of speaking, is the "good news."

The "bad news" is that were he or she to speak candidly, not one witness really thinks you can do this work, before, or in the beginning stages of the sketch.

At the very best, the witness seriously doubts the sketch can possibly capture the face of the suspect sufficiently to help solve the case. Added to this is the fact that many witnesses are immensely traumatized. Thus the forensic artist is faced with a frustrating combination of a highly traumatized witness who doesn't believe there is any reason to be working with that artist.

> The amazing paradox is that 100% of the time, when a sketch is done from a witness who is not lying about the incident, if the artist is reasonably talented and reasonably trained, the sketch will come out looking *at least similar* to the person being described. Having said that, there are some poor likenesses that have helped identify the perpetrator. Therefore to succeed, the composite artist must ignore the negative expectations of the witness, and be satisfied that an imperfect sketch can bring success.

The first consideration is that 100% of the information the forensic artist has is in the mind of the witness, so the artist must do everything possible to make it conducive for his or her witness to remember the face of the perpetrator. However, almost all witnesses will say some version of the following:

- I don't know why you think I can do this…
- I don't think I can remember enough to do a sketch…
- It was too quick…
- All I saw was the gun…
- I was too scared…
- It was too dark…
- It's been too long…

If forensic artists believed these kinds of comments, there would be no composites created. Instead of being dissuaded, realize the witness is doing some needed venting. Never argue with these kinds of comments. Talking this way helps the witness get rid of frustrations over the whole situation and become more relaxed. Since relaxation of the witness is one of the most important goals for the interviewer, listen patiently and pleasantly—but don't believe him or her. Thousands of successful composites have been created from witnesses who were adamant in declaring in the beginning of the interview that they would not be able to remember enough to do a sketch.

Knowing this, you must deduce the following to be able to work in this profession. First, you will have to be extremely patient with reluctant, agitated witnesses. Expecting their attitude that they can't work with you should put you at ease and help you not to take it personally. Witnesses resist the efforts of the forensic artists; anticipating this will help you keep on track in spite of the protestations.

Other effective methods used to pull out the vision of attackers from witnesses will be described in the following pages. These are methods and hints I have gleaned from more than 24 years sketching with witnesses where the images created have helped identify over a thousand perpetrators of crime. My hope is to save you from learning many lessons the hard way—by making mistakes. Besides saving you from mistakes, I hope to provide methods perfected over time that will put you far ahead of previous forensic artists.

In Brief
Sketching a face from a witness's description is the most frequently needed task. It is also the most difficult forensic-art duty, since the witness is traumatized and almost never thinks the task can be performed. Knowing to expect this can help the artist succeed no matter what barriers the witness puts up.

GETTING RELAXED

The session of sketching from a witness memory can be so difficult that every effort should be made to make that encounter as comfortable as possible. Knowing that you should ignore the witnesses' doubts should keep your nerves soothed during their protestations. But there are other obstacles to overcome. In the early days artists and investigators would not do sketches when they heard the litany of reasons the witness had for not doing the sketch. Individuals who survived events, after which conventional wisdom would dictate they could not help create a usable sketch, nevertheless have been able to remember enough to make a recognizable image with the forensic artist. Understanding the seemingly impossible situations where favorable sketches resulted will take away the most uncomfortable feeling an artist can have—self-doubt.

For the purpose of discussing the forensic art profession, the term *successful sketch* must be defined.

A forensic sketch is successful if it helps identify the perpetrator of the crime.

Forensic artists should know successful sketches were obtained from:

■ A witness who was a 5-year-old sexual assault survivor[2]

Figure 1.2

The sketch on the left was done with a 5-year-old who was sexually assaulted by the man on the right. His arrest later for public intoxication led to a line-up that identified him as the perpetrator. The exact age of the witness was 5 years 3 months (courtesy of the Houston Police Department).

■ A witness who was inebriated[3]

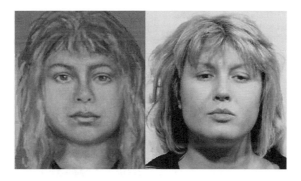

Figure 1.3

The sketch on the left was from a man who was drugged and robbed by the woman on the right. Her fingerprint at a scene and striking resemblance to the sketch identified her to detectives, and the witness picked her out in a line-up (courtesy of the Houston Police Department). See color plate.

■ An unarmed security guard shot three times during a homicide[4]

Figure 1.4

The sketch on the left was done in a hospital intensive care unit from a security guard shot three times by the man on the right. This shooter wore a wig and glasses during the crime. He received the death penalty for killing a jeweler that same night (courtesy of the Houston Police Department).

■ An officer shot twice and run over and dragged under a vehicle 60 feet[5]

Figure 1.5

The sketch on the left was done in a hospital intensive care unit with an officer who was shot twice, run over, and dragged over 60 feet by the man on the right. His resemblance to the sketch led to a lineup that identified him (courtesy of the Houston Police Department).

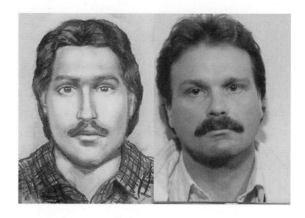

■ A mother whose 10-hour-old baby had been kidnapped by a stranger[6]

Figure 1.6

The sketch on the left was done in a maternity ward from a mother after her 10-hour-old baby was kidnapped by the woman on the right. The sketch was released and a friend of this kidnapper called authorities. The baby was returned safely that night (courtesy of the Houston Police Department). See color plate.

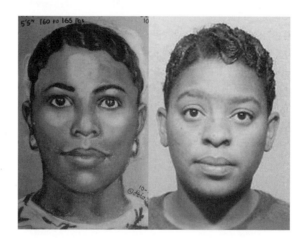

■ A witness who saw the perpetrator drive by while shooting, at 65 miles per hour[7]

Figure 1.7

The sketch on the left was done with three young men. While driving at 60 mph, they saw the man on the right drive up along side them and shoot their driver in the head. A caller identified him when the case aired on Crime Stoppers *(courtesy of the Houston Police Department).*

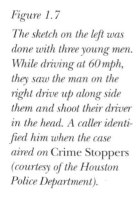

- A witness who was trying to lie[8]

- A witness who had only one-fourth of a second glance of a face in motion (at 45 mph)[9]

- A witness who was completely disinterested in the perpetrator observed[10]

- A 9-year-old girl who saw her mother raped and strangled to death, and was herself raped by the same man[11]

Figure 1.11

The sketch on the left was done with a 9-year-old girl who saw this man hogtie, rape, and strangle her mother to death before assaulting her. Detectives used the sketch in identifying him. He received the death sentence and was executed the year the witness turned 16 (courtesy of the Houston Police Department).

- A witness who saw the perpetrator's profile only in her peripheral vision[12]

Figure 1.12

The sketch on the left was done with a bus driver who saw the man on the right in profile in her peripheral vision as he followed his victim, a 6-months-pregnant blind woman, off the bus. The sketch led to his identity (courtesy of the Houston Police Department).

- A 9-year-old boy who described a person wearing a hat and sunglasses who kidnapped his 6-year-old brother[13]

Figure 1.13

The sketch on the left was done with a 9-year-old boy who saw his brother kidnapped by the man pictured on the right. The sketch was shown on TV in jail, and a woman told her cellmate his name. The cellmate notified detectives and the case was solved (courtesy of the Houston Police Department).

■ A witness who saw his parents shot to death, then was himself shot twice as he crashed through a screen door to escape[14]

Figure 1.14

The sketch on the left was taken from the memory of a witness who had seen this man's partner shoot his elderly parents to death. The partner then shot the witness twice as he crashed through a screen door to escape (courtesy of the Houston Police Department).

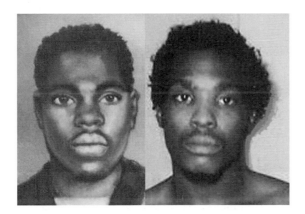

Figure 1.15

The sketch on the left was taken from the memory of a witness who had seen the man on the right shoot his elderly parents to death. The man then shot the witness twice as he crashed through a screen door to escape (courtesy of the Houston Police Department).

■ A woman who was shot 15 times, two in the head, four in the neck, and who lost an eye and seven teeth[15]

Figure 1.16

The sketch on the left was done with a woman who was robbed, taken to a field, and shot 15 times. The shots took out her eye and several of her teeth. The man on the right was tried and sentenced to life in prison (courtesy of the Houston Police Department).

■ A witness who insisted she never saw the perpetrator's face[16]

Figure 1.17

The sketch on the left was done with a woman who had an assault rifle pointed in her face by the man on the right. She insisted she never saw the rifleman's face. He was identified, charged, made bail, and is now a wanted fugitive (courtesy of the Houston Police Department).

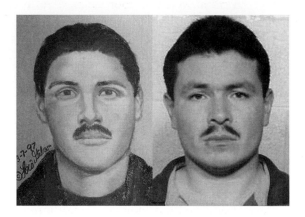

This is not an exhaustive list of seemingly impossible forensic sketching situations. Every law enforcement artist has new stories to tell of witnesses who endured unspeakable trauma and yet were able to help them develop a usable sketch.

Methods of sketching in these difficult cases will be examined in great detail in later chapters. A description of what the witness experienced while viewing the perpetrator's face, and what methods the artist used to develop an image from that witness's memory will be detailed. The sketch and mug shot of the person described will be included for examination.

In Brief

Witnesses have been able to give successful sketches after enduring the most harrowing emotional and/or physical trauma.

THE MOST BASIC RULES OF COMPOSITE SKETCH CREATION

Sketch in private with the witness in order to maximize his or her comfort.

Since relaxation is the best enhancement to memory, the sketch should be done with only the witness and the artist in the room.

One exception would be a child younger than 5 years of age. In that case, the mother or other adult relative *with whom the child feels most comfortable* might need to be in the room. The other exception would be if the artist is a female or male and the witness is the opposite sex and of the Islamic faith. There is a verse in the Quran that essentially states it is evil for a man and a woman who are not married to be alone in a room with the door closed. The interview can be conducted alone in a room with the door open. The interviewer should notify surrounding personnel of the need for quiet.

The detective or other officers should not be allowed in the interview room to observe the sketching process. If the artist is new to the profession and/or law enforcement agency, the detectives' curiosity about the process might override the need for a comfortable interview. But the worst persons to have in the room during a forensic sketch are authority figures from the department. Even practiced artists who are officers try to dress in casual civilian clothes to avoid this kind of "authoritarian" appearance.

Many tasks, which take good quality concentration, are best done alone. Some of these tasks would be studying for an exam, reading complicated directions, or bathroom activities. The last is mentioned because of the embarrassment that would be caused if someone were watching. The act of talking about being sexually assaulted or even robbed at gunpoint can be extremely embarrassing. Add to the embarrassment the mental strain of trying to recall a face that represents terror to the interviewee and this renders the situation as being doubly in need of privacy.

The way to minimize disturbing the witness's concentration is for the artist to be as unobtrusive as possible. Start with voice tone; use the softest voice possible. Speak as if you wanted to lull the witness to sleep or into a meditative state (obvious exceptions to this rule are persons with hearing impairments).

Special care should be taken with children regarding voice. Children usually have an acute sense of hearing compared to adults. A good rule is to speak far more softly than what you think is normal when interviewing children. When a child seems to be straining to hear, pick up the volume a bit and keep it at that level.

Children appreciate being talked to like adults. They consider you to be "talking down" to them if you use baby talk or speak to them in a motherly or fatherly manner. Act like they are adults, but keep the vocabulary simple enough for them to understand.

Conversely, if the witness is an adult who seems to need a louder voice, try your best to find the optimum level without going too far.

POSITION THE WITNESS AND ARTIST TO MAXIMIZE PRIVACY

The placement of the witness in relation to the artist in the interview area should be done with the goal of maximizing the witness's relaxation. To reach this goal the witness needs to feel as private as possible. Having survived a near-death experience during an aggravated assault, I can give concise advice on this part of the sketching process.

> The artist should sit far enough away from the witness so that were he or she to extend his or her hand, it would not reach the witness.

Since almost all witnesses probably thought they were going to die during the crime they survived, they are understandably skittish about people being near them. Some survivors might not mind someone they just met sitting next to them. However, many crime victims feel revolted by others and even have irrational urges to physically attack their own loved ones as a reaction to their ordeal. Considering the added stress that could be imposed by working near a witness who is too polite to ask them to move away, the artist should not take a chance and sit next to *any* witness. This small incursion into the witness's personal space could affect the quality of the sketch created in ways that would diminish its impact on the case. See Figure 1.18 for an arrangement of the witness and artist that works best for maintaining the comfort and privacy of the witness.

Figure 1.18

Here is the suggested arrangement for maximum witness comfort. The artist is far enough from the witness so that he or she could not be reached with an outstretched hand. The easel creates a barrier between witness and artist and allows attachment of visual aids directly to the drawing board (photo by author).

> The artist should use an easel.

The basic, time-honored piece of equipment, the easel, is indispensable for serious drawing.[17] For the forensic artist, an easel has special features that greatly enhance the interview with a witness. When the easel is set between the witness and the artist, it serves as a "shield" that keeps the two from seeing each other unless the artist leans slightly to the side and peers around the drawing board. This barrier helps witnesses feel as if they are somewhat alone and enhances their concentration as they peruse the visual aids. The drawing board on the easel keeps the witness from focusing on the artist's face, and keeps the witness from feeling like he or she is being stared at.

Besides the comfort of the witness, an easel gives the artist maximum comfort during the stressful forensic sketch interview. Additionally, true professional artists know the best drawing mechanics dictate positioning between drawing and artist that only an easel offers. Brian Curtis, in his 2002 drawing textbook, *Drawing from Observation* (McGraw Hill), states, "When you draw it is important to position the surface of your

paper at a right angle (90°) to your line of sight. The center of the paper should be at your shoulder level. Establishing this 90° relationship with the drawing surface occurs naturally when you are standing or seated at an easel…. If you do choose to work at a drawing bench, be sure to keep the end of the drawing board out of your lap. Putting the board in your lap causes serious deterioration of the viewing angle."

> Witnesses should feel comfortable enough to close their eyes as they activate their visual memory.

The feeling of being observed is distracting while trying to remember the face of the attacker, since that activity almost always requires the individual to close his or her eyes. Since it is nearly impossible to close one's eyes if it is perceived one is being stared at, the interviewer should close his or her eyes when peering around the easel to ask questions during the witness's use of the visual aids. An effective practice during the interview is to ask as many of the questions as possible with your eyes *closed*. If witnesses see the interviewer closing his or her eyes, it gives them permission to close *their* eyes. This closed-eye look should be accompanied with your body and face aimed away from the witness. Face in a direction off to the side of the witness's line of gaze, and with your head tilted slightly down, ask the questions with closed eyes. Even if the witness starts out looking at you, eventually he or she will close his or her eyes, too, and be more relaxed. All of this adds to a relaxed, private atmosphere in the interview room. Never let the witness open his or her eyes to find you staring.

> Use visual aids.

It is much easier and quicker for witnesses to see a photo that reminds them of the face they are trying to remember than for them to create numerous words to describe the features. Even the most nonverbal witness can see a photo of a complicated feature and by simply pointing to that feature, convey dozens of words to the artist. It should be obvious visual aids are mandatory when the person cannot speak, the language barrier is prohibitive, or the person is too young to possess the verbal skills to describe the facial features. However, even the most intelligent, articulate witness will find it far easier to convey what he or she remembers to the artist by using photos of various features as references to aid recall.

The neurological explanation of why visual aids should be used to help witnesses recall the face of their attacker is illustrated in Figure 1.19 and can be summed up as follows:

1. When the witness sees an attacker's face, that image is recorded in the part of the brain known as the *visual cortex*.
2. To come up with the language necessary to describe the face that he or she saw, he or she has to use a different part of the brain, known as the *angular gyrus,* which transforms the visual image into a sound pattern, which is then sent by the brain to yet a third part, called *Wernicke's area.*
3. For the witness to take that language and then speak it out loud, all this information then needs to be transmitted to yet another part of the brain, known as *Broca's area*, which issues instructions for the necessary muscle movements needed to create speech.
4. After that, the part of the brain known as the *motor cortex* orders the muscles of the speech organs to move and alerts the cerebellum to coordinate their movement.[18]

That is, *if the correct words are even known*. With young children, for instance, or people who've suffered head injuries or other incapacitating wounds, the verbal description of what they see in their mind may not be available for all these various brain transactions to take place.

In the beginning of my career, I created forensic sketches without visual aids. Such a process can be done; however, even with an eager, articulate witness, without visual aids the sketch can take hours longer and is an exhausting process for both the crime victim and the artist.

On the other hand, when someone is shown a picture similar to what he or she saw, that information is received in the same part of the brain—the *visual cortex*—as when he or she saw the attacker's face. This recognition happens instantly and the witness needs only to point at that photo and the information is conveyed.[19]

Figure 1.19

On the left is the direct process of visual information entering the eye and being received by the visual cortex. The diagrams second and third from the left show the tasks needed to describe that feature. For a detailed explanation see text under "Use visual aids" (drawing by author).

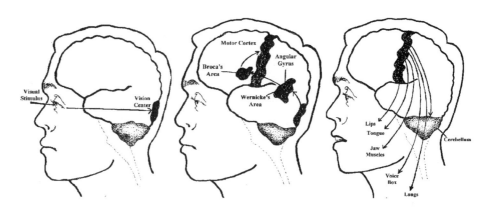

Lastly, the visual aids give a more accurate communication of the visual information needed by the artist. An individual could say many words about a mouth and yet no words can accurately describe *all* areas of the mouth. With a photo reference, the artist can see every square millimeter of the mouth. The guesswork for the artist is eliminated, thus saving precious time. An example of this is Figure 1.20. This is one of the first sketches I did using visual aids. Juxtaposed are photos of the face and lips of the woman described. Notice all the accurate shadow patterns in and around the lips.

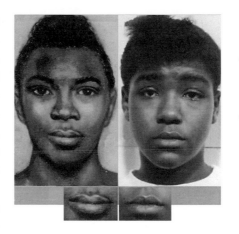

Figure 1.20

On the left is one of the first sketches I did using visual aids; on the right is the person who was described. The witness for this sketch saw this woman for less than 5 seconds, during which time this woman was shouting obscenities (courtesy of the Houston Police Department).

THE FBI FACIAL IDENTIFICATION CATALOG

The Federal Bureau of Investigation's Graphic Design Unit of the Special Projects Section of the Laboratory Division created the *FBI Facial Identification Catalog* in the 1980s. This reference is commonly used in forensic art and has helped artists in the profession identify thousands of suspects. Figure 1.21 shows the cover of this catalog and Figure 1.22 is the "Bulging Eyes" page.

This compact compilation of visual aids for features needed when sketching suspects is a good tool to start the forensic interview. For photos of ethnic types that might not be in this catalog, the artist should obtain mug shots of those types of individuals residing in the area worked by that particular artist's agencies. There would be no one book that could possibly cover all nationalities, nor is there a need for one. Instead, the best method would be to have photos of persons who reside in the population the artist serves. If mug shots are not available, an artist can make good copies of high school and college yearbooks. Since the majority of criminals are far under the age of 40 years, these populations would almost always fit into the age group of the perpetrators described.

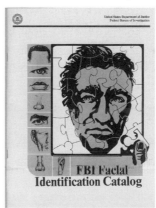

Figure 1.21

The cover of the FBI Facial Identification Catalog, *a compact collection of features commonly used by forensic artists (courtesy of the Federal Bureau of Investigation).*

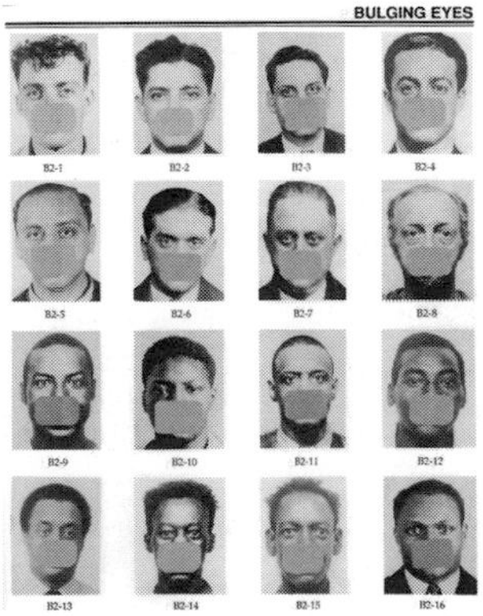

Figure 1.22

Here is the "Bulging Eyes" page from the FBI Facial Identification Catalog. *This catalog has 208 different sets of eyes from which to choose (courtesy of the Federal Bureau of Investigation).*

OTHER VISUAL AIDS FOR FACIAL FEATURES

Many forensic artists have gathered a collection of mug shots and categorized them for use similar to, but more expansive than, the FBI catalog. As an example they will have a stack of "white males," "Latino males," "white females," and so on. Some of these collections can be quite elaborate, with various stacks for hairstyle types, nose types, eyebrow types, and others. This method can allow for a larger array of features and ethnicities. There is probably an optimum amount of examples that can be shown before the witness becomes exhausted. A general approximation of too many mug shots for the witness to look at would be over 100 per feature. Another indication for this mug-shot method is that some witnesses prefer color photos. Also, the mug-shot method has the entire face without the blocking out of various features as in the FBI catalog.

Samantha Steinberg of Miami, Florida, is the lead forensic artist at the largest police department in the southeastern United States. She spent a great deal of time compiling a catalog with ethnic features from her area of South Florida; this book is called *Steinberg's Facial Identification Catalog* (the cover is shown in Figure 1.23). I obtained several copies and was thrilled to have them around when, the day after receiving them, I had a witness who described a suspect with dred locks. Using the "Dreded Hair" page as shown in Figure 1.24, I saved a lot of time when the witness was able to just point out one of the photos instead of spending a long time showing me how the dred locks were short over the cheeks, a few just hung down on the forehead, then the locks were longer in the back, and so on. Instead the witness picked out example J6-12, and I was able to start drawing immediately.

Samantha has made these catalogs available on her web site: SamanthaSteinberg.com. Some other sample pages are seen in Figures 1.25 and 1.26, the "Heavy Brows" and "Close Set Eyes" pages, respectively. Ideally all regions of the country should have this type of book. Samantha Steinberg is to be commended for exerting such a great amount of time and effort to compile this helpful visual aid.

Here is a special caveat when using mug shots. Make it abundantly clear to the witness that the suspect in his or her case is *not* in the examples he or she will be examining. First of all, if the witness thinks he or she is looking for *his or her* suspect, the witness

Figure 1.23

The cover of Samantha Steinberg's Facial Identification Catalog, *which was created to customize her visual aids to reflect the population of her area. Other artists would do well to follow Steinberg's lead in their area (courtesy of Samantha Steinberg).*

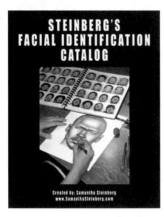

Figure 1.24

The page from Steinberg's Facial Identification Catalog *depicting individuals wearing various "dred-lock" hair styles (courtesy of Samantha Steinberg).*

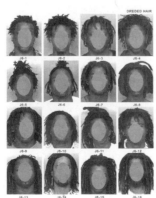

will not search for similar features to construct the face of their perpetrator for a drawing. Time will be lost as he or she goes through hundreds of mug shots trying to find the exact person. Second, if the witness finds his or her attacker among the photos, his or her search can be considered a valid "photo-spread line-up" since you told him or her the suspect was *not* among those through whom he or she would search.

This has happened to several forensic artists on rare occasions. If the interviewer says the suspect *is* among the group of photos, that would be considered faulty instructions for a photo line-up. Conversely, if the witness is told *not* to expect to find the suspect, it becomes an unbiased photo line-up if the right photo *does* turn up. If this unusual event happens to you, the artist, be prepared to gather up the mug shots the witness viewed prior to finding the suspect to submit to the court as part of the photo line-up that just occurred. In other words, the detective submits the group of photos shown to the witness before he or she picked out the suspect. This proves the extensive line-up you performed. If your witness looked at 65 photos before spotting the actual suspect, gather the previous 65 photos to show the court the group from which the accused was selected.

Another warning is that some detectives may become unjustifiably angry when this unusual event occurs. The detective has no reason to be angry. The case has simply been solved in a manner unfamiliar to him or her. Most detectives will realize if you first told the witness his or her suspect wouldn't be among the photo group, and you further ended up showing that witness far in excess of six photos before the perpetrator was picked out, you have conducted an extremely fair photo line-up.

Figure 1.27 is a case study where just such a mug shot search allowed the witness to discover his attacker. The artist had tried to draw this particular aggravated robber three times with witnesses to three other crimes. Detectives estimated he had committed more than 30 robberies over a period of five years. During a session trying to sketch an

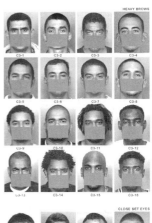

Figure 1.25

The "Heavy Brows" page from Steinberg's Facial Identification Catalog *(courtesy of Samantha Steinberg).*

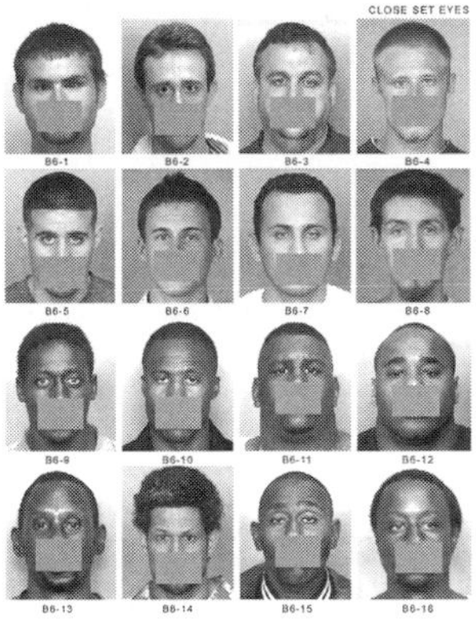

Figure 1.26

The "Close Set Eyes" page from Steinberg's Facial Identification Catalog *(courtesy of Samantha Steinberg).*

Figure 1.27

The sketch on the left was done with a witness robbed by the man on the right. He was identified when I gave a stack of photos to another witness, who identified this man after looking through more than 100 pictures (courtesy of the Houston Police Department).

aggravated robber on August 21, 1996, the artist gave the witness a stack of mug shots after she had completed half the sketch and the witness had made all his choices of features from the *FBI Facial Identification Catalog*. The detective had informed the artist he was certain the robber being described was the same individual for whom he had been searching for years. Because of the detective's urgency, the artist handed the witness a stack of over 200 mug shots of African-American males and said a close approximation of the following:

"Your robber is not in this stack of pictures. I have a good idea of the features from the ones you picked from the book. I want you to just look through here and see if there is any feature—a nose, some lips, whatever feature you might find—that is *especially* similar to the man who robbed you. You have plenty of time before I finish the sketch, so relax and just look through the photos."

After looking through over 100 photos, the witness notified the artist that one photo was the man who robbed him. When the detective learned of the development, he looked up the man's address and found a vehicle parked outside that matched the car description from the scene of the robbery. He obtained a warrant for the suspect's residence, where the detective found items stolen from many of the previous robberies. After filing charges, he returned to the artist's office and took possession of the stack of photos through which his witness had searched. At the detective's request, the stack had been kept in the same order as when the witness had perused them. The suspect was convicted of seven robberies, two sexual assaults, and one shooting. He was suspected in 70 other robberies in surrounding counties. He received three life sentences. This is an example where an artist conducted a somewhat unconventional but valid photo line-up that identified a perpetrator, and further, where the line-up held up in court.[20]

When using visual aids, I prefer to start with the compact FBI catalog and then go to the mug shots to fine-tune the feature choices. As an example, the witness might look through the stack of mug shots to find a hairstyle not found in the FBI catalog. While looking for the hairstyle, the witness might come upon a face shape or eyebrows that have a striking resemblance to the suspect's. If the witness is exhausted, highly traumatized, or in the hospital, the interview might not get as far as the mug-shot stage and still be a successful drawing. For just such a composite, see Figure 1.28. This perpetrator had such thick glasses

Figure 1.28

This composite was created using only the FBI Facial Identification Catalog *since the thick glasses and drastic features didn't need any refining from the witness searching through mug shots (courtesy of the Houston Police Department).*

and other drastic features that there was no need to further refine the image by having the distressed witness search mug shots for additional details. He was caught by patrol officers within hours after they received the sketch on a bulletin during rollcall.[21]

Always be ready to sketch with no visual aid if the witness wants to describe a feature in detail.

If the witness makes any type of sketch, even if it is crude, never hand the drawing back. This drawing is an important piece of visual information, no matter how poorly it is rendered, and to give it back is a needless act of rejection on the artist's part. The fact that the witness has put him- or herself into a visual mode and attempted to communicate with the artist in this manner offers a strong line of communication. Always take the drawing and study it attentively. Then, using a piece of masking tape, attach the witness drawing to your drawing board, giving it the status it deserves: a piece of visual information to which you can refer during the creation of the suspect sketch.

Figure 1.29 shows three drawings done by complainants before their sessions with me. The top left drawing was from a woman in her 70s who was attacked by the man in the photo to the right who was 6' 11". The middle witness sketch on the left was from an assault victim who got caught in the middle of a shootout between the man in the photo in the center of the page and an off-duty arson investigator. The bottom left sketch was by a talented artist who was nearly beaten to death by the man pictured mid-bottom; he was caught after the sketch on the bottom right was circulated among patrol officers in the area of the attack.

Each drawing was given to me by the witness as an opening gesture in a sincere effort to help create the sketch from memory. Even the crudest drawing was treated with utmost respect; notice how the drawings truly do bear a resemblance to the identified suspect. These sketches all convey helpful visual information. To put the witness's drawing on the drawing board during the interview is an ingratiating gesture that at the very least improves the mood of the interview, and obviously in some cases offers good visual help for the artist.

Figure 1.29

Left, top to bottom, sketches drawn by witnesses and given to the me before the sketch interview. Middle, photos of the perpetrators. Right, top to bottom, sketches by author (courtesy of the Houston Police Department and witnesses from Houston Police Department Incident Numbers from top to bottom, 54461791, 5642792, and 37673203).

Be deliberate and purposeful when using visual aids. Most importantly, the artist must replicate the feature chosen as perfectly as possible. This visual aid is the closest the artist can come to seeing what the witness saw. It is of no use if the features chosen are not respected and are drawn inaccurately.

Early in my career, a child chose some features for the sketch of his attacker from visual aids. When the perpetrator was caught, it was noticed that there were some features that, had I adhered strictly to the visual aids, would have provided an amazing likeness. All the portions that were dissimilar were instances where the visual aid had not been replicated as exactly as possible. Avoiding this mistake from that sketch onward has contributed to the success of subsequent sketches.

> **Be able, skillful, and willing to modify the sketch at the witness's direction.**

The sketch should be done on an easel with the drawing board facing away from the witness. Thus the first part of the sketch is done out of the sight of the witness. Since the witness cannot see the sketch in the beginning stages, you can struggle with the most awkward part of this drawing ordeal in virtual privacy. This most challenging early stage of the drawing, which is lining up the features in the right size and distance from each other, is easier without the distraction of being watched. Not watching the beginning drawing stages also keeps the witness from being "led along" by the drawing. Instead, the witness is constantly trying to delve into his or her memory. This keeps the artist from contaminating the witness's memory, and from a legal standpoint, if the easel is turned away from the witness while the features are being decided, then all the information comes from the witness.

When the hard-to-manage part of constructing a human-looking face from patching together the various features indicated by the witness is done, you can turn the lighted easel around and show the witness what should be termed the "rough sketch." Referring to the work at this point as a rough sketch gives the impression you are ready to work on the drawing some more. This is a good thing, since even little changes the witness feels comfortable enough requesting can make a big difference in the appearance of the face drawn.

Before turning the easel around, make it *abundantly clear* that you are ready and willing to change *anything the witness indicates* in order to make the drawing look as much like the perpetrator as possible. This is crucial, as some witnesses will be too shy or otherwise inhibited about telling the artist to do anything different. If you do not make this concept clear, the witness could end up, after the sketch is finished, telling the investigator the sketch was OK, except this or that needed to be changed. Keep this from happening by communicating you are willing and open to change. Do not intimidate the witness by your mannerisms in this regard. Be confident, but convey that you are the vessel that creates the image and the witness is the person with superior knowledge as to what the sketch should look like. Never forget, the witness has all the information. You are only a vehicle to produce the visual information the witness possesses.

One enemy to this last part of the sketching session is slow work. As witnesses attempt to retain the image of the face they saw in their mind while looking at an artist's sketch, they will be frustrated and confused if the changes for which they ask take too long. No matter how difficult the change or uncomfortable it is to sketch rapidly, you must appear as if the work is effortless. Maintaining an easy demeanor while making requested changes will signal to witnesses that any and all changes are welcome if it will bring the sketch to a closer likeness of the person they've seen.

Compare this appearance of carefree sketching to Olympic ice skaters. These skaters show pleasant expressions as the music plays and they carry out their incredibly difficult routines with seeming ease and grace. It is certain they are stretched to the limit, barely able to concentrate on one amazing move after another, yet the appearance to observers is smooth professionalism. The artist who is asked to change a drawing to bring it in line with the witness's memory has more at stake than a skater. If the witness is made to feel comfortable with guiding the changes, a murderer can be taken off the streets, which can save lives. If the effortless demeanor of the artist allows the witness to feel comfortable with making that one last change that helps bring in his or her attacker, then the artist's composure is worth it.

In conclusion, the last part of the sketch, where the artist makes changes at the witness's bidding, is the most difficult, and yet must be done with speed, agility, and patient willingness.

In Brief
The three most basic rules of composite sketch creation are:
1. Sketch in private with the witness.
2. Use visual aids and replicate them as exactly as possible.
3. Be able, skillful, and willing to modify the sketch at the witness's direction.

GETTING STARTED—MATERIALS AND SUPPLIES

The majority of forensic artists use graphite pencils on white paper, usually Bristol board with a vellum finish. I use different shades of warm gray pastel on felt gray Canson Mi-Tientes paper (often simply called "Canson"), using the smooth side. Since the vast majority of artists use the graphite pencil method, those materials will be described in depth here. Since the act of drawing from a witness's memory is such a difficult, uncomfortable, unnatural act, the medium used should be the one with which you are most comfortable. Use the medium you can control the best. The only rule is you should not use a medium that is difficult to erase or change. Since the witness needs to see changes done quickly, the medium should be easily and effectively erased, and changes should be added rapidly and in a seamless manner. Therefore, any medium you find that meets this criterion and with which you are supremely comfortable can be used.

PAPER

Paper used for composites must last for dozens of years. In fine art this is termed *archival paper*. For instance, oil paintings are considered archival in nature because they can last many hundreds of years. Since there is no statute of limitations on murder, your sketch on such a case might be entered into evidence in courts of law to be viewed many years after your work is done. For this reason newsprint or any cheap drawing paper is unacceptable for forensic art. Bristol board is a thick, durable paper that withstands vigorous and multiple erasures and is archival in nature. For those wishing to use pastels, be aware there are mid-eighteenth century drawings on Canson Mi-Tientes paper that hang beautifully intact in museums today, so this paper is definitely archival.

The majority of forensic artists prefer the *vellum* or textured surface on their Bristol board. An artist who uses the smooth surface is usually after fine details. The act of sketching a composite should be fast and generalized. The urge for tiny details would be an enemy to sketching in this situation. Additionally the texture tends to hide flaws in the drawing, a much-needed feature in the tense, time-sensitive situation of forensic sketching. For these reasons, sketching on the textured (vellum) side will probably yield the best results.

The smooth side of Canson Mi-Tientes paper is actually as textured as the vellum Bristol board. Some artists use the *pebble* side of Canson. However, this texture is very deep and could be distracting to artists and witnesses. "Felt gray" is the Canson Mi-Tientes color that seems to lend itself to a black-and-white sketch best. However, Canson comes in five shades of gray and they are, from lightest to darkest, Pearl, Felt Gray, Flannel Gray, Moonstone, and Steel Gray. A good strategy for paper color choice would be to find several shades of dark to light pastel sticks in a neutral color and then choose the paper color that matches that brand of pastels the best.

Artists who use these colored papers are able to draw in the highlights and create a three-dimensional look in their two-dimensional drawings.

Size of Paper

In general the image should be sketched life size. Any attempts to sketch smaller will make the act of sketching unnecessarily difficult. If at first you draw your faces smaller than the distance from the heal of your palm to the tip of your fingers (the approximate length of your face), then quickly compel yourself to sketch larger until your image is this "face" size. This will make it easier to create changes and construct the tinier facial elements such as eyelids and lashes. For this size, the paper's drawing surface should be approximately 12″×9″.

Since various people such as investigators, photo-lab, and courtroom personnel will handle the sketch, it needs to be protected from smearing. The perfect way to accomplish this is to sketch on a double-wide size of paper so a fold-over cover sheet is in place to protect the drawing. In other words, use a piece of paper twice the size of the sketching surface. Fold the left half behind the right half, which becomes the drawing surface as it is taped to the drawing board. This way, half of the paper is behind the drawing, serving as a pad. Then when the drawing is done, the folded back portion is simply folded on top of the drawing like the front of a greeting card, thus protecting the drawing from any distortions caused by handling.

Here is how to create the right size sketch with its own cover sheet. Bristol board is commonly sold in pads of 18″×24″ sheets. Take one of these sheets and cut it in half horizontally as shown in Figure 1.30. This leaves two sheets of 18″×12″ paper, which if folded in half yields a 12″×9″ drawing surface with a sheet underneath that can be folded on top for protection when finished with the drawing, as seen in Figure 1.31. Since the Canson Mi-Tientes dimensions, at 25½″×19½″, are almost identical to the Bristol board, the same procedure would yield an almost identical sketching surface area and shape. The process

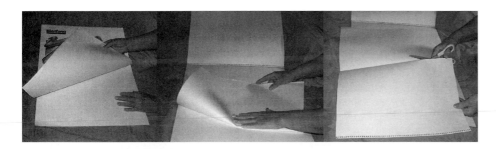

Figure 1.30

To equip your drawing with a built-in cover sheet, take an 18″ ×24″ sheet of Bristol board and cut it in half.

Figure 1.31

Fold the half sheet in half and tape this double thickness to your drawing board. After creating the sketch, bring the back sheet forward and fold over your drawing. This built-in cover sheet will keep the drawing from being smeared during handling.

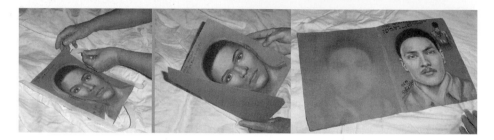

Figure 1.32

Take a full sheet of 25½″×19½″ Canson Mi-Tientes paper and cut it in half. Fold that half sheet in half again and tape to your drawing board.

Figure 1.33

After finishing the sketch, fold the sheet from behind over the front of the drawing. The sketch on the far right was stored for more than seven years. The "ghost" of the drawing on the inside of the cover sheet is the sole pigment disturbance that occurred, and the drawing still appears pristine.

of cutting the sheet in half, then folding the half sheet in half again where the drawing will be made, is illustrated by Figures 1.32 and 1.33.

> Failure to create the sketch without the easily built-in cover sheet would invite defacing of the drawing. Another benefit of this method is the freedom to use charcoal or even pastels with no fear of smudging.

DRAWING UTENSILS

Graphite pencils come in a wide range of darks and lights. The lighter pencils are the "H" type, with higher numbered H being the lightest. The darker pencils are labeled "B," with the higher numbers being the darkest; the higher-numbered B leads are softer. A full range of graphite is shown in Figure 1.34.

Figure 1.34

Here are 10 gradients of graphite pencils. The gradient of each pencil is printed above it and just below a scribble made from that pencil.

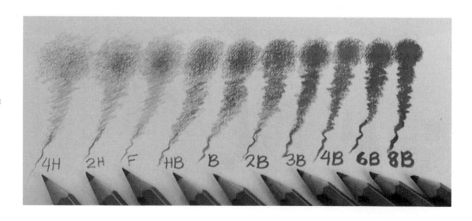

There are "woodless" pencils, which are sticks of graphite shaped like a pencil. Like pencils, these come in various types, from hard to soft. They can be broken into smaller pieces and laid on their sides like pastels to shade large dark areas such as hair and clothing, or cheeks and foreheads of darker complexioned subjects. Graphite also is sold in sticks resembling some pastel stick shapes. A variety of graphite utensils are shown in Figure 1.35.

Figure 1.35

These various sticks of graphite are from left to right: Creta Color Monolith 4B, Creta Color Monolith 8B, Creta Color Extra Large round graphite stick 8B, and General's GRAPHITE 986-6B.

A sandpaper paddle can help to grind the right-shaped surface on the graphite stick; this can also be used to sharpen the graphite stick to a fine point for tiny details like eyelashes. Figure 1.36 shows a sandpaper paddle and a sharpened 4B graphite stick with the thin line drawn after sharpening.

Some of the most successful forensic artists use charcoal in the last stages of their graphite drawings to enhance the darkest areas. Several varieties of charcoal are shown in Figure 1.37.

If you employ the built-in cover sheet method shown in Figures 1.30 through 1.33, there will be no problem with smearing, and adding charcoal will be feasible. You can also employ touches of white acrylic paint to enhance the lightest areas such as the shine in the eyes. Figure 1.38 shows just such a sketch. Done by the exceptionally prolific Marla Lawson of the Georgia Bureau of Investigation, this sketch has charcoal deepening the darks and white acrylic

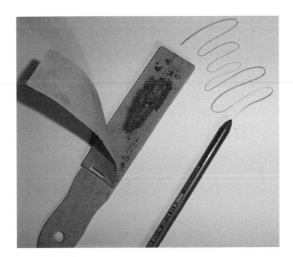

Figure 1.36

A sandpaper paddle was used to sharpen this Creta Color graphite stick 8B. The sharpened graphite drew the slender line shown.

Figure 1.37

These sticks of charcoal are from left to right: Coates #6 medium willow charcoal, Coates #3 thick willow charcoal, Coates extra thick willow charcoal, and Creta Color compressed charcoal no. 49403.

Figure 1.38

Marla Lawson of the Georgia Bureau of Investigation uses charcoal and graphite, with white for highlights to create a realistic look with a broad range of values. For the white Marla uses either acrylic paint or even common office correction fluid (courtesy of Marla Lawson and the Georgia Bureau of Investigation).

paint enhancing the lights. All these most intense pigments are added after the witness has finished asking for changes.

Since Marla Lawson produces what could be considered some of the finest artistic images of any forensic artist, I will quote her from a personal communication written in 2006 describing her technique:

> "…Materials:
>
> I use any erasers I can get my hands on! (I also use) white charcoal pencils, Wite-Out, stumps, charcoal pencils (General's) HB, 2B, 4B, 6B. I use 18" × 24" charcoal paper pads.
>
> I start out and sketch lightly w/extra soft pencil, then move up to soft, then finish up with medium and hard leads to add details. I just prefer the huge paper pads because I can prop them up on chair back or desk corner, etc. They copy the image OK in copy machines usually if you shrink them to 65%.
>
> I use stumps to blend—but most of the time I forget to use them and just use my finger. When I'm finished, I spray with Final Fixatif… I sometimes do add Wite-Out or white charcoal pencils to cover up some of my eraser marks. Sometimes I can't resist just adding a little here and there on the face too."

Erasers and Blenders

The best eraser for this kind of work is the white plastic kind, either the rectangular hand-held or the cylindrical type used in a holder as seen in Figure 1.39. This type gives the cleanest erasure. The pink- or golden-type erasers commonly used in grade schools can smear, so they are not suitable.

Kneaded erasers are not recommended for graphite as they absorb body oils that transfer to the paper, making erasure irregularities that show through the corrections. However, a kneaded eraser *is* ideal for purposefully smearing pigments to make them look like hair as demonstrated in Figure 1.40, or smoothing out rough edges when there will be no further erasures or do-over sketching.

Figure 1.39

Two kinds of white plastic erasers are, from the top: the hand-held rectangular type and a holder loaded with a round stick of white plastic eraser.

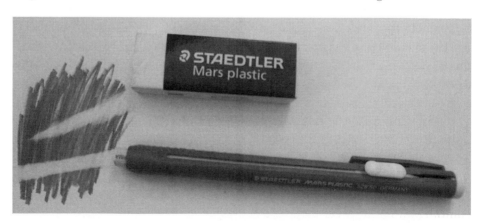

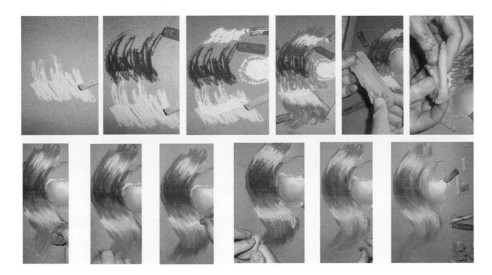

Figure 1.40
*Method of depicting hair
by smudging pastels with
a kneaded eraser.*

The method for rendering hair in pastels shown in Figure 1.40 is as follows. Top left: apply light colored pastel. Next three photos to the left: applications of various lights and darks laid on perpendicular to the direction of the hair strand. Photos next to top right and far top right: the eraser is kneaded into an oblong shape to use as a uniform smudging surface. Bottom left: the lights and darks are smudged together following the curvy direction of the hair strand. From left to right in the following five bottom photos: the area is alternately stroked and smudged with the eraser and the light and dark portions are re-established until the area looks like a shiny strand of hair.

These smearing techniques should not be used until all the possible changes are finished. The kneaded eraser is suitable for pastels since those pigments are much thicker than graphite.

Pigments need to be blended to best depict flesh. This is especially true for forensic art portraits since most criminals are under the age of 40 and have smooth skin. Tortillions or "stumps" are a favorite tool for blending, since they can be held like a pencil. Many artists like to blend their graphite with a chamois. For maximum control you can use a facial tissue wrapped around the index finger of the drawing hand. This combines ultimate control with the texture of the softest stump or tortillion. Blending done with all three of these items on a graphite sketch of a sphere is shown in Figures 1.41 and 1.42.

It is not advisable to blend with a naked finger. This will introduce body oils into the graphite and paper. The body oils will make the blending uneven and inhibit or make uneven any later erasure. If you have the urge to blend with your finger, simply wrap a common tissue around the finger and blend oil-free.

Some uniquely talented artists are able to indicate subtle shadings of facial contours with pencil technique alone and need no blending tools. However,

Figure 1.41

Pictured are three graphite sketches of spheres done with an 8B Creta Color Monolith. I attempted to sketch the spheres to be as identical as possible.

Figure 1.42

From left to right the graphite sketching on the spheres was blended with: a Royal Langnickel Artist Chamois small, a blending stump no. 8, and a 2-ply white Kleenex tissue wrapped around my right index finger.

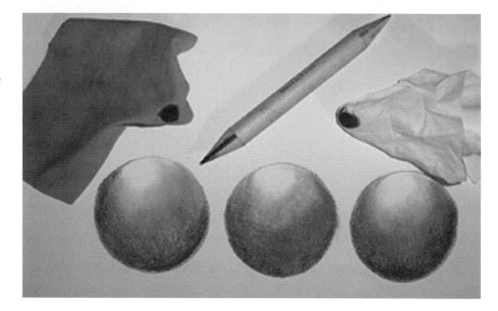

in the high-pressure, time-sensitive forensic sketching situation, the ability to depict flesh without blending would be a rarity. It is therefore advisable for the fine artist who is trying to sketch with a witness for the first time to make himself or herself familiar with the quickest, if not the most virtuous, method possible for creating a face on paper. It must be stated here that the goal is to catch the perpetrator of the crime. Any urge to create a virtuous work of art should take a back seat to creating an image most like what the witness remembers.

Of most importance is the comfort of the witness, since his or her memory is affected adversely by discomfort. For this reason, sketch as quickly as possible. It is far better to have a sketchy, haphazard drawing that brings in the perpetrator of the crime than to drive the witness to distraction and burn out by spending too much time making the sketch "look good." Therefore, choose the blending method that is most rapid.

Pastels

Pastels with no oil or wax content can be used for composites. Choose a brand or mixture of brands that suits you. The most basic rule of working with pastels is to blend areas of pastels on the paper using another stick of pastel. Simply stated, you should lay down areas of color where you want them and take a stick that is neutral, or the same or similar to one of the colors, and rub it back and forth over the area. With a little practice this technique renders smooth, flesh-like areas. If you choose a group of colors that are different shades of gray with a near-black and a near-white at either end of the spectrum, you can easily make a black-and-white sketch. A sample group of pastels that could be used is shown in Figure 1.43.

It takes some work to be able to control pastels, but the payoff is that you can complete the work much faster than with graphite. A stick of pastel can be laid on its side and large areas can be rendered in seconds, whereas with the pencil lead it might take much longer. Since the paper is darker than the whites of the eyes, teeth, and highlights on hair and face, pastels give a more three-dimensional look to the drawing.

Here's a quick and easy method for easing into pastels, even if you have previously drawn only in pencil.

Virtually every color found in pastels is also offered in pastel pencils. Make certain you buy colored pencils with no wax or oil content. Some of the best are Carb-Othello, Cretacolor, Derwent, and Conte pastel pencils. You should be able to start drawing immediately just as well with pastel pencils as with your graphite. Buy some sticks of pastel that resemble the colors of your pencils for the larger areas such as hair, cheeks, neck, and forehead. Most artists find it a breeze to do the small details in these pastel pencils. For the finest lines use the sandpaper paddle to sharpen the lead to a tiny point. You get the advantage that your pencil marks blend easier and farther than graphite. Notice in Figure 1.44 above each pencil is a scribble of that pencil's color and a half-circle blended from left to right with a leather-gloved finger. These pencil markings were made on the smooth side of felt gray Canson Mi-Tientes paper. Notice how the Derwent pastel Sepia 53D is almost the match for the color of the paper. This pencil can thus be used as a cover-up for mistakes.

Soon many artists find they are drawing with the pastel sticks (particularly the smaller NUPASTELS) and they use the pencils less and less. This results in a shorter sketching time, which is better for the witness's comfort. If an artist never feels comfortable with using the sticks of pastels, the pastel pencils will still afford smoother blending and a three-dimensional look that comes from using a gray-toned paper.

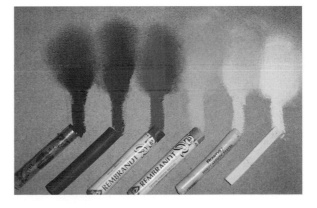

Figure 1.43

These are six shades of pastel on Canson Mi-Tientes paper. Above each, a sample scribble with the top blended. Left to right: Sennelier-Paris pastel Al'acue no. 456, Yarka Pastel #10 Brown, Rembrandt Soft pastel raw umber no. 408.3, Rembrandt Soft Pastel raw umber no. 408.9, Daler-Rowney raw umber Tint 3 Series A no. 247, and Nupastel color no. 249 P.

Figure 1.44

*Left to right is an assort-
ment of pastel pencils:
Conte Pastel Pencil 1355
no. 9, Conte Pastel Pencil
1355 no.42, Derwent
Pastel Pencil French Grey
70B, Conte Pastel Pencil
1355 no. 33, Derwent
Pastel Sepia 53D, Derwent
Pastel Umber 79F, and
Derwent pastel French
Grey 70H. Above each is a
sample scribble and blended
drawn circle.*

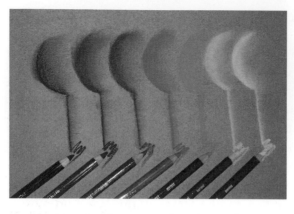

Figure 1.45

*Top: A brief sketch of an
eye with a dark pastel
pencil. Middle: The same
eye refined with lighter
pastel pencils; some match
the color of the gray paper.
Bottom: The same eye
with highlights and other
refinements imposed by
the medium and lighter
shades of pencils onto
the original dark pencil
markings.*

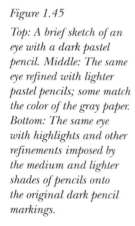

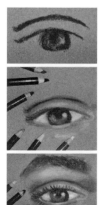

Since the pastel pigments are so dense, they should be used on a gray-colored piece of Canson Mi-Tientes. Erasure can then be done two ways. Erase with the kneaded eraser or simply cover up the "mistake" with a pastel that matches the paper. The match of this cover-up color with the paper does not need to be exact—it only needs to vaguely match the background and be *lighter*, as demonstrated in Figure 1.45. This manipulation available with pastel is the ability to "shave" off the edge of lines that are too thick or other darker areas with the cover-up color. The lower part of Figure 1.45 shows how a lighter color pencil, almost the color of the paper, is used to shave off the edges of the eyelid crease that are too thick. These lighter pastels can also draw in the highlights.

Whatever medium you use, spray the drawing with fixative when all the changes are done. Spray in a ventilated area to avoid breathing toxic fumes. For legal purposes, perform this spraying function in view of the witness and/or the detective to verify you have finished the drawing at that time and will not work on it later, out of sight of the witness. Even though all artists know the spray can says "*workable* fixative," we also know it is much harder to change a drawing after it is sprayed. The "workable" part means you can do more work *on top* of the pigments already in place. However, your erasure is greatly inhibited by the spray. Lastly, since you have drawn on a double-wide piece of paper, you do not need to spray too much fixative on your image. You simply fold the cover over the drawing, and even the messiest pastel or charcoal drawings will be protected from smearing.

USE AN EASEL

Sketching a face from a traumatized witness is one of the most difficult, uncomfortable tasks any artist can undertake. The comfort of using an easel in this situation is a must. In addition, there are numerous indispensable features sketching with an easel can offer that using only a drawing board cannot. First, an easel holds the drawing board perpendicular to the artist and witness's view so the image is not distorted. Second, a light attached at the top of the easel makes for the most effective viewing of the drawing. This light also helps the artist view the visual aids selected by the witness. The modestly priced Stanrite 500 easel comes with an attachable gooseneck light that can be adjusted to aim anywhere. The easel (weighing 7 pounds) and light can be folded into a compact T-square 51 inches in length for easy portability.

With an 18″×18″ drawing board, the visual aids can be clipped around the edge of the drawing, facilitating the viewing of any and all features during the construction of the face. Figure 1.46 shows two views of me working at the easel with pages of features clipped along the edge of the drawing board. In practice, as many as six catalogs and photos of hats, glasses, and other visual aids can also be attached for view along the edge of the drawing board since it is secured by the easel. This ability to simultaneously view all visual aids allows the artist to draw faster. Readjusting features so they are in proportion with each other is eased greatly by having them all in view at once. This cannot be done using only a drawing board. An easel frees up both hands, which further hastens the sketching process. The easel also acts as a shield between the often-traumatized witness and the artist. The benefit of this situation to the witness will be dealt with in great detail in later chapters. Suffice it to say here, a barrier will benefit the relaxation of the witness. Artists can work on an easel-held drawing completely out of view of the witness. This situation facilitates sketching successfully from a witness who saw a perpetrator's face but does not want to create the image, and witnesses who are too terrified to face the image of their attacker until the final phase of sketching.

Figure 1.46

Pictured are two views of me using an easel to sketch a composite. Notice the many visual aids clipped on the drawing board and the goose-neck light. The bottom photo replicates the dimmer lighting of some locations (photo by Tiffany Gibson).

Artists know that lighting is everything. Notice in Figure 1.46 the Stanrite 500 easel has an attachable, gooseneck light that allows the artist to view the drawing and visual aids no matter how dark the room or where the easel is set up. The artist can install any bulb brightness desired for his or her working comfort. In the final stage of the sketch, when the witness views the artist's work, the light intensifies the concentration on the drawing.

The light also helps the pervasive mood of the witness, which is despair and frustration. Since the sketch appears remarkably better with light focused on it, the mood of the witness is elevated when he or she views a successful sketch. The artist will gain much-needed confidence in his or her work since it is enhanced by being shown in the best light.

Finally, easels have been in use since before the Renaissance. Therefore it is a centuries-old piece of drawing equipment. No serious artist would create a major two-dimensional work without an easel. If anything, the creation of a drawing that might bring in a murderer could be considered the most serious work of all. With the Stanrite 500 Easel weighing only 7 pounds, about the same as a woman's purse, and the attachable goose-neck light that folds all together into a compact T-square for portability as shown in Figures 1.47 through 1.52, there is no reason not to use this well-established piece of equipment.

In Brief
- Most forensic artists use various gradients of graphite pencil on vellum-finish Bristol board.
- Pastels on gray Canson Mi-Tientes paper offer a quick method for forensic sketches. Use easily controlled pastel pencils to transition from graphite pencils.
- Use an easel for distortion-free drawings, attached light source, and maximum comfort for artist and witness.

The easel shown in Figures 1.47 through 1.52 is lightweight but can be awkward to carry if it is not secured correctly with the cord from the light. Figures 1.47 through 1.52 show the convenient way the electrical cord can be used to keep the legs and light strapped to the main shaft of the easel for smooth portability. If the cord is not wrapped around the light and legs of the folded easel, they will hang down and make the easel ungainly to carry for a distance. However with these simple maneuvers, which take less than 60 seconds to perform, the easel can be carried effortlessly.

Figure 1.47

On the left is the easel standing, fully assembled with the attached light. To break it down for transport, first loosen the wing nut at the top of the back leg as shown in the center. Slide the top of the back leg up the main easel shaft as shown on the right.

Figure 1.48

Left: The top of the back leg has been slid to the top, parallel and flush with the main shaft. Center: Turn the easel upside down. Right: Loosen the center and left wing nuts on the crossbar that holds the other two legs in place, as shown (photos by Tiffany Gibson).

Figure 1.49

Once the wing nuts are loosened, the legs and crossbar swing free as seen above left. Drop them down flush with the main shaft of the easel as seen above right (photo by Tiffany Gibson).

Figure 1.50

Left to right: Wrap the cord around the head of the light several times. Pull the cord until the light is close to the main shaft of the easel. Notice the flexible goose-neck will allow this to be done no matter where the light is attached to the easel (photos by Tiffany Gibson).

Figure 1.51

Wrap the cord around the legs and the main shaft of the easel as seen in the first three photos on the left. Lastly, wind the remainder of the cord around the crossbar of the easel, as seen on the right (photos by Tiffany Gibson).

Figure 1.52

The 7-pound easel is perfectly balanced if held in the center as shown above, leaving the other hand free to carry supplies. By using a shoulder bag for supplies, I have been able to carry everything for house calls, even when those trips involved walking considerable distances (photo by Tiffany Gibson).

REFERENCES

1. Houston Police Department Incident Number 4522490.

2. Jennifer Liebrum, "Man charged in assault on fourth child," *Houston Chronicle*, March 8, 1989. "Suspect, 25, arrested," Staff, *Houston Chronicle*, February 16, 1989. Houston Police Department Incident Number 88542288.

3. "Woman who drugged men, stole from them gets 17-year term," Staff, *Houston Chronicle*, September 1, 1993. Houston Police Department Incident Number 75127892.

4. S. K. Bardwell, "Jewelry heist well planned, officers say," *Houston Chronicle*, January 30, 1996. S. K. Bardwell, "Diamond suspect in sketch," *Houston Chronicle*, January 31, 1996. Jerry Urban and S. K. Bardwell, "Two charged in killing of diamond merchant," *Houston Chronicle*, February 25, 1996. S. K. Bardwell, "Police look for missing jewels in robbery-shooting death case," *Houston Chronicle*, February 27, 1996. S. K. Bardwell, "Three suspects held in connection with jeweler's murder," *Houston Chronicle*, February 24, 1996. Stephanie Asin, "Guard identifies jeweler in murder

case," *Houston Chronicle*, August 19, 1997. Stephanie Asin, "Jeweler convicted of killing diamond dealer in robbery," *Houston Chronicle*, August 29, 1997. Stephanie Asin, "Jury sentences jeweler to death/Execution by injection ordered in theft, killing of gem broker death," *Houston Chronicle*, September 5, 1997. Houston Police Department Incident Number 10330996.

5. Jo Ann Zuniga, "Traffic stop turns tragic for officer/Policeman shot twice, run over," *Houston Chronicle*, January 6, 1991. Eric Hanson, "Suspect in shooting of officer arrested," *Houston Chronicle*, January 10, 1991. "Prison escapee charged with attempted capital murder in attack on officer," Staff, *Houston Chronicle*, January 11, 1991. John Makeig, " 'Galleria rapist' gets life in police shooting," *Houston Chronicle*, July 18, 1991. Houston Police Department Incident Number 1449791.

6. S. K. Bardwell and Eric Hanson, "A babe in arms/Kidnap suspect may have been delusional," *Houston Chronicle*, October 25, 1995. Houston Police Department Incident Number 12217669512.

7. Houston Police Department Incident Number 74896194.

8. S. K. Bardwell, "Death orders from prison?/Alleged gang leaders accused in murders," *Houston Chronicle*, September 10, 1999. "Motive sought in shooting," Staff, *Houston Chronicle*, August 3, 1999. Houston Police Department Incident Number 997390997.

9. Patti Muck, "Capital murder charges planned in deputy slaying," *Houston Chronicle*, March 22, 1988. Patti Muck, "24-year-old alien charged in death of area deputy," *Houston Chronicle*, March 23, 1988. Patti Muck, "Confession in deputy's killing shown," *Houston Chronicle*, July 19, 1989. Fort Bend County Sheriff's Incident Number 88032106.

10. Lisa Teachey and Stephen Johnson, "Off-duty officer slain at family's store," *Houston Chronicle*, April 7, 1997. S. K. Bardwell, "HPD hopes $21,000 reward helps to solve officer's killing," *Houston Chronicle*, April 8, 1997. S. K. Bardwell, "Help asked in solving murder," *Houston Chronicle*, June 12, 1997. Jerry Urban and Ron Nissimov, "Suspect charged in slaying of HPD officer," *Houston Chronicle*, August 15, 1997. Jo Ann Zuniga, "Vietnam refugee sentenced to die for clerk's killing," *Houston Chronicle*, March 12, 1998. Houston Police Department Incident Number 43386597.

11. S. K. Bardwell, "Girl, 9, choked by intruder, discovers mother murdered," *Houston Chronicle*, October 28, 1994. Felix Sanchez and S. K. Bardwell, "Girl helps ID suspect in slaying/Man, 23, held in woman's death," *Houston Chronicle*, October 30, 1994. "Neighbor arrested in slaying/Nine-year-old girl identifies suspect," *The Houston Post*, October 30, 1994. John Makeig, "Girl tells how killer choked her after slaying her mom," *Houston Chronicle*, September 4, 1995. Houston Police Department Incident Number 122312494.

12. "Pregnant blind woman victim/Man, 25, sought in aggravated rape case," Staff, *The Houston Post*, August 4, 1988. Felix Sanchez, "Blind woman identifies rape suspect," *The Houston Post*, August 5, 1988. Houston Police Department Incident Number 57430188.

13.   Ed Asher, "Groups uniting in effort to find abductor of boy," *Houston Chronicle*, February 19, 2001. Peggy O'Hare, "Ex-con charged in sexual assault of 6-year-old boy," *Houston Chronicle*, February 27, 2001. Peggy O'Hare, "System didn't stop sex offender/ Assault suspect was on parole but broke rules, records show," *Houston Chronicle*, June 3, 2001. Houston Police Department Incident Number 18924701.

14.   Eric Hanson, "Two gunmen executed couple, police say," *Houston Chronicle*, December 15, 1990. "Pair held in execution slayings of elderly couple," Staff, *Houston Chronicle*, December 16, 1990. "Police charge 2 in deaths of area couple," Staff, *Houston Chronicle*, December, 17, 1990. Ruth Piller, "Killer, 25, sentenced to death," *Houston Chronicle*, October 26, 1991. Houston Police Department Incident Number 129389990.

15.   "Sketch of shooting suspect," Staff, *Houston Chronicle*, December 10, 1999. S. K. Bardwell, "2 arrested in robbery, shooting of woman who was left for dead," *Houston Chronicle*, December 23, 1999. Steve Brewer, " 'I was not going to quit'/Woman refuses to let 15 bullets silence her," *Houston Chronicle*, June 2, 2000. Steve Brewer, "Teen gunman gets life for brutal '99 robbery/Victim shot 15 times, left for dead," *Houston Chronicle*, July 11, 2000. Houston Police Department Incident Number 152410199.

16.   Houston Police Department Incident Number 28701497.

17.   Brian Curtis, *Drawing from Observation*, New York, McGraw Hill, 2002, pp. 18–21.

18.   C. J. Price, R. J. S. Wise, E. A. Warburton, C. J. Moore, D. Howard, K. Patterson, R. S. J. Frackowiak, and K. J. Friston, *Oxford Journal of Neurology*, 1996, Volume 119, Number 3, pp. 919–931.

19.   Gabriel Horn, *Memory, Imprinting, and the Brain: An Inquiry into Mechanisms*, Oxford University Press, 1986, pp. 286–287.

20.   Houston Police Department Incident Number 80539795 and 107399594, Harris County Sheriffs Case Number 9608080831, Humble Police Department 9513312, S. K. Bardwell, "Photo of suspect leads to charges in three robberies/Police say fired city worker may be behind many more," *Houston Chronicle*, August 31, 1996. Barbara Newman, "Armed robber draws third life sentence," *The Humble Echo*, December 10, 1997.

21.   Harris County Texas 262 District Court Case Number 048626701010.

CHAPTER 2

DRAWING IN FORENSIC ART

There are unique problems intrinsic to forensic art. Even the casual observer can see that many sketches in the news or on "true crime" shows do not appear to be of the finest artistic quality. It is absolutely acceptable for any *forensic* artist to produce inferior drawings if those drawings help the detective discover the name or location of a perpetrator. This is because the atmosphere in which the drawings are created is fraught with stress unimaginable to artists not in this profession. When you see a sketch on the news, you can assume that the artist has drawings at home of far superior quality, drawings created in an atmosphere of thoughtful study. The drawings put on public display from forensic artists, however, are done with distressed witnesses under time pressure.

The identification of violent criminals depends on the artist's skill at drawing something he or she cannot see. The forensic artist is desperately trying to create a face from a witness's memory while clinging to rules of good draftsmanship. It is no wonder there will be imperfect passages of drawing and shading in the various composites the public sees. However, I have worked extensively in high-stress situations and have developed an array of suggestions for improving the quality of art that is produced in these distracting drawing sessions. Following these guidelines can enhance the quality of sketches.

The suggestions that follow address faults that appear most frequently in forensic sketches seen in circulation. The hope is that improvement of quality will accomplish two goals. First, a more realistic, artistically virtuous sketch could more likely help solve the case. Second, the continuing improvement of quality in sketches appearing in the media will enhance the respect toward the profession by the general public. This respect should further generate more sketch artists' work solving more cases. Since the beginning of forensic art in earnest in the late 1970s and early 1980s, there has been a steady increase in quality and quantity of forensic artists and sketches. This has resulted in an increase of crimes solved because of our profession's work. These guidelines can help in that fortunate trend.

Many of these suggestions are common fine-art principles; some are unique to forensic art. Don't be insulted by these humble suggestions; at least some of the knowledge presented here, peculiar to this specific field, can help even the most talented artist improve. If you are a fine artist entering the field, you will be shocked at how distracting the interview situation can be in your efforts to sketch even the most basic drawing.

LIGHT SOURCE

One important decision affecting all the shading on the facial features is the direction of light on that face. Where should the lighting source be placed? I decided early that the ideal lighting angle to use on faces sketched from witness memory should duplicate arrest photo lighting. The reason is that when a criminal is arrested and the sketch is compared to the photo, he or she will appear more similar *if the lighting is the same.*

The arrest lighting situation is quite similar to standard high school yearbook photo lighting, so most artists will find it common and easy to replicate. Occasionally a witness will describe some drastic lighting situation or odd angle of light or almost no light at all. In the thousands of sketches I have created, no witnesses have insisted that the lighting be changed on the drawing to replicate the lighting during their experienced crime.

GUIDELINES FOR SKETCHING COMPOSITES

We will first examine the most common mistakes seen in composites that are purely errors in drawing, not memory retrieval. First, the drawing style should be as realistic as possible. It is unavoidable that an artist's "style" will show through. Showing a drawing style in a composite is both unavoidable and fortunate. The public needs to be aware the image they see is a sketch and not a photo; otherwise, they will assume the image should be *exactly* like the perpetrator, and virtually no tips will be relayed to authorities. If the public is aware the suspect image is an artist's sketch, they will broaden their observations to anyone who looks *similar* to the sketch, thus *increasing* the chances of identifying the suspect.

THE LIPS

Unless the perpetrator is a man dressed as a woman with makeup, or a woman with extremely heavy makeup application, the lips should not be outlined. Rather, the artist must depict the shape of the lips by showing the shadows and highlights around and on those lips. See Figure 2.1 for a comparison of the right and wrong way to draw lips.

Most artists who outline the lips are attempting to "place" the lips in the right area with the right size and shape. This should be done in the beginning with very light pencil strokes until the shape and placement seem right.

Then the darker, more decisive strokes can be made, but only as shadings that show the protrusion of the three-dimensional lips. The way to make these various shadings should be determined by the feature your witness has pointed out from the visual aids. You should attempt to replicate these shadings as closely as possible to the example chosen by the witness.

The one continuous line that exists on the mouth is the crease where the two lips come together (assuming the mouth is closed,

Figure 2.1

The top shows an incorrectly drawn mouth where the lips are outlined. The bottom lips are correctly drawn; their contours are indicated by shading, with the only line being the crease between the lips.

which is almost always the case in suspect sketches). This "crease line" should never be drawn as a continuous curve with uniform line thickness. Rather, all dark lines where the lips meet are varied in their curves and thickness, as seen in Figure 2.2. Notice how the outer rim of the mouth is described by shading those areas *around* the lips as well as *on* the lips, as seen in Figure 2.3. Notice in these lip drawings how oftentimes the bottom lip reflects enough light that the darkest shadows are *under* the bottom lip. In fact, correctly shaped lower lips aren't finished unless the shadows underneath are there and done correctly.

The far left image in Figure 2.4 is a pair of lips drawn incorrectly with outlines. The second from left are lips that are drawn correctly, using shadows. Next are some lips drawn from a real homicide witness. Last in the row are lips belonging to the murderer identified from the artist's sketch.

THE NOSE

Even if the face being sketched is of an elderly person, there will never be a continuous line around the nose. Once again, the artist who makes the error of

Figure 2.2

Here are six drawings of various lips done with shading and no obvious outlines around the mouth. The only lines are the dark creases where the lips come together.

Figure 2.3

Three photos of lips on the left with the correctly done drawing to the right. Notice there are no outlines on the lips; instead shadows and highlights indicate the contours. Sometimes the darkest areas are the shadows under the lips. The dark crease where the lips meet varies in curvature and thickness/darkness.

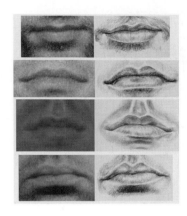

outlining the nose is trying to place the nose and describe its shape and size on the face. This placement should start with light, almost invisible lines. Soft shadings that describe smooth flesh should then indicate the nose.

Figures 2.5 and 2.6 show both a poorly done outlined nose and a correctly shaded nose compared to the photo of that nose. Notice when the shading is used to describe the protruding nature of the nose, it appears much more three-dimensional and realistic than a nose that is outlined. The shading is needed since the nose is a foreshortened protuberance of the facial plane when a person is viewed frontally.

Difficulties in drawing noses should not be underestimated. Essentially the nose is shaped like a mountain that is being looked at from above. It is a sort of peak, or triangular protuberance, that is being foreshortened since one is staring at it from the top looking down.

To illustrate the difficulty of depicting such an object, first imagine how easy it is to draw a hand that is viewed with the palm facing the artist and the fingers spread out as shown in Figure 2.7. Now imagine drawing a hand looking straight down the fingers with the tips closest to the viewer as seen in Figure 2.8. The second is incredibly more difficult to draw.

Figure 2.4

From left to right are lips drawn incorrectly with outlining, lips drawn correctly using shading, lips sketched from the description given by a homicide witness, and the lips of the proven perpetrator of that homicide.

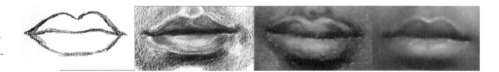

Figure 2.5

From left to right are a nose drawn incorrectly with outlining, a nose drawn correctly by shading in the contours, and the photo of the nose depicted in the drawings. Notice the shadings usually have no precise beginning or ending.

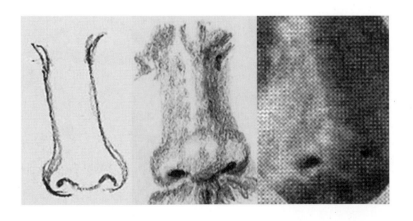

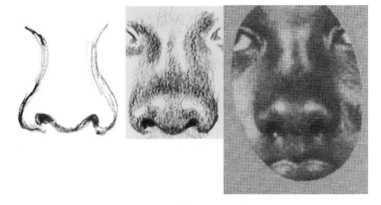

Figure 2.6

From left to right are a nose drawn incorrectly with outlining, a nose drawn correctly by shading in the contours, and the photo of the nose depicted in the drawings. Notice the shadings usually have no precise beginning or ending.

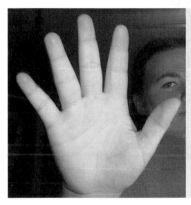
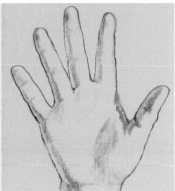

Figure 2.7

Drawing a hand from the view of a flattened palm is easy. Simply draw the outline and add some minor shading (photo by author).

Figure 2.8

Drawing a hand from a view looking down the fingers is very difficult. The only way to indicate the foreshortened fingers is with shading in around the fingers. No obvious lines can be used to show the fingers thrusting toward the viewer (photo by author).

For the open-handed palm view, one can simply outline the fingers and thumb and throw in a minor amount of shading. For the view looking down the fingers, however, the only way to describe the fingers would be with subtle shading; almost no lines can be utilized. Drawing the nose poses a similar problem. Thus the nose can be drawn well only with subtle shading. The only lines are the dark edge of the nostril holes, and sometimes short horizontal crescent-shaped dark areas under the tip of the nose and the outer nostril folds. To decide just how these subtle shadings should be done in order to describe the contours of the nose, the artist should adhere as precisely as possible to those in the example picked by the witness from the visual aids.

Do Not Make the Nose Too Long

The single most common proportional mistake in both compositry and fine art portraits is making the nose too long in relation to the face drawn. The museums are full of portraits done before the invention of the camera,

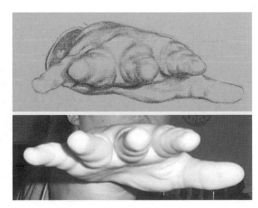

where the noses of persons painted or drawn by the finest artists are longer than possible in human anatomy. Likewise one can observe that even the best forensic artists produce sketches that, when compared to the person depicted, display a nose that was drawn too long. It is not explainable in concrete terms why this mistake is so pervasive in artistic renderings of the human face. But knowing this is a common mistake can help you avoid it. The logic is that a forensic sketch should be as close as possible to the person depicted.

This problem is very pervasive; many other artists have expressed difficulty in fighting the habit of drawing the nose too long. Some other artists as well as I independently have come upon one method that can help in this most pervasive portraiture mistake. First, lay out the eyes and nose as you think you should. Then erase the bottom of the nose as you have placed it and move it up a notch. As irrational as this method may seem, it has consistently alleviated the problem for many practicing artists.

Figure 2.9 shows a sketch where this technique was employed when the witness said the suspect had a really short nose. The bottom of the nose was sketched in the right place as best as the artist could calculate. Then the artist forced herself to erase the dark nostril holes and shadows underneath and simply placed new nostril holes immediately above the erased nostrils. Once the suspect was caught, a comparison of his photo with the sketch seems to prove the efficiency of this method. The proportions of the face are very similar; however, this suspect's nose is *so* short, the drawing still depicts the nose as a bit longer than the one in the photo.

Figure 2.9

For this sketch I was determined not to make the nose too long since the witness said the man had a very short nose. The technique involved drawing the nose like normal, erasing the bottom, and drawing it again just above the earlier nostril marks (courtesy of the Houston Police Department).

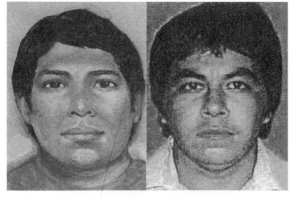

THE EYES

Unless you are sketching a man who has applied makeup to appear like a woman, or a woman with a lot of makeup, the eyes are not outlined. Once again, the artist who makes this mistake is attempting to draw lines to establish the size, placement, and shape of the eyes. This kind of outlining should be done first with light, almost invisible pencil lines. Then the eyes should be described by subtle shading around the upper and lower lids. Eyelashes also describe the contour of the eyes as they are drawn in place. Figure 2.10 shows three examples of eyes drawn correctly next to the photo source for the drawings—you can see there are no continuous lines surrounding the eyes.

All eyelashes change size and curve direction as they grow around the perimeter of the eye. To

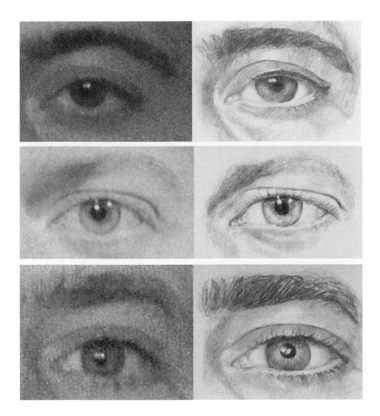

Figure 2.10
Left: Three photos of
eyes. Right: Drawings
of those eyes done with
correct technique, no
outlines of the eyes. The
irises intersect with the
eyelids; they are never
seen as perfect circles.
Eyelashes vary in length,
curvature, and direc-
tion of growth. Notice
the eyelid crease has a
different shape from the
eyelash line.

determine how those eyelashes should be drawn, look to the visual aid choice of your witness. Ideally, forensic sketches are drawn life size. The reason an artist's image needs to be at least that large is to accommodate all these tiny details involved in drawing eyes. These minute items are prohibitively difficult in a drawing smaller than life size. Notice that the eyelashes are on a ridge of rubbery flesh that separates them from the eyeball surface. Never depict the lashes as coming straight out of the eyeball or iris. Also notice the fold of the eyelid is a different shape from the eyelash line (see Figure 2.10).

The iris is never depicted as a full circle. Rather the upper and lower lids cut off its bottom and top edges horizontally. Exceptions are individuals whose bottom lid does not intersect the iris. However, the upper lid will still cover some of the iris. The way to determine how to shade all the eye structures is to duplicate as identically as possible the eyes chosen by the witness from the visual aids.

Eyebrows

Eyebrows appear unrealistic and poorly done when the artist does not rep-licate the direction of the hair growth. This is less important for extremely dense, dark eyebrows, but it is crucial to get this right with lighter colored

Figure 2.11

The top eyebrow drawing is not realistic because it doesn't show correct hair-growth direction. Below is an eyebrow that replicates the changes in hair-growth direction as the eyebrow travels above the eye, creating a more realistic drawing. To determine the direction of hair growth, observe the photo of a real eyebrow.

eyebrows or those with dark hairs where the skin shows through. Even with dark eyebrows, if hair-growth direction is understood, replication of the correct eyebrow shape will be superior. A careful perusal of the hair direction in the feature selected by your witness will give you the guidance to sketching those eyebrows realistically, as illustrated in the bottom drawing of Figure 2.11.

In Brief

Lighting in the sketch should be like that in arrest photos.
- Never outline the lips.
- Never outline the nose.
- Never outline the eyes.
- Use the chosen visual aid example to guide your drawing.
- Replicate eyebrow-hair–growth direction for a realistic drawing.

AREAS SURROUNDING THE SENSORY FEATURES

A common deficiency found in forensic sketches is a lack of any structure besides the sensory features of eyes, nose, and lips. Two examples of this are illustrated in Figures 2.12 and 2.13. Both photos of the suspect have the sketch done correctly on the left, and a sketch done without any detail besides the core features on the right. Composites like these, with only the core anatomy, are seen often because of dire rush on the part of the artist, or because the traumatized witness has little patience for much detail during the interview.

There is a cure for this sketching malady, and there is good reason to take steps to assure the entire face is done as completely as possible. First, a more complete composite with more detail in a sketch could result in a higher chance of helping identify the criminal. Additionally, it has been my experience that many of those nonsensory features such as the chin, cheeks, forehead, and neck can be strikingly similar to the person eventually identified. Often these features surrounding the facial core can be *the* striking element that brings the sketch more in line with the appearance of the subject. It is a fact that some of the more obvious features, the things that make a person unique, are not always the eyes, nose, or mouth. As an example, I observed the suspect's photo for the linear drawings in Figures 2.12 and 2.13. I copied all the proportions and

Figure 2.12

Far right: A linear drawing with no details besides the outline, eyes, lips, and nose. This is an inadequate composite sketch. Left: A sketch from a witness that includes information about the entire face including the cheeks, chin, and areas surrounding the eyes, lips, and nose (courtesy of the Houston Police Department).

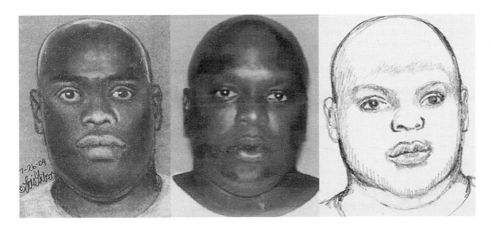

Figure 2.13

Right: A sketch similar to faulty sketches created by artists who do not draw anything but the outline, eyes, lips, and nose. I drew this sketch looking at the subject's photo. It is not as similar as the sketch on the left from a witness which included filling in the entire facial area (courtesy of the Houston Police Department).

correct anatomy from that specific individual's photo. The sketches to the left of the photo were done from witness memory, so the proportions and shapes of the features are less perfect. However, the filled-in drawings give a stronger likeness, because they give more information besides just the sensory features.

The remedy for the unfinished looking sketch is to decide before you work that you need to get that information from the witness. I confess to having sketched in a situation where the witness was so frenetic that in the end a "generic" chin or other peripheral feature was added without much thought. However, you at least need to try and flesh out the face as much as possible, no matter how frantic the interview becomes. The solution is to use your visual aids and have the witness guide you to the right forehead, chin, and cheeks. And if the subject being described has short enough hair, ask about the ears. Be willing and able to change any of these features at the witness's request.

CHIN, CHEEKS, AND FOREHEAD

After comparing over one thousand sketches from witnesses' memories to the people depicted, I have found the chin most often is drawn incorrectly. Some blame for this common problem must be assigned to the witnesses. The reason for this might be that the number one feature witnesses tend to describe, and subsequently artists sketch most accurately, is the eyes. Regardless of why, be aware that the chin can be the most often fumbled area of a sketch, and thus intensify your efforts when sketching that part of the face.

One of the major areas differentiating a teenaged suspect from a suspect in his or her 20s is chin structure. Even an individual of average weight will add bulk in the chin and jowl area as he or she grows past the earliest 20s. If you have sketched an individual and the witness remarks he or she looks "too old," try making the chin slightly smaller. Dozens of times when the witness has remarked about the sketched face appearing too old, the simple shrinking of the chin immediately makes the face look younger. An example of this can be seen in Figure 2.14. The photo on the left shows my father at approximately 17 years old; on the right he appears again at age 19. He appears many years younger in the left-hand photo, yet the only difference in facial structure is a chin and jowl area that is smaller.

If the witness remembers a receding chin, it can be a great identifier but only if the artist can sketch this feature correctly. A receding chin is so difficult to portray, I recommend that you practice the shading on this type of face before a witness requests that task during an interview. Even though the chin is a feature that protrudes from below the mouth, and usually catches light in normal lighting situations, a receding chin is often completely in the shadows. Figure 2.15 is the "Receding Chin" page from the *FBI Facial Identification Catalog*, showing a fairly comprehensive collection of this difficult-to-draw feature.

Figure 2.14

The individual on the left (aged 17) looks much younger than the subject on the right (aged 19). The smaller chin makes the difference since all the other features (except the hair) are the same.

Figure 2.15

This "Receding Chin" page from the FBI Facial Identification Catalog *shows a comprehensive collection of a difficult-to-draw features (courtesy of the Federal Bureau of Investigation).*

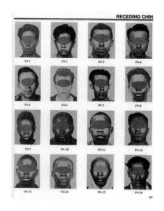

The forehead is another area often portrayed incorrectly by forensic artists. The term "forehead" usually refers to the shape of the hairline since offenders are young enough to have hair that is not drastically receding. This intersection of the hair to the forehead plays greatly in the appearance of the individual face. You either should gather a wide range of visual aids depicting foreheads or hairlines, or make certain to utilize the pages far in the back of the FBI catalog during the interview. The three forehead pages are shown in Figures 2.16, 2.17, and 2.18. Notice that on the page labeled "Average Forehead," each hairline is different. The hairline on your suspect is a large feature and a distinct, easily noticeable identifier. Thus it is important to ask the witness about this area of the face and sketch it accurately.

Cheeks cannot be sketched with lines, so to draw the cheeks and surrounding areas, you must be able to convey smooth, rounded areas of flesh. Even if the suspect is older, wrinkles will not cover the entire cheek and jowl area. The majority of these parts of the face will still need to be smoothly depicted, with meaningful lines and folds done in the older individuals. Even an extremely slender-faced individual will have features in the jowl area that cannot be drawn with lines. One area of a slender individual's face that proves difficult to draw is shown in Figure 2.19.

This feature is found on a male with a substantial mandible (chin) and slender build. In this type of face there will be a vertical shadow between the chin and cheeks. In an older individual, you can draw a line or lines in this area. However, in the younger face, like those of the common-aged suspect, this vertical fold has no lines. Resist the urge to draw lines; instead, skillfully indicate that vertical shadow with smooth shading. Since many suspects are not practicing robust nutrition in their lives, they will often exhibit this feature. Practice this difficult shading or be able to accurately depict this feature from the visual aid when the witness indicates. Figure 2.20 shows two examples with that feature from the "Square Chin" area of the *FBI Facial Identification Catalog.*

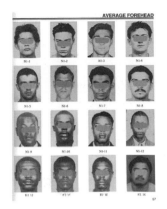

Figure 2.16

This is the "Average Forehead" page from the FBI Facial Identification Catalog. *Notice that, even though they are supposedly "average," each forehead has a different shape, especially the hairline. Determining this large, easy-to-see feature from your witness is important to depicting a likeness with the sketch (courtesy of the Federal Bureau of Investigation).*

Figure 2.17

This is the "Low Forehead" page from the FBI Facial Identification Catalog. *Notice that each one is different from the others, especially the shape of the hairline. The forehead is a large, easy-to-see feature, which a forensic artist should attempt to depict accurately (courtesy of the Federal Bureau of Investigation).*

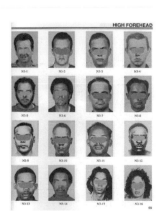

Figure 2.18

This is the "High Forehead" page from the FBI Facial Identification Catalog. *A high forehead is a large, easy-to-see feature, which a forensic artist should attempt to depict accurately (courtesy of the Federal Bureau of Investigation).*

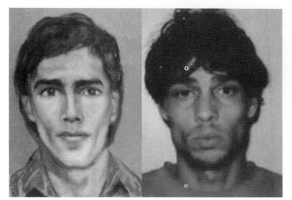

Figure 2.19

For the sketch on the left I needed to depict the slender vertical shadow on this slender suspect's face pictured on the right. This feature cannot be depicted using lines since the subject is youthful enough to have no wrinkles on that area of his cheeks (courtesy of the Houston Police Department).

Figure 2.20

Below are two examples from the "Square Chin" page of the FBI Facial Identification Catalog *that show the vertical shadows on the cheeks like those on the sketch and suspect shown in Figure 2.19 (courtesy of the Federal Bureau of Investigation).*

Everyone has seen the effects of acne on faces. If the witness indicates the suspect had acne, find out if the acne was active, with open sores, or healed with the resultant scars. Active sores are easy to draw. The acne-scarred face, however, is more difficult to sketch than you might assume. Take some time to find a technique that works for you to show cheeks and other areas with acne scars. You must be able to quickly and deftly lessen or increase the severity of this scarring to the witness's satisfaction.

Do not overdo the creation of the scarred area until the area of the face upon which the scars occur has been shaped to the witness's satisfaction. In other words, if the witness tells you the suspect had more acne, ask first if the features upon which the acne scars lie are completed correctly. For instance, get the chin, cheek, forehead, and nose to the right width and shape before creating the right texture of acne upon those surfaces. When the shapes are correct, *at that time* proceed to establish the right amount of acne scarring.

Figure 2.21 shows a suspect with healed acne scars depicted in two different sketches on each side of his photo. The witnesses for each sketch saw this individual two months apart in very different circumstances. The sketch on the left was from a female who was kidnapped from a vehicle late at night and taken to a field and raped. The witnesses for the sketch on the right were victims of an incredibly brutal home invasion/robbery.

Also use caution when adding an unshaven look to a sketch. If the witness wants the face to show a beard that is partially grown out, first make certain the *underlying features* upon which the hair will be drawn are done to witness satisfaction. The texture of small hairs that do not yet comprise a dense beard is difficult to sketch. See Figure 2.22 for three examples of suspects with an unshaven look. All the unique chin contours were done correctly before the light covering of facial hair was added.

NECK AND SHOULDERS

Forensic artists working in colder climates where populations wear coats for six or more months of the year are understandably reticent to include a neck and shoulders in their sketches. However, in the warmer months when perpetrators of crime dress so the neck and shoulder contours are visible, these artists should take advantage of the extra information that can be portrayed by a sketch that includes a neck and a bit of shoulders.

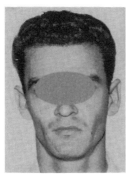

F5-6

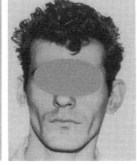

F5-7

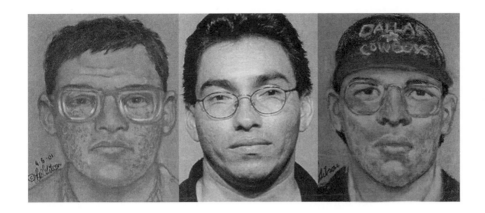

Figure 2.21

The sketches on the left and right of the proven perpetrator's photo were taken from different witnesses in separate incidents. All witnesses saw acne scars, but had the artist sketch them differently (courtesy of the Houston Police Department).

Figure 2.22

These sketches depict men with a few days' growth of facial hair. The artist should make certain the underlying structures are done to the witness's satisfaction before adding this texture to avoid redoing the chin and the texture again.

Necks are all shaped a little differently, showing fat and muscle content. Shoulders are also shaped differently, each individual's being unique. Shoulders can also show fat and muscle content. This inclusion of a small amount of shoulder area also reveals individual dressing style. There has been more than one sketch where the clothing worn when the suspect was spotted is the same as that in the sketch (see Figure 2.23 for four examples of this fortunate similarity). The relatives and friends of the suspect who might want to help solve the crime can be further aided when shoulders, and thus clothing, are added to the sketch since this displays a personal style. Add this to the tendency of males to dress the same in their daily life once past their early 20s and this makes another case for sketching past the chin and neck. Once again, these sketches have the potential to help stop felons. Not to perform that extra bit of work by adding the neck and a bit of shoulders is not rational.

Though the neck appears to be a simple feature, it can be difficult to draw correctly. Before doing any sketches from a witness, the beginning forensic artist should practice drawing necks with commonly worn clothing

Figure 2.23

Top: Suspect preferred a white-collar shirt under another with bold geometric print. Second down: Suspect likes to wear a dark casual cloth coat over a light colored button-up shirt. Third down: Suspect's shirt choice is a black knit collar style worn unbuttoned. Bottom: Suspect chooses bold striped shirts (courtesy of the Houston Police Department).

on the adjoining shoulders. Further, when constructing a composite, ask the witness to point out a neck that is similar to the person he or she is trying to remember. Or if the clothing described is similar to that of one of the visual aids, sketch the clothing and ask if the neck was thin, thick, and so forth, and sketch that kind of neck with the clothing indicated by the witness. Since there are clothing catalogs with photos of men in shirts and coats everywhere, and 960 photos in the *FBI Facial Identification Catalog* that show necks on clothed men, there is an abundance of visual aids for this area of the body.

Some articles of clothing found on the shoulders can be more difficult than others to sketch. Forensic artists just beginning should practice sketching a plaid shirt before getting a witness who sees that kind of shirt on a suspect. Either work from a model wearing a plaid shirt, or sketch from a photo of someone in a plaid shirt. It is nearly impossible to attempt to portray a plaid shirt without a visual reference until you've sketched hundreds. The step-by-step process of how to draw a plaid shirt as shown in Figure 2.24 is as follows.

1. First draw the general structure on the shirt. For the sake of this demonstration, the body under this shirt is bulky.
2. Draw the vertical lines on the collar. They follow the angle of the collar like the sides of a roof. Draw the lines closer together as they appear farther away toward the individual's back.
3. Draw diagonal lines on the strip of material where the buttonholes and buttons are attached.
4. The lines on the back travel in an outward curve away from the shoulder seam. The lines on the front appear to travel straight down.
5. Now draw the perpendicular lines, curving them around the neck and back of the shoulders. For added depth, darken the lines under the collar. It helps to smudge some of the areas with an eraser. Areas at the top of the collar that would catch light can be partially erased for highlights.

I drew this in a hurried manner so as to replicate the situation of sketching with a witness. The time to sketch an entire shirt for a composite in this manner can be less than 60 seconds with practice.

If the subject of the sketch has no shirt on, this is an opportunity to home in on the body type. Here is a situation where the artists who have studied in the classical way can shine since they have spent dozens of hours sketching from live nude models. For forensic artists who are not classically trained, spend some time sketching some shirtless male friends or relatives. In the hotter climates, this is a must for sketching men wearing tank tops or muscle shirts. Since the practice is for composites, you need to go down only a few inches below the top of the shoulder.

An unexpected difficulty is the man wearing a suit with tie. This garb poses its own unique difficulties, with the neck hardly being seen and the need for the tie and collar and jacket to line up a certain way. If you have not done a fine art portrait of a man in a suit and tie, practice this outfit in anticipation of a well-dressed criminal. The sketch in Figure 2.25 was of a man who would dress in a suit and tie to gain the confidence of women showing condominiums for lease.[1] Depicting the suit was a must since that clothing choice was an integral part of his method of committing his crime.

All these clothing styles can easily be gathered in a visual aid file you can bring to the interview in case they are needed. Additionally, the *FBI Facial Identification Catalog* has numerous examples of almost all types of clothing styles. Simply learn the type from the witness, and use the visual aid to guide you in your sketch.

It is understandable why artists located where criminals wear coats half the year might not see the virtue of sketching the added physical information below the chin. However, since these sketches can be such a vital part of bringing in dangerous felony criminals, it is illogical not to do this last bit of work to create what could be the defining feature that helps solve the case. During the cold months the sketch of a small portion of the jacket around the neck could give a unique identifier of the individual. Unless the criminal is wealthy enough to have several jackets, the coat sketched will most likely match what the perpetrator wears daily. It takes only a few moments to sketch the difference between a leather jacket and various cloth jacket styles.

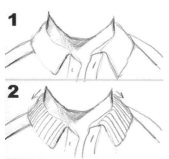

Figure 2.24
How to draw a plaid shirt in 60 seconds.

Figure 2.25
Right: Suspect always wore a suit and tie when approaching his victims, making them necessary in the sketch. This kind of outfit allows only a fraction of the neck to show. You need to be capable of drawing a suit and tie for some perpetrators (courtesy of the Houston Police Department).

In Brief
- For a more professional sketch, draw details of areas outside eyes, nose, and mouth.
- Include the neck and tops of shoulders for maximum suspect information.

Figure 2.26

Six examples of unusual hairstyles seen on suspects. Replicating an unusual look is worthwhile as it could be the key to identifying the perpetrator.

HAIR

Witnesses notice hair readily and tend to have the artist make changes until it is the right volume, shape, and texture. By its nature, hair is the feature that has the potential to differ the most from person to person. Figure 2.26 shows six sketches from actual cases exhibiting radically different hairstyles. Sketching such divergent styles is worth the effort since tipsters to authorities would have no problem remembering a suspect with such unusual hair. And since this is a feature that can hold the most unique qualities, accurate depiction of hair can make or break an appearance for the witness. Most artists find drawing hair enjoyable; following are a few caveats.

Bald or Close-Shaved Hair Styles

One of the most difficult and time-consuming styles to draw is the almost-bald head with stubble. This style is so noticeable a witness will find it easy to remember. The forensic artist needs to be adept at this style to save time during the sketch. Always show a shiny area somewhere on a head with this style. The most universal shiny area with this style of hair will be on the very top. The challenge is to show the skin, both shiny and shaded, through the hair stubble. Figure 2.27 shows two sketches done from witnesses to crimes with just such a hairstyle.

Observe the Latest Hair Styles in Your Community

One example of this practice paying off is the advent of persons braiding their hair and wearing it close to the skull like the sketch on the middle left of Figure 2.26. I observed this style in my community, and when I was asked to draw that style on a suspect, I was able to accomplish that. However, the difficulty of doing this without a visual aid was exhausting. Try to gather photos of any new hairstyle that becomes popular, especially among younger males, in your area.

Some Basic Hair-Drawing Rules

The light reflections, or highlights, on hair run *perpendicular* to the strands. Those same highlights curve around the head. The easiest way to create realistic hair is to lay down the light and dark areas and stroke them with an eraser. The stroking with the eraser must be in the direction of the hair strands. This stroke can only be done once or twice. After that the light and dark areas can become muddy and might need to be reestablished. The highlights can also be erased with the white plastic eraser if the smudging by the kneaded eraser makes the area too muddy.

Steps in creating realistic hair as shown in Figure 2.28 are as follows.

Figure 2.27

Two sketches done on real cases of one of the most difficult hairstyles to draw—a shaved head with stubble. Always show a shine on the top of the head.

1. Light and dark areas are laid down perpendicular to the direction of the hair strands while curving around the head.
2. Stroke across the bands of dark and light in the direction of the hair, including following the curves with a kneaded eraser.
3. A plastic eraser can also be used to stroke the hair.
4. The finished hair drawing.

These are finishing moves and should not be performed until the witness has conveyed that the hair volume and texture are to his or her best recollection. Once these kinds of moves are performed, erasure is difficult and uneven since such procedures emboss the pigment into the paper.

There is one helpful caveat for sketching the darker hair tones with a witness. Since it is easier to *add* hair than erase, it is wiser in the beginning to draw a conservative amount of hair. If the witness indicates the amount of hair should be increased, this is a quick and easy addition to make. On the other hand, if you fill in a too-large area, the erasure and reestablishment of the outer contour take much longer. If you use a white paint in your composites, you can clean up this outer contour after the final sketch is done for better reproduction, but the best plan is to place a conserva-

Figure 2.28

How to draw realistic hair.

tive amount of that dark hair in the beginning. Figure 2.29 shows a sketch by the prolific Marla Lawson where she has used Wite-Out™? on the right side of the drawing to eliminate excess dark areas, showing this can be done effectively.

Do not allow the witness or yourself to become overly concerned that the suspect

Figure 2.29

Marla Lawson with the Georgia Bureau of Investigation used white paint to refine the right edge of the drawing at right. Her medium in this and other composites is graphite pencil, charcoal, and Wite-Out (courtesy of Marla Lawson and the Georgia Bureau of Investigation).

Figure 2.30

Right: A sketch done with some children who were playing on a bayou when they saw the man follow a woman later found murdered. Several individuals in the neighborhood remembered the man had the hairstyle from the sketch, but changed it after the sketch was released (courtesy of the Harris County Sheriffs Department).

will change his or her hairstyle, thus looking less like the drawing. Be aware the suspect's acquaintances or informants will remember the suspect had that particular hairstyle *before* the crime or that the person of interest changed hairstyles after the sketch appeared in the media. There have been several occasions when detectives have taken a sketch to the area where the suspect lived and were informed he did have the hairstyle shown in the sketch, but changed it right after the time of the crime. Figure 2.30 illustrates one such case. The sketch on the right was constructed from children who saw this man follow a woman jogging along a bayou. When the woman was found later raped and strangled to death, detectives had the artist work with these witnesses. A canvass of the neighborhood turned up several acquaintances of the man, pictured on the left, who insisted he had his hair braided on top similar to the drawing. After the sketch came out in the media, these acquaintances recall the suspect combed his hair out. This allowed the detectives to focus on the suspect who suddenly changed a long-standing hairstyle. After a confession and DNA match, the case was solved.[2]

Facial Hair

Facial hair is a boon to the forensic artist. These areas are easy to sketch and easy for the witness to remember. Gather examples of beards and mustaches to save time pointing to various areas of your face where you think a beard might grow, and to help the witness more accurately describe what he or she saw.

Figure 2.31

Page 52 of the FBI Facial Identification Catalog *is one of two "Mustache and Beard" pages. Any artist can easily collect his or her own photos of various beard and mustache types for useful visual aids (courtesy of the Federal Bureau of Investigation).*

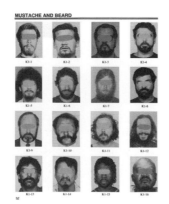

These will help you replicate the most varied area of the beard, which is the pattern of hair growth below the lips. Some men have a small point of hair under the middle of the lip with the full beard starting at the bottom of the chin. Some have no hair under their lip; others have hair growth along the entire border of the lower lip. It helps if there are plenty of photos for the witness to point out this easy-to-sketch feature. Figure 2.31 is one page from the *FBI Facial Identification Catalog* showing beards and mustaches.

People of Northern European descent often have dark head hair and different colored facial hair, including one color for eyebrows, a different color for beards, and still another for the mustache. Simply because the witness says the hair on the head is one color, don't assume the facial hair is the same. With Anglo and even Latino suspects, ask if the eyebrows appear lighter, darker, or the same as the hair on the head. Even if the eyebrows are the same color as the hair on the head, the hairs can be finer, or spaced apart so the flesh shows through, making them *seem lighter* than the head hair.

Do not be overly concerned about a suspect shaving his facial hair. For legal and practical purposes, you can sketch only what was seen during the crime. If the perpetrator shaves his beard or mustache, his acquaintances will still remember his facial hair and notice the change.

A helpful note is that facial hair grows approximately an eighth of an inch per week. Additionally, it has been my observation that some men will never shave their facial hair for *any* reason.

HATS

In the United States, the most common hat a forensic artist will draw is the baseball cap. Since it seems to be a favorite item worn by suspects, it's a good idea for you to be able to quickly and efficiently sketch this type of hat. Since the bill is a foreshortened object, it can be challenging to draw it realistically.

You should have pictures of various hat styles worn in your area as visual aids to help the witness convey the type of hat the suspect was wearing. It becomes extremely difficult even for articulate witnesses to describe the "golf hat" if they don't have a name for it. Even if there is a meeting of minds on the name of that hat, there are several styles of golf hats, making it even more confusing. If you have photos or pictures of hats, all the confusion will be gone. Some artists find it much more helpful to take photos of friends in the various hat styles; that way there is a head already inside the hat. I have drawn hats on Texas men for more than 20 years and maintain that cowboy hats are almost impossible to draw realistically without a picture for a guide. Even the khaki fisherman-type hat can be difficult to draw without a picture reference. Figure 2.32 is an array of various sketches for real cases where the suspects wore hats. The artist used photos of hats to help do all the sketches except the upper left; that type of hat is drawn so frequently, no visual aid was needed.

One excellent way to show body size is with a hat. Since most hats are made about the same size, you can indicate really large or rather small suspects by sizing the hat proportional to their head in the drawing. This "hat trick" is shown on Figure 2.33. Notice how big the hat looks on the slender

Figure 2.32

Sketches of various suspects wearing a variety of head gear. All the drawings were done from descriptions by witnesses to actual crimes. See color plate.

Figure 2.33

The "Hat Trick": since all hats are manufactured about the same size, you can show one individual (left) to be small framed, and the other individual (right) large framed, by having the hat fit loosely or tightly, respectively. The ratio of head size to hat emphasizes his build type without obliging the artist to draw the suspect's entire body.

suspect and how tight and much smaller the same kind of hat appears on the larger suspect. Without drawing the body, you can easily indicate drastically different sized individuals by emphasizing the relationship of their heads to their hats.

EYEGLASSES

If the suspect is wearing glasses, you need visual aids both for the witness to recall the correct shaped frames, and for a reference to aid drawing. Optometrists have photos of various styles that will be current to the population of your area. If you take time to obtain pictures of a variety of these eyeglass styles for your witness, this item worn by the suspect can be chosen quickly and sketched with accuracy.

The rules for drawing glasses are simple. First of all, both sides need to come out looking the same. Try to indicate some kind of shiny areas on the glasses. An effective practice for realistic looking glasses would be to have the shiny areas appear on the same location of each side of the frames. For instance, if there is a shiny point indicated on the top right of one lens frame, place a shiny area on the top right of the other lens frame.

The method for drawing thick glasses is to add more highlights at the outer edges of the lenses, especially near the ears. The thicker the glasses, the more the highlights you should add to the lens area. The thickest glasses have such wide highlights they seem to cut into the outer edges of the face. Various examples of glasses drawn with witnesses during sketch sessions can be seen in Figure 2.34, including a sketch with extremely thick glasses that helped patrolmen catch the suspect pictured. Take some time to look at people with various eyeglass thicknesses, and notice the effect they have on the eyes and the surrounding features of the face.

Dark glasses should reflect some kind of light. Those reflections can be any kind, but it will be wise to practice doing the highlights on dark glasses before you have a case where that item must be sketched. For the bank-robber sketches, practice replicating office lighting reflections on dark glasses. Pay close attention to the shape of those sunglasses so as to remind the suspect's acquaintances of his or her appearance.

It is a natural instinct for a forensic artist to become discouraged when the witness mentions that the perpetrator was wearing a hat *and* dark glasses. But many suspects still have been identified from those kinds of sketches, even with that much of their face covered. Some examples of sketches that were successful with this handicap are seen in Figures 2.35 and 2.36. In this situation, home in on the visible features and maximize your drawing skills to replicate them accurately. If you did your homework and became skilled at

Figure 2.34

Seven sketches and one photo of individuals with glasses. Top right: Image of a man identified by an officer on patrol who saw the sketch, second from right on top, at roll call. Bottom left: An attempt to sketch glasses with attachable shades in the up position (courtesy of the Houston Police Department). See color plate.

Figure 2.35

Top left: A sketch from a 9-year-old boy who saw his 6-year-old brother kidnapped by the man pictured top right. Another witness gave the description for the bottom sketch of this man with glasses and no hat. Notice that highlights on the dark glasses match highlights on the face (courtesy of the Houston Police Department). See color plate.

drawing the features *surrounding* the eyes, nose, and mouth, this sketch can still give lots of information about the suspect.

If detectives reach out in this situation, the crime is usually quite egregious. Be ready and willing to subdue your pessimism and sketch everything your witness *can* see well, and do a great job on that hat and glasses.

In Brief
- Collect appropriate visual aids and be ready to skillfully sketch many types of hair, hats, and glasses.
- Don't be discouraged if the suspect is wearing a hat and dark glasses. Skillfully draw what the witness *can* see.
- Facial hair grows approximately an eighth of an inch per week.

EARS

Since before the Roman Empire, men in societies that have been depicted in visual media typically have worn short hairstyles. Furthermore, since the vast majority of violent criminals are men, the forensic artist must be capable of drawing ears. Ears, however, are the most convoluted, complicated feature on the head. The difficulty of drawing this feature is witnessed in the many otherwise well-done composites with anatomically incorrect ears.

Besides being extremely complicated in its structure, the ear appears vastly different when viewed from the front as when viewed from the side, as shown in Figure 2.37. For purposes of sketching from witness memory, you must be adept at this front view. As shown in Figure 2.38, the ear is so convoluted that a diagram indicating its various anatomical points is more complicated than the surface anatomy of eyes. Take some time and practice this complicated item so as not to be left wanting. The absolute best practice would be done while observing a live, three-dimensional model and will give a better understanding

Figure 2.36

The sketch on the left was done from the description of witnesses who experienced a brutal home invasion. Even though the suspect had on a hat and sunglasses in the sketch, it was nevertheless instrumental in identifying the perpetrator pictured on the right (courtesy of the Houston Police Department).

of the shadings of the folds of flesh than would sketching from a photo of an ear. Sketching the ears of people in your residence as they watch television, read, or do some other sedentary activity can be worked into both the artist's and model's schedule. At the very least, practice the easier front view of ears for the pose most frequently needed in composites.

For unknown reasons, witnesses tend to pick out accurate ear shapes from the visual aids. Some artists waste this by putting the right-shaped ears with faulty anatomy in the interior areas. Take advantage of the witness's accuracy and make the anatomy like that of a real human ear.

Figure 2.39 is a sketch next to the identified suspect. One of the hardest forensic sketches with which to strike a likeness is of a normal face with no outstanding features. Notice how, even though the witness said he didn't see the suspect's face very well, the shaved head and the ears are fairly similar. This particular sketch was taken to a college near the crime. An officer who worked almost exclusively at that school was able to put a name with the sketch immediately upon viewing it.[4] The suspect had quit going to classes suddenly and told his friends the reason was he had done a "really bad thing." The date he said he had done this bad deed was the same as the date of the offense. The artist was very surprised at the effectiveness of the sketch since she considered the face one of the most commonplace she had ever drawn.

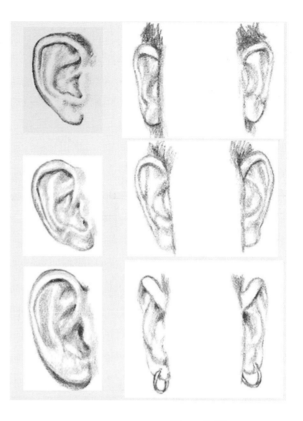

Figure 2.37

Left: Three ear shapes drawn in profile. Right: Ears drawn as they would appear in the majority of forensic sketches, viewed from the front. The ear is the most convoluted, complicated feature on the human head; therefore, you should practice its depiction until the ears in your drawings appear anatomically correct.

If the suspect is overweight enough or has a thick enough face, the ears will hardly be noticeable. However, the anatomy still needs to be understood to complete even this slender part of the ear. If the witness says the suspect has long hair, make certain to find out if the hair covers the ears entirely or only partially. A man's hairstyle that completely covers the ear is uncommon, so you will probably still be drawing at least half of this feature. Lastly, don't forget the placement of the ear as being, in general, from the top of the eye area to the bottom of the nose, as shown in Figure 2.39.

PROPORTIONS

Getting the correct proportions on a portrait from a model or a photo can be difficult. Success is determined by the artist's ability to combine these features in the right size and placement relative to each other. When the proportions are not done right, it is obvious to the viewer since the face does not look human.

Getting the correct proportions in forensic art, where the subject is *not* seen by the artist, poses far more difficulties. First, you must determine the correct shapes of eyes, nose, and lips. Then the act of combining those features into a believable, correctly proportioned face poses an almost insurmountable predicament.

Figure 2.38

Above are the anatomical points of the ear; below are the anatomical points of the eye.

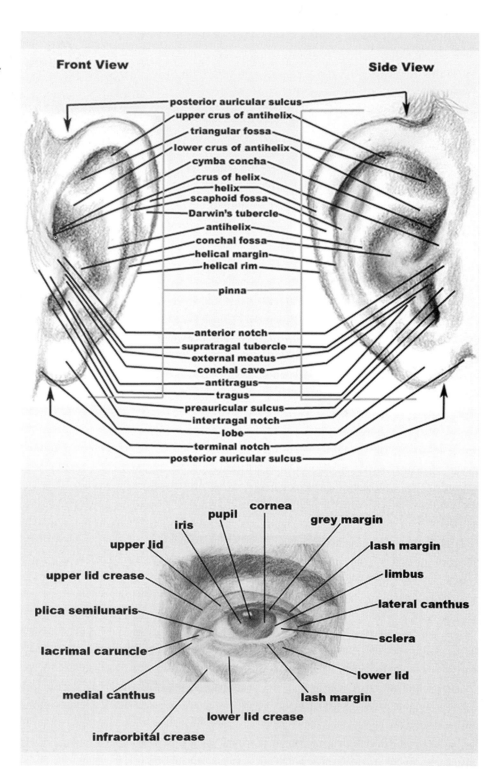

The visual aids instantly take care of the first task of finding the right-shaped features. For the correct size and placement, you can study the schematics for human facial proportions such as shown in Figures 2.40 and 2.41. Since there are obviously variations for individuals, these templates of feature placement are only guides. However, some artists use templates with all their sketches. Other artists study the placement and are able to draw it naturally. Still other artists claim individual faces vary too much and decide templates should not be used. Use the method that is most comfortable for you.

The unique proportions that give people their individual looks, the kind political cartoonists exaggerate, are those that vary from this standard layout

Figure 2.39

The most difficult forensic sketch to do effectively is that of an extremely normal face. Though the witness said he never saw this person's face, the sketch aided in finding the suspect and the resulting ears bore a good resemblance to the perpetrator's (courtesy of the Houston Police Department).

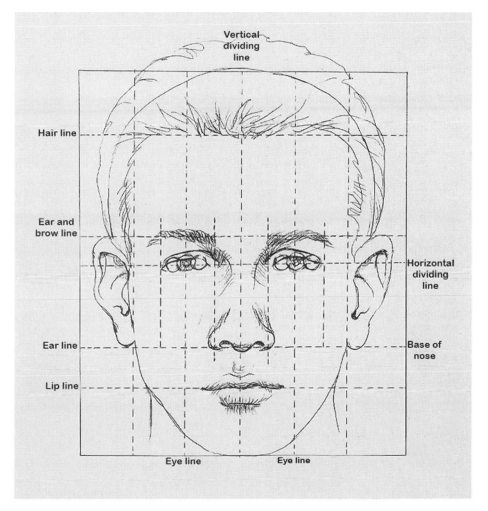

Figure 2.40

Here is a typical template for facial proportions of the frontal view. Not all faces have these exact proportions, and some forensic artists claim this is an incorrect technique. However, if a forensic artist decides using a template can help create a better sketch, that artist has a valid reason to use a template.

Figure 2.41

At right is a facial-proportion diagram for the profile.

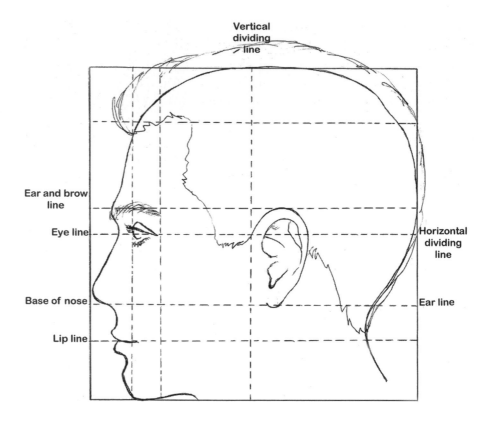

Figure 2.42

Below left: A sketch done with an 11-year-old girl who was sexually assaulted. Though the sketch developed a lead that led the detectives to find the man on the right, the proportions were so faulty as to make a poor resemblance (courtesy of the Harris County Sheriffs Department).

in Figures 2.40 and 2.41. The way to create those special variations in the sketch is by having the witness choose features from all areas of the face, not only the eyes, nose, and mouth. It is the distance *between* the features and their size relative to the other features that often make a unique resemblance.

One obvious example is seen in Figure 2.42. This sketch was taken from an 11-year-old girl who was sexually assaulted. The sketch did indeed generate a tip that led to the perpetrator's arrest, the detectives lauded the forensic artist, and the man received a life sentence.[5] To the artist, the sketch seemed horribly dissimilar. The problem is the features by themselves were similar, but their placement and size ratio to the other features were faulty. The eyebrows are too close together. The nose is the right shape at the bottom, but is far too long. The lips are too far away from the mouth. The mouth is the right shape but is too large. The man has similar hair, but the volume of his hair is much larger compared to the facial area. The most obvious dissimilarity in proportions is the layout of the features on the face. The suspect's features are clustered in the center of his face, whereas in the sketch those same features are spread out on the facial area. Said another way, the witness did not give the lower and outer fat content surrounding the eyes, lips, and nose. Added to the fact that the volume of hair was given as far less in the sketch, the result is a face where the core of eyes, lips, and nose are correct, but the outer perimeter of facial features is far off. Excuses for this are the witness was much smaller than this man and she was looking up at his face and was terrified. For law enforcement, the function of this sketch with many faults was, nevertheless, perfect. However, a study of how to avoid these pitfalls was undertaken by the artist in hopes of creating better likenesses in the future.

I have compared more than a thousand sketches and found the most common disparity in proportions of a sketch compared to the subject described: The facial core (eyes, nose, and lips) will be very similar, but there will be a great disparity in the peripheral features such as cheeks, chin, forehead, and hair. Said differently, the outer periphery of the face will be out of sync with the inner core of the face. Several examples of this are shown in Figures 2.43, 2.44, and 2.45.

In Figure 2.43, the sketch on the right was done very early in my career. The witness was a surgeon. The suspect pictured on the left was with a group of robbers who beat the doctor so severely, the bones in his hands were crushed and he thought he might never perform surgery again.[6] This doctor/witness was intensely angry because, as he lay pinned to the floor and gravely injured, the suspect on the left pushed his face so close he and the doctor were touching noses. While in this face-to-face position, the suspect swore he and his friends were going to kill this victim. Perhaps this is why the surgeon insisted the nose and lips on the sketch be made extremely bulbous and large. The sketch generated a tip that led to the robbers' capture and conviction. For years I believed the sketch bore a poor resemblance to the perpetrator in the photo, but after careful study, I realized that, if the facial cores of the sketch and the photo were isolated, the eyes, nose, and lips bore a remarkable resemblance.

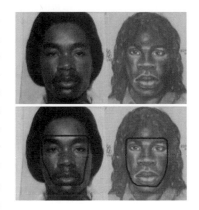

Figure 2.43

A sketch early in my career (top right) resulted in identification though the resemblance was poor. A closer examination (below left and right) shows the facial core, eyes, nose, and lips, are similar, but the periphery of the face is out of proportion with the center (courtesy of the Harris County Sheriffs Department).

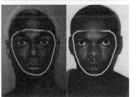

Figure 2.44

Top left: A sketch done with an elderly couple who were violently attacked in their home. The sketch led the detective to the man shown top right. Bottom left and right: The facial core of eyes, nose, and lips are similar but the outer periphery of the face differs (courtesy of the Friendswood Police Department).

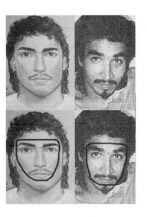

Figure 2.45

Top left: A sketch done with witnesses who saw a 10-year-old boy shot over his new bicycle. The man pictured top right was identified to authorities after being killed while attacking other people. The facial core is similar but out of sync with the peripheral facial features (courtesy of the Houston Police Department).

Figure 2.44 was done later than Figure 2.43, but still early in my career. This seemed to be an even more glaring and bothersome example of the proportional malady. Although this sketch, done from an elderly couple who were beaten, robbed, and the woman sexually assaulted in their home, led the detective to the perpetrator immediately after the sketch was released,[7] the flaws are obvious. The head in the sketch is long and slender; the suspect's head is decidedly short and round. Having already become aware of this flaw from the case in Figure 2.43, I knew immediately what was wrong and began formulating a strategy to correct this kind of flaw. The same problem occurred much later in the case worked for Figure 2.45. I believe this is because the witnesses were almost 100 feet away and saw the suspect only as his head was down (thus viewed in a foreshortened manner) as he threw a 10-year-old boy whom he had just shot from his bicycle before riding away on it.[8] Soon after, I came up with the following strategy to avoid this pervasive problem while sketching from witnesses.

This most pervasive of forensic sketching problems can be solved by paying special attention to the following guidelines. The majority of these methods involve plumbing the witness's memory for those peripheral features and their size and positioning compared to the core features of the face.

Figure 2.46

The "Average Forehead" page from the FBI Facial Identification Catalog *(courtesy of the Federal Bureau of Investigation).*

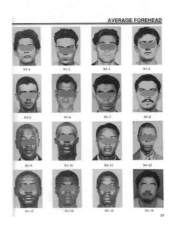

Figure 2.47

The "Low Forehead" page from the FBI Facial Identification Catalog *(courtesy of the Federal Bureau of Investigation).*

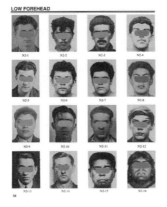

Figure 2.48

The "High Forehead" page from the FBI Facial Identification Catalog *(courtesy of the Federal Bureau of Investigation).*

The Forehead

One feature that can vary widely is the forehead. This feature can be twice as tall in individuals of the same size. The hairline on the sides of the forehead can grow more than four inches wider apart or closer together in individuals of the same size. The hairline shape along the top of the forehead has many variations. For these reasons the artist needs to gain accurate information from the witness as to the height and shape of the hairline. The best method is to have visual aids for this large facial feature. Figures 2.46, 2.47, and 2.48 are the three forehead shape pages from the *FBI Facial Identification Catalog*.

Notice on the page labeled "Average Forehead," every single example of a forehead has a different shape, especially regarding the hairline.

Go to these pages, or have your own visual aids showing foreheads, to make certain the witness is able to convey the proper shape of the hairline and size of the forehead relative to the rest of the face. The forehead, compared to the rest of the face, is a large feature and should not be ignored when searching the memory of the witness. Since this part of the anatomy takes up approximately one-third of the facial surface, it will be easily remembered by even the most traumatized witness.

Figure 2.49 is a sketch done from a man who witnessed the murder of a father and the man's 8-year-old daughter. This witness was traumatized and fearful that, since the homicide was a cult killing, he also would be murdered.[9] It seemed impossible to get this witness to concentrate at all on the drawing during the sketch interview. This sketch being early in my career, the common rookie mistake is present in that the irises were made too large. Additionally, this man was wearing a full beard when he committed the murder; he shaved while a fugitive. However, the large, unusual, and visually dynamic forehead/hairline were remembered and thus drawn with great accuracy.

Forensic artists should know hair on the head grows from a half to a third of an inch per month. Thus, if the subject being sketched has a shaved head, artists can take heart the subject has a hairstyle that is quite noticeable and slow to change. This will hopefully make up for the fact it is a difficult style to sketch.

The Philtrum

The philtrum is one feature that has great bearing on the unique proportions of an individual. This is the area between the bottom of the nose and the top of the upper lip. This distance varies so little between individuals that a baby two years of age can have the same distance between the nose and lips as a 6-foot-tall adult. Since the variance of this area is so small, getting it right plays an important role in creating an individual's unique look. Figure 2.50 shows two adults genetically related to a very small baby.

Figure 2.49

The witness for this sketch, left, saw this man, right, kill a neighbor and that neighbor's 8-year-old daughter. Though the witness was nearly hysterical, the forehead was remembered with great accuracy; the detectives even held up the suspect's hair during the photo to make a record of the resemblance. A beginner's mistake of making the irises too large is obvious (courtesy of the Houston Police Department).

Figure 2.50

The 5-year-old boy pictured at left has a philtrum (the distance/area between the bottom of the nose and top of the upper lip) almost the same length as the adult male beside him despite being less than one-fifth his height or weight. The philtrum is crucial to proportions since it varies so little (photo on left by Diane Denton, center and right photos by author).

Even though the adults are far more than five times the height and weight of the baby, the length of their philtrum area is the same. Even in the far right photo, where the baby is less than 2 months old and has no teeth, the length from the bottom of his nose to the top of his lips is almost as long as the same area on the adult male.

The time for determining philtrum size from the witness comes when you have finished the nose and the witness has chosen the lips from the visual aids that best resemble those of the suspect. At that time, point out some philtrum areas, or lip to nose-base relationships, and ask about the perpetrator's. Witnesses almost always have been able to give guidance when these questions are asked. Referring to Figure 2.51, the "Average Lips" page in the FBI catalog, we see how mouths can rest at varying distances from the above nose.

As an example of how to zero in on the correct distance covered by the philtrum in question, suppose the witness picks E1-16 in the catalog. Ask the witness if the lips are *that close* to the bottom of the nose, *further away* as in E1-9, or *closer* like E1-11. Of the hundreds of witnesses asked this kind of question, all were able to give an opinion. Or, after the witness picks either some close-up lips like E1-11, or far-away lips like E1-9, ask if the suspect had lips closer or farther away than the example. Once again, witnesses almost always can answer this question, giving you an important clue to your subject's proportions. A finishing thought is that men with mustaches that are wider on the horizontal plane have longer philtrum areas; narrower mustaches indicate shorter philtrum areas. As can be seen in Figure 2.52, the mustache was so thick, getting that easily noticed feature correct insured a correct philtrum size and a fortunate resemblance.[10]

The Distance between Eyes and Eyebrows

Witnesses often will choose eyes from the visual aids and tell you they should be closer together or farther apart. The fact is, your witness will be sensitive to

Figure 2.51

The "Average Lips" page from the FBI Facial Identification Catalog *(courtesy of the Federal Bureau of Investigation).*

Figure 2.52

The sketch at far right was taken from a description by a worker who was robbed by the man on the right while working at a bank. When a suspect has such a thick mustache, it can be assumed the philtrum length is fairly large (courtesy of the Harris County Sheriffs Department).

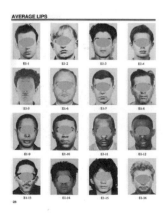
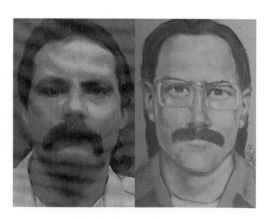

these traits. Listening and responding to this kind of remark can save a lot of time and difficult effort moving the eyes when the witness sees the sketch for the changes in the end stage.

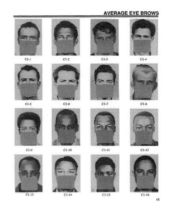

Figure 2.53

The "Average Eyebrow" page from the FBI Facial Identification Catalog (courtesy of the Federal Bureau of Investigation).

Another feature about which witnesses almost always can give an opinion as to placement and spacing is the distance from the eyes to the eyebrows. For example, say the witness chooses the eyebrows from C1-12, as shown in Figure 2.53. Whether the witness chooses those eyes or another eye shape, ask him or her if the eyebrows are that far above the eyes or closer down as in C1-16. Again, witnesses almost always can answer that question, giving you another important clue to the proportions of the face you are sketching. Conversely, if the witness picks eyebrows like B4-2 as seen in Figure 2.54, ask if those brows should be that close to the eyes or farther away. Often the witness will say to move them a bit higher off the eyes.

An important note is the fact that hundreds of witnesses who insisted they did not see the face well enough to do a sketch later were able to give these accurate calibrations for the proportions or positioning of features in relation to the other features. The reasons for this paradox will be explained extensively in following chapters.

In Brief
- Be capable of drawing the ear, the most complex feature on the head.
- The forehead plays a large role in proportions.
- Head hair grows approximately one-half to one-third an inch per month.
- Correct proportions are often about the distances *between* the features. Have the witness use the visual aids to point out the nuances of feature placement.

DEEPSET EYES

Figure 2.54

The top line of the "Deepset Eyes" page of the FBI Facial Identification Catalog (courtesy of the Federal Bureau of Investigation).

| B4-1 | B4-2 | B4-3 | B4-4 |

EDUCATIONAL ACTIVITIES CONDUCIVE TO FORENSIC ART

Life drawing classes, where a live model is provided, are the best way a forensic artist can enhance his or her skills at a university or college. Students place themselves around the model and draw that person as realistically as possible. Usually the model is completely nude. The forensic artist could focus, as many students do, on the face of the model. Drawing down to the neck and shoulders will definitely be beneficial.

The reason artists learn to draw the body without clothes is that you cannot do the best depiction of a clothed person unless you understand the underlying body shape. Since the models for these classes are usually young and thin, the most common criminal body would be replicated. Fine artists believe in this practice so universally that almost all large cities have some place where artists pay a fee and a live model is provided. In this venue professional artists who no longer attend a university can still practice "life drawing" without enrolling in an institution. It is recommended that a quality practice for a forensic artist would be either to take life drawing at a college or university or find an organization where like-minded artists hire a model for life drawing.

ESSENTIAL EXERCISES

Before you find yourself alone in a room with a distraught witness and a high-profile case hanging in the balance, there is one essential exercise you should do. To best replicate the witness-interview sketching situation, find someone willing to "act" as a witness in a simulation, to take the time to help create a sketch. Have that individual look at someone he or she has never seen before. That person should be a male between the ages of late teens to 40s. This demographic will represent 99% of the subjects you will sketch during your work. After viewing this stranger, your "witness" should take a photo of that subject. The photo should be sealed immediately in an envelope. If a digital camera is used, simply wait until after the exercise to download the image.

After seeing the stranger, the witness should describe him to you. You can employ all the techniques you choose from this book or other training and try to draw the person the simulated witness saw, from his or her memory. It goes without saying that you should not go with the "witness" and see the stranger, and neither the witness nor you should "peek" at the photo of the subject until after the exercise.

If you have never done a sketch from memory before, your results will be better than you imagine *while* you are trying to draw the face. No matter what the results, take a photo of your sketch for comparison to the individual described. If you are disappointed, it is of little consequence. Notice your weaknesses and repeat the exercise with a new subject. Keep in mind what went wrong before and try to correct whatever that might be.

It cannot be emphasized enough how beneficial this sketching-with-a-simulated-witness exercise can be. To actually try and pull an image from the mind of a "witness" is like no other drawing experience. Potential forensic artists can study theories and methods for hours. However, that is like studying how to swim. Doing this exercise with a simulated witness is like jumping into water and swimming. The theories can go only so far. The best way to successfully learn how to do something is actually to *do* it.

Good forensic art training will include this kind of simulation. Usually the class pairs off and one person is the witness while the other acts as the artist. Subsequently the pair trades places and the witness becomes the one who interviews and sketches while the previous artist plays the role of witness.

This exercise can be a great experience builder to the civilian who is not employed by a law enforcement agency. Persons who are employed by law enforcement agencies, but who are not in a position where they are ever placed with witnesses to crimes for the purpose of sketching the perpetrator, can benefit from these simulations. Individuals in either of these situations can collect a portfolio of sketches compared to photos that can be shown as proof they can do this important, challenging work.

One way to show great expertise is to use a simulated witness who is 10 to 12 years old. I'm not sure why, but this youthful age produces some of the best witnesses with whom to sketch. Since some early artists incorrectly assumed these adolescent witnesses would be too young, a sketch done from this source will appear to be quite an accomplishment to adult investigators. There is one warning: the younger the witness, the more necessary it is to use visual aids.

How to Conduct This Essential Exercise

Have a friend and his or her child agree to spend the time and effort with you to do your sketching-from-witness-memory exercise. The friend can arrange to take the child to another friend's or acquaintance's house to meet a male of adult age the child has never seen before. This adult male can be someone from out of state or simply across town. The only criterion is the child cannot have seen this person before. After the child has briefly viewed this individual, have your friend take a photo from the same angle as the child's view.

The friend now brings his or her child to you and a sketch can be created from the child's memory. After the sketch is done, the photo can be revealed for comparison. This exercise can be done with the "witness" being any age. The single reason I suggest a child is because children make terrific witnesses, and make picks from the visual aids three to five times more quickly than adults!

Conducting the Exercise

Some rules for conducting the sketching-from-witness-memory exercise are as follows.

- Do not have the "witness" simply look at a photograph. In forensic artwork, your real witnesses will see a live, three-dimensional person who is breathing, moving, and usually talking. Having a person describe a face he or she saw in a photo does not replicate the forensic sketching situation.

- Do not have the "witness" look at a female, at least at first. The vast majority of violent criminals are males, so at least the first practices should be done of men's faces. Having stated that, it is advisable to sketch at least one female for the rare but egregious infant-kidnapping case. The first and majority of practices should be of male subjects.

- Do not have the "witness" look at an elderly person. The vast majority of criminals will be aged from late teens to early 40s.

- Do have the "witness" look at someone unusual. A man with a large mustache is easy to remember and sketch, and the beginner deserves this advantage.

- Do keep copies of the sketch and photo of the subject described. All artists know they are their own worst critic. Instead of denigrating your efforts if the sketch is off here or there, take the opportunity to focus on the mistake. Then do the exercise again, concentrating on correcting that specific mistake. Store the comparisons away, no matter how disappointing. Experience has shown that, when viewed later, rejected artwork always looks better to the creator. Understand the important potential for the novice artist. If you do many of these practices and save the comparisons, those can be assembled as a portfolio to prove proficiency to detectives who might need forensic art services.

- Do feel free to construct the sketch right after your "witness" has viewed the subject. The practicing forensic artist is called out immediately after the incident on many cases, thus lending validity to practicing right after the subject of the drawing has been viewed.

Years ago I received a call from someone wishing to become a forensic artist. After being presented with the proposition that the caller should perform these exercises, the caller refused. She related the concept that she should be "…paid to practice." This attitude is not conducive to a successful forensic artist. This individual wanted to practice on a real victim of crime.

In the real world, probably most beginning cases *are* done by artists with hardly any practice. However, any practice as realistic as explained earlier most certainly can improve the quality of sketches, even for artists who are already working in the field. The only thing the artist has to lose is a couple of hours. This seems a small price to pay if the next call could be a high-profile murder or other felony. If persons are already employed as classified officers in a law enforcement agency, it should not be difficult to gain permission to practice in this manner while on duty. An agency could logically justify the two or three hours a month it would take for them to cultivate their forensic artist, especially if there is no other such artist available nearby.

By the way, the previously mentioned caller attempted several sketches, the last of which the witness walked out of without finishing. This artist who refused to practice gave up trying to be a forensic artist after a few months.

Be a Witness to Learn from the Inside Out

This brings up another important exercise. There is great understanding to be had by playing the role of the "witness." Forensic artists of varying experience levels always gain great insights by walking in the shoes of someone who glances at a face, and then must describe the features to someone for a sketch. If you are not planning on attending training, set up a situation with another artist with whom you can play the role of the witness. This exercise is guaranteed to give some understanding of how a witness feels, which can be gained in no other way. This role reversal is so enlightening that even if the artist has sketched from witnesses previously, he or she almost always changes something about how he or she interviews due to new insights.

WORK EXPERIENCES CONDUCIVE TO FORENSIC ART

The occupation that will radically enhance drawing skills and closely mimic the sketching situation in forensic art is not suited to all temperaments. However, this kind of work has been so instrumental in making me agile at the drawing part of the forensic-art profession, it must be mentioned in detail. Employment as a public artist who does fine-art portraits in a one-time sitting for an immediate fee can do wonders for an artist's ability to sketch the human face quickly and accurately.

I sketched thousands of live portraits on the River Walk in San Antonio. That experience forces the artist to draw the individual accurately with attention to good speed, two key components of a successful forensic artist's abilities.

Marla Lawson, the forensic artist for the Georgia Bureau of Investigation, also was employed as a public portrait artist in her state of Georgia. Marla is arguably the best forensic artist in the world. Her sketches show a virtuosity not seen elsewhere and her large yearly workload that she handles with ease, speaks of an artist who is imminently comfortable sketching faces with witnesses. Viewing

Marla Lawson's experience, it can be deduced that sketching portraits in public can forge an artist into the kind of portraitist most suited for forensic art. For a view of just a few of Marla Lawson's sketches done from witness description juxtaposed with the proven perpetrator of the crimes, refer to Figure 2.55. Marla also does amazing work with sketching portraits postmortem of unidentified homicide victims (see Figure 2.56).

Notice how her extensive work sketching live models enabled her to imbue these faces with an extraordinary life-like quality. Observe also that these are not works of art that took dozens of hours; rather they are obviously sketched quickly, similar to the method necessary for sketching live models in public before they tire of the pose.

Figure 2.55

Four examples of sketches done from witnesses by the renowned Marla Lawson of the Georgia Bureau of Investigation. Juxtaposed to each sketch is the perpetrator. Marla Lawson engaged in creating portraits of live models in public, likely aiding her in her forensic artistry (courtesy of Marla Lawson and the Georgia Bureau of Investigations).

Figure 2.56

Sketches of unidentified deceased persons done from post-mortem photographs by Marla Lawson of the Georgia Bureau of Investigation. Lawson's occupation of sketching portraits of live models in public likely aided her ability to make even these quick sketches of deceased persons seem quite life-like (courtesy of Marla Lawson and the Georgia Bureau of Investigations).

The method for doing this kind of work is straightforward. Every mall at Christmas time would be a location teaming with potential patrons of this kind of art. Simply make an alliance with a frame shop or gallery. Ask to set up in front of their shop, but not blocking the walkway. When you are sketching portraits, a crowd will always gather. Therefore, it is a win-win situation for the shop. The crowd you attract will increase customers browsing in their shop. Your patrons will probably need to buy a frame from the shop for the portrait you create, as it will need to be covered with glass for protection. Therefore, there is a frame sale for nearly every portrait. Also, most artists give the hosting shop a percentage of the money taken in. Often the artist attracts so much commerce that this percentage is waived.

Many artists have been able to set up in shops that are not galleries. Some shops that have aligned with portrait artists have nothing to do with art. The shop owner simply realizes the attention will increase business. Obviously, if you live near a tourist area, you can create a business liaison with a shop in that area.

Figure 2.57 is a collage of me doing a portrait on the San Antonio River Walk. The Stanrite 500 easel shown can allow more than one light to be attached along its main shaft. You should employ at least two lights, one aimed at the model and the other at the work in progress. It is almost mandatory for advertisement to have a third light aimed at some examples of your work. For these examples, pick a person that everyone walking by will recognize. Displaying this famous person's portrait proves you can create a likeness of someone's face. The lights on your work and the model will spotlight an activity that people find fascinating. As can be seen in Figure 2.57, a crowd will always gather to watch the drawing take form. A plus for the ambiance of the locale is that drawing is silent and need only be noticed if the viewer chooses.

If you can withstand the pressure of this situation, you will develop into an accomplished portrait artist. Additionally, the time pressure of customers waiting in line, the distractions of the crowd, and the need to create a likeness replicate almost all the important elements of the forensic art situation. As a fortunate offshoot, working in this capacity, the artist can earn a substantial income per hour. For that reason, and because of the speed and ease you can gain for the occasion when you eventually work with a witness to help solve a crime, this occupation is unparalleled in enhancing a forensic artist's skills.

If you cannot stand the pressure of sketching in this capacity for money, try sketching at parties. To further shelter your sensitivity, the party could be for an adolescent of a distant acquaintance. Another shelter for sensitivity could be placing your easel so that your back is toward the corner of the room, where

Figure 2.57

Three photos of me sketching tourist portraits on the San Antonio River Walk. Notice how the use of an easel is key to this kind of activity. This occupation closely replicates the need for speed and accuracy found when sketching from the memory of a witness to crime (courtesy of the Cobalt Manufacturing Company).

passersby cannot easily view the sketch. The point of the exercise is to draw faces where there is time pressure, the sketch needs to be finished in one sitting, and there is motivation to create a good likeness of the subject.

It is true; you can be a great forensic artist without having sketched in public. However, this occupation compels you to be fast and efficient at portraiture. It could be likened to a portrait-artist boot camp. There is only one way to do the work; it must be fast and efficient. The money made usually causes such an artist to sketch dozens more subjects than would a student in art school during the busiest of semesters.

In Brief
- Drawing live models where the focus is on the face is good training for forensic artwork.
- An indispensable exercise is to use a friend to simulate sketching from a witness's memory of a face.
- Acting as the witness for an artist to sketch from your memory offers insights gained no other way.
- Drawing portraits in public replicates the pressures of drawing faces from witnesses and will hone your portraiture skills to a remarkable degree.

STEP-BY-STEP DRAWING FOR A REAL CASE

The following is a detailed explanation of what a highly traumatized witness to a real crime conveyed verbally, with the help of visual aids and other means. This explanation will be accompanied by stages of the sketch as it progressed from the information given. Each step of the drawing will be explained as to why it was constructed in such a way. To show the progression from start to finish, I have copied my original drawing. No mechanical means were used to trace. I used the most common medium, which is graphite pencil on Bristol board with a vellum finish, for this demonstration. The original was done in pastel on felt gray Canson Mi-Tientes paper. An almost exact copy was made, including all the mistakes and the proportions, which were dissimilar to the perpetrator's photo when he was caught. It is most important to note that the sketch, with all its imperfections, was directly responsible for identifying this man.

The case that generated the need for this sketch unfolded like this. Officer Paul Deason was on patrol and stopped a man in a vehicle for a routine moving violation in an affluent part of town. The man, who was an escaped felon, immediately exited his vehicle. He shot Officer Deason once in the head and once in the back. As Deason lay on the ground, the felon got back into his car and ran over the officer, dragging him more than 55 feet. Deason broke free of the undercarriage, walked back to his patrol unit, and called in his own assist. He was rushed to the hospital and stabilized.

Approximately 34 hours later I arrived at the hospital bedside of Officer Deason at the behest of the detectives working the case. After the resulting sketch was released to the media, a man was arrested trying to shoplift a chainsaw from a hardware store. One individual who helped apprehend the shoplifter from the parking lot of the hardware store and two jail personnel where the thief later was taken, all suggested that the offender looked like the sketch of Officer Deason's shooter. A video line-up was held in Officer Deason's hospital room and he positively identified Donald Eugene Dutton. A later search of the hardware store parking lot turned up a vehicle with pieces of Officer Deason's skin and uniform hanging from the undercarriage. Dutton was tried, convicted, and sentenced to life in prison.[11]

What follows are the actions of the witness and artist, and the sketch as it unfolded. Reasons as to why the features were drawn as they were are explained.

THE SCENE OF THE SKETCH

I found Officer Deason lying in a hospital bed, completely covered with bandages except some openings over his mouth, lips, and eyes. He appeared to be heavily sedated.

I quietly set up the easel and materials, taking care not to awaken the injured officer. When I was ready to begin sketching, I whispered in Officer Deason's ear that I wanted to sketch the man who did this to him. I concentrated on having the most pleasant voice tone possible.

Officer Deason said that he did not see the face of the shooter, only the flash of the gunfire.

I did not argue with the witness. Instead, I talked soothingly about how well he had survived. I mentioned other pleasantries about living through the ordeal and what the future held. Then almost as an aside, I asked what kind of terrible person would do such a thing. "What kind of expression did he have?" I asked.

The officer said, "He didn't have any expression. He looked like a shark, like he didn't care about anything at all."

Since the witness described the expression, it could be determined that he *did* see the face.

I asked Deason to please just look at some features and see if anything seemed similar to that man. I held the *FBI Facial Identification Catalog* horizontally above Deason's face so he could see clearly and turned the pages when he wanted. After indicating the shooter was a white male aged late 20s to early 30s, of average height and build, Deason picked B1-3 as the eyes and eyebrows

AVERAGE EYES

 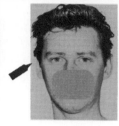 

B1-1   B1-2   B1-3   B1-4

Figure 2.58

At right is the top line of examples from the "Average Eyes" page of the FBI Facial Identification Catalog. *The gravely injured officer picked the third example, B1-3, out of all 144 examples on nine pages (courtesy of the Federal Bureau of Investigation).*

(shown as the third from left in Figure 2.58). Asked about the forehead and hair, Deason said those features were also like B1-3. When asked, the officer said there were no stray hairs like those in the example. Deason indicated rather that the hair was slightly shorter and smoother on the sides.

Since I tried to show the injured officer all the pages of eye examples from the catalog, Deason's choices of almost the first example for eyes, brows, and hair, made me think the officer was simply trying to get the sketch over with or not taking the choices seriously, or that he was so heavily medicated he was not truly responding. I pushed the doubts aside and continued to sketch, resulting in an image almost identical to the image on the left of Figure 2.59.

Deason was shown several pages of noses and chose example D1-1, the very first nose example on the first of nine pages from the FBI catalog. The top row of nose examples from that page is shown in Figure 2.60. I asked if there was a rounded "ball shape" at the end of the nose since Officer Deason showed an interest in nose example D1-3 before settling on D1-1. Deason said there was no "ball shape" at the end of the shooter's nose. Deason then fell asleep, leaving me to sketch on those bits of information.

I sketched as quickly and efficiently as possible while the injured officer dozed off into a drug-induced nap. When the nose portion of the sketch was

Figure 2.59

On the left is how the sketch appeared with the eyes drawn; to the right is with the nose sketched in.

finished, as on the right side of Figure 2.59, I gently awakened the officer and asked if the attacker had a mustache. Deason indicated he did, and I held the "Mustache and Beard" section of the catalog over his face for his perusal. The officer picked mustache K2-4 shown in Figure 2.61, and I sketched the image on the left of Figure 2.62. Once again, the gravely injured officer picked an example from the top row of the FBI catalog, causing me to feel doubts about the sincerity of his choices.

AVERAGE NOSE

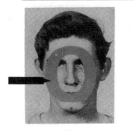
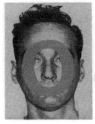
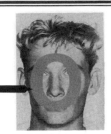
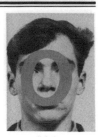

| D1-1 | D1-2 | D1-3 | D1-4 |

Figure 2.60

The gravely injured officer chose D1-1 first on left as looking like his assailant's nose. Since the officer showed an interest in D1-3, I asked him if his attacker had a ball shape on the end of his nose (like D1-1) and the officer indicated he did not (courtesy of the Federal Bureau of Investigation).

MUSTACHE

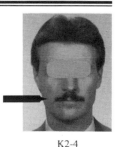

| K2-1 | K2-2 | K2-3 | K2-4 |

Figure 2.61

The highly medicated officer picked K2-4 as looking like his attacker's mustache (courtesy of the Federal Bureau of Investigation).

At this time the officer was wheeled suddenly out of the room, and I had to scoop up my gear and follow him to another floor. After gaining clearance from the personnel in the magnetic imaging area where the officer waited on his bed in line with other patients, I continued my work.

The officer agreed the sketch of the mustache was satisfactory. After being shown many pages of lips, Deason chose E1-1 as shown in Figure 2.63. After being questioned about the chin, he indicated the E1-1 example closely resembled the chin also.

Since the injured officer had picked the first example for the nose, lips, and chin, I harbored doubts about the sincerity and/or clarity of his choices and attention to the task of sketching the shooter.

Forensic art rule: Always finish the sketch no matter how difficult the interview, if you think the witness saw the face.

Early in my career it was proven that no matter how difficult the interview, if the witness saw a face, the artist should continue the interview until the sketch is finished. Some of the best likenesses have resulted from some of the most

Figure 2.62

Left: The sketch after drawing in the mustache. Right: The sketch with the mouth drawn in after the witness picked example E1-1. The lips and nose were each the first example of over a hundred choices, and the eyes were from the top of the first page of eye choices.

difficult interviews. Many successful sketches were created in situations that made me want to abandon the interview at almost every step. To be a successful forensic artist, you must ignore doubt on the part of yourself and the witness.

Because I had learned this lesson, I finished the sketch up to a point shown in the left of Figure 2.64. At that time I asked the final question as to what kind of shirt the officer's attacker wore. The officer indicated a medium-toned plaid shirt, and I constructed that garment as seen on the right of Figure 2.64.

The officer was now shown the sketch for the first time by holding it horizontally above his gaze. I asked if any changes would help the sketch more closely resemble the attacker's face. After a very long pause with no reply from the officer, I queried whether the drawing appeared similar to the shooter's face. Deason would not reply verbally. Instead, he raised his hand and pointed his finger at the face in the drawing. Once again, I gently asked if there were any changes. Officer Deason weakly mumbled a negative answer to that question.

I gathered my gear, exited the patient area, and set up in the hall where I intensified the darks and lights in the drawing without changing the shapes of the features. I then sprayed fixative on the drawing as shown on the left of Figure 2.65. The detective met me in a hospital hallway and retrieved the sketch.

The sketch was released immediately to the media. An escaped convict named Donald Eugene Dutton was caught shoplifting two days later. One officer at the scene of the shoplifting capture and two personnel who received Dutton at the city jail told detectives they thought he looked like the sketch of Officer Deason's shooter. A video line-up was held in Officer Deason's hospital room and he identified Dutton as the man who shot him and ran over him, dragging him under the shooter's vehicle. A search of the parking lot outside the shoplifting scene turned up Dutton's vehicle with pieces of Officer Deason's skin and uniform hanging from the undercarriage.

Figure 2.63

The injured officer picked E1-1 left as the lips that most resembled his attacker's (courtesy of the Federal Bureau of Investigation).

AVERAGE LIPS

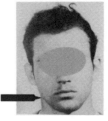

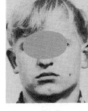

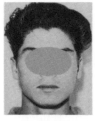

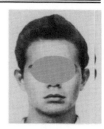

E1-1 E1-2 E1-3 E1-4

I compared the mug shot of Dutton with the sketch, and found the following flaws regarding how similar it was to the perpetrator:

- The nose was too long.
- The mustache was not large enough or long enough.
- The forehead was not quite wide enough.
- The irises were too large.
- The face was a little too chubby.
- The chin was not quite the right shape.

I further discovered that Dutton had features quite similar to those chosen by the injured witness, which coincidentally, were almost all the first feature in each category. Therefore, the rule about ignoring doubts and finishing the sketch, in spite of obstacles, paid off.

The drawing technique was simple, once the witness began choosing features from the visual aids. I simply drew the features indicated, combining them in the right place and proportion for a human face. I happen to start at the top and go down; however, most artists first block out the face with light marks and then draw in the details. Some artists would use a template to guide feature placement. Either method will work. Simply plug in the features indicated by the witness.

Figure 2.64

The nearly finished face is sketched on the far left; to the right is an image of the sketch with the plaid shirt drawn in.

Figure 2.65

Above left: The sketch with finishing touches. Above right: The man caught shoplifting a chain saw. The light colored plaid shirt in his arrest photo shows a consistency in his clothing choices (courtesy of the Houston Police Department).

In Brief
- Endure all difficulties to the completion of the sketch if you think the witness saw the face of the perpetrator.
- When the witness insists he or she did not see the face of the perpetrator, never argue. Instead, make pleasant conversation about uplifting topics. Then pose the rhetorical question: "What kind of expression did he/she have?" If the witness answers that question, he or she saw the face, and the interview can proceed.

CONCLUSION

With visual aids, the drawing part of this forensic sketch was straightforward. Using the rules of sketching portraits, any artist could perform the task of drawing this face with ease. It is rather the other part of the drawing, extracting information from the witness's memory, that becomes very problematic. This witness was shot twice, run over, and dragged beneath a vehicle for a great distance. The witness told the artist he did not see the face of the shooter. He further was obviously on medication that dulled his senses. Another complication was that the perpetrator of the crime had features that resembled the first picks in the 180 examples of each feature in the catalog. Only patience and persistence in the face of all these obstacles allowed me to finish the sketch. Additionally, I needed to disregard all doubts, both internal and external, to continue to the successful completion of the shooter's image.

You must believe you can draw a face you cannot see from a witness memory or you will never complete a sketch. There will be no vote of confidence from the witness in this effort. Therefore, the only source of confidence that this task can be done, before you have amassed a track record of successful sketches, will be the supportive nature of other like-minded forensic artists.

Remember this counterintuitive fact: 100% of the time when a reasonably talented, reasonably trained forensic artist sketches from the memory of a witness, the sketch will be at least *similar* to the person being described. Therefore, the most important lesson to be learned from this book might be that you should continue through to the end, no matter how much you or the witness doubts the process can succeed.

REFERENCES

1. Staff, "Police warn leasing agents, ask help to catch serial rapist," *Houston Chronicle*, March 15, 1988. Houston Police Department Incident Number 10404088.

2. Lisa Teachey, "Lawmen find jogger's body/Nightly run along bayou ends in assault, death," *Houston Chronicle*, July 31, 1997. Eric Hanson, "Suspect, 27, is charged in jogger's death," *Houston Chronicle*, August 10, 1997. Steve Brewer, "Witnesses recall scene before jogger's slaying/Testimony places defendant on same trail the victim used just prior to her abduction," *Houston Chronicle*, June 17, 1998. Steve Brewer, "Confession tells victim's last words/'She was asking me did I know God'," *Houston Chronicle*, June 18, 1998. Steve Brewer, "Man who strangled jogger convicted of capital murder," *Houston Chronicle*, June 20, 1998. Steve Brewer, "Man receives death sentence in jogger's abduction, slaying," *Houston Chronicle*, June 24, 1998. Harris County Sheriffs Case Number 9707292767.

3. Jo Ann Zuniga, "Traffic stop turns tragic for officer," *Houston Chronicle*, January 6, 1991. Eric Hanson, "Suspect in shooting of officer arrested," *Houston Chronicle*, January 8,

1991. Robert Stanton, " 'Galleria Rapist' receives life sentence in shooting," *The Houston Post*, July 18, 1991. Houston Police Department Incident Number 1449791.

4. Humble Police Department Case Number 1-04-005580.

5. S. K. Bardwell, "Authorities search for serial sex offender," *Houston Chronicle*, May 31, 1997. Lisa Teachey, "Man faces 11 counts of child sex assault," *Houston Chronicle*, June 3, 1997. Jo Ann Zuniga, "Man receives life sentence for sexually assaulting children," *Houston Chronicle*, February 3, 1998. Harris County Sheriffs Case Number 9703041828.

6. Houston Police Department Incident Number 8249088.

7. Friendswood Police Department Case Number 92-3431, Texas State District Court 212, Case number 92CR1383, State of Texas vs. Jake Williams, sentence: 196 years.

8. Lisa Teachy, "10-year-old shot in bike robbery may never walk again," *Houston Chronicle*, July 12, 1998. Lisa Teachey, "Sketch issued of suspect in shooting of boy/Youth reportedly shot for his 10-speed bicycle," *Houston Chronicle*, July 17, 1998. Eric, Berger, "A painful message to deliver/Family telling wounded boy he likely won't walk again," *Houston Chronicle*, July 15, 1998. Lisa Teachey, "Suspect in shooting of boy killed by car," *Houston Chronicle*, October 7, 1998. Houston Police Department Incident Number 87199298.

9. Jerry Urban, "Six in sect indicted in four slayings/8-year-old girl among 1988 victims," *Houston Chronicle*, August 25, 1992. Patricia Manson, "Jury indicts 6 in execution-style slayings within polygamous sect," *Houston Post*, August 25, 1992. Jerry Urban, "Ex-LeBaron cultist admits two slayings," *Houston Chronicle*, September 16, 1992. Houston Police Department Incident Number 50598888.

10. Houston Police Department Incident Number 133948197.

11. Jo Ann Zuniga, "Traffic stop turns tragic for officer/Policeman shot twice, run over," *Houston Chronicle*, January 6, 1991. Eric Hanson, "Suspect in shooting of officer arrested," *Houston Chronicle*, January 10, 1991. "Prison escapee charged with attempted capital murder in attack on officer," Staff, *Houston Chronicle*, January 11, 1991. John Makeig, " 'Galleria rapist' gets life in police shooting," *Houston Chronicle*, July 18, 1991. Houston Police Department Incident Number 1449791.

PULLING FACES FROM WITNESS MEMORY

ATTITUDE IS EVERYTHING

The mood of the witness is the paramount priority during the interview. Every effort should be made to help the witness feel as happy, relaxed, and comfortable as possible. This can be daunting since almost all witnesses will have experienced the most horrible event of their lives before they meet with the forensic artist. Added to this is the fact that the subject of your sketch will be the face of the person who caused this terrible event. Then one last obstacle is the fact that most witnesses lack confidence that the artist's sketch can help solve their case.

GETTING THE ARTIST'S ATTITUDE IN SHAPE

Following are ways to bolster your confidence. Your attitude is the one thing that can be controlled and nurtured from within by understanding that even the most imperfect work can be a factor in solving the case. To combat the pessimism surrounding your efforts, I have assembled some documented incidents where the sketch helped to solve the case. The following are varied descriptions of scenarios where sketches helped the investigator discover the person responsible for a crime. If the beginning artist knows how many varied ways a sketch can help the investigator identify the criminal, it will give him or her a confident attitude. If investigators reading this understand these scenarios, it will increase their usage of forensic artists. They will further understand how having sketches done from their witnesses can help them find their suspect. This list is meant to help instill in you a positive attitude that will produce the best efforts. This positive attitude is essential since you cannot instill confidence in a witness if you don't first feel confident yourself.

For clarification of what works in forensic art, I constructed a definition of a successful forensic sketch early in Chapter 1. That definition bears repeating here before this extensive list of successful scenarios.

A forensic sketch is successful if it helps identify the perpetrator of a crime.

Forensic artists have discussed for years what defines success in their profession regarding the results generated for the investigator by using a forensic sketch. I believe the earlier definition is straightforward enough. If others in the profession wish to disregard or replace this definition with their own, they are welcome to do so. However, since attitude is indeed very important to any effort, it is important for artists in this most challenging field to envision possible successes. For this reason a definition of success needs to be installed in order to understand the ultimate goal of the forensic sketch.

The following list is an effort to help you envision a myriad of ways in which you might find a satisfying ending to your efforts. While in the midst of this struggle to create a sketch with a witness, knowledge of the varied opportunities for success can buoy your mood and thus improve your efforts to create the elusive image of that suspect's face.

When possible, the following scenarios have case numbers and news reports cited as references. Some scenarios are changed to protect the innocent.

After the sketch generated these identification tips, the detective held line-ups, got confessions, found ancillary evidence, or otherwise confirmed the identification enough to bring charges in a court of law. This list is not an exhaustive selection of how sketches work during investigations; there are hundreds of other unique true stories. The possibilities for other successful scenarios where sketches can help a detective would be as numerous and varied as the twists and turns of future crime investigations.

Some scenarios where forensic sketches helped identify the perpetrator are as follows.

- A live-in girlfriend sees the sketch on the news that resembles her significant other and calls authorities to give them his name and location.
- Relatives of a perpetrator see a sketch on the news and call authorities with information on their suspected kin.
- An officer makes a domestic disturbance call and thinks the abusive son looks like the sketch of a rapist in the area. The witness for this sketch was attacked and sexually assaulted in her home after returning from high school. A line-up done for the victim who helped the artist construct the sketch identifies the domestic disturbance suspect as the neighborhood rapist.[1] The comparison of the sketch with the mug shot can be seen in Figure 3.1.
- A person visiting another home overhears someone say, "I'm better looking than that!" when

Figure 3.1

Left: A sketch, done September 1, 1999, from a teen who was sexually assaulted in her home. On September 14 officers were called to the suspect's home when he became violent toward his family. His resemblance to the sketch led to a line-up and his identification (courtesy of the Houston Police Department).

he sees the sketch on television. The visitor calls authorities after returning to his own home. The witness who gave the description for this sketch was in her late 70s and knocked to the ground during a purse snatching.[2]

- A detective lays a sketch of a murder suspect on his desk. His officemate looks at the sketch and produces a photo and a name of someone wanted for other crimes but not in custody. The comparison of that photo and the sketch is shown in Figure 3.2. Upon apprehension, the suspect is put in a line-up and the murder is solved.[3] Therefore, this sketch allowed the detective to solve the case without leaving the office or even making any calls.

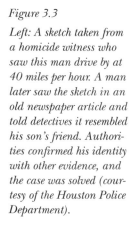

Figure 3.2

Left: A sketch created with a woman who saw the man shown right shoot her husband to death while stealing her purse. Upon apprehension, this man was picked out in a line-up by three witnesses from the scene and the woman who helped create the sketch (courtesy of the Houston Police Department).

- An elderly man recycling his newspapers sees the sketch of a murder suspect and thinks it looks like his grandson's acquaintance. He calls the detective and the murder is solved. This sketch was drawn from a witness who saw the shooter drive by at 40 miles per hour.[4] See Figure 3.3 for a comparison of the mug shot with the sketch.

Figure 3.3

Left: A sketch taken from a homicide witness who saw this man drive by at 40 miles per hour. A man later saw the sketch in an old newspaper article and told detectives it resembled his son's friend. Authorities confirmed his identity with other evidence, and the case was solved (courtesy of the Houston Police Department).

- A college coed recognizes a sketch posted on campus as being that of a guy who flirted with her and then gave her his number, which she relays to the authorities. Several rapes on campus are solved.[5] See the comparison of the sketch to the mug shot in Figure 3.4.

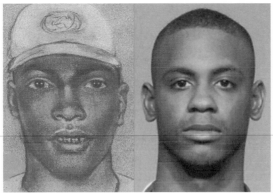

Figure 3.4

Left: A sketch created with the victim of a rape at a large university. The sketch was posted around the campus. A woman who had rebuffed the advances of the man shown right recognized the sketch as him and gave his number to police (courtesy of the University of Houston Police Department).

■ A large, overweight robber is shot during a robbery and left in a coma. A detective visits the robber's hospital bedside and thinks he looks remarkably like the sketch of a prolific serial robber in his jurisdiction. After the detective shows the bedridden robber's mug shot to many victims, over a dozen cases are cleared. The robber subsequently dies. It is discovered he was a hit man for the Mafia, had turned state's witness against the Gambino crime family in New York, and was relocated to Texas with a new name and identity.[6] Compare the photo of this man with the sketch in Figure 3.5.

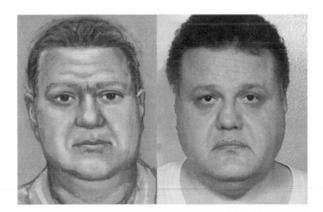

Figure 3.5

Left: A sketch done with a shop owner who was robbed by the man shown right. This man was shot during a subsequent robbery; while hospitalized a detective on the case thought he resembled the sketch. He was later able to connect the man with over 20 cases (courtesy of the Houston Police Department).

■ An 84-year old woman recognizes a sketch as the 19-year-old son of her friend whom she hasn't seen since he was 14. See the comparison of this sketch to the mug shot of the perpetrator in Figure 3.6. The witness was kidnapped and taken to a wooded area where her attacker engaged in a shoot-out with an investigating officer who happened upon the scene.[7]

■ Two men are repairing a fence. The boss sees a poster on the fence that looks like his helper. The helper tears the poster off, abandons the work site, and goes to his mother's home demanding money so he can go to Mexico. The mother sees the poster and calls police.[8] It seems the woman he sexually assaulted got together with 40 friends, made 3,000 posters, and plastered the neighborhood with them because she

Figure 3.6

Left: A sketch created from a witness who was being sexually assaulted by the man on the right when an officer interrupted them. A woman in her 80s recognized the sketch as being a boy she hadn't seen since he was 14 (courtesy of the Houston Police Department).

couldn't stand being a victim. Her plan worked out. The man was arrested, tried, and convicted. An image of one of the posters and a comparison of the sketch and photo of the suspect are shown in Figure 3.7.

Figure 3.7

The sketch on the poster and in the center was created from the victim of a particularly brutal sexual assault. She and 40 friends plastered the neighborhood with posters like the one shown left. Within hours of the postings the man's mother called in his identity to authorities (courtesy of the Houston Police Department).

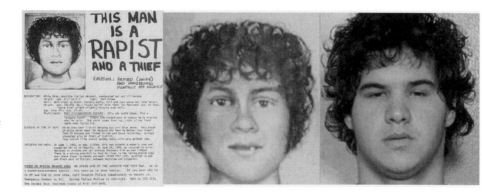

■ A man who raped a 10-year-old girl sees the sketch on a television *Crime Stoppers* segment. He calls the police and turns *himself* in.[9] See the sketch compared to his photo in Figure 3.8.

Figure 3.8

A 10-year-old girl was sexually assaulted and helped me create the sketch on the left. The man on the right saw the sketch on a Crime Stoppers *segment on TV and called the police to turn himself in. He was tried and convicted of the crime (courtesy of the Houston Police Department).*

■ A man watering his lawn sees a man drive by that he thinks looks like a sketch of the suspect who raped a woman on his street. He takes down the tag number, and a man who robbed hundreds of people is caught. He liked to rob entire crowds at restaurants, bars, and churches wearing a bandana. He was not wearing the bandana during the sexual assault.[10] The sketch can be compared to his photo in Figure 3.9.

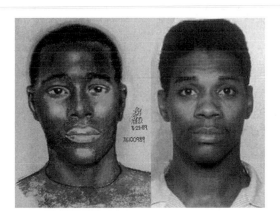

Figure 3.9

A woman who survived a sexual assault helped create this sketch. A man observed the man on the right drive past and saw a resemblance to the sketch. He took down the tag number of the vehicle. The man was identified in the woman's assault and in dozens of robberies (courtesy of the Houston Police Department).

■ A woman walking out of a store thinks a man walking in looks like the sketch of a serial killer in her up-scale neighborhood. With her child's crayon, she writes down the tag number of the vehicle he has exited. A few days later a trooper runs the tag of a sleeping motorist at a rest stop into the system and it comes up "wanted for homicide in Houston." The gun used in two shootings is found next to the driver. The witness for this sketch was shot through the chest but survived.[11] This killer's photo can be compared to the sketch in Figure 3.10.

Figure 3.10

A woman was shot through the chest and survived to give a description for the sketch on the left. A woman saw the man shown right, thought he resembled the sketch, and wrote down his tag number, which eventually led to his arrest (courtesy of the Houston Police Department).

■ An off-duty DEA agent helps chase down a shoplifter at a mall. He points out that the shoplifter looks like the sketch of a man who shot an officer twice and ran over him, dragging him over 55 feet. While being booked in the jail, two guards tell officers they think the shoplifter looks like the sketch of the man who shot the officer. The suspect is shown in a video line-up in the officer's hospital room and the officer positively identifies him. A search of the scene of the shoplifting yields a vehicle with pieces of the officer's flesh and uniform caught in the undercarriage.[12] The sketch compared to the photo of the man who tried to kill an officer of the law can be seen in Figure 3.11.

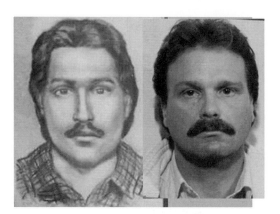

Figure 3.11

An officer was shot once in the head and back, then run over and dragged over 55 feet until he was able to break loose. The sketch, left, was done at the officer's hospital bedside. Days later the man pictured at right was caught trying to shoplift a chainsaw (courtesy of the Houston Police Department).

■ A man calls *Crime Stoppers* saying his across-the-street neighbor is the man in the sketch. The detective sets up surveillance on the identified house for 6 hours waiting for the suspect's vehicle. The suspect and vehicle never show up. The detective goes to the nearest convenience store and the man behind the counter is almost identical to the sketch. The detective calls for backup and a subsequent interview leads to an arrest, identification, and conviction.[13] Compare the sketch to the photo of this kidnapper/rapist in Figure 3.12.

Figure 3.12

A sexually assaulted woman gave the description for the sketch shown left. A tipster called in his address to the detective on the case. After a fruitless surveillance, the detective drives to the nearest convenience store for refreshment and finds the man pictured on the right behind the counter (courtesy of the Houston Police Department).

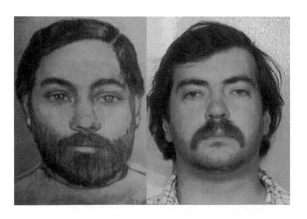

■ A group of adults at a convalescent home see a man dropping off his wife to work and think he looks like the sketch in the newspaper dispenser at the front of the business. The sketch is of a shooter who killed a 3-year-old boy who was running past a group of adults who were probably the target. The crowd at the convalescent home surrounded the car so he couldn't leave, while someone called the police. All the people in the car with him were also with him when he committed the murder. They were separated and all implicated the driver in the murder. The shooter received 38 years in prison.[15] This sketch and photo are compared in Figure 3.13.

Figure 3.13

The man on the right was apprehended when a crowd surrounded his vehicle and called police because they thought he resembled the sketch on the left. He confessed and received 38 years in prison for shooting into a crowd and killing a 3-year-old boy (courtesy of the Houston Police Department).

■ A man is robbed of his truck that is fully loaded with furniture at gunpoint. The truck has a global positioning device and the detective tracks it to a house. An older couple that answer the door deny knowing the person in the sketch. A young female in the house tells the detective to wait for a moment. She returns to the door with a male who closely resembles the sketch. The suspect says the sketch looks like him, but he is taller. After an interview catches the young man in several lies, a photo line-up is conducted and other ancillary evidence solves the case.[16] Compare his photo to the sketch in Figure 3.14.

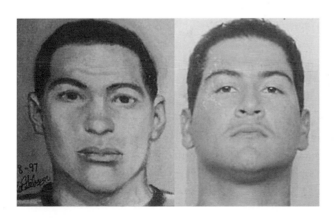

Figure 3.14

The sketch shown left is of a man who robbed a furniture-laden truck. A detective came to a house where residents denied recognizing anyone from the sketch. Moments later when the man shown right was spotted coming to the door, the detective was able to solve the case (courtesy of the Houston Police Department).

■ A sergeant with a county sheriff's office was catching a ride to lunch with a detective in the sex crimes unit. The sergeant notices one of the composites on the seat between them looks like a former employee of the department. The detective puts the employee-in-question's photo in a line-up and he is positively identified. Other evidence matches and the former employee is convicted and gets a 17-year prison term.[17] This sketch can be seen next to his photo in Figure 3.15.

Figure 3.15

A sergeant going to lunch with a detective saw the sketch, left, in the investigator's vehicle and thought it looked like a former employee. A line-up and other evidence proved the man pictured right, who had bragged to his victim he was a cop, was telling the truth (courtesy of the Harris County Sheriffs Department).

■ A man and wife experience a brutal torture-filled home invasion. They take a flyer with the sketch of their attacker around their neighborhood. A woman at a nearby business tells them she thinks the man in the sketch dates a coworker and gives them his name and address. The couple relays this information to their detective. After ancillary evidence is a match, the case is solved.[18] This home invader's photo is compared with the couple's sketch from memory in Figure 3.16.

Figure 3.16

A couple who gave the sketch on the left were tortured and robbed by the man on the right during a brutal home invasion. They were able to use the sketch and track him down by showing it to people who worked in the neighborhood (courtesy of the Houston Police Department).

- A young woman is found strangled to death after she leaves a restaurant with a man she just met. Her friends help the artist create a sketch the next day. The officers are still processing her murder scene and are in possession of photos of the sketch when a man drives by slowly, staring at the activity. The officers notice he resembles the sketch and stop him for questioning. They find he is on parole for a violent felony. Further investigation proves he is their suspect.[19] See how close the victim's friend's description was to his photo in Figure 3.17.

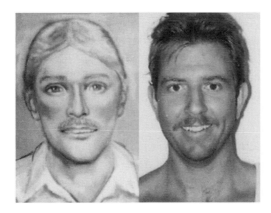

Figure 3.17

Friends of a murder victim gave the description for the sketch on the left of the man with whom they last saw her. Detectives recognized the man on the right when he returned to the scene of the crime as they were still processing it (courtesy of the Friendswood Police Department).

- A huge naked man in the wilderness trails of an affluent neighborhood chases two 12-year-old girls. They get away and days later work with a forensic artist at a nearby police department. Even though the department where the sketch was done was not in the jurisdiction where the crime occurred, an officer there took a photo of the sketch and laid it on his desk. Three days later, that same officer was returning from a fishing trip when he saw a man that closely resembled the sketch driving a van. The officer took down the van's tag number. The man was identified in a line-up, and ancillary evidence combined to help convict him.[20] His photo can be compared to the sketch in Figure 3.18.

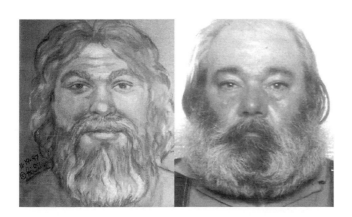

Figure 3.18

The sketch, left, was taken from two girls who were chased through the woods by a naked man. A detective from another police department saw the sketch and later recognized the man shown right driving near his house. With his tag number and a line-up, the case was solved (courtesy of the Houston Police Department).

The perpetrators of all these crimes were identified due to imperfect sketches. Even though some of these sketches barely resemble the person described, the important lesson to be learned is that these drawings from witness memory, faulty as they are, nevertheless were the tool that led to the crime being solved. Some of the worst sketches generated the most forceful lead for solving the case.

I wish that in the beginning of my career I could have envisioned the myriad of scenarios where a sketch could help detectives identify their witnesses' attackers. Instead, early forensic artists toiled in an atmosphere of doubt that did not help the work product. Remember this collection of successful, true stories when the detective, the witness, or anyone expresses doubt about the effectiveness of forensic drawings.

Rather than be consumed with negativity, you need to believe there is every possibility that your sketch can make a difference, no matter what the witness says. The possibilities of how the drawing will help can help you to maintain a great attitude in a stressful situation. Once you believe in the effectiveness of your work, you can truly focus on helping the witness's attitude.

Figure 3.19

The witness for the sketch, left, was sprayed with tear gas, blindfolded, handcuffed, and sexually assaulted while being stunned with a taser gun. When the sketch was released, a detective in another jurisdiction called in the identity of the man on the right and solved the case (courtesy of the Galveston Police Department).

THE WORST STILL WORKS

In a final effort to shore up the confidence of forensic artists, I will lay bare two of the worst composites of my career. Thankfully, this first terrible likeness helped the detective find the man pictured next to it. When the detective released the sketch in a Texas Department of Public Safety crime bulletin, he got a call from a detective in another part of the state that led to the man pictured in Figure 3.19. The suspect was subsequently tied to the assault by two fingerprints and DNA evidence. It turns out he was a career serial rapist.[21] The detective was pleased enough to write me a letter of commendation, seen in Figure 3.20.

THE ARTIST'S HANDICAP, OR WHAT THE WITNESS EXPERIENCED

The witness who gave the description for this sketch experienced a particularly brutal, torturous attack. She was working in a small business alone when the suspect entered. After asking her a quick question, he sprayed her face with pepper spray. He then blindfolded her, clamped metal handcuffs on her, laid her on her back, and sexually assaulted her, while repeatedly using a taser gun on her. She told me she never saw his face.

City of Galveston Police Department

Identification Division
P.O. Box 568
Galveston, Texas 77553-0568
(409) 797-3733

Figure 3.20

A letter of commendation because my sketch, even with its multiple defects, helped the detective find the sadistic attacker in Figure 3.19.

February 15, 2000

Lois Gibson

Dear Lois:

You did a composite for me in September 1998 on a particularly violent sexual assault. I was able to solve the case by placing a copy of the composite and a synopsis of the crime in the Department of Public Safety crime bulletin. A detective in east Texas saw the bulletin and called me with a lead on a suspect. I have subsequently tied the suspect to the sexual assault by two fingerprints and DNA evidence. The offender is a career serial rapist and maybe now he will stay in prison where he should have been when he attacked the young lady in Galveston.

I am submitting a photograph of the offender that was taken approximately one month after the Galveston offense. I am also submitting the written description that I released with the composite, after several of my local witnesses looked at the composite — but before the offender was identified. Thank you very much for your help, the crime would not have been solved without your typically excellent work.

Sincerely,

Norman Giles

Norman Giles
Lieutenant

WHAT IS WRONG WITH THE COMPOSITE

The chin is three times too long, the lips are far too thick, the nose is tilted out not down, the hairline is too low, and the suspect is not wearing glasses in this photo. However, the success of this fault-ridden sketch is 100%.

STILL MORE GOOD FROM BAD

Figure 3.21 shows another terrible drawing that gave a perfect assist to the detective working the case. The Houston Police Department released this sketch on TV and in the newspapers of a man who sexually assaulted two girls, aged 8 and 9. The detective received more than 25 calls naming the same person, "Al," and the same place of employment, a grocery store. The detective took the sketch and walked into the grocery store wearing plain clothes and holding the sketch up in front of him. When the detective approached him, the store manager asked what he was doing with a picture of "Al," his night stock boy. An interview with Al yielded a thorough confession, the girls picked him out of a line-up, there was other ancillary evidence, and the man was given a life sentence.[22]

Figure 3.21

The sketch, right, prompted 25 calls giving the same name to the detective when he released it to the media. At the store where the 25 tipsters said this man worked, the manager also named him upon seeing the sketch. The man shown left confessed to the crime (courtesy of the Houston Police Department).

The Artist's Handicap

The 8- and 9-year-old girls were playing in an apartment after school waiting for their mom to get home from work. A man knocked on the door claiming to be the maintenance man. The girls told him to go away, but when they opened the door a little bit, he forced his way in. He then sexually assaulted both girls and further took a knife from their kitchen and stabbed both in the stomach area. The artist did the sketch in the hospital at the girls' bedside 20 hours after the attack. The little girls were distracted by pain and the detective pulled the sketch away from the artist before it was truly finished.

What Is Wrong with the Composite

The artwork in general is poor. The lips are far too large. One side of the hair is unfinished. The chin is too big. The face is too long. The top of the head is too wide. The chin is too wide. The irises are too large. The ears are too long. However, this poorly executed sketch was also 100% successful.

RELAX

I have offered documented examples of various ways a sketch can lead the detective to the perpetrator of the crimes he or she needs to solve. There are more than a thousand other unique stories not mentioned here. If we were to add other successful scenarios from forensic artists around the world there are no doubt thousands. As we just saw, drawings can be poor caliber and not bear the most striking resemblance to the perpetrator being described and still be successful.

This knowledge is offered so that the beginning forensic artist can relax enough to make it through the sketch regardless of self-doubt or harassment from the witness. Just as dancing, singing, or playing an instrument will be done poorly if the creator is crippled by fear and tension, so too does the visual artist need relaxation to create effectively. Any reasonably talented artist can draw as well as any of the earlier examples that helped bring in violent offenders. So, approach your drawing board with confidence. The other part of your job, pulling the memory of a face from your witness, will be handled next.

FOCUSING ON WITNESS NEEDS

THE INTERVIEW

Previous chapters proved that drawing a forensic sketch takes a portraiture ability possessed by many artists. The various supplies and techniques are in common use among artists around the world. It is extracting a description from the witness's memory that is an esoteric skill. The difficulties in this portion of the work to the beginning forensic artist can seem insurmountable. It is this task that will be addressed at length in the following pages.

Having compared over a thousand sketches to photos of the proven perpetrators of the crime, and having further understood what went right, what went wrong, and why, I offer the following techniques. Feel free to use one or many of these hints. Others in this profession might disagree with these suggestions, which is understandable and even expected. However, it should be obvious that some techniques work in certain situations, and not in others, so take what is useful.

The relaxation of the witness is the most important consideration during the interview, although you need to be comfortable as well. The best enhancement to memory is mood elevation and relaxation.[23] It follows, therefore, that if you want your witness to remember the attacker's face, you must put his or her mood ahead of all considerations.

The previous chapters have dealt extensively with the artist's comfort during a forensic sketch. Turning now to the witness's comfort, remember that the witness has all the information. In any situation, therefore, the witness's comfort takes precedence over yours, or any other individual's comfort, during the act of drawing the suspect's face from the witness's memory.

PHYSICAL PROPERTIES OF THE SKETCH SITUATION

The witness needs a quiet, distraction-free atmosphere during the sketch session, so you should do the sketch alone with him or her. Even though loved ones and friends mean well, if they are included in the sketching session they will place a distracting emotional burden on the witness. The witness at this time is trying to delve into his or her inflamed memory of what was probably the worst experience of his or her life. Proof of this is that all witnesses, including small children, express relief when their relatives are gently escorted out of the room before work on the sketch begins.

SEPARATING A WITNESS FROM PARENTS OR COMPANIONS

Parents of children, or even close friends or spouses of adults, are often reluctant to leave the witness alone. These individuals usually have been acting as a support system during the witness's trauma and might act in a protective way. However, using the following method, I have never failed to be able to smoothly and pleasantly separate the witness from those individuals who have accompanied him or her to the interview. Never simply insist that the sketch really must be done alone with the child (or adult with clingy companions), even though this is true, and pull the child away from his or her family. Instead, to create a peaceful environment beneficial to the witness's retrieval of the face from memory, perform a creative separation ceremony. This genteel act will be worth the extra time in the warm mood it creates for the beginning of the sketch interview.

Bring *everyone* into the interview room, and show them around cordially. Seat the witness in the proper chair. Make some friendly small talk; mention how your goal is to create the best sketch possible, and for that, the witness needs to be as relaxed as possible. For that purpose, gently suggest that being alone with the witness would produce the best sketch, while walking slowly to the door. Tell the witness you will be right back and walk the companions/parents to a waiting area. Give them hints on how to pleasantly occupy their time while waiting, like where the snack bar and vending machines are. Tell them how to find the bathrooms. Let them know their loved one is in good hands, and how long until the drawing will be done. Tell them they are welcome to buy the witness a snack or a drink and bring it to the door, and you will give it to their loved one.

Upon returning to the interview room, tell the witness that his or her parents/companion(s) are just fine and how they will probably be spending their time waiting. Make complimentary comments about their loved ones who have just left.

Juvenile witnesses are generally glad to get their parents to wait outside. Female witnesses will almost always be glad to get husbands or boyfriends out of the interview room. Even a 5-year-old will sigh with relief when the parents leave him or her alone.

It seems there should be no reason to mention this, but the subject has come up so often with beginning forensic artists it must be addressed. Possibly the worst persons to be included in the interview room would be law enforcement personnel such as detectives. These are the persons who often ask novice artists to observe the process since they are most acutely curious as to what goes on during the interview. However, the presence of authority figures would be a decidedly disruptive influence on the witness's concentration. Truthfully, tell curious individuals that for the best sketch, the witness needs to be alone in order to concentrate. Since no rational person would put his or her curiosity needs above the goal of solving the case, this explanation should suffice.

EXCEPTIONS TO SKETCHING ALONE WITH THE WITNESS

If the witness is a child 5 years old or younger, a parent or sibling *can* be included in the interview room if that individual will make the child feel more comfortable. The reason for the last caveat is that some parents *would not* make the child feel more comfortable, but a sibling might. Sometimes it would be an aunt, a cousin, or another person who would be best. Simply state to all involved that the comfort of the witness is paramount and the best individual should be included, even if the person who believes he or she loves the witness the most might not be the companion needed during the interview.

Another exception to the rule would be a witness of the Islamic faith if he or she were of the opposite sex of the artist. There is a scripture reference in the Quran that says it is wrong for persons of the opposite sex who are not man and wife to be in the same room with the door closed. One way to handle this situation would be to keep the door open, but essentially be alone in the room. The only necessity would be to notify anyone outside the room not to disturb the interview.

PHYSICAL ARRANGEMENTS DURING THE INTERVIEW

Since the witness probably thought he or she was going to lose his or her life at the hands of an attacker, sit a reasonable distance away from the witness. Even witnesses who were not shown a weapon, or even touched, express fear they might have been killed during their incident. Having been attacked myself when living alone in my apartment, I can testify that crime victims often do not want people to be near them, sometimes for a very long time after their experience. Even if the witness experienced what some would consider a low-key crime, do not take a chance of disturbing the witness by assuming you can sit close by.

One proof of this wisdom is the fact that individuals have a wide range of abilities to withstand being victims of crime. Seasoned investigators know the most hysterical witness might *not* be a witness to the most serious crime. Some witnesses to robberies can be more devastated than those who have witnessed multiple homicides. Therefore, if the reaction to traumatic incidents can vary widely, you must assume your witness might be highly traumatized no matter what he or she experienced. No matter how comfortable you may feel sitting next to the witness, and no matter how much you think it is a show of comfort to the victim, to stay on the safe side, you should always allow the witness his or her personal space.

A good rule is to sit far enough away that, were you to reach out your hand, you could not touch the witness. Also, use an easel so that the drawing board can act as a "shield" or barrier between you and the witness. This setup will maximize the comfort and relaxation of the witness. See Figure 1.18 for a view of a typical sketching arrangement with enough personal space for the witness.

Obtain the most comfortable chair possible for the witness. Put a box of tissues in plain view and within easy reach of the witness chair. Obtain a nice floor lamp or a lamp for the table next to the witness's chair. This will give the witness tungsten lighting, the kind commonly found in homes. The fluorescent office lighting enhances the greens and blues of objects observed. This is why your skin does not appear as attractive in office lighting as in outdoor (full-color reflection) or home (tungsten bulb) lighting. Tungsten lighting brings out the yellows, reds, and oranges, giving a warm, homey feel when the witness needs to look at the visual aids.

Walls should have soothing posters, artwork, or photos—avoid photos of men or mug shots. Have a small blanket or throw on hand for witnesses who might be in shock. Try to have a small office refrigerator where cold water and disposable glasses can be kept. At the very least have a box of crackers for upset stomachs, pregnant witnesses, and others. Any array of snacks can be a good thing, depending on the varied needs of the witnesses. A candy dish that is always full can help you through with child witnesses or if the witness brings children.

Dress in a way that will maximize the witness's comfort. If you are an officer, wear civilian clothes if possible. If the witness is a child, dress in a manner that the child expects adults in his or her life to dress. If the witness was sexually assaulted, do not wear clothing that could in any way be construed to be "sexy." If the witness is an adult, try to dress the way you think the witness would dress so everyone "fits in." Don't wear strong cologne or perfume.

No matter how hurried you may feel, give a relaxed appearance. Don't bring up time-pressure items in conversation. Schedule the interview so the witness does not feel time pressure as much as is possible. Have a clock in full view to eliminate the feeling on the part of the witness that he or she is losing track of the time. This will also keep the witness from looking at a cell phone or watch to check on the time.

In Brief
- Sketch alone with the witness for maximum concentration.
- Use the proper technique for separating relatives and friends from your witness.
- Sit a bit more than arm's length away from the witness, facing him or her with the easel between.
- Dress with the witness in mind.
- Avoid feelings of time pressure.

FIRST IMPRESSIONS

If you call the witness to make an appointment, take full advantage of this duty to maximize this first impression. Speak with warmth and compassion. Give the best directions possible if the witness is driving to your location. Tell the witness that the interview will be therapeutic (a correctly conducted forensic sketch interview *is* therapeutic), and that he or she will feel better once the drawing is finished. Before the witness asks, give an idea of how long the sketch will take. Strongly suggest he or she arrives with a full stomach, and let the witness know that it is to maximize his or her comfort. Let the witness vent during this phone conversation, and never interrupt the witness unless he or she has finished, or you have an urgent need to get off the phone.

Often the detective will bring the witness to you. Somehow the detective needs to say very positive comments about your work and ability. Once your reputation is established, detectives will tell the witnesses these types of comments automatically. In the beginning of a forensic artist's career, the detective may need to be prompted to say these kinds of things. If the detective praises you, it can only help, and it might help a great deal. Often, the witness will listen and believe more readily a testimony of your ability from the investigator on the case. Therefore, the detective has nothing to lose and everything to gain by endorsing your abilities. With this goal in mind, either keep in good graces with the detectives, or convince them of the wisdom of praising you simply because instilling confidence can help the witness create a better sketch.

Don't let personnel with whom you work know what has happened to your witness before he or she shows up. This will keep people from staring and making the witness feel even more uncomfortable. Many a witness is sensitive enough that he or she will be able to tell the significance of certain kinds of body language and the gazes of people in your office if they know what happened to that particular witness. If the crime was terribly embarrassing or brutal, these gazes might ruin the witness's mood before you even get started.

Never make the witness wait more than a few moments for the interview, unless you are with another witness working on another case. This is the one excuse witnesses seem to understand.

COPING WITH THE DREAD

From comments gathered during 24 years of this work, and from thousands of witnesses, I can assure you that the witness dreads coming in to do a sketch. For that reason, you must greet the witness in the warmest possible way. Begin immediately to verbally comfort him or her, and make him or her feel welcome. Act as if the witness is the most important person at that time. Do not engage in small talk with coworkers when retrieving the witness, unless it seems it will make the witness feel more comfortable. Ask about the drive in, how his or her luck was at parking, any subject about *the witness.*

These suggestions may well sound like methods for a salesperson to be successful. The most difficult sales job has to be convincing someone who was almost killed to describe the perpetrator of that horrible act. Creating an image of that terrifying person is probably the very last thing a victim of crime would *want* to do. Therefore, you must be as charming as you can possibly be. The witness might try to be socially acceptable and appear pleasant and congenial in order to make it into the interview without embarrassing him- or herself. However, there is a great chance the witness is fighting back tears as he or she approaches the office. If you behave in the most charming way possible, it will signal to the witness that you can be trusted with his or her bruised feelings.

Once alone with the witness, the best memory enhancer is the witness's comfort—letting down his or her defenses. To facilitate this, you should act differently when finally alone in the room with the witness. Make a show that *you* feel more relaxed and relieved to be away from everyone. You can do this by acting in that manner, or simply by remarking that it is good to be alone and away from all those people. Almost always, the witness will agree and become more relaxed than in the open office area.

As soon as the witness is settled, explain how the sketch will be created. Make this explanation as brief and simple as possible so that the witness can imagine the sketch process being brief and simple. I like to explain the process to the witness something like this:

> "You sit there where you can't see the drawing at first. I'll have you choose features that seem similar to that guy from here (holding up the *FBI Facial Identification Catalog* and some mug shots). When I get a rough sketch done, I'll turn it around and show you. At that time I can change anything you want, any way you want me to change it. The changes are quick and easy. Then we'll be done."

Briefly describe the process as you see fit. It is highly recommended to portray the end of the task as something that will happen soon.

The witness will commonly remark how much he or she wants to do a good job and may express distress that he or she doesn't think he or she can do very well. In reply, let the witness know that the witness who does the best job is the witness who is able to relax the most. Point out how everyone was sent out of the room because his or her relaxation was so important. While saying this, slow down the rate of speech and talk as quietly as possible. Mention if he or she relaxes enough, he or she can remember grade school friends. Most everyone is grateful for a reason to simply relax. Let the witness know that relaxation is the most important tool used to create the sketch, and do whatever it takes to help that witness relax.

In Brief
- Make the best first impression possible with the witness even if it is only a phone call.
- Detectives can help the production of the sketch with positive remarks regarding your abilities.
- Understand all witnesses dread the interview and doubt a sketch is possible from their memory; deal skillfully with these negative attitudes.
- Once alone with the witness, acknowledge by actions and words to the witness that his or her relaxation is of the utmost importance.

MAKING THE HOUSE CALL

Going to the witness's residence is always more inconvenient. However, a house call can be a huge enhancement to the witness's relaxation and therefore can be conducive to creating a better likeness from his or her memory. If it would be worse to do it at the witness's residence, the detective will know and keep it from happening. Also, the witness should always have the option of *not* having the sketch done at home. Some of the reasons might be a house that is too noisy with small children, terrible housekeeping by other members of the household, the lack of a room in which to sketch where you can be alone, and so on. But if the witness is willing, and the maximum relaxation can be had there, the true professional artist will be willing to pack up all necessary equipment and do the sketch at that location.

Obviously, witnesses who are badly injured during the incident and are recuperating at home can be interviewed *only* at their residence. If the witness has no choice about doing the sketch at home, he or she may be embarrassed if the surroundings are humble. In that case, use all your social skills to nullify this embarrassment as much as possible. Normal socialization will enable you to assuage the witness's discomfort, saying the right things he or she needs to hear in order to feel comfortable enough to concentrate on the work together, no matter what the surroundings.

Never make a house call on a homicide case unless capable, armed, sworn officers who are familiar with the case accompany you. If you are also an officer, you should still have at least one companion along to "watch your back" if making a house call for a homicide case. Remember, sketching from a witness is one of the most difficult, if not *the* most difficult, artistic act anyone can perform. You need the concentration that having backup can bring.

More frequently than not, a detective can take you to the residence and wait outside, talk to relatives and friends, or canvass the area. This usually accomplishes three tasks at once for dedicated investigators. They get to touch base once again with their witnesses. They get to canvass the area if need be. They are able to get the image done and leave with a copy the same day. Also, if a house call is necessary because of a recuperating homebound witness, the detective can act as an armed bodyguard. In one such instance, I was accompanied by three armed homicide detectives when sketching at the home of a nephew who was recuperating from a gunshot wound suffered when he witnessed the murder of his uncle. It wasn't so much that I needed guarding—the sketch session gave the homicide investigators the opportunity to look around the neighborhood, make the witness and family know they were working the case with a full force, and head out with the sketch immediately to search some nearby areas with the image in hand.

Figures 3.22 and 3.23 are two examples of sketches done during house calls.

SKETCHING AT THE HOSPITAL

Forensic artists often need to sketch at the hospital bedside of a witness. All persons involved are faced with unique difficulties in this setting. On the negative side, there are often difficulties with achieving privacy and relaxation for the witness, and in some instances, that would be putting it mildly. On the bright side, if the crime is so egregious as to land the victim in the hospital, then the heightened attention by media, authorities, and the public often means a higher rate of success for the sketch effort. Figures 3.24 and 3.25 are examples of successful sketches done at hospitals.

Always take along an officer or the detective when sketching with a witness in a hospital. For many valid reasons, hospital personnel can cause obstructions to an artist's effort to sketch with a witness that also happens to be a patient in their care. Having the detective along smooths out nearly all those problems without your saying a word. It is heartening to see the guardianship of a dedicated nurse when it comes to a patient, but the need for the authorities to capture the man who injured the patient so terribly can be explained wordlessly by

Figure 3.22

This sketch was conducted in a meeting room at the mall where the witness worked. The witness sculpted pewter figurines and sold them in her shop. This man robbed the witness at gunpoint. He did not actually touch her, but she felt certain he was capable of killing her[24] (courtesy of the Houston Police Department).

Figure 3.23

I traveled to the apartment of the witness for this sketch. She had been kidnapped by this man and sexually assaulted for several hours. This man's identity was called in immediately after Crime Stoppers *released this sketch[25] (courtesy of the Harris County Sheriffs Department)*

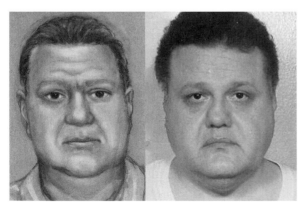

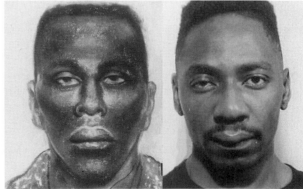

the presence of the officer working the case. Some people with fairly high levels of intelligence really don't believe it is possible to sketch a face from someone's memory. Some of those same people require several minutes of explanation to understand the concept of what a forensic artist is trying accomplish in a hospital with a drawing board and art supplies. More than once I've been

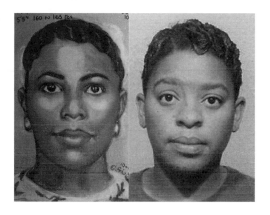

Figure 3.24

The witness for this sketch was a mother whose 10-hour-old newborn baby was kidnapped from her hospital bedroom. The sketch was done at the hospital 6 hours after she last saw the kidnapper. A friend of the kidnapper called in her identity when the sketch aired on the news[26] (courtesy of the Houston Police Department).

asked if I were there to sketch the portrait of the patient. All these queries and objections can be handled by the investigator while you are working your way through the sketch as quickly as possible.

One other reason to have an official companion with you is to help carry your gear and find the bedside location. In many cities, the hospitals can be very large, and you can walk for long distances and take up lots of precious time if you don't know the exact location of the witness/patient. On particularly violent cases the patient cannot be seen unless a visitor has a code word or knows a pseudonym. Some departments have rules that specify that only the investigator is allowed to know this information.

When you finally reach the witness's hospital room, make the approach and introduction as warm and cheerful as the situation will allow. As soon as possible, sit down so you are eye-to-eye with your witness. In other words, try not to stand over the witness and talk down to him or her.

If the witness is in obvious pain, acknowledge that fact and let him or her know the sketch will be done as rapidly as possible. Then, if you have ever put some speed behind your sketching, this is the time! Remember all those art

teachers who proclaimed that drawing faster is better technique than drawing slowly, and believe it.

The hospital is where the easel is a must. Since it can weigh only 7 pounds and can fold up, it can be carried to the bedside easily. When the drawing board is in place, adjusting the height can place the drawing straight up and directly in

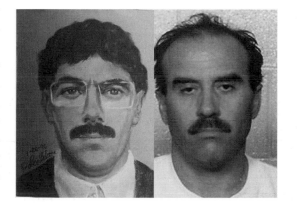

Figure 3.25

This sketch was done in the intensive care unit of a hospital. The witness was a security guard who had been shot twice during a multimillion-dollar jewelry robbery. He was in excruciating pain and said he really didn't see the face of the shooter[27] (courtesy of the Houston Police Department).

the line of vision of your bedridden witness. An attached light makes for good viewing even if the room is dark in whatever place you are drawing. Also, since you can clip all the visual aids to the sides of the drawing board and look at them simultaneously, the drawing process goes faster.

Many hospitalized witnesses will doze in between selecting features because they are under varying degrees of pain and/or sleep medication. Wise detectives will coordinate these kinds of medications with the staff to help the witness be conscious for the sketch session when possible. I have experienced many witnesses who demanded they not be given incapacitating medications until after the sketch was done. Some witnesses in horrible pain made it through almost all the sketch, and then asked desperately for some medication relief when they knew the sketch was almost done. Further, I have noticed all persons—the doctors, nurses, patients, family members, and even officers—team up in an effort to have the beleaguered witness conscious for the time it took to do a sketch.

Having said all that, it must be noted that Figure 3.26 was done from an officer who had been shot twice, once in the head and once in the back, driven over, and then dragged under a vehicle for more than 55 feet. This witness was so medicated that he seemed barely conscious. Evidently this appearance of incoherence was authentic as this officer steadfastly maintains that he does not remember doing the sketch. The sketch nevertheless went on to be a rapid identifier of the shooter after his arrest for shoplifting. The lesson to be learned is this: even a heavily sedated witness in great pain can give a description for a sketch in a hospital setting. The overall warning is that sketching from a witness takes patience, and sketching from a hospitalized witness takes an even higher degree of patience.

Two special situations can occur in hospitals. First is the desire on the part of doctors and staff to perform various procedures on the patient. Have the detective do his or her very best to stave off these interruptions while the sketch is being done. If the staff of doctors and nurses know how long the sketch will take and are told how important its creation is to the community and victim, they almost always will comply and avoid interrupting your work.

Early in my career, I worked with a small boy in a hospital to sketch his attacker who had almost stabbed him to death after killing a woman. A doctor who simply wanted to look at the healing progress of the boy's wounds interrupted in the middle of the sketch. The "examination" was so painful the boy was unable to proceed to the end. The attacker was caught but the sketch proved to be a very poor likeness, directly due to the interruption. Looking back, the detective or even I could have convinced the doctor to wait to examine until after the sketch was finished. His viewing of the wounds was no heroic, life-or-death procedure that absolutely had to be done at that moment. Were it to be done over, the doctor should have been convinced to wait until the sketch was finished before he probed the stab wounds of the small boy. Hopefully, other artists can learn from this mistake and assert themselves.

If the doctor or other hospital personnel are advised how long the sketch will take and that the concentration and comfort of the witness is paramount, those medical professionals will do their best to help in the sketch creation. Remember, this is their territory, their workplace. Bring an investigator or officer along and enlist them in helping the effort, if by doing nothing more than leaving you and the witness alone.

Figures 3.26 and 3.27 are examples of sketches created at hospital bedsides.

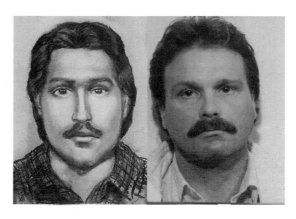

Figure 3.26

The witness for this sketch was shot in the head and back, then run over and dragged more than 55 feet, putting him in intensive care. The sketch helped identify the shooter when he was caught shoplifting three days later.[28] The officer does not remember doing the sketch (courtesy of the Houston Police Department).

COPING WITH WITNESS DENIAL

Almost every witness during my 24-year career has said some version of "I don't think I can do a sketch with you." Lots of witnesses wait until they are alone in the room and ready to begin before they voice these protestations; some say them during the walk to the room. Witnesses have said these comments in Chinese, French, Spanish, and baby talk. They have screamed it, whispered it, or insisted in a firm voice it was true. Almost all witnesses say they don't think it is possible for them to remember enough for you to somehow draw a sketch of the face they have seen. However, hundreds of successful forensic sketches have been created from witnesses who denied it could be done, so obviously these comments are not to be believed.

However, even though you know these comments are not true, never argue with the witness when he or she says these kinds of things. Realize that the witness is doing some much needed venting of emotions. Allow him or her to go on, all the while explaining how important this effort will be. As soon as is courteously possible, let your witness know this is what all witnesses say.

Figure 3.27

The witness for this sketch, left, was shot 15 times, losing an eye and some teeth. She was able to walk 950 feet and get help.[29] The sketch was done at her hospital bedside 10 days later. The man, right, was caught, tried, and given a life sentence (courtesy of the Houston Police Department).

TAKING AWAY THE TASK

One good method to cope with these protestations is called *Taking Away the Task*. This term means

Figure 3.28

The witness for this sketch was sprayed with tear gas, blindfolded, handcuffed, then had a stun gun used on her while being sexually assaulted. She insisted she never saw his face. A parole officer recognized and identified him as soon as the sketch came out[30] (courtesy of the Galveston Police Department).

Figure 3.29

The man shown right shot a woman through the chest. She survived and helped me create the sketch shown left. A woman who thought he looked like the sketch on flyers she had in her vehicle took down his tag number and called it in to authorities[31] (courtesy of the Houston Police Department).

you should tell the witness he or she doesn't have to do a sketch of the face—he or she is not obligated to help make an image of that person. Rather, he or she needs only to help narrow down the field of suspects. For instance, was the person male or female? What race was the attacker, and what kind of hair did he or she have? Then let the witness know if you do create a face, it can be very imperfect. Just ask for a little of his or her time, and say that *you* will do all the work—all he or she has to do is relax.

If the witness is oppressively motivated to do a good sketch, as in a witness to a multiple murder or an infant kidnapping by a stranger, let him or her know some poorly done sketches nevertheless were able to help solve cases, so even a bad sketch can help. This is not advocating bad sketches. Rather, it should be noted when witnesses were so painfully motivated that it was required that I made these comments, the sketches created resulted in good likenesses. It is just good technique to take away the pressure by letting them know, truthfully, that a bad sketch *can* help. For proof, see the poor sketches in Figures 3.28 and 3.29. As faulty as they are, both were directly responsible for identifying the perpetrator to the detective working the case.

In Brief

Sketching on location with the witness will be necessary on occasion. Be prepared for the special needs of various cases and the challenging hospital setting.

Be prepared with effective techniques to cope with the witness's inevitable negative attitude toward the task of creating the forensic sketch.

MOOD ELEVATION TECHNIQUES FOR THE CRIME VICTIM

Mood elevation is the most substantial enhancement to memory.[32] Some witnesses are so distressed and doubtful they will not *begin* to work on a sketch unless they are made to feel much better. Therefore, somehow you must be able to converse in a way that will pull the witness out of this mood by employing skills specific to sketching from memory.

Do your best to lead the witness into conversation about positive things in his or her life, or subjects of interest. Ask about children, work, school, and such, whatever is important to him or her, and let the witness talk as much as he or she wants about that subject. Remember to show genuine interest.

One way to understand how you should conduct yourself is to imagine the witness is a neighbor or a friend who has just experienced a near-death event. Further imagine that this is your first conversation together since that frightening occurrence. It would be of utmost importance to comfort that friend, and most likely you would bring up the subject and allow the friend to describe what went on and his or her feelings about it at length. You would keep a sympathetic demeanor during all the emoting, describing, agonizing, and carrying on. Simply act in this same manner with the witness to a crime, and he or she should relax and warm to the situation.

There is scientific proof for the success of this technique. The clinical name for this way of retrieving information from a witness has been termed *Cognitive Retrieval Mnemonics* by researchers R. Edward Geiselman, Ronald P. Fisher, David P. MacKinnon, and Heidi L. Holland.[32] These researchers proved what a good friend knows: don't interrupt when a friend is describing a terrible experience. In other words, these scientists proved that if law-enforcement professionals act with sympathy about the traumatic incident, they will conduct the kind of interview that will retrieve the most information.

One of the first tenets of their interviewing technique is entitled *Reinstate the Context*.[33] This method allows the witness to verbally recreate the environment before, during, and after the traumatic incident. The witness is encouraged to describe both his or her feelings and impressions before, during, and after the incident. This has proven to help the witness remember more details. The old-fashioned interview where the witness is asked questions limited to the exact incident to save time for the interviewer has been discredited. Researchers found when the witnesses instead were allowed to relive the day as it progressed, starting before the traumatic portion and continuing afterward, they remembered much more.

The next tenet is entitled *Change Sequence*. The witness is encouraged to describe the events out of chronological order. This out-of-order recall keeps witnesses to the facts and diminishes embellishment.

Another concept is *Specific Retrieval*, where witnesses are encouraged or allowed to relate the things they saw to someone or something familiar to them. An example of this would be a witness who said the suspect looked like a well-known actor. Another example would be clothing descriptions. Almost always a witness describes clothing on the suspect by relating those items to clothing he or she has observed on other individuals at some other time. This allows the witness to draw from a lifetime of experience and make comparisons instead of making it necessary to create the description. Instead he or she can draw on the familiar observations from his or her life as a source of information.

The last component of the *Cognitive Retrieval Mnemonics* style of interview is labeled *Time Factors*. This scientifically proven technique determines the interviewer should not rush the interviewee. Science has proven that if a witness is not allowed to respond, is interrupted, or is made to feel rushed, he or she will shut down the retrieval of the information. Conversely, if the witness is allowed to speak, pause and ponder, then speak again, he or she will bring forth more information to the interviewer.

Instead of trying to memorize all the jargon and terms, I have found the way to automatically perform this scientifically proven interview is simply to have compassion for the witness. In other words, if you care about someone who is describing a traumatic event, you will automatically:

- Let him or her ramble on as long as he or she wants about what happened, which would be following the *Reinstating the Context* and *Time Factors* components.
- Ask him or her different questions about the event, causing him or her to talk about things out of chronological order, which would be the *Change Sequence* component.
- Ask him or her who the person looked like, or what the clothing resembled, compared to persons and items in his or her past. If you let the person sharing the event talk at length about these kinds of comparisons, this would include some *Specific Retrieval* on his or her part.

Therefore, the interviewer who wants to gain the most information possible can approach the interview two ways. One, you can memorize the academically proven *Cognitive Interview*.[34] The second method would be to perceive the witness as someone for whom you have compassion and caring and act in a manner befitting that situation. I have found the latter method came naturally and allowed for successful interviews that are customized to every witness's needs. Only after acting like a person who has normal compassion for a grieved victim did I learn how researchers had proven the methods successful and given them scientific names. Whichever approach you choose, there is a simple phrase that concisely describes the best interview. The following is a quick definition of an ideal interview.

Successful forensic sketch interview: The most enjoyable conversation for the witness, considering what the witness has been through.

Happily you have an advantage over the friends and relatives with whom the witness might have shared his or her feelings before the interview. Since you are a perfect stranger, the witness can unload feelings more freely. The witness is not being judged or second-guessed by someone who might love him or her so much he or she is also devastated by the event. Also, those who are not versed in conversing with a victim of crime might question that person's actions leading up to the incident. This is a common attitude that leaves the victim feeling at the very least as if he or she were to blame for the attack, and at the most, infuriated. You should know not to call into question the victim's acts leading up to the incident. This can only engender hurt and anger in someone who obviously did not want to be a victim.

ACKNOWLEDGE THE WITNESS'S NEAR-DEATH EXPERIENCE

Since almost all witnesses will have felt they faced their own death, go ahead and bring up that subject. The witness needs someone to bring that subject up to relieve any feelings of isolation.

Having been a victim of a violent crime, I can say with certainty, witnesses are likely walking around silently repeating one theme inside their minds—they are saying something like, "…I almost died! I was almost killed!" These thoughts will boil around in their minds while the world goes on as if nothing happened. Others are going about their normal lives, yet there is no way victims can forget the terrible incident that happened. The worst thought they had during that incident was that they were going to die. This is, without question, the biggest fear anyone can have. Yet, if they are constantly remembering those thoughts, and others around them are thinking of normal life concerns, the crime victim feels isolated. This isolation can create negative feelings in the crime victim such as fear, anger, frustration, and grief. When the witness is unable to talk about this life-altering experience, those negative feelings grow.

A simple, easy, and effective way to relieve this feeling of isolation in your witness is to bring up the subject so he or she can talk about it. As soon as you bring up the subject, follow immediately with the fact that the witness didn't die and add positive thoughts about that fact. Usually this will bring forth a cascade of how terrible that feeling was and the positive feelings toward loved ones and what the witness has planned for the future.

If you haven't experienced almost being killed during a crime, it might sound strange, but bringing up this subject works wonders. This ends the witness's feelings of isolation and can create a bond with you.

The conversation can go something like this. Say a phrase like "…I understand you were almost killed [say this with reverence], but you weren't, you're here!" or "You are alive! You made it through!" Emphasize these positive last thoughts and be prepared to dwell on this good outcome. This will open a floodgate of positive thoughts from the witness about future plans and new perspectives on life. If the witness is so new to the shock of almost being killed, do your best to bring up the positive things the witness can do now that he or she still has a future. Most witnesses will be greatly relieved to hear someone else mention the thought that has been occupying all their conscious moments while everyone around them is making small talk. This conversation will establish an immediate footing with the witness and the positive thoughts of the future will be a mood elevator.

The only negative thoughts that might occur during this kind of conversation will be those concerning what the attacker did to him or her during the incident, or what the attacker might do to the witness in the future. Seize this opportunity to point out how the witness's help in creating the sketch can help capture the attacker, eliminate his or her fears, and greatly ease grief and anger when justice is served. One positive truism that can be mentioned here is that the witness who is most emotionally injured often is the witness who creates the best sketch, due to the vivid experience.

REAL CASE SCENARIO

A real case where this tactic came into play was when I went to the hospital bedside of a woman who had been shot in the chest at close range. She was a third-year medical student. She had gone for ice cream and was robbed at gunpoint in the parking lot. Because she was not quick enough to exit her vehicle, the robber shot her. The bullet was miraculously slowed by a rib and just missed her heart. She was recuperating nicely, but everyone, including the patient, knew she nearly died.

When I entered the hospital room of this young vibrant-looking medical student/patient, her friends were standing around her bed talking about what she would have for lunch and the weather. She seemed disinterested as I set up my gear. I sat down while the friends continued the idle chatter and locked gazes with the shooting victim. I said, "You almost died, but you didn't. It is *so good* to see you alive."

The witness brightened visibly and almost laughed out loud. She quickly got her friends to leave, and a successful sketch was done in less than an hour. During the interview the witness dominated the conversation with excited plans for

Figure 3.30

The sketch on the left was taken from a third-year medical student who was shot in the heart by the man pictured on the right. She survived and I was on an immediate footing with her by mentioning my near-death experience immediately upon meeting her in the hospital[35] (courtesy of the Houston Police Department).

the future and her astonishment and anger at someone who would shoot her just for her car. She was also angry with loved ones who decided it was her fault for going to have ice cream after dark. I assured her it was not her fault, and that loads of people go for ice cream after dark. It was the fault of the robber and no one else. The shooting victim obviously enjoyed talking to me more than her friends since I brought forward the one subject that dominated all her thoughts. The sketch created during this interview juxtaposed with a photo of the man who shot her can be seen in Figure 3.30.

The phrase "misery loves company" is absolutely true. However, I assert a more positive version is closer to the truth, especially as it relates to interviewing victims of crime. The phrase instead should be, "talking about a terror relieves the terror." Sometimes the witness is so overwrought with not being able to talk about his or her feelings about almost dying, that it would be impossible even to start the sketch without bringing up the subject. Once those all-consuming thoughts can be said out loud, the interviewer can turn them into the positive imaginings of what will now be done with the rest of the witness's precious life.

This is "turning a negative into a positive," which is a must-have for almost all sketch interviews. Said in different terms, the witness has experienced what might be the most negative occurrence of his or her life. If you can turn his or her feelings about that negative experience into a positive, that would be a great emotional accomplishment. Point out that if the sketch is good enough, it can get the perpetrator of his or her worst ordeal caught. The sketch can gain justice; it can help the witness get back his or her life, which will make the effort seem like a most desirable activity. Added to the positive thoughts that flow after the near-death experience is mentioned out loud is the satisfaction of knowing the attacker can be put behind bars if the sketch is created.

Now is the point where reasonable pessimists caution that the sketch might *not* come out well, and that the perpetrator of the crime may *not* be caught. But surely you and the witness won't make the best effort to get a sketch if pessimism is allowed to stifle the interview. If you use optimism to elevate the mood of a witness, a sketch still might not lead the detective to the person responsible. But if you don't try optimism, and the perpetrator isn't caught, you will never know how much better it could have been using positive comments with the witness.

The witness for the sketch in Figure 3.31 saw a man kill a business owner to whom he was making a delivery. For compelling reasons he did not notify authorities he saw this murder committed. Through delivery records the detectives eventually made their way back to the witness. Of necessity, the detectives had suspicions he committed the murder. After long interviews and detective work, it was determined he did not shoot the owner.

When I finally encountered the witness, he was so distraught he refused to be engaged in the effort of creating an image of the shooter. In less than a few minutes I was able to enlist his memory for the sketch by bringing up his biggest issue. Before the owner was shot, the shooter aimed the gun at him. After the shooting he was told to "…keep his mouth shut" or he would also be killed. Once this witness was able to rage and grieve over being put in such a position, he was ready to help make the sketch. I also convinced the witness there was no way the killer could find him and that he was likely long gone.

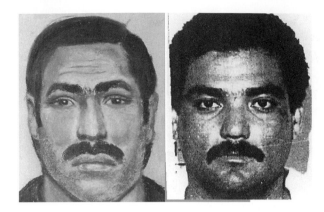

Figure 3.31

The man shown right killed a business owner and threatened to kill the witness. The witness spoke only Spanish so, using broken Spanish, I created the sketch shown left. This drawing subsequently helped detectives capture the killer[36] (courtesy of the Harris County Sheriffs Department).

Additionally, I convinced the witness the detectives no longer blamed him for the crime and they would probably find the shooter and solve everyone's problems.

The detectives were able to arrest the murderer using the sketch.

The technique of letting the witness vent about his near-death experience was the only way to get him to work with me. The proof this technique is easy to implement is evidenced by the fact that I am a native English speaker who studied three years of Spanish in high school, and the witness spoke Spanish and almost no English. This technique works so well, I needed only to bring up the subject and let the witness ramble on to a sympathetic person. Even though I did not understand everything the witness said, I understood the feelings and commiserated. I knew the phrases in Spanish for "they can catch him" and "he can't find you," which brought obvious comfort to the witness. Surely you can employ this method easily with a person who speaks the same language.

GETTING THE WITNESS TO LAUGH: THE HOLY GRAIL OF A GREAT INTERVIEW

Imagine being with a friend who has been through a near-death experience, and wanting to help him or her recover emotionally. One of the best ways to regain happiness in life after a tragedy is to laugh. Obviously you can't bring another to laughter the instant after the incident, or if that person is injured and still in pain. However, once the witness has accepted the fact the incident has occurred and he or she is out of immediate danger, laughter can be a most-welcome experience. Proof of this is the reaction by witnesses when they are brought to laughter. Once I learned how effective laughter was in relaxing the witness, the comments heard were something like these:

"That is the first time I have laughed since that happened; this is great!"

"I can't believe I'm laughing, but it *is* funny!"

Remarks that will bring a witness to laughter would be as varied as individual personalities. If you can meet new people in social situations and find ways to engender mirth in conversation, surely you can use those same skills to bring joviality to the interviewee during the sketch. Many individuals employ these social skills to stay in good stead with their bosses and work mates. Laughter is even more important if it can elevate the witness's mood and help create a sketch that might stop a felon.

The Science of Laughter

Psychologists, neurologists, and physiologists have been discovering the value of laughter since Norman Cousins wrote *Anatomy of an Illness* in 1979. In this book Cousins credits watching humorous videos with helping him reduce pain and recover from ankylosing spondylitis, a life-threatening degenerative spinal disease. Researchers were inspired to examine whether laughter really did aid in recovering from illness and coping with pain.[37]

Researchers at Loma Linda University School of Medicine studied the effects on medical students who watched a 60-minute videotape of a popular comedian. After watching the video, researches discovered their subjects had a measurable decrease in stress hormones, including epinephrine and dopamine in their blood. There was also an increase in endorphins, the body's natural painkillers. The most changes were found in the subjects' immune systems. They exhibited:

- Increased levels of gamma interferon, a hormone that "switches on" the immune system, helps fight viruses, and regulates cell growth.
- Increased "Complement 3," a substance that helps antibodies destroy infected and damaged cells
- Greater numbers of "helper T-cells," which help the body coordinate the immune system's response to illness
- An increase in activity and number of "natural killer (NK) cells," which the body uses to attack foreign cells, cancer cells, and cells infected by a virus.[38]

Peter Derks, a psychologist at the College of William and Mary, did a study that more directly proves how laughter can help a witness who is trying to remember the face of an attacker. Derks conducted a test to see how the brain stimulates laughter. He hooked up his subjects to an EEG (electroencephalogram) topographical brain mapper. He then told the subjects jokes until they laughed.

Derks found almost the entire "higher brain" or cerebral cortex became involved as the subject tried to understand the joke. Functions such as problem solving or experiencing emotions are carried out in only one region. Laughing causes a wave of electricity to sweep through the entire cortex. Problem-solving abilities are increased since the emotional, rational, and sensory parts of the upper brain are all carpeted with stimulation during laughter. Hormones are produced that make the subject more alert. Stress levels go down. The muscles loosen up and digestive systems work better. The blood becomes more oxygenated due to increased respiration, heart rate, and blood pressure.[39]

In other words, witnesses who can laugh will be more in the mood to help with the task. Finding themselves engaged in laughter will allow them to believe they have begun to conquer the situation. It will instill optimism in a situation that is overloaded with pessimism. Drawing on the large scientifically valid study of what has worked well in over 3,700 forensic-sketching interviews, I can state that getting the witness to laugh is the best vehicle to engaging the witness's help in creating an image of the perpetrator.

No specific phrases can be given, or jokes relayed that can help an interviewee find laughter. Rather, it is like conversations in real life; the humor must be thought up as the situation dictates. I am glad to relate that persons who have almost lost their lives are more readily disposed to laughter. It goes without saying the exceptions would be persons in extreme physical pain and those who have just lost close loved ones. Witnesses who sincerely thought they were going to die, once they have concluded that they will live and that they are safe, laugh more readily than casual conversants. The recent survivor will also feel more gratitude about being able to laugh and will be eager for more mirthful comments once the mood has turned in that direction during the interview. College of William and Mary psychologist Dr. Peter Derks studied this "predisposition to laughter." He showed that once a person starts laughing, the brain is prepped and ready to laugh more. Joseph Richman, M.D., professor at Albert Einstein Medical Center, New York, has determined laughter counteracts "feelings of alienation, a major factor in depression...."[40]

We can deduce from these scientific findings that an interviewer can break down the isolation and depression of witnesses by getting them to laugh. To maximize concentration and clear thinking, the best method would be to keep the laughter coming as much as possible.

An Example

The following scenario is an example of a time laughter helped a witness create a successful sketch. I was called to a hospital to sketch from a woman who had been carjacked and robbed in a particularly violent manner. The detective related that the robbers first took the woman to an automated teller machine and forced her to withdraw money. The robbers then drove her to a remote area and walked her out to a field. They told her to kneel down on her knees, but she refused. One of the robbers then shot the woman 15 times with a 22-caliber weapon. The robbers then walked away and drove off in the woman's car, leaving her for dead.

The woman awoke and realized she could walk and breathe, but that she was most likely bleeding to death. She walked the equivalent of three football fields and came to a gated apartment complex where she got help. She lost one eye and several teeth, but survived.

When I arrived to create the sketch at the hospital, it had been 10 days since the shooting. The witness appeared to be a healthy woman in her early 30s.

Her parents were in the room with her. She seemed to be slightly uncomfortable, but not in any obvious pain. One of the first things the witness did upon meeting me was to laugh a bit at the proposition she was supposed to help do a sketch. She expressed (as all witnesses do) that she didn't think she would be of much help. She followed that immediately with a joke something like "…I guess if I can handle getting shot all up, I can handle trying to do a drawing of the guy. I don't have anything to lose and I'm stuck here and not going anywhere anyway!" I picked up on this line of humor and we both laughed intermittently during the entire sketch shown in figure 3.32.

Figure 3.32
The witness for the sketch shown left was shot 15 times by the man, right, losing an eye and some teeth. She walked 950 feet and got help.[29] *I used humor to make the interview easy since it was obvious the witness was glad to be alive after coming so near death.*

Much of the humor related to how great it was to be alive. The kind of humor used in these situations would never be jokes of the kind you might memorize, with punch lines contrived to be funny. Rather the humor must be customized to relate to that witness's situation, temperament, and recent experience. Therefore, there is no one line of humor that can be taught by anyone for this kind of work. You should imagine the witness is a friend, and further envision how you would bring that friend to laughter if you experienced the same thing.

One of the biggest laughs from the witness of this case came when she made a remark that the shooter was not bad looking. I stared at her with a blank expression and said, "Yeah, but when he's trying to shoot you to death, that really puts a kink in how cute he looks!"

I am certain persons who haven't been shot 15 times but did not die might not think this remark is funny. However, the witness laughed so hard, she began moving around in the bed, would groan, and then start laughing again. The laughter went on for quite a while. Then the witness shook her head up and down slowly and continued to laugh and make her own jokes during the rest of the sketch. The only time she quit laughing came when the sketch was turned around for her to view and make changes. At that time, she remarked how much the sketch resembled the shooter. The witness was so relieved and in such a great mood, she insisted on getting out of her bed to hug me. Even though the woman's mother protested loudly for her not to get out of bed, she did anyway. At the end of the interview she had her mother take a photo of us in the hospital room, as can be seen in Figure 3.33. The note the witness wrote on the front of this photo proves how effective bringing the witness to laughter is. Even though this woman was shot 15 times and left for dead, she truly enjoyed laughing about it just days later, thanking me for utilizing that technique during the sketch interview.

I knew instinctively in the beginning of my career that bringing witnesses to a jovial state during the sketch interview was a valuable tool for their

Figure 3.33

The writing says, "Thank you so much for the Job you do and the Gentle manner in which you apply it—Tracey L. Deel, June 7, 2001." The date, bottom left, is, "Dec. 8, 1999, Ben Taub Hospital." This message makes it obvious this witness felt my technique of getting her to laugh was effective (photo used by permission).

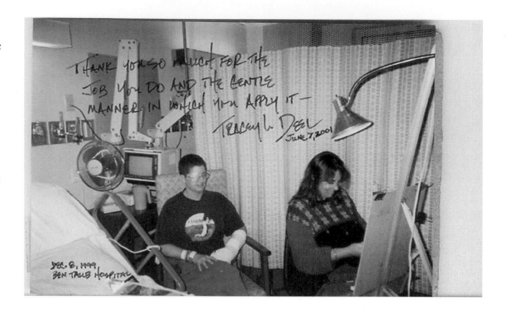

relaxation. As we can see from the scientific studies, it has been proven how beneficial laughter is to sharpening the mind and elevating the mood. Certainly there might be those artists whose style does not lend them to being humorous. However, if you are *able* to bring individuals whom you have just met to laughter, I highly recommend that you use those skills to enhance your forensic artwork.

In Brief

- A sympathetic interviewer will automatically perform the scientifically proven Cognitive Interview.
- Bring up the near-death aspect of the witness's experience since that concept is occupying much of his or her waking thoughts; the subsequent venting will relieve tension.
- Whenever possible, as much as possible, get the witness to laugh.

HOW LONG AFTER THE CRIME SHOULD THE SKETCH BE DONE?

Ideally all sketches done from witness memory should be done immediately after the incident. However, some studies indicate that trauma may inhibit memory and that it would be best to wait until after 24, or even 48, hours. This needed "waiting period" would pertain to those witnesses who are highly traumatized.

In the real world of working with witnesses and detectives, the fact is you will be allowed to work with the witness when factors out of your control determine you will have the opportunity to sketch. The most traumatized witnesses will often be those you see first. This is due to outrage on the part of the media, the public, and the detectives. On the other end of the spectrum, the first thing the detectives do immediately after many crimes is follow promising leads to their conclusion. By the time these leads prove to be dead ends, often many days, weeks, and even months have passed. Then, sometimes as a last resort, the artist is brought in to work on the case. Don't despair about situations over which you have no control.

Witnesses do forget some information as time ticks by after their incident. The good news is that after 72 hours, the details retained by witnesses will stay in their memory for many years. Actually, barring Alzheimer's or other age-induced dementia, witnesses will retain these memories the rest of their lives. I have experienced witnesses who gave superior descriptions many weeks after the crime. During 1999 at the Houston Police Department, the average session with a witness occurred about three weeks after the incident.

Table 3.1 is a list of the number of days after the incident I did the sketch on the first two months of 1999.

January	February
115	7
25	15
19	10
11	18
29	29
46	25
7	3
33	17
85	0
14	9
10	46
4	51
	24
	27

Table 3.1

Days after Crime Sketch Created (1999)

Average time elapsed from crime to sketch: 22 days.

These two months were 17 years after I began working with the area law enforcement agencies, so I was well established. All detectives knew me and my services. As you can tell, sometimes my schedule caused me to delay an interview, or as in the zero days waited on one case in February, the witness was obviously brought to sketch immediately after the crime. In this large metropolitan area (fourth in size in the U.S.) the average time of 22 days elapsed between crime and sketch is not ideal. However, during that year, I had a 43% clearance rate.

Some highly specific examples of what can be remembered and thus sketched after considerable periods of time are too numerous to mention. Figure 3.32 was done nine days after the crime, and furthermore the witness had the unbelievable trauma of being shot 15 times by her assailants. The sketch on the upper left of Figure 3.34 was done 77 days after the 6-year-old witness was stuffed into a closet by the man pictured on the right, who then murdered her mother while she listened. Her 5-year-old friend was with her in the closet and also helped with the sketch. Notice the choice both girls made independently, in separate interviews, from the *FBI Facial Identification Catalog*. Both little girls chose a nose that exhibited perfectly circular nostril holes when in frontal view. I unwisely assumed these round nostrils were a function of the little girls' viewing the man from below and changed them to a more normal elliptical

Figure 3.34

The sketch, top left, was done 77 days after the 6-year-old witness was stuffed into a closet by the man pictured top right, then waited in fear while she listened as he murdered her mother. Her friend, a 5-year-old girl, also helped with the sketch in a separate interview (courtesy of the Newton, Kansas, Police Department).

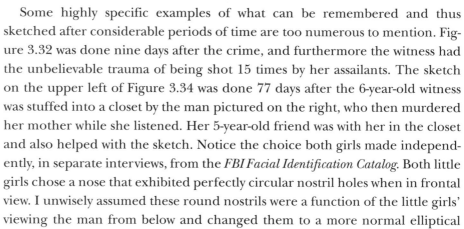

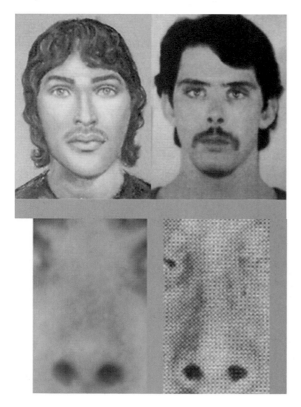

shape. Had I respected the little girls' memory, the drawing would truly have reflected the extremely accurate memory of these tiny details, even after the 77 days since they viewed the face of the killer. In defense of this imperfect drawing, it led directly to the identification, apprehension, and conviction of the murderer.[41]

The sketch in Figure 3.35 was done 239 days after the witness saw the man on the right kidnap a woman on a freeway. Because of his hostility toward law enforcement, he refused to come forward to authorities. After the parents of the missing girl erected billboards begging for her to be found, the witness relented and called police. The suspect was arrested for another crime 13 months after the abduction, and confessed to kidnapping the woman.[42] This sketch, done a few days short of 8 months after the witness saw his face, at a distance of several yards, is nevertheless accurate as to proportion, eyebrow shape, and hair type. It must be noted the witness was extremely depressed and hostile during the sketch.

Proof of how much a witness can remember for a sketch 6 years after viewing her attacker can be seen in Figure 3.36. The other handicap for this sketch was that the witness had cerebral palsy so she could not talk. She communicated by blinking for "yes" and "no." She was confined to a wheelchair, and was 7 years of age when the attack occurred. With visual aids, the girl gave a description for the sketch on the left. She was also able to specify a date of the attack by relating the distance in days from certain holidays and special events at her school. She described being taken to a storage room and assaulted. It was discovered the individual pictured had access to her school, keys to a storage room, and had made a delivery on the day she was attacked.[43]

Figure 3.35

I met with the witness for the sketch on the left 239 days after he saw the man on the right, from a distance of several yards, kidnap a woman from her car on a feeder of a freeway (courtesy of the Federal Bureau of Investigation and the Galveston Police Department).

In Brief

- Ideally the sketch should be done immediately after the crime.
- Do not ruin your attitude about a sketch when it takes time for the detective to bring a witness to you. A negative feeling about something that is beyond your control serves no purpose. Rather, remember successful sketches have been done long after the crime, and accept and do the best with what you are given, when you are given it.

The ideal would be to get all witnesses immediately afterward. I vigorously endorse any efforts by any forensic artist to prompt all their detectives to bring them their witnesses as soon as possible. When sharing successes from sketches done long after the incident, I am only trying to give other forensic artists coping skills to deal with what will happen in all departments of which I am aware.

If, however, there is an artist who has developed a technique to changing detectives' mind sets, creating a situation where all witnesses are brought to the artist's side with great speed, I join all forensic artists in saying we are eager to learn this technique.

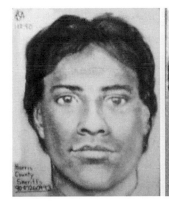

Figure 3.36

The sketch, left, was done 6 years after the incident. The witness had cerebral palsy, could only blink for "yes" and "no," was 7 years old at the time of the attack, and in a wheelchair. The man, right, had keys to the room where the assault took place (courtesy of the Houston Police Department).

However, the all-important mood of the artist will be kept harmonious, and thus the work will be enhanced, if we accept all the gross imperfections of this kind of work. These imperfections are the reluctant witnesses, the heart-wrenching crimes, and lastly, the fact that you might not get witnesses until some time after they have seen the face they must help the artist to draw.

REFERENCES

1. S. K. Bardwell, "Police link license ID to sketch," *Houston Chronicle*, October 7, 1999. Steve Brewer, "$250,000 bail set for man charged in sexual assault of Houston teen," *Houston Chronicle*, October 8, 1999. Houston Police Department Incident Number 110674299.

2. Houston Police Department Incident Number 41190397.

3. Rosanna Ruiz, "Awash in grief and rage," *Houston Chronicle*, August 5, 2001. Houston Police Department Incident Number 106339501.

4. Houston Police Department Incident Number 12435288.

5. Staff, *Houston Chronicle*, "UH police seeking assault suspect," November 7, 2000. University of Houston Police Department Incident number 00-61386.

6. Geoff Davidian, "The Gay Hit Man," *Houston Chronicle*, August 10, 1991. Houston Police Department Incident Number 44008890.

7. S. K. Bardwell and Gayness Terrell, "Galleria abduction has shoppers a little jittery," *Houston Chronicle*, January 18, 1992. "Police release drawing of abduction-rape suspect," Staff, *The Houston Post*, January 21, 1992. "18-year-old man charged with assault," Staff, *Houston Post*, January 23, 1992. Patti Muck, "Ex-Galleria clerk held in abduction, assault," *Houston Chronicle*, January 23, 1992. "Kidnapping count added in Galleria abduction," Staff, *The Houston Post*, January 24, 1992. "Hockley man, 19, convicted in assault," Staff, *Houston Chronicle*, February 12, 1993. Katy Hall, "Hockley teen sentenced in kidnapping, assault," *The Waller County News Citizen*, February 17, 1993. Houston Police Department Incident Number 5642792.

8. James T. Campbell, "Rape victim's plan helps nab suspect," *Houston Chronicle*, July 4, 1990. Houston Police Department Incident Number 57711990.

9. Houston Police Department Incident Number 4522490.

10. "Arrest may solve series of sex assaults, robberies, police say," Staff, *Houston Chronicle*, August 31, 1989. "Rapist given 99 years," *Houston Chronicle*, April 9, 1991. Houston Police Department Incident Number 76100989.

11. Mike Glenn and Dale Lezon, "Tip from shopper leads to an arrest in Rice shootings," *Houston Chronicle*, April 7, 2004. Houston Police Department Incident Number 43259504.

12. Jo Ann Zuniga, "Traffic stop turns tragic for officer," *Houston Chronicle*, January 6, 1991. Eric Hanson, "Suspect in shooting of officer arrested," *Houston Chronicle*, January 8, 1991. Robert Stanton, "'Galleria Rapist' receives life sentence in shooting," *The Houston Post*, July 18, 1991. Houston Police Department Incident Number 1449791.

13. "Police seek information on abductor," Staff, *Houston Chronicle*, February 4, 1991. Houston Police Department Incident Number 114461490.

14. Staff, "Man posing as security guard knifes young girls in apartment," *The Houston Post*, January 23, 1988. Jack Douglas, "Suspect charged in attack of 2 girls," *The Houston Post*, January 26, 1988. Janet Elliott, "Attacker gets 99-year prison term," *The Houston Post*, August 19, 1988. Houston Police Department Incident Number 5540588.

15. "Witnesses describe boy's killer/Artist's sketch of suspect," Staff, *The Houston Post*, June 6, 1987. Eric Hanson and Andrea D. Greene, "Man held in slaying of boy, 3," *Houston Chronicle*, June 7, 1987. Staff, "Man gets 38 years in tot's death," *Houston Chronicle*, August 22, 1987. Houston Police Department Incident Number 31515687.

16. Houston Police Department Incident Number 127802197.

17. Mary Lynn Young, "Ex-sheriff's deputy arrested in rape case," *The Houston Post*, October 1, 1993. Jennifer Liebrum, "Former sheriff's deputy convicted in rape," *Houston Chronicle*, July 2, 1994. Jennifer Liebrum, "Former deputy gets 17-year prison term for rape." Harris County Sheriff's Case Number 9308080463.

18. Roger Smith "Good job, performance with a plus," *City Savvy Magazine*, April, 2002. Houston Police Department Incident Number 6282694.

19. Friendswood Police Department Case Number 914811.

20. Houston Police Department Incident Number 91136597.

21. Galveston Police Department Case Number 492220.

22. Staff, "Man posing as security guard knifes young girls in apartment," *The Houston Post*, January 23, 1988. Jack Douglas, "Suspect charged in attack of 2 girls," *The Houston Post*, January 26, 1988. Janet Elliott, "Attacker gets 99-year prison term," *The Houston Post*, August 19, 1988. Houston Police Department Incident Number 5540588.

23. Peter Doskoch, "Happily Ever Laughter," *Psychology Today*, July/August, 1996.

24.   Geoff Davidian, "The Gay Hit Man," *Houston Chronicle*, August 10, 1991. Houston Police Department Incident Number 44008890.

25.   Harris County Sheriffs Case Number 92031901116.

26.   S. K. Bardwell and Eric Hanson, "A babe in arms/Kidnap suspect may have been delusional," *Houston Chronicle*, October 25, 1995. Houston Police Department Incident Number 12217669512.

27.   S. K. Bardwell and "Jewelry heist well planned, officers say," *Houston Chronicle*, January 30, 1996. S. K. Bardwell, "Diamond suspect in sketch," *Houston Chronicle*, January 31, 1996. Jerry Urban and S. K. Bardwell, "Two charged in killing of diamond merchant," *Houston Chronicle*, February 25, 1996. S. K. Bardwell, "Police look for missing jewels in robbery-shooting death case," *Houston Chronicle*, February 27, 1996. S. K. Bardwell, "Three suspects held in connection with jeweler's murder," *Houston Chronicle*, February 24, 1996. Stephanie Asin, "Guard identifies jeweler in murder case," *Houston Chronicle*, August 19, 1997. Stephanie Asin, "Jeweler convicted of killing diamond dealer in robbery," *Houston Chronicle*, August 29, 1997. Stefanie Asin, "Jury sentences jeweler to death/Execution by injection ordered in theft, killing of gem broker death," *Houston Chronicle*, September 5, 1997. Houston Police Department Incident Number 10330996.

28.   Jo Ann Zuniga, "Traffic stop turns tragic for officer/Policeman shot twice, run over," *Houston Chronicle*, January 6, 1991. Eric Hanson, "Suspect in shooting of officer arrested," *Houston Chronicle*, January 10, 1991. "Prison escapee charged with attempted capital murder in attack on officer," Staff, *Houston Chronicle*, January 11, 1991. John Makeig, " 'Galleria rapist' gets life in police shooting," *Houston Chronicle*, July 18, 1991. Houston Police Department Incident Number 1449791.

29.   "Sketch of shooting suspect," Staff, *Houston Chronicle*, December 10, 1999. S. K. Bardwell, "2 arrested in robbery, shooting of woman who was left for dead," *Houston Chronicle*, December 23, 1999. Steve Brewer, " 'I was not going to quit'/Woman refuses to let 15 bullets silence her," *Houston Chronicle*, June 2, 2000. Steve Brewer, "Teen gunman gets life for brutal '99 robbery/Victim shot 15 times, left for dead," *Houston Chronicle*, July 11, 2000. Houston Police Department Incident Number 152410199.

30.   Galveston Police Department Case Number 492220.

31.   Mike Glenn and Dale Lezon, "Tip from shopper leads to an arrest in Rice shootings," *Houston Chronicle*, April 7, 2004. Houston Police Department Incident Number 43259504.

32.   R. Edward Geiselman, Ronald P. Fisher, David P. MacKinnon, and Heidi L. Holland, "Eyewitness Memory Enhancement in the Police Interview: Cognitive Retrieval Mnemonics Versus Hypnosis," *Journal of Applied Psychology*, 1985, vol. 70, No. 2, p. 403.

33.   Margo Bennett and John E. Hess, "Cognitive Interviewing," *FBI Law Enforcement Bulletin*, March 1991, pp. 8–12.

34. R. Edward Geiselman, Ronald P. Fisher, David S. Raymond, Lynn M. Jurkevich, and Monica L Warhaftig, "Enhancing Eyewitness Memory: Refining the Cognitive Interview." *Journal of Police Science and Administration*, December 1987, vol. 15, No. 4, p. 292.

35. Deborah Quinn Hensel, "Med student gets violent lesson in being a patient," *The Houston Post*, April 16, 1994. "Suspect jailed in Rice kidnap-rape, shooting," April 27, 1994. S. K. Bardwell, "Kidnap suspect probed in spree," *Houston Chronicle*, April 28, 1994. Houston Police Department Incident Number 37589794.

36. Harris County Sheriffs Case Number 9309031777.

37. Maurice J Elias, "Lighten up your life; laugh with someone," *Houston Chronicle*, June 16, 2000.

38. Norman, Cousins, *Anatomy of an Illness as Perceived by the Patient*, W. W. Norton & Company, New York, reprint edition, July 11, 2005.

39. "Laughter Research Conducted at LLUMC," *Loma Linda University School of Medicine News*, March 11, 1999.

40. Peter, Doskoch, "Happily Ever Laughter," *Psychology Today*, July/August, 1996.

41. Kelly McGuire, "Inmate charged with '94 murder/Chester L. Higginbotham, serving time for a 1995 murder, faces first-degree murder charge for death of Newton woman more than four years ago," *The Hutchinson News*, August 13, 1998. Bill Wilson, "A battle hard won/Police say Krehbiel murder solved," *The Newton Kansan*, August 13, 1998. Laviana Hurst, "Suspect charged in 1994 murder case/Chester Higgenbotham is accused in the beating death of Rhonda Krehbiel of Newton," *The Wichita Eagle*, August 15, 1998. Newton Police Department Case Number 94N1424.

42. Ken, Lanternman, "Pair accused of kidnapping Sikes indicted/Murder evidence lacking," *The Houston Post*, July 29, 1987. Stanton, Robert, "Witness identifies defendant as man who abducted Sikes/Bare hand used to break out window," *The Houston Post*, June 23, 1988. Staff, "Earthmovers dig pasture in body hunt/Authorities get tip about Shelly Sikes," *The Houston Post*, September 26, 1990.

43. Harris County Sheriffs Case Number 9003260493.

CHAPTER 4

SPECIAL REFINEMENTS TO THE INTERVIEW

A TECHNIQUE FOR THE DESPERATE INTERVIEW

The most desperate situation a forensic artist can encounter is working with the witness who adamantly insists he or she did not see the face of the perpetrator. These remarks often come in the highest profile cases. They come from a witness who has been put with the artist by detectives who are feeling great pressure to solve the case. The witness is also usually feeling pressures from many directions. Witnesses for cases that might not be of the highest priority will also make this claim.

Dozens of witnesses who claimed they never saw the face of the perpetrator nevertheless gave descriptions for successful sketches early in my career. The interviews were long and frustrating. The witnesses would exclaim they were only guessing when they chose features from the visual aids. Then they would insist on *detailed changes*. After the suspect was identified, a comparison of the sketch with the photo would prove a good likeness. Further, dozens of sketches taken from witnesses who proclaimed they didn't see a face helped get the person identified.

Soon it became apparent that witnesses who experienced a situation where you would *assume* they saw the face of a suspect most likely *did* see the face. The protestations were ways to try to get out of performing the task and to vent their frustration at the situation.

The quandary was to develop a way to quickly engage the witness who actually *did* see the face of the suspect in the work of creating an image. The other need was to find a way to determine which witnesses really *didn't* see a face. I came upon a magic phrase to ask in the midst of a desperate sketch interview: What kind of expression did the suspect have?

If the witness remarks about the expression, he or she saw the face. You cannot obtain impressions about an individual's expression by looking at the back of the head. There is not even much information about the expression when observing a face in profile.

Never ask about the expression immediately after the witness has declared he or she never saw the face. This would appear as if you were arguing with the witness. Arguing will only increase the tension, which will diminish the witness's ability to access his or her memory.

Instead, the way to work this technique is to change the subject. Talk sympathetically to the witness. Talk enough so that the witness thinks the subject of the suspect's face is not being discussed any more. Then, in a soothing manner, remark about the terrible crime and suspect. Gently ask," What kind of person would do such a thing?" Then say, "What kind of expression did he (she) have?" Remain quiet and listen to the reply.

Almost all witnesses start talking about the expression. They were riveted by that expression because they were likely pondering whether they were going to die at that person's hands. The witness who starts talking about the expression of his or her attacker will be emotional. Talking about the expression on the face they saw will have them reliving the experience. At that time, you know *the witness did see the face.* The interview is at a very crucial phase. As gently as possible, present the visual aids to the witness. Be positively meditative while asking the witness to please give a look and see if anything is similar to the features.

This technique has elicited information about the suspect's face from witnesses who have insisted repeatedly that they never saw the face. Because of consistent success, this question is a mainstay of the interview. It was first discovered in a situation where the interview was at a standstill and the detectives and public were desperate for a lead. Then it became obvious that it was an effective tool for almost all witnesses to help jog their memory of a face they truly did not want to recall. This question is so helpful it can speed up the interview process when the witness shows the slightest resistance. You must only couple it with a warm and sympathetic attitude that makes witnesses feel certain you are on their side.

This phrase works so well that many witnesses indicate several changes be made to the sketch when it comes time for the corrections phase. Although logically valid, never remark, "I thought you said you didn't see the face!" Although it may be true, do not gloat about having gleaned a sketch from a witness who earlier was so adamant that he or she couldn't help. Rather, simply note this phenomenon understood by seasoned forensic artists, and be glad there is a way around this seemingly insurmountable obstacle to the interview.

Figures 4.1 through 4.4 are all sketches taken from the memories of witnesses who adamantly declared that they never saw the suspect's face. Of particular note is Figure 4.2. The man on the bottom right approached a young female while driving a black van and offered her money to get in his vehicle. She refused and ran away. After the sketch was done, a crime analyst ran all the black vans cited for traffic violations in the area of the incident. This man came up as the van owner in one traffic violation. Since his photo bore a strong resemblance to the sketch, the detective searched and found other evidence linking him to the area that was

Figure 4.1

The sketch, left, was done in the intensive care unit with an officer who had been shot twice, run over, and dragged more than 50 feet by the man pictured on the right.[1] The officer insisted he never saw the shooter's face (courtesy of the Houston Police Department).

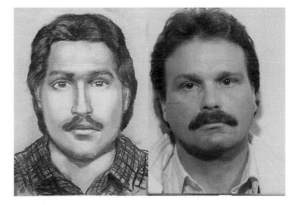

far from his home. Several other witnesses he had approached picked him out of a lineup. In the beginning of the sketch, the witness claimed she never saw his face,[2] yet this sketch is almost identical to the face of the suspect.

Figure 4.2

From left to right along the top is the photo of the man described, with each image to the right a progressively less transparent overlay of the sketch superimposed atop. The sketch on the bottom left was taken from an 11-year-old girl (courtesy of the Houston Police Department). See color plate.

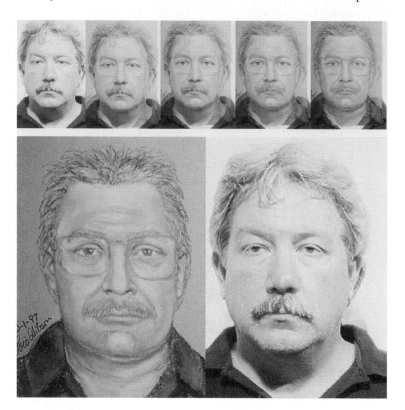

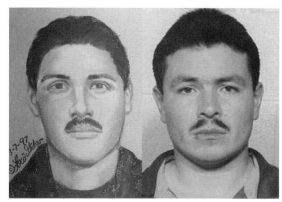

Figure 4.3

The sketch on the left was taken from the memory of a woman who was fueling her truck when the man on the right stole her truck at gunpoint. She insisted she never saw the rifleman's face. He was identified, charged, made bail, and is now a wanted fugitive[3] (courtesy of the Houston Police Department).

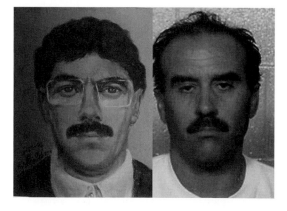

Figure 4.4

The sketch on the left was done in a hospital intensive care unit with a security guard who had been shot three times and insisted he never saw the face of the man pictured on the right.[4] This shooter was wearing a wig and glasses when he committed the crime (courtesy of the Houston Police Department).

Figure 4.5
The witness for the sketch on the left saw the man on the right steal her bag with over $630,000 in jewelry from a conveyor belt at an airport security checkpoint.[5] She and her assistant insisted they never saw his face (courtesy of the New York Port Authority Police).

ANOTHER EFFECTIVE PHRASE

Another phrase for witnesses who claim they never saw the face or who claim they don't know anything about the suspect is: What kind of hair did the suspect have?

This works with witnesses who say they didn't see the face and are also demonstrative that they didn't see *anything* about the suspect. Again, do not argue with their protestations. Engage the witness in congenial conversation. Assuage their anxiety by "taking away the task" and saying they need to communicate only two or three things. Then have the witness relate the gender and race of the suspect, and then ask what kind of hair the suspect had.

Witnesses will remember hair more readily than other features. Hair is the largest feature on the head. If the person is bald, that is an easily observable trait. Most witnesses who speak as if they didn't see the face will give complete information on the hair.

After gaining the hair description, gently ask the witness to look at the visual aids. Make minimal comments at this stage. Ask if he or she could simply give a guess at the eyes or eyebrows. Almost always the witness will start choosing features of the face once the hair description is established. Hundreds of witnesses who were handled in this manner went on to give descriptions for successful sketches. Again, witnesses are not lying when they say they can't remember; rather they need to vent and declare their frustration. Once they are allowed to do this without confrontation by the interviewer, they can begin to engage in the recall of facial features by observing visual aids. An effective introduction to the central facial features is remembering the hair. The hair surrounds the features and pulls the witness into the facial area.

It is not known how this works. What is certain is that it *does* work. There is not enough space to show all the successful sketches where this technique has worked, but a sampling can be seen in Figures 4.6 through 4.9. All these sketches were taken from witnesses who said they never really looked at the suspect's face,

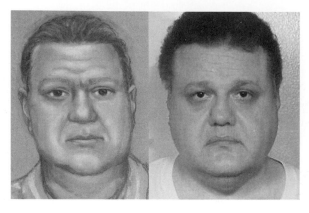

Figure 4.6

A shop owner was robbed by the man on the right and gave the description for the sketch shown left. This man was shot during a subsequent robbery and landed in a hospital where the detective on the case thought he resembled the sketch[6] (courtesy of the Houston Police Department).

Figure 4.7

The sketch on the left was created from the victim of a particularly brutal sexual assault. She and 40 friends plastered her neighborhood with posters bearing the image of her attacker. Within hours of the posting the mother of this man called in his identity to authorities[7] (courtesy of the Houston Police Department).

but when asked what kind of hair the suspect had, went on to remember the rest of the features.

When interviewing a witness who says he or she did not see the attacker's face, and you are reasonably certain he or she *did* see the face, be patient. When you ask about the expression or hair, give the impression that you are only discussing that. Believe it is acceptable that there will be no face described. Instead, act as if you are not going to sketch a face, but instead want to know about the hair or what kind of emotion was exhibited by the suspect's face. When the witness feels the pressure of creating a sketch removed, he or she will become relaxed enough to work. This attitude in the interview has led the way for the witness to continue with the visual aids, selecting an entire face to be drawn.

Figure 4.6 is a perfect example. The witness swore she did not see this man's face. After being asked about the hair and the expression, she began working with the visual aids. Not only did she pick out features, but she became so obsessive with making changes that the sketching session lasted 2 hours longer than normal. The point is, the witness *did* see the face, unlike her beginning protestations, or she wouldn't have made so many changes. Therefore, this sketch, which bears a remarkable resemblance to the suspect, was done in spite of the fact the interview seemed doomed to failure in the beginning.

Another example is Figure 4.8, which contains a sketch from two girls who claimed they never saw the man's face because he was completely naked as he chased them down a wooded trail. An officer in a nearby jurisdiction who had solved crimes with my sketches over the years put the sketch on his bulletin board. Three days later he saw the man on the right driving a van. The officer took down the van's tag number. A positive identification in a line-up by the girls and other ancillary evidence solved the case.[8]

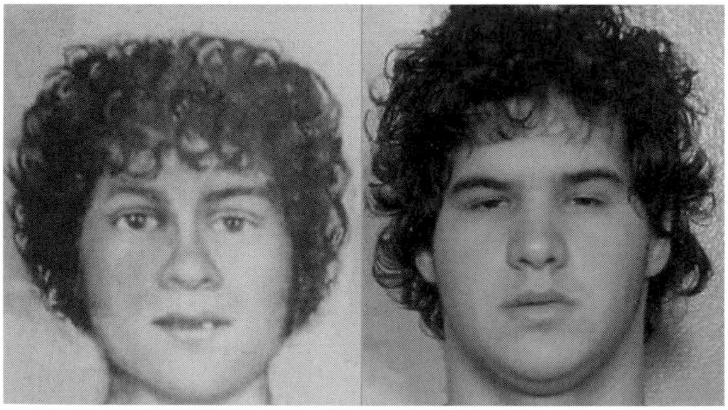

WHEN THE WITNESS IS "JUST GUESSING"

Another phenomenon is sketches done from witnesses who declare during the entire interview that they are "just guessing" after every selection of a feature from

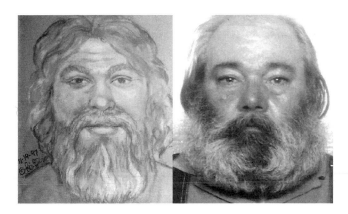 

Figure 4.8

Above left: The witnesses for the sketch on the left were riding their roller blades when the man on the right came out of the woods wearing no clothes and chased after them.[8] In the beginning of the sketch session, they claimed not to have seen his face (courtesy of the Houston Police Department).

Figure 4.9

Above right: A young couple that was home invaded, tortured, and robbed by the man on the right created the sketch on the left.[9] In the beginning of the interview, they insisted they did not see his face (courtesy of the Houston Police Department).

the visual aids. After doing hundreds of successful sketches from witnesses who made these kinds of remarks, one fact became certain. Do not abandon the interview if this is the attitude of your witness. Instead, stay patient and keep asking for the various pieces of information. Once the rough sketch is done and the witness views it in order to make changes, it will be evident that he or she was not really "just guessing."

These types of witnesses will make numerous changes. The sketches they help construct can look remarkably like the person they describe. We might deduce this is the way some witnesses react to the pressure of having to help authorities find the suspect. One common denominator is that these types of witnesses are from cases where there is incredible pressure, such as an infant-kidnapped-by-a-stranger case. This type of witness also seems to be more negative and depressed than other witnesses. However, no matter what the reason, if you know not to abandon the interview because of these types of comments, you will have a chance to help solve a high-profile case.

Figures 4.10 through 4.13 are sketches done with witnesses who declared during the entire interview they were "just guessing" about the features on the suspect's face.

The witness for the sketch in Figure 4.10 said repeatedly during the interview that he was just guessing about the features of the man on the right who stole a Corvette from him. *Crime Stoppers* segments aired with the sketch, telling how this man would test drive a vehicle and never bring it back. The next day a detective who had arrested this man for the same crime years earlier and thought he looked like the sketch gave all the needed information to the detective and the case was quickly solved.[10]

Early in my career there was an infant kidnapped from a day-care center by a stranger. The witness was the day-care owner who was one of the most distressed, angry, frustrated, and grieved witnesses ever encountered. She insisted during the entire sketch that she couldn't possibly remember the face

Figure 4.10

Above left: The sketch on the left was created with a witness who claimed he was "just guessing" about all of the man's features.[10] I knew this was a common remark from a frustrated witness and completed the sketch in spite of the witness's remarks (courtesy of the Houston Police Department).

Figure 4.11

Above right: The witnesses for the sketch on the left worked at a day-care center where a baby was kidnapped.[11] These witnesses felt profound frustration, anger, and pressure to help find the baby and insisted they were "just guessing" at all the man's features (courtesy of the Houston Police Department).

of the kidnapper. She proclaimed after every feature was described that she was "only guessing." An incredibly frustrating interview produced the sketch in Figure 4.11. I had little hope it would bear any resemblance to the suspect. The kidnapper was discovered within 24 hours and a photo was obtained. Since the sketch is quite similar to the face of the suspect, it can be deduced these kinds of remarks do not need to be taken literally. Another way to perceive these remarks is that the witness is guessing, but it is likely their guesses can be right.

Many similar interviews followed as the years went by with subsequent witnesses making almost identical remarks that they were guessing about their answers to questions. The sketches always looked similar to the person described when the perpetrator was apprehended. After dozens of interviews and results like this, I have deduced this: Continue to sketch and hope for the best even though it seems these remarks would make you believe there was no good reason to keep sketching.

WHEN WITNESSES INSIST THEY SAW THE PERPETRATOR ONLY IN PROFILE

Many witnesses insist they saw the perpetrator only in profile. After constructing hundreds of successful front view sketches from witnesses who made these kinds of remarks, I have these thoughts on the subject.

First of all, this protestation seems to be a method by which witnesses assume they might be able to get out of doing the sketch. This might also be a subconscious desire to get out of "facing" the suspect again since that face is central to a terrifying experience. This conclusion was reached when it became obvious from the incidents described that it would be impossible for the victim to have seen the assailant *only* in profile. In fact there are few incidents in life where

two human beings interact in a physical way where they see each other *only* in profile. I have listened to hundreds of witnesses who were:

- Approached by a gunman who asked for their property and then fled.
- Sexually assaulted (numerous sexual assault victims claim they closed their eyes *every time* they could have seen the suspect from the front; some say the suspect covered their eyes).
- Engaged in a fight including blows with fists and wrestling.
- Kept captive in an apartment and raped for days.
- Engaged in a heated cussing fight with the suspect.

When hundreds of witnesses to these types of incidents claimed to have seen only the profile, yet successful composites of front views of faces were created, it became obvious the witnesses' claims were impossible. It also became obvious there was a strong common urge among them to make this outrageous claim. The sexual assault victims just mentioned allowed they saw the profile to explain why they knew his age and race, and about mustaches, eye colors, and such. Some times these witnesses waffle between saying they never saw the face; then when it became obvious they knew details, tried to claim they saw only the profile.

Rather than argue with these claims, simply use the techniques outlined in previous paragraphs. Include the phrases "what kind of hair did they have" and "what kind of expression did they have" and obtain sex, race, age, and body type information. Then, hand the witness the *FBI Facial Identification Catalog* and say that it is possible to extrapolate the front view of a human face by seeing the side view. Ask the witness to look and see which features look most like the attacker from whatever portion of the face he or she saw. This allows for those witnesses who actually did see the front of the face, but for whatever reason need to claim having seen only the profile, to join in the sketch creation without confrontation with the artist.

Figure 4.12

Above left: The witnesses for the sketch, left, were a couple in their 60s who had been home invaded by the man pictured on the right. He knocked the man unconscious and sexually assaulted the wife. Immediately upon the sketch release, a parole officer recognized the perpetrator[12] (courtesy of the Friendswood Police Department).

Figure 4.13

Above right: The witnesses for the sketch, left, worked in the lobby of a motel and observed the man, right, talking to a woman later found murdered. All the witnesses claimed they never looked at the man's face and that they were only guessing at his features[13] (courtesy of the Montgomery County Sheriffs Department).

Those individuals who actually *did* see the attacker only in profile can still help describe the features. Since individuals can easily recognize persons they have not seen for years when viewing only a profile, we can assume people can extrapolate a front view from a profile. Additional proof of this ability is the fact that individuals see strangers in profile all the time and make many important determinations about the faces they see. They decide the age, attractiveness, ethnicity, fat content, and any number of facial facts from only a profile. I have engaged in an exercise where I viewed profiles of individuals whom I had never seen before and attempted to draw the front view. Those front views were almost perfect matches to the front views revealed at the end of the exercise.

A remarkable example of a sketch created with a witness who probably did see only the profile of a suspect is shown in Figure 4.14. The witness for this admittedly poorly done sketch was a bus driver who I truly believe might only have glanced at the man pictured next to the sketch in profile, and also only in her peripheral vision. There was immense pressure since this man had raped a blind woman who was 6½ months pregnant. The rapist had followed her off the bus. As he exited the bus he made an outrageous remark to the blind woman. The bus driver remembered that remark, and the blind girl told the detective the man who had made that remark and followed her off the bus was the same man who attacked her. Therefore, the bus driver's vision of the rapist was the only thing the detective had to go on.

The bus driver was so adamant about her profile-only view of the rapist that she became hostile during the interview. I used the technique of gaining a description of the sex, race, age, body type, and hair first from the witness. I then had the bus driver choose features she considered to resemble the rapist from the *FBI Facial Identification Catalog*. When I turned the easel around so the witness could see the sketch and make changes, the bus driver remarked that she never saw the man from the front and made me put the sketch in the wastebasket in the corner of the interview room. I took care not to fold, wad up, or tear up the sketch.

Figure 4.14

The sketch, left, was done from a witness who saw the man on the right in profile. The witness was so frustrated she made me put the sketch in the trash. Even so, the detective used it to identify the man on the right[14] (courtesy of the Houston Police Department).

After the witness left, the detective came into the room and asked for the sketch. I took the sketch out of the wastebasket and handed it to the detective. When the detective showed the sketch to the manager of a grocery store near the location of the rape, he gave him the name of an employee he was planning to fire because he was showing up at work under the influence of alcohol. The rape victim and the bus driver described the rapist as smelling like alcohol at nine in the morning. An arrest, identification in a voice line-up, and a DNA match solved the case.[14]

Obviously the sketch is of poor quality. The anatomy is so poor the face does not seem human. Since I was made to place the art in the trash, the sketch was not finished, dated, or signed. However, I adhered to the wise policy of not attempting to evaluate the sketch. The witness's evaluation of the sketch was clear. She considered it to be a total failure; proof of this is that she made me place it in the trash. Nevertheless, the detective was able to gain a successful identification from this image.

Figure 4.15

Both of these sketches were created from witnesses who claimed they saw the subjects' faces only in profile. These witnesses were either trying to avoid doing a sketch by making this claim, or they were able to extrapolate the front view by choosing features while remembering the profile view[15] (courtesy of the Houston Police Department).

We can deduce from this case that individuals *can* imagine the front view of someone's face from a profile. After sketching dozens of successful front views from profiles, I am certain of this fact. Figure 4.15 shows sketches compared to mug shots that were created from witnesses who insisted they saw the men pictured only from the side.

Figure 4.16 shows a sketch done with an even more remarkable handicap. The witness hysterically insisted that he saw the man pictured only from behind as he threatened his uncle and a customer at a liquor store. He then slipped out the back of the store and ran the length of a football field to another business for help. He then looked back the 100 yards as the gunman exited his uncle's business. He insisted the distance was too great to allow him to see the gunman's face. His uncle and the customer were found shot to death.

The witness convinced me he saw this double murderer only from behind. After consoling the young man who had just lost his uncle and felt guilty he couldn't stop the killing, I declared I would simply get what information I could about the shooter. The witness offered the man was white, with a large build standing at least 6.2 feet tall. He had a baseball cap on, but the witness could tell he had blond hair. Then the witness admitted he did see the man from the front when he was more than a football field away at a restaurant trying to get help. He declared it was impossible to see the face very well because of the great distance. I asked if the killer had a beard or mustache and the witness

Figure 4.16

The witness for the sketch on the left insisted he saw this man only from behind immediately before the suspect killed two people. The witness ran for help, then looked back and saw the man from the front at a distance of 100 yards (courtesy of the Harris County Sheriffs Department).

was certain he did not. By this time the witness had become quite relaxed and I offered him the *FBI Facial Identification Catalog* and asked if he would venture a guess at some features. The sketch on the left of Figure 4.16 was completed to the tepid satisfaction of the witness.

Detectives took the image around the neighborhood along with a description of the get-away vehicle. One detective spotted a similar vehicle parked in a nearby apartment complex. The detective set up surveillance at that location all

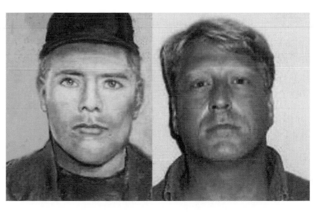

night until the man pictured on the right of Figure 4.16 came out of the apartments and began unlocking the vehicle. The detective approached and asked for identification. After evasive answers and a demeanor indicative of deception, the suspect's apartment eventually was searched, and bottles of liquor and cash from the double murder scene were found. This suspect was subsequently tried and convicted.[16]

The detectives confirmed that the witness was a little more than 100 yards away from the front of the liquor store when he went for help and looked back. We can deduce that the witness was able to give correct information about the race, sex, hair color, and body type just from seeing the suspect from behind. The frontal view offered at least the knowledge that there was no facial hair. The chin is too long in the drawing, but of the same large type as the suspect. The nose and lips are vaguely similar; the eyebrows are drawn too dark. However, as a whole, the face holds together as appearing similar enough that a detective was able to delve further into the suspect's identity when he saw him begin unlocking a vehicle like the one described leaving the scene of the double murder.

After sketching on this difficult case and seeing the successful results, I sketched dozens more where the witnesses were adamant they saw the suspect only from the side. No police department captures 100% of the persons for whom they search. However, 100% of the time when a sketch was done from a witness who claimed he or she saw the perpetrator only in profile and the subject was caught, the subject looked at least *similar* to the drawing.

Figure 4.17

Drawing a profile of this suspect was necessary for Michigan State Police Forensic Artist/Trooper Sarah C. Krebs, since the suspect had an extraordinary ponytail that could not be seen from the front (courtesy of the Michigan State Police Department).

Figure 4.18

Detail of Figure 4.17, the miniature portrait shows a profile with the suspect's extraordinary ponytail that could not be seen from the front (courtesy of the Michigan State Police Department).

WHEN PROFILES ARE A MUST

When an item of identification can be seen only in profile, the forensic artist needs to do what it takes to create the lateral view. Michigan State Police Forensic Artist/Trooper Sarah C. Krebs adeptly conveyed essential information about suspects as seen in Figures 4.17 through 4.20. First she rendered the important front view with a diastema on the female suspect, and a goatee on the male. Then, with brevity and precision, she created concise miniature profiles to the side, showing unusual hair that was impossible to view from the front. These profiles were both necessary to convey information that could be seen only from the side. The creation of miniature profiles as virtuous as these in Figures 4.18 and 4.20 requires a high level of fine artistic skills.

Figure 4.19

Drawing a profile of this suspect was necessary for Michigan State Police Forensic Artist/Trooper Sarah C. Krebs, since the suspect had a curly pony- tail that could not be seen from the front (courtesy of the Michigan State Police Department).

Figure 4.20

Detail of Figure 4.19, the miniature portrait shows a profile with the suspect's curly ponytail that could not be seen from the front (courtesy of the Michigan State Police Department).

In Brief

- When witnesses say they did not see the face and you are reason- ably certain they did, "Take away the task" by telling them they need to communicate only the most basic traits such as sex, race, and hair; make it seem as if creation of a face is not necessary.

   When witnesses say they did not see the face and you are reason- ably certain they did, there are two phrases that can help with recall if they are asked in a nonconfrontational manner after changing the subject of whether the witness did, or did not, see the face of the sus- pect. Those phrases are (1) What kind of expression did he or she have? and (2) What kind of hair did he or she have?
- Hundreds of successful sketches have been created from witnesses who insisted they were "just guessing" at their answers.
- Front views can be extrapolated by witnesses who claim to have seen only a profile.
- Sometimes a profile must be constructed to show identifiers observ- able only from the side view.

PRAISE THE DETECTIVE WORKING THE CASE

Even if you really don't know everything about the detective, it is a winning situ- ation to always praise the detective who is working the witness's case. There is everything to gain and nothing to lose by remarking positively about the detec- tive's abilities. This can be one of the most substantial ways to elevate the mood of the interviewee.

Law enforcement personnel often are taciturn and not given to grand ges- tures of nurturance. Some witnesses might mistake these qualities to be an indication the detective does not care about solving their case. Additionally, the officers who first made the scene are often in an emergency mode of inter- action and have likely treated the witness to terse questions and commands. The forensic artist has a great opportunity to show the witness a completely different kind of treatment. Once the ambiance of the interview has been established as a kind, warm, and comfortable one, the subject of the detective can be brought up.

Whatever the witness comments about the detective or other law enforcement personnel, if the remarks are negative, it is relatively easy to explain how necessary those officers' attitudes were at the time. Then it is a positively superb mood elevator to tell the witness that the detective is masterful at his or her job. The witness will often pull up in the chair and ask you to repeat the remark or explain more. At this time you should say any and all remarks about how long you have known the detective and how good he or she is at tracking down suspects. Even if you haven't known the detective for long, say he or she has a great track record (in most departments, an officer has to have a great track record to make detective). Tell the witness about any other personnel, such as other detectives, crime analysis technicians, commanders who are concerned, and virtually any persons or activities that are working to solve the victim's case. Since everyone who works solving crimes knows that sometimes even a rookie can have great luck and solve a case, it is valid to make any positive remarks about any detective.

Besides improving the mood of the witness, saying positive remarks about the detective handling the case will cause the victim to work more closely, respectfully, and positively with the investigator. That enhancement to the victim/detective relationship might cause the detective to canvass one more store, knock on one more door, and give him or her that break that helps bring in the victim's attacker.

An example of this can be seen in Figures 4.21 and 4.22. A crime victim described two men for the artist to sketch, one of whom had crooked teeth, and sketches were constructed. The witness felt like no one cared about the case. The artist assured him the detective was one of the best sleuths in the state and detailed a past successful case for which the detective performed in a heroic manner. The detective called to say thanks because he was so gratified by the witness treatment and respect he noticed as an effect of the positive remarks.

The detective set up surveillance at motel near the area of the suspect's operations. After many hours with no vehicle matching the witness's description showing up, the detective headed for home. Along the route to leave, the weary detective spotted a vehicle similar to the kind for which he had been searching, sitting in another motel parking lot. Even though he was in dire need of a break, the detective made that one last stop. He showed the motel manager the sketch.

Figure 4.21

A detective, whose complainants treated him with great respect because of positive remarks from the forensic artist, went the extra mile using the sketch on the left to find the man in the photo on the right (courtesy of the Houston Police Department).

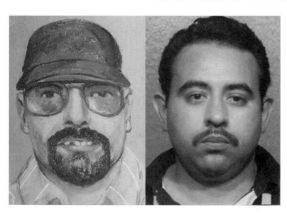

The manager noted the image resembled the man who owned the vehicle noticed by the investigator. Obtaining the room number, the exhausted detective knocked on the door and found the two suspects in the room. One of the men's teeth matched the composite, and even though they both had on hats and glasses in the sketch, ancillary evidence and line-ups identified the suspects and many cases were cleared. The detective remarked to the artist how much it mattered that he found justice for the grateful complainant who had worked with the artist on the sketches, and that was the reason he made that last stop inquiring about a suspicious vehicle at the motel. This is one example where the artist generating a respectful relationship between the detective and the crime victim helped solve the case.

Figure 4.22
The sketch of the second suspect used by the same detective[17] (courtesy of the Houston Police Department).

CLOSE YOUR EYES AND UNDERSTAND WHAT THE WITNESS SEES

As much as possible when with the witness, close your eyes. This will help the witness do what he or she needs to facilitate his or her memory of the face—which is to close *his or her* eyes. Closing your eyes while someone else is staring is universally uncomfortable. Therefore, the best way to ask the questions is to do so with your eyes closed. Another way is to start closing your eyes while you are asking the question so they are completely closed at the end of the question. After watching the interviewer with his or her eyes closed, the interviewee will be drawn to close his or her eyes. This is far superior to mentioning out loud to the witness to close his or her eyes.

The method of getting witnesses to close their eyes by letting them see the interviewer's eyes closed is an old trick mothers have been using for hundreds of years. As a mother holds a baby she wishes would relax or go to sleep, she will let the baby see *her* with her eyes closed. As with the baby, most individuals will give in to the urge to close their eyes and sink into the relaxed state that automatically ensues if they are alone with an interviewer who consistently closes his or her eyes.

Once the witness has begun the habit of closing his or her eyes to help remember the face of the attacker, never let the witness open them to see you staring. This is also a great time to keep the barrier of the easel holding the drawing board between you and the witness. If you want to know why this is necessary, try to picture your first friend in grade school. You will most likely need to close your eyes.

Another consideration is to understand what the witness "sees" when trying to remember the suspect's face. The image of the face that can be remembered usually is seen only inside the mind for a fraction of a second, or at most, a few seconds. Then the image of the face fades away. The good news is this process can be repeated hundreds, even thousands, of times. For instance, you can picture the face of a memorable person in your past hundreds of times a year during the course of your life.

Here is why you should consider how this works. First of all, witnesses who are under stress might incorrectly assume their memory is defective if they see the image in their mind and then it fades instantly to nothing. Reassure them that *all* witnesses remember in that manner, and that *thousands* of successful sketches have been created from memories that worked just like theirs. This will help them feel up to the task.

Second, imagine how difficult it is for the witness to pull up the image in his or her mind's eye and constantly compare those features with visual aids. This will be a huge motivation to sustain a quiet, meditative atmosphere during the sketch interview. Knowing the witness has only fractions of a second to see the face in his or her mind's eye, you should devoutly avoid disturbing the witness's concentration. Almost all witnesses need a peaceful time while they look at the visual aid and close their eyes repeatedly to compare what they see in the visual aid with what is in their mind.

An effective enhancement to thoroughly understanding this process is to take on the role of a "witness" as a form of training. Find another artist with whom to work and try to describe a face he or she cannot see. Soon you will understand the mechanics and limitations of what the witness goes through.

MAXIMIZE COMFORT FOR NON-ENGLISH SPEAKERS

If the witness speaks another language fluently, use this fact to your advantage. Ask what the word for "relax" is and use it. Ask what the word for "eyes" and the other features are, and use those terms. This makes witnesses feel like the communication is more thorough. Additionally, you will soon learn to speak that language if many successive witnesses speak it. Conversely, if you refuse to try to meet the witness halfway regarding language, it will make the witness weary and even more alienated than before the interview started. A forensic artist who engages in trying to learn those familiar terms when handing the visual aids to the foreign witness will enhance the warmth and comfort in the interview room like nothing else can. Besides, this follows the one-sentence definition of a successful interview: "...the most enjoyable conversation possible, considering what the witness has been through."

If you know that one particular ethnic group occupies a significant segment of the population you serve, the best effort toward successful interviewing would be to endeavor to learn that population's language. In my case, Spanish is the predominant language spoken after English in my area. Early on there was a case that caused me to decide that learning Spanish would be a necessary goal in my profession.

A young lady was kidnapped at gunpoint while on a date. She was clothed in dressy evening wear when two men forced her out of her boyfriend's vehicle. The two kidnappers took her to a mobile home. She could see where they were driving for much of the way, but as they got near their residence, they forced her to the floorboard and covered her head. They sexually assaulted her and kept her captive for almost 2 days.

She was released on a street near the abduction site and the Spanish-speaking homicide detectives began interviewing her immediately. They kept her up all night driving around until they found the area of the abduction. Unfortunately, she was unable to lead them to the exact residence where the assaults occurred. She was brought to my office the next morning, still wearing the same evening dress, to create a sketch of the abductors.

I learned the witness spoke only a few words of English. Having studied Spanish in high school for 2 years, a rudimentary conversation developed. I did everything possible to comfort the witness, including wrapping her in a small blanket kept in my office. Soon the witness conveyed that the most disturbing feature of her abduction was that she could not return to her employer where she lived as a nanny. The kidnappers had convinced her they would kill her employers and their baby if she called the police.

I had already started sketching a white male at the witness's direction. However, it became apparent the witness was too distracted over having lost her job to concentrate. The interviewer discovered the kidnap victim was so certain she would not be returning to her job caring for a baby she loved, she had not called the woman of the house for whom she was a live-in nanny. I sprung into action and insisted the witness call her employer immediately.

The woman for whom the witness worked was so relieved she cried for joy. This woman, the baby's mother, insisted the girl return to her house as soon as possible. She exclaimed that both she and the baby missed the nanny. She squelched all the witness's fears of retaliation against the household and family by assuring her they had installed an alarm system, changed the locks, and bought two Doberman pinscher guard dogs. The conversation was entirely in Spanish except the last sentence when the witness said, "I love you" in English several times, seemingly in reply to the employer on the other end of the phone.

As soon as the witness got off the phone, it was obvious she was immensely relieved. She admitted she was lying about the abductors being Caucasian. She relayed that she felt as if I were her true friend, and that the abductors were black men. These men had brainwashed her into lying to police about their appearance. She kept describing them deceptively for their benefit until I broke down their grip on her by helping her feel safe about her future.

When the sketch was finished, the witness requested I listen to something she had been trying to tell the Spanish-speaking detectives all night. She related that she had memorized the address on a piece of paper. After a long explanation and hand signals, I understood she knew the address of a business on a "check stub" but didn't know that term in English. Once this was known, I had her write on a piece of paper the name of the business, as it was not clear from the witness's pronunciation of the business what she was saying. As soon as the witness wrote the name down, it was immediately recognizable as a common fast-food restaurant.

I instantly called the detectives and let them know there was a check stub in the room where the victim was held captive and further that the witness had memorized the address and name of the business. The detectives swept up the witness and the sketch and went to the fast-food restaurant. The manager there recognized one of the sketches as a former employee. The address on the employee's file was in the area pointed out earlier to detectives by the kidnap victim. Soon, the kidnapper in the sketch was in custody.

I spoke pitiful Spanish. The technique that helped solve the case was multifaceted. First, the comfort of the witness was the paramount concern. I swallowed my pride over poor skills in the witness's language and conducted the interview in her native tongue. A blanket was used to cover the witness's awkward clothing. A piece of paper and pencil were supplied to fill in the lack of complete communication because of the language barrier. I discovered the issue that concerned the witness most—she believed she had lost her job in a strange country. By convincing the witness to call the concerned employer, that issue was quickly solved in a most satisfactory manner for the witness, elevating her mood and greatly enhancing her ability to relax. Finally, I listened patiently and allowed the victim to say what she wanted, as advised by the "Cognitive Interview." The operative concept is that the witness didn't care how much the interviewer knew; it was how much the interviewer cared. Once the witness knew the interviewer had sympathy, humility, and patience, she was able to give all the information needed to solve the case. Figure 4.23 shows the sketch created by this session.

Through the years I have had abundant Spanish-speaking witnesses and have used every opportunity to enhance my conversational abilities. Some sketches from Spanish-speaking witnesses created after those language skills had improved can be seen in Figures 4.24 and 4.25.

Figure 4.23

The witness who gave the description for the sketch on the left spoke Spanish and almost no English.[18] She was kidnapped, held prisoner in a house, and sexually assaulted for 2 days (courtesy of the Houston Police Department).

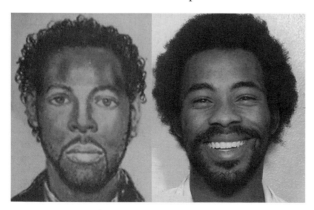

Figure 4.24

The sketch on the left was taken from a 9-year-old girl who was sexually assaulted by the man on the right. The little girl spoke only Spanish, so I employed phrases and words I had learned on the job to create this sketch[19] (courtesy of the Houston Police Department).

Figure 4.25

The sketch on the left was taken from a witness to a home invasion who spoke only Spanish. I utilized phrases and words in Spanish I had learned on the job and created this likeness[20] (courtesy of the Houston Police Department).

Learning a language can be one of the most difficult efforts encountered by the adult mind. However, if it might help bring in a felon, the effort seems worthwhile.

Lastly, if you have an interpreter, prepare a handout in advance that outlines the basic mechanics of doing the sketch and/or discuss this with the interpreter before the interview. Let the interpreter know the philosophy of the interview, that the witness's comfort is the most important consideration. Have the interpreter understand the interview should be as enjoyable a conversation as possible, considering what that particular witness has been through.

Figure 4.26 shows a sketch I created with interpreter Christina Espinoza. Ms. Espinoza is a masterful interpreter because she is fluent in Spanish and instinctively understands how to conduct an effective forensic sketch interview. She converses in a warm, ingratiating manner. She brings the witness to laughter when possible and steers the conversation to items the witness wants to talk about. She

Figure 4.26

The witness for the sketch on the left watched the man on the right sexually assault her 11-year-old daughter before he sexually assaulted her.[21] During the entire sketch she said she never really saw her attacker's face and was only guessing at each feature choice from the visual aids (courtesy of the Houston Police Department).

also allows witnesses to vent emotions as much as they want. In this particular case, the witness watched her 11-year-old girl be sexually assaulted. Then the assaulter cut her across the legs with a machete. She then had to threaten to kill her own infant to keep the man from sexually assaulting that baby.[21] Ms. Espinoza cried and grieved with the witness for much of the interview, yet brought her to a happy state whenever possible. As one can see by comparing the sketch in Figure 4.26 with the photo of the proven perpetrator of the crime next to it, there is a successful resemblance.

FEAR OF RETALIATION: ENEMY TO WITNESS CONCENTRATION

A pervasive fear among witnesses, gripping them long after their incident has occurred, is the thought that somehow the criminal who victimized them will return and hurt them again. This fear can be so consuming that the witness is incapable of concentrating. Of course the *perfect* answer to all this worry would be to construct a sketch good enough to help take their attacker off the streets! However since witnesses think it is unlikely they can do a successful sketch, this fear can control their thoughts and make relaxation and concentration extremely difficult. One example is in the previous section concerning non-English-speaking witnesses. The kidnap victim could not concentrate on the sketch until her boss had assured her that she could come back to work since they had instituted several anti-crime measures at their household, which was her place of work.

Most victims' imaginations run wild thinking of how the robber or sexual assaulter or murderer will find out where they live and come back to hurt or kill them. A forensic artist must have a ready repertoire of ways to soothe these fears. First, it should be pointed out that almost never in the annals of crime has a perpetrator come back later to revictimize the victim. The main reason is the criminal has the strongest urge in human nature, which is self-preservation. The attacker does not want to be killed. The criminal thinks the victim has obtained a weapon and will attack and/or kill the attacker if he or she sees him or her again.

However, this fear of retaliation is so pervasive in witnesses and takes so many irrational forms that the forensic artist should go to an expert source to find ways to soothe the witness's fears. Go to any seasoned detective and reiterate the fearful declarations witnesses have expressed. All detectives who work crimes-against-persons cases will have heard these same types of comments during their careers. If the detective is effective at handling complainants, he or she will have a vast array of rebuttals to these fears that are robbing the witness of peace of mind. The area detectives will have confident reasons why the witnesses' fears are unfounded that are custom-made for the type of crime those witnesses have survived. Use as many detectives' advice as possible to fight these fears and gain the relaxation needed to get a good sketch.

On one occasion a witness who was trying to begin a sketch with me was so distracted by her fear of retaliation, it was impossible to start working. Since the witness had experienced a common robbery, I asked if she would like to talk to a large group of seasoned detectives about her fears. When the witness agreed, I brought her into the main robbery office where about 25 detectives were sitting in cubicles. Combined they had worked on more than 40,000 cases over their careers. The witness articulated her fears to the detectives. Instantly, to the person, all the detectives firmly insisted she had nothing to fear. They all shook their heads no with kind knowing looks. There was a cheerful, warm outpouring of testimony to her that she had nothing to fear. This only took one minute, and then the witness was able to return to the interview and complete the description for the sketch.

Another way to handle each witness's fears of retaliation would be to hear him or her out, then call a detective who handles those kinds of cases and pose those exact fears for answers. The detective can give specific rebuttals over the phone. The lesson here is that you should use the experience of detectives in the law enforcement agency to help the witness get enough peace of mind so the sketch will not be compromised. After a while, any seasoned forensic artist develops methods and lines of reasoning for effectively calming these agitations.

In Brief

- Always praise the detective working the case. This could give him or her the motivation to do that one last task that could solve the case.
- Close your eyes and try to remember a face and understand what the witness "sees" in his or her mind.
- Conduct the interview so it is conducive for the witness to close his or her eyes.
- Learn to speak as much of the language as possible of ethnic witnesses in your area.
- Understand how to deal effectively with a pervasive obstruction to your witness's relaxation, which is fear of retaliation by the offender.

HOW TO KNOW WHEN YOU ARE DONE

You need to know when the sketch is done. During early sketches, I would expect and almost insist the witness ask for changes in the sketch. Some of these early changes were detrimental as they made the sketch less similar to the person being described. It became evident there is an optimum stopping place during the creation of the sketch.

The sketch is done when the witness says that it is not perfect, there is *something* more that needs to be changed, but the witness cannot think of what that *something* is. This is a universal sentiment expressed in various ways at the end of thousands of sketches. Once the witness has reached this point, there is no need to continue. Declare an end and expect the witness *not* to feel a sense of perfection. He or she will feel relief because the sketch is similar. However, both the artist and witness should know they will never have perfection. The creators of the suspect image need to realize they have done their best and now it is the detectives' turn to do their work with the image.

EVALUATING THE SKETCH

Never have the witness assign a numerical score to the sketch's accuracy. First of all, a defense attorney will latch onto this kind of scoring and use it against you. The defendant's attorney could argue that if the sketch were "graded" to be an 8 out of 10, that means out of 100 men, 20 would not be guilty. As strange as this argument seems, it has been used by a defense attorney to attack a sketch that had been numerically evaluated. There would be many other ways to take logic and cast doubt on any numerically evaluated sketch.

Instead, don't put this added burden on the witness. Do the best effort, and give the sketch to the detective. Tell the detective the sketch is as good as any others done previously. The reason you should remain out of the "evaluating the sketch" game is that the witness is not always a good judge of how good the sketch really is. There are many cases that illustrate this point.

A man robbed one witness with a hunter's crossbow at an automated teller machine. After the robbery victim created the sketch, she told me it was such a poor likeness it should not be given to the detective. The witness was insistent about the sketch being a failure and made me promise I would not allow it to be released. I agreed and never gave the sketch to the detective working the case. Months later the "crossbow robber" was arrested. Once it was determined that the witness for the sketch was robbed by this individual, I obtained a photo. The comparison of the sketch and photo in Figure 4.27 shows it to be as good as, if not superior to, many successful sketches seen throughout this text. Comparing this sketch reveals that a witness is not the best judge of how good a sketch is.

Another glaring example can be seen in Figure 4.28. This is arguably the closest likeness I have ever created of someone's face from a witness description. However, the session ended with the witness feeling as if the sketch was a

Figure 4.27

Below left: The witness who provided the description evaluated the sketch on the left as useless and totally wrong. When the man pictured on the right was identified as the person who robbed the witness, I learned that witnesses are poor evaluators of sketch quality[22] (courtesy of the Houston Police Department).

Figure 4.28

Below right: The sketch on the left took hours longer than usual and the witness who gave the description considered it a failure. Nevertheless, the sketch helped the detective identify this robber[23] (courtesy of the Houston Police Department). See color plate.

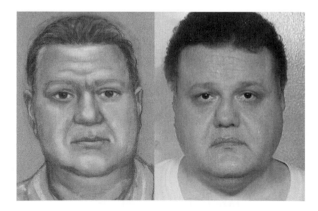

complete failure. The witness had me make changes for almost 2 hours. After the witness had made changes where all the features were made larger one at a time and then they were all made smaller one at a time, I finally called a halt. After I pointed out that I was sketching the same face over and over and the only changes were to make the face larger and then smaller, the witness reluctantly agreed we were at an end. The witness expressed the opinion that the sketch probably wasn't any good. She shook her head in a negative way and said the only reason we should quit is she couldn't think of what else we could do. She apologized that I had done so much work, only to create such a poor sketch. I could only imagine her numerical rating of the sketch would be a very low number.

Weeks later the robber depicted in the sketch was in a shootout and landed in a hospital. After the witness identified the man pictured in Figure 4.28, I obtained a photo of the robber from the detective. I am perfectly capable of declaring my sketches to be poor likenesses (see remarks on Figures 3.19 and 3.21). However, this sketch, declared a rank failure by the witness, bears a remarkable likeness. Once again, if the witness were to rank the sketch numerically after its completion, the score would have been very low.

Another successful sketch where the witness was certain the effort was a failure is shown in Figure 4.29. The witness for this sketch had her 4-month-old baby in a car seat inside her vehicle. While she was fueling her vehicle, a man approached from behind and asked her for a ride. She turned to tell him she didn't have the time and was confronted with the barrel end of an assault rifle inches from her face. She immediately ripped her baby from the child seat and told the man to take her truck, purse and all.

Before beginning the sketch with the artist, she claimed she never saw his face; rather she insisted she only saw the barrel of the rifle. After using the techniques described in previous chapters, the sketch on the left in Figure 4.29 was created. The witness ended the session ambivalently, saying she didn't know if it looked like the man who took her vehicle at rifle point or not. At best she would have given a mediocre score to the quality of the sketch. However, even the most critical observer would say the sketch bore a close resemblance to the man in the photo, who is the proven perpetrator of the crime.

Many other sketching sessions have ended with the witness declaring the image to be a wonderful likeness, yet the results were very poor. For example, Figure 4.30 is a really poor likeness done from a witness who raved at how close the resemblance was. This sketch is both a poor likeness of the perpetrator, and a poor sketch of a

Figure 4.29

The witness who gave the description for the sketch on the left claimed she never saw the man's face.[24] When the sketch was done, she was ambivalent and expressed doubt it was a good likeness (courtesy of the Houston Police Department). See color plate.

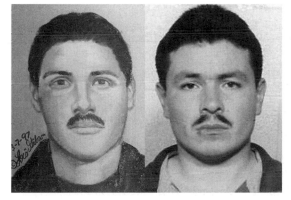

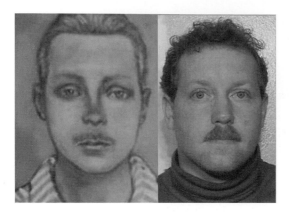

Figure 4.30

The witness for the sketch on the left declared it to be a terrific likeness of the man on the right. The witness's declaring enthusiastically that this sketch was positively a success is another proof that witness evaluations of sketches cannot be depended upon (courtesy of the Houston Police Department).

human face. The witness wanted the eyes and particularly the eyelids enlarged beyond that of any human being's normal proportions. The witness also had me shorten the chin about three gradients (as can be seen in the shadows of erasure under the chin) until the chin was far shorter than the perpetrator's. The witness had me continue to thin the bridge of the nose again and again until it appeared almost feminine and did not fit the face. Finally, at the end, the witness raved about how great the sketch was. I made a note about how enthusiastic the witness was over the outcome of the drawing.

When the perpetrator of the crime in question was finally arrested, I was acutely disappointed to see how dissimilar the sketch was to the man in the photo on the right side of Figure 4.30. The likeness was so poor, I questioned the detective handling the case to discover whether the witness was sincere or practicing deception. The detective was positive the witness was completely invested in the suspect being caught and had no motive to throw the investigation off track. The crime was egregious enough to earn the man a life sentence.[25]

I will avoid further ridicule over poor sketches and trust you to believe I have no motive to lie when I assert other witnesses have helped create poor likenesses for which they expressed great enthusiasm at the final drawing. Therefore, experience proves the witness evaluation of the potential effectiveness of the sketch at solving the case is faulty and inaccurate at best. At its worst, a witness evaluation can be completely wrong. Add to this the fact that poorly done sketches have helped the detective identify the perpetrator and we can deduce there is no value in having the witness evaluate the sketch. For certain, the worst evaluation would be to have the witness assign a numerical score to the quality of the sketch. There is abundant proof that witnesses cannot accurately evaluate the quality of the sketch, and if they are forced to decide on a numerical grade, it can cause harm to the case when it goes to court.

Put another way, many persons would give actual photographs taken of themselves low evaluations as to the quality of the likeness. Add to that the fact that no one can predict what circumstances will help a forensic sketch identify the perpetrator to the detective. Since no one can predict the future events that may help solve a case, and people cannot evaluate actual photos of their own face, having a witness who has just done the tedious work of creating a likeness from memory evaluate the work product is not logical. This is not considering other influences on the witness—the witness might want to please the artist or detective by saying the sketch is good. Conversely, the witness might vent frustrations, anger, or other negative feelings by saying the sketch is not good.

Perhaps one of the best testimonials that forensic artists should *not* have the witness evaluate the sketch is from K. Taylor in *Forensic Art and Illustration*, where she states:

> "…Over the years, I have found a lack of constant predictability of the results of my composite drawing likenesses to described faces.… Occasionally, drawings produced from witnesses who gave highly detailed, confident descriptions seemed to bear less likeness to the subject than drawings based on descriptions of less confident witnesses. I have learned to expect surprises!"[26]

Taylor noticed the demeanor of her witnesses was not an accurate gauge of the quality of her sketches.

In conclusion, the evaluation of the sketch by the witness cannot be a measure of whether it will help solve the case. Since solving the case is the goal, the detective should realize the best effort has been made to create an image of the suspect and move on with the efforts to investigate the case.

WORKING WITH A CHILD WITNESS

Children can be the best witnesses. If a few special techniques are used, the best images can be taken from the memory of a child who has seen the face of a suspect. A 10-year-old girl gave me the description for a sketch that produced the most successful results of my career.

The sketch seen on the left of Figure 4.31 was placed on television with a description about the crime, which was the assault of the little girl in a parking garage stairwell. When the man pictured on the right saw the sketch, he called the police and told them he was the person for whom they searched. He named a street corner where he would be waiting. The officers came by and picked him up as planned. His confession, identification by the victim, and his trial resulted in a conviction.

A 5-year-old girl gave the description for the sketch seen in the upper right of Figure 4.32. The man pictured next to that sketch was arrested for public intoxication weeks later. The officers who arrested him thought he looked like the sketch on the bulletin board at their substation. A line-up was held, there was an identification, and evidence found at the man's domicile led to his conviction.

The witness for the sketch on the middle left image pairing in Figure 4.32 was a 9-year-old boy who saw his 6-year-old brother abducted. The sketch in the middle right was taken from a 9-year-old girl who saw her mother

Figure 4.31

A 10-year old girl who was assaulted by the man on the right gave the description for the sketch on the left. The man on the right called police and turned himself in when he saw the sketch on television news (courtesy of the Houston Police Department). See color plate.

Figure 4.32

All these sketches at right were created from the descriptions of children, and all aided in the identification of the men in the accompanying photos. The witnesses for the sketches, from left to right, top to bottom, were 10, 5, 9, 9, 9, and 11 years of age[27] (courtesy of the Houston Police Department). See color plate.

raped and killed. The rapist then turned on the little girl. He assaulted her and beat her so badly her tooth was knocked loose. The sketch on the bottom left of that same figure was taken from a 9-year-old sexually assaulted girl. The bottom right sketch was gleaned from the memory of an 11-year-old girl who was abducted from a sidewalk and brutally raped. All the sketches in Figure 4.32, taken from children, helped the detective identify the suspect.

GUIDELINES FOR WORKING WITH CHILD WITNESSES

1. Dress modestly and in a style the child witness would expect adults to dress.
2. Greet the child cheerfully, but do not talk too loudly. Children usually have better hearing than adults. Talk as softly as possible. Treat the child's parents or companions with warmth and respect. Act as if they are visiting dignitaries. This will calm the child and help him or her feel secure.

3. Do not talk in a child-like manner to a young witness. Children are gratified if an adult talks to them as if they are grown. Conversely, children can become angry and feel insulted if they are talked to like babies.

4. Use the "Proper technique for separating a child from their parents…" as outlined in Chapter 3. If you make a house call, make certain to diplomatically discuss the process with a parent who will be present during the sketch, emphasizing the need for the child's peaceful concentration. One of the best situations for a child is to have the mother of the house let him or her know she will be ironing or doing some other household chore in another room. That way the child has a sense the mother is in the house, but not listening to every word, since she is in another room. Children need to talk freely and not be watched, but the comfort of their parent present at a distance can relax them.

5. Once alone with the child, show a spontaneous sense of humor if possible. Ask how he or she is doing and then listen. One truism children love to hear is that the child takes these terrible events better than the moms and dads. Most children enjoy hearing this and that, further, they are not as upset as their parents. This comment accomplishes many things. It usually makes the child smile and feel superior to the parents. It has been my experience that the parents show much more distress after a tragic criminal attack on their child than the child him- or herself. The child is ready to move ahead to a new day, even one day after the incident. The adult loved ones, on the other hand, tend to dwell on the attack constantly and show no signs of moving past the event even weeks later. This is another good reason to remove the parents or loved ones from the interview room. Children always seem relieved of some heavy emotional burden when their relatives leave them alone with the artist.

6. Begin the sketch by saying the truth, which is that children find it easier to remember and help do a sketch than adults. This begins the interview with optimistic expectations.

7. Have toys, candy (if the parents allow), and paper with coloring utensils for the child to while away his or her nervous energy. Give the child witness the visual aids and watch how he or she chooses more quickly than adults—about five times more quickly! It is recommended the *FBI Facial Identification Catalog* be used since it is compact and easy to handle.

8. Draw as fast as possible to accommodate the shorter attention span. Any skill at handling children will buy even a slow artist enough time, but for optimum results, sketch quickly.

9. Laugh with the child as much as possible. Tell the child everyone wants that yucky person caught and his or her detective is smart and strong and great at the job of solving this crime. Let the child vent any fears and try to resolve them honestly and soothe him or her.

10. Watch to see if the child might need to go to the bathroom and is afraid to ask. If the child seems extra fidgety, go on a fun walk to the soda machine or to the copy machine to get some paper. Let the child run down a hall for a break halfway through the sketch. Make doing the sketch a fun adventure.

For the sketch in Figure 4.33, I took the witness on an adventurous walk to break the tension and help my concentration. The witness was 6 years old and had been stuffed into a closet by the man pictured next to the sketch. He told her not to come out or she would be killed. She then listened as he bludgeoned her mother to death.

I was flown to another state to sketch with the little girl 3 months later. Before the girl arrived for her interview, I located a distant break room with a soda machine in the building in which I had never worked before. When the little-girl witness began fidgeting in the beginning of the interview, I asked if she would like a soda. When the girl said yes, I took her down halls and stairs and through several doors remarking all the way about how fun it was to find a place I had found only once before. After the convoluted trip, the little girl was content to drink her soda and sketch with the artist.

Although the sketch is flawed, it caused the detective to suspect the man pictured on the right when he was arrested 3 years later for another similar murder. When the detective asked the man's wife to come in for an interview, she brought along her 6-year-old son. When the boy saw the sketch on the bulletin board, he told his mother "…look mommy, there's a picture of daddy." The parents of the murdered woman thought the man looked like the sketch also. DNA and other ancillary evidence presented at his trial convicted him.

Figure 4.33

The witnesses for the sketch, top left, were a 6-year-old girl who was stuffed in a closet along with her 5-year-old friend, by the man pictured on the right.[28] The bottom left is the identified man's nose; bottom right is the nose chosen by both witnesses (courtesy of the Newton Kansas Police Department).

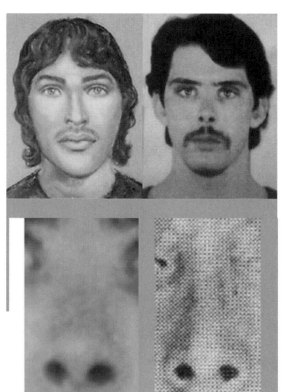

One lesson learned about sketching with children can be seen in Figure 4.33. Children should be listened to and taken seriously about their opinions on features of the perpetrator's face. The witness in this case picked nose D8-2 on page 24 of the *FBI Facial Identification Catalog.* These nostrils display an almost perfect round hole. I even asked the little girl if his nostrils were like those in the example, and she indicated they were.

I decided to take matters into my own hands. I reasoned that since the little girl was so short, she was looking up at the nostrils. Almost all individuals' nostrils make round holes when gazed at from below. I changed the shape of the nostril holes slightly, making the dark openings more elliptical in shape. As can be observed in the bottom of Figure 4.33, if I had adhered to the choice made by the 6-year-old witness, the nose would have come out almost identical to the murderer's nose pictured on the bottom left.

When it is time for the changes, do not be devastated if the child witness tells you it doesn't look anything like the person. Many times children make this comment. Then, after only a few tiny changes, they declare it looks just like the person. So, make the changes quickly and cheerfully, and be glad for the child witness's honesty.

DEALING WITH A CHILD CONSUMED WITH GRIEF

If a child is consumed with grief, such as one who has witnessed the murder of his or her mother, there are ways to calm him or her.

Sometimes the child is crying convulsively and giving a comforting touch seems like the only appropriate thing to do. Avoid touching witnesses in almost every case; however, if the occasion seems as if physical comfort is the only thing that will work, touch the child very lightly at the outer edges of his or her upper shoulders. While using this feather-light kind of hug, lightly touch the top of your forehead to the top of the child's head and talk in soothing tones. This touching should be done with the slightest pressure, so the child knows he or she is being comforted, but can pull away in an instant. With this position, the child can still feel like the front of his or her body is not going to be touched, but that someone is trying to comfort him or her physically. Also, you are not speaking into the child's face; rather you are talking toward the floor.

Another tactic in a desperate crying situation is to help the child travel in time in his or her mind. Bring up topics of the future that are positive, like a first dance or date he or she will have. One of the best topics for boys is to wonder out loud about what their first vehicle will be like. These kinds of comments can be prefaced with the happiness over being left alive. After saying how good it is they are still here, make observations and speculations about what they will do on positive occasions in their future. This works wonders when children take the cue and begin talking about those future events themselves. This helps them to accept their loss and view it from a happier time in the future. This technique of time traveling to a positive future works great with children since they are far better at this type of imaginary thinking than adults.

If the tragedy has just occurred, you might need to employ a technique of telling children how they should feel. Tell them they are safe now and it is over. The bad thing that happened is in the past and now they are safe and with people who will protect them and help them. You can also simply state that they can relax now and feel safe, and they will almost always stop crying and feel relaxed. This also works on adults. It is a simple technique where you tell people how they should feel, and they will respond by feeling that way. This works if someone is in deep despair. They will usually be open to genuine suggestions like this, especially the more impressionable child witness.

These techniques were used to create the sketch shown in Figure 4.34 with a 12-year-old boy whose mother had just been stabbed to death in front of him.

This boy tried to offer the killer money to save his mother, but the man threw the money to the ground and continued stabbing her. The boy witness joined the artist at the police station 4 hours after he saw his mother killed.

Once alone in the room with the witness, I acknowledged that I knew what had happened. The boy began crying uncontrollably. I held him lightly on the back of his upper shoulders and he seemed comfortable crying with his face on my shoulder. After a while he sat back and kept repeating the scene of his mother's murder over and over with emphasis on the frustrating part where he tried to stop the stabbing but couldn't. Then he made the sounds his mother made as she was dying. I realized he needed to travel in time to the future in order to accept the fact his mother had died.

I told the boy he would be fearless and be able to succeed in the business world since nothing he experienced would ever be this frightening. The boy began to relax. Then I asked if he took tests at school or played sports; he answered yes to both questions. I pointed out that after this, the most terrifying experience anyone could have, he would never be afraid of taking a test or playing in a big game again. The boy smiled in agreement. Then I mentioned that most people work for a wage or salary, but that some people who were less fearful would save money or borrow it and invest it in a business. If the business went well, they could make back hundreds and often thousands of dollars for every dollar they invested. I then told him the only thing he would have to worry about was what color of Jaguar to buy. The boy actually smiled. He then began talking about how his mother would be looking down at him and watching his success. I agreed about his bright future and listened intently as he talked about his plans. Once the boy had accepted his mother's death by being led into the future, the work on the sketch in Figure 4.34 finally could begin.

After the sketch was finished, the boy left the room. Some neighbors were brought in to look at the sketch. Those neighbors identified the sketch as looking like the man pictured on the right in Figure 4.34. At trial months later, that man was convicted of murdering the boy's mother.

Before the trial began, the boy insisted the district attorney come to visit me. The district attorney delivered the message from the boy that he had borrowed money, purchased hair clippers, and was giving haircuts for schoolmates at his house for money. He wanted me to know he already had enough money to buy a car, even though he was only 13.[29]

Therefore, the method used with this boy who was crying uncontrollably in the beginning of the interview was two-fold. First, since it seemed

Figure 4.34

The witness for this sketch was a 12-year-old boy who had seen his mother stabbed to death 6 hours before he met with me. Neighbors recognized the sketch as being the man pictured on the right[30] (courtesy of the Houston Police Department).

appropriate, I touched the witness in a light hug and held him that way while he cried. Second, I engaged the boy in imagining positive things in his future, which allowed him to accept his mother's death. Those actions allowed the witness to vent and to view his mother's death from a happier time. This dream of the future I conjured up was so genuine, the witness incorporated it into his life after surviving the crime. He did as I suggested and through entrepreneurship, earned enough money to buy a car.

CRYING CAN HELP

If it will help get an effective sketch, crying can be incorporated into the forensic sketch interview. If the act of crying will help the witness relax and reinstate the context of the experience, thus vivifying the image of the attacker's face in his or her mind, a dedicated forensic artist should welcome weeping by the witness. In fact, if the witness needs to cry, the interview goes faster and the sketch comes out better when it becomes a time and place that welcomes the release of grief.

From D. Heimstadt in the *Archive of Psychohistory*, we learn that "Crying is not grief; it is a way of getting over your grief."[31] Indeed, during the incident, the witness will almost always suppress the crying mechanism as a reaction to extreme stress. The ability to cry signals that the incident is over and there is at least an emotional resolution.[32] This means a witness who is allowed to cry feels like the traumatic incident is finished and it is safe to vent in a most basic way, by crying. Relaxation is enhanced and the witness's crying is directly linked to recovering from the painful experience.[33] Therefore, the skilled forensic artist/interviewer will facilitate an atmosphere where the witness feels welcome to cry.

Officers and detectives will often handle witnesses in a terse, taciturn manner. Answers are asked quickly of them and the answers need to be to the point. Often witnesses are numb and still suppressing their emotions during the first outcry phase of their incident.

When a witness reaches the artist and is left alone to perform a task he or she has never done and he or she does not believe can be done, it is the perfect time for the witness to break down. The wise forensic artist will welcome this reaction and make it as comfortable as possible for the witness to cry. Have plenty of tissues noticeable next to the witness chair. By every action and word, make it clear that grief is welcome. You can even try to launch the witness into weeping if it seems necessary to release tension.

An example is a case of a 14-month-old baby who was kidnapped from her bed in the middle of the night. The kidnapper was a stranger whom the family had taken in because she was homeless. The mother and father of the baby were at the police station where the artist met them to help sketch their baby's kidnapper.

As I set up my gear, I noticed the non-English-speaking mother was holding in her emotions with all her might. She appeared as if she were going to explode. When the detectives told her in Spanish she was supposed to help create a likeness of the woman who took her baby, the woman appeared even more distressed.

As soon as we were alone, the mother indicated it was impossible for her to help create a sketch, even though she had seen the woman for hours. I realized the mother needed desperately to cry in order to relax enough to do a sketch. Unfortunately, it was early in my career and my Spanish was limited. I picked up a photo I knew was of the kidnapped baby since it had just been shown on the news. I asked the mother if that was her little girl and the mother said it was.

I then genuinely cried out "no, no, no!" and held out my arms as I began crying. The mother stretched out her arms and began crying loudly while holding onto me. She cried convulsively and soon was joined by the father from another office, and they both cried until they were fairly exhausted. Then the sketch was begun. The mother and father witnesses were fluid and mellow and the sketch went quickly using visual aids and hand signals and my broken Spanish.

When the sketch was released in Mexico, where the kidnapper originally resided, the case was solved. The mother of the kidnapper lived in a remote village. When she saw the sketch in the newspaper, she realized it was her daughter and that the baby she had mysteriously brought home was the kidnapped infant. The mother walked 5 miles to the nearest phone and contacted the authorities, who returned the baby to her parents.[34]

The sketch might have been done without encouraging the witness to cry in the beginning. However, after crying, the witnesses were remarkably more relaxed and cooperative. Since I knew the couple needed to cry eventually, I decided to let the venting of this grief aid in my creation of the sketch. In fact, many witnesses who need to cry will say they cannot do a sketch. Then, after they have been enabled to cry in a comfortable way, the information for the features on the face of the suspect comes quickly and they give no resistance.

In Brief
- You are finished with the sketch when the witness cannot think of what else to change. No sketch will end perfectly.
- Neither the witness nor the artist should attempt to evaluate the sketch.
- Children witnesses can give the best sketches if techniques customized especially for their needs are used. Delicate physical comfort and imagining happier times in their future can help children consumed with grief make it through the sketch.
- Enabling a witness to cry during the sketch is an enhancement to memory. Crying might be the only release that will enable a witness to help create an image of the suspect's face.

THE MYTH OF THE DISINTERESTED WITNESS

For years the conventional wisdom among forensic artists was that if a witness was disinterested in the person he or she saw, the sketch he or she helped create would be inferior. Early in my career I found this not to be true. Many successful sketches have been created from persons who were not under duress or had little or no investment in the perpetrator being caught. Two obvious examples of this are shown in Figures 4.35 and 4.36. The sketch on the left side of Figure 4.35 was taken from a man walking down a sidewalk carrying a large basket of laundry from the laundromat. He thought he heard the faint sound of a firecracker. He then saw a man exit a liquor store nearby; the man then walked past him. It was later discovered the liquor-store owner had been shot to death at that moment. The detectives were able to deduce that the man doing his laundry had seen the murderer.

The man first claimed he never saw the perpetrator's face. He then emphasized why he had no reason to look at the face or care what the face looked like. I used several of the techniques outlined in the previous chapters and created the sketch on the left.

After the sketch was published in the papers, a caller notified the homicide detectives a man matching the sketch was "hanging around" a certain location. Four homicide detectives traveled to the area. They saw a man standing on a corner in the area mentioned by the tipster. Because he resembled the sketch enough, they stopped to identify him. When the detectives exited their vehicle, a shoot-out ensued, during which the man pictured on the right was wounded four times and taken into custody.[35] He was later convicted. The sketch was drawn early in my career so the beginner's mistake was made of making the irises too large. However, it is significant to note the extreme accuracy of the shapes of the chin, lips, nose, and eyebrows from such a totally disinterested witness. I am certain the perpetrator got a haircut right after the murder. That conclusion can be made because of the fresh-cut look of the man's hair in the photo, and the fact that even the *worst* witness would not be mistaken about the long scraggly hair shown in the sketch.

Figure 4.36 shows another sketch compared to the proven perpetrator of the crime taken from the description by a witness who was even more disinterested and farther away from the subject than the case previously mentioned. The sketch on the left was taken from a woman who was washing dishes when she looked out the window in front of her sink to see a man exit the convenience store directly across the street. She had lived at this residence a little more than 2 years. Seeing someone exit the convenience store would have to be one of the most mundane sights

Figure 4.35

The witness for the sketch on the left was carrying a huge basket of laundry when he saw the man on the right exit a liquor store. He said the laundry was too high, he never saw the face, and he didn't really want to get involved (courtesy of the Houston Police Department).

Figure 4.36

The sketch on the left was done with a disinterested witness who saw the man on the right walk out of a convenience store across the street 100 feet away from the window of her kitchen sink (courtesy of the Houston Police Departent).

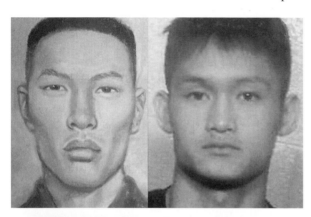

Figure 4.37

The sketch on the left was created from a witness working the window at a fast-food restaurant. The man on the left drove through mumbling, allowing only a slight glance as he paused briefly below the witness's window before speeding off (courtesy of the Houston Police Department).

possible. She said the only thing that made her notice the man pictured on the right was he dropped something, bent over to pick it up, and looked around nervously. I asked what kind of item he dropped, and the witness replied it must have been very small, like a coin. The witness did not realize the man she saw had just shot a Houston police officer to death and stolen his ring.[36] The witness for this sketch insisted she never really looked at the face of this man. She also conveyed that she had little or no interest in helping.

I used the technique of "taking away the task" by telling the witness we didn't need to do a detailed portrait; rather we would try to distinguish the individual she saw in only a general way from the people in the area. The witness narrowed the suspect down to being an Asian male, thin and young, and then I handed the witness my stack of visual aids for Asian males.

Although the sketch on the left has lips that are thicker than the suspect on the right, who was subsequently convicted of the crime, all the features are consistent when comparing the drawing with the photo. Put differently, this sketch bears a better resemblance to the subject than some other sketches done with witnesses who were vastly more invested in finding the suspect.

Figure 4.37 shows a sketch from one of the most disinterested witnesses imaginable. The witness who gave the description for the sketch on the left was working at a fast-food drive-thru window. Early one morning when business was slow, he told a drive-up customer at the speaker, whom he could not see, what he wanted to order. The driver made some unintelligible sound. After being asked several times for his order and never getting a coherent answer, the worker saw the car pull up alongside the window. The customer in his vehicle glanced at the witness for a fraction of a second, said something unintelligible, and drove off. A deliveryman who was inside stacking buns left seconds later and discovered a woman who had been strangled to death and dumped near the drive-thru speaker. Since it was surmised the mumbling customer in the drive-thru had dropped off the body, I interviewed the restaurant worker for the sketch on the left.

Eleven years later, DNA from under the fingernail of the murdered woman in that case was matched through CODIS (Combined DNA Index System) to the man pictured on the right. This man was subsequently linked to four other murders.[37] The sketch is not the best ever created in the annals of forensic art. This sketch did not help detectives identify the murderer of the woman dumped in the drive-thru because those investigators decided not to release the image made by the artist to the public. However, most of the features are consistent, and the sketch is a superior likeness compared to some done with highly motivated witnesses. Additionally, this sketch is superior to others that have led directly to the suspect sought.

The deduction here is this: Simply because a witness is not interested in the case, do not assume his or her description will render an inferior drawing. Rather, the wise approach would be to treat the description from a disinterested witness as having all the possibilities of any description. To do otherwise would be to needlessly infuse the effort with counterproductive pessimism.

SKETCHING WITH MULTIPLE WITNESSES

Beginning forensic artists are often fearful of working with more than one witness. If you create sketches for a considerable number of cases, the possibility of having multiple witnesses will eventually arise. You should become comfortable with interviewing more than one witness. What at first might seem an obstacle can become an asset for creating better sketches, if a few logical rules are followed.

If the witnesses experienced the incident together, then it is proper to do the sketch with them together. However, do not sketch with witnesses in the same room if you are not absolutely certain they saw the same person. Examples of this would be a person who sees a man commit a crime inside a room. Immediately after committing that crime, the man runs down a hall or a street and another witness sees him run by. It does not matter if the man has the same clothing and both witnesses describe him the same way—there is no absolute way to prove these two witnesses, separated by a wall, saw the same person. A defense attorney could cast doubt on the idea your witnesses saw the same person when the case goes to court.

Some exceptions to this rule would be if the witnesses were extremely close to each other, the witness *outside* the room heard the activity *inside* the room immediately before the suspect ran out, and/or the suspect had unique clothing or appearance. An example of this was a suspect who was wearing a purple shirt and orange pants. One witness saw this man inside a room; the other witness saw him run out of the room. It should be noted the race, age, sex, height, body type, and hair also matched. In these types of situations where the witnesses are separated in space and by a tiny bit of time, the artist can sketch with them together. The reason the term "can" is used is because having help doing the sketch with someone else almost always comforts witnesses, so it is desirable to sketch with the witnesses together.

Obviously, if the witnesses are all in view of the suspect at the same time and place, the sketch can be created with the witnesses together.

Since the comfort of the witnesses is the first consideration in arranging a sketch, the prospect of doing the sketch with others helping is without a doubt going to relieve the pressure a witness feels over doing the work. Another advantage of having multiple witnesses is that one witness might remember one feature very well, and the other or others might remember a different feature. Therefore, theoretically you can obtain more information from multiple witnesses.

Many methods for working with multiple witnesses are the same as with the single witness. Start the sketch where the witnesses cannot see. When working with the visual aids, it is best with multiple witness to use the compact *FBI Facial Identification Catalog* so they are all looking at the same collection of features. Hundreds of times I have observed that one witness will find a feature, and then wait for the other witness(es) to make *their* picks. At that time the witnesses tend to share what they have found. There is almost always a consensus. If there is not an outright consensus, one witness will say something like, "that nose looks like it, but this other one does, too." Then the witnesses will tend to work it out among themselves as to the one that is *most* similar.

During this kind of multiple-witness interview, the witnesses usually show relief and comfort in the camaraderie of working toward a common goal. I have never seen multiple witnesses who did not try to work with each other to help create a likeness of the suspect they saw. The possible explanation of why this happens is the goal of capturing the suspect is such a universally serious one felt by all involved.

One warning for sketching with multiple witnesses is to make it clear that input from all witnesses will be considered. Do not allow a witness who is more assertive to make all the choices. Be aware that the less-assertive witness might be able to give a better description. I have found that even when witnesses pick different features, if you observe the choices, they will usually be very similar. Declare this fact out loud so the witnesses will realize they are confirming each other's choices.

One positive outcome of working with multiple witnesses is that you will realize the superiority of children if one witness is a child and the others are adults. I worked with two adult married couples and one couple's 10-year-old son. The two families had gone to a restaurant that was robbed by two armed men. One of the men discharged his firearm, striking one family's baby with a ricocheted bullet. The baby was not seriously injured.

None of the adults could verbalize what kind of hair the suspect had. The boy exclaimed that the suspect had on a hat. When the adults happily agreed that the suspect did indeed have on a hat, the artist asked if there was any design or writing on the front of the hat. The adults seemed puzzled and said they could not remember. The boy then confidently proclaimed that the hat was black with the word GIANTS written all in white capital block letters. The boy was also certain about all his choices from the visual aids.

Doing the sketch alone with the boy would have made him less comfortable, and he would have felt incredible pressure to succeed since his baby sister sustained the nonfatal wound from the ricochet. Sketching with his family gave him comfort enough to show how well a child witness can perform when creating a forensic sketch.

Another helpful revelation about the superiority of the child witness came during a multiple-witness interview involving three 5-year-olds who all saw a man who later molested one of them. The artist gave a single FBI catalog to each girl separately while the other two girls played with toys in another corner of the room. It is remarkable that each girl picked out the same eyebrows, eyes, lips, and chin from over 100 choices for each feature. I was relieved to find each little girl confirmed the features chosen by the others. The point must be emphasized that none of the girls influenced any of the other girls during her perusal of the FBI catalog. Instead they were entertained with a large box of toys kept in the interview room for just such a purpose. Even more remarkable is the fact that each 5-year-old girl separately told me that the suspect had a nose just like mine. Faced with this unusual source of a nose type chosen by my three witnesses, I taped a mirror from my purse to my drawing board and drew my own nose into the sketch.

The sketch was released and posted on the bulletin board of the department's substation in the area of the attack. Almost a month later a man was arrested for public intoxication. The arresting officers thought he looked like the sketch in Figure 4.38. The little girls who gave the description were brought in for a line-up.[38] All the little girls positively identified the man pictured in Figure 4.38. Looking at the noses from the sketch, to the identified perpetrator, and my face, they do appear very similar.

Therefore, the perceived handicaps of sketching from multiple witnesses who are also only 5 years old proved no obstacle to creating an image that was capable of alerting officers they had arrested a child predator.

Another case where multiple witnesses helped create a successful sketch was the armed robbery of a beauty parlor. Four hairdressers were present when the man pictured on the right in Figure 4.39 entered and stole their money at gunpoint. I met with the stylists and created the sketch on the left of Figure 4.39. The witnesses were loud and angry, but easily described the robber.

I displayed the sketch at a criminal investigators' luncheon a few days later. One of the attendees recognized the sketch as looking like a man he had recently arrested. A line-up was held and the hairdressers identified the man

Figure 4.38

All three witnesses, little girls, independently chose the same features for the sketch top left and said the suspect's nose looked like the mine. The middle top photo is of the suspect and the top right is me. Below are all three individuals' noses in the same order (courtesy of the Houston Police Department).

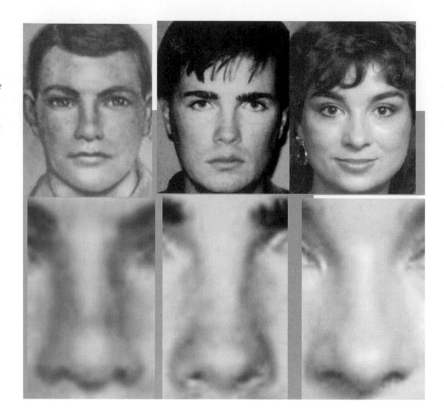

Figure 4.39

The sketch on the left was created from the descriptions of four hairdressers who were robbed by the man pictured on the right. There is a close likeness even though the witnesses' loud expressions of anger created a chaotic sketch session (courtesy of the Pasadena Texas Police Department).

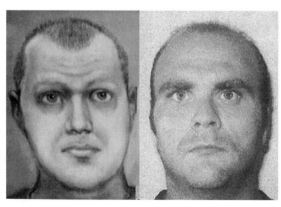

and the case was solved.[39] I must note that hairdressers tend to be great witnesses for creating forensic sketches.

Another multiple-witness sketch interview was conducted under some pressure after a man had stolen an airplane from a small airport near the large Houston metropolitan area. The witnesses had seen the man walk away from the wrecked airplane after the crash. The sketch was done around midnight, and the witnesses had been up since 5 A.M. I needed to interview a man, his wife, his sister, and daughter. All involved grappled with the task in a desperate push to be finished so everyone could return home and to sleep. I had been called more than an hour's drive from home, after 10 P.M., so I shared the mood and goals of the witnesses. The witnesses worked out their differences together in an efficient fashion, and the sketch was completed in 45 minutes.

The next day after the release to the media, the sketch in Figure 4.40 prompted an acquaintance of the man pictured there to call in his identity to authorities, and thus the case was solved in 24 hours.[40]

Again, the methods for working with multiple witnesses are similar to those used with a single witness. The witnesses tend to work out among themselves the choices, and then later the changes, needed when they view the sketch. On the rare occurrence when there is an overly assertive witness who tends to overpower the other witness, it is easy to elicit the more recessive witness's input by simply asking.

CREATING ONE SKETCH FROM TWO WITNESSES DURING SEPARATE INTERVIEWS

If you are reasonably certain two different witnesses saw the same perpetrator, but the cases are separated by time and location, there is a simple method for compiling just one sketch while maintaining the witness separation. First, take what is considered the better witness (the one who more recently saw the suspect, or saw the suspect longer, or in better lighting, etc.) and do a complete sketch. It is all right if the first witness is not the better witness; sometimes that determination is difficult to make. After this first sketch, cordially escort the first witness out of the room. Make certain before, during, and after the interviews that the witnesses do not talk about the suspect appearance together. Bring the other witness into the room, making certain to cover the already created sketch so it cannot be seen. After making this second witness comfortable, obtain the same types of information. Once this second witness describes the sex, race, age, and body type, provide visual aids to focus on the features. Once again, the FBI catalog is preferable, since both witnesses are viewing the same collection of features.

Almost always the second witness, if he or she did indeed see the same perpetrator, will choose the same or very similar appearing features from the catalog. If these descriptors are the same, or similar, you might not need to initiate a new sketch. Instead, tell the second witness he or she will be shown a drawing. Make certain the witness knows the goal is to depict the man that he or she saw, and to be honest if there is a likeness or not.

Almost always the detective will be right and the second witness will agree with the image already created with the previous witness. Other times the second witness will concur with the image, but will be certain about some small change. At this time, you can decide to change the sketch or not, depending on your appraisal of the individual witnesses. Since the change asked for can be slight, it will not have an all-encompassing effect on the case, so don't assign an inordinate value on making a minor change. Lastly, almost all sketch artists will be good enough that the witness will know if the sketch is of the same suspect,

Figure 4.40

The sketch, left, was created around midnight with a man, his wife, sister, and daughter who had all been up since 5 A.M. that morning. The release of the sketch to media prompted a friend of the suspect to turn in his identity to authorities within hours (courtesy of the Brazoria County Sheriffs Department).

or if a completely different sketch needs to be made. I have found that usually only one sketch ends up being done in this situation.

However, there have been cases when a whole new sketch was done because the second witness proved to be far superior. Still another case found me sketching three different armed robbers, even though the detectives thought they were looking for one man since his height, race, and modus operandi were the same. In that case, I sketched three different sketches because my interviews uncovered the details that one robber had a large birthmark, one was very thin, and still another was lighter skinned than the others.

A few weeks later, a house was raided, and found inside were large amounts of stolen goods. All three suspects sketched were found among the residents who fled during the raid. After their capture, detectives were able to distinguish them by robbery scene locations connected with the sketches, even though the jailed suspects refused to give their names. The robbery suspects assumed the detectives had photos of them since the detectives were able to describe the location of each individual's robbery. The suspects were separated and all confessed while implicating the others as the main perpetrators.[41]

WHEN THE WITNESS IS UNDER THE INFLUENCE

Many witnesses have been under the influence of alcohol or other stimulants or depressants at the time they viewed a face that they later had to describe to a forensic artist. Although the conventional wisdom for years was that persons who were intoxicated at the time they experienced the incident should not be witnesses, I have found in my practice that sketches are possible from witnesses suffering from this type of impairment.

The first sketch in this genre is Figure 4.41. The witness who gave the description for this sketch met this woman at a drinking establishment. At some point it was decided she would accompany the witness home to fix both of them breakfast. The woman surreptitiously added a strong drug to his scrambled eggs. The

Figure 4.41

A man who shared drinks with the woman pictured on the left helped create the sketch on the right. This witness was therefore under the influence of alcohol when he viewed her face (courtesy of the Houston Police Department).

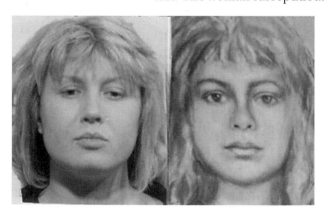

witness fell asleep immediately. He awoke the next day to find he had been robbed. There is no doubt the man was under the influence of alcohol when he saw this woman; further he experienced a deep drug stupor after viewing her for the last time.[42] Yet, this is one of the better likenesses sketched from a witness description.

The second case of this kind produced the sketch shown in Figure 4.42. The description for this drawing was taken from a mother and son who had been drinking at a bar until it closed, only to come upon this man in the act of murdering someone. As they drove home they had to crash past his vehicle, sustaining body damage to their car, in order to get away from the scene and avoid being shot. They were so much under the influence they waited until 9:00 the next morning to call authorities and tell of the murder they witnessed. It must be assumed by all indications these witnesses, who got a quick glance at the man pictured in Figure 4.42, were very intoxicated when the incident occurred.[43] The sketch appears similar, and it helped identify the perpetrator, even though it appears somewhat like a cartoon of the suspect.

Figure 4.42

A mother and son who had been drinking at a bar until it closed came upon the man pictured on the right murdering someone. They were so inebriated when they saw him they waited until 9 A.M. the next morning to call the police (courtesy of the Harris County Sheriffs Department).

The third sketch taken from a witness who viewed a suspect's face while under the influence of alcohol can be seen in Figure 4.43. This witness who helped with this image admits to being so intoxicated, he was fearful of driving his truck back to his house. Since he lived only a few blocks from the bar, he left the vehicle parked there and walked home.[44] This likeness is somewhat successful, though this drawing is also a sort of cartoon of the suspect.

Although I have never sketched with a witness who was under the influence of alcohol at the time of the interview, Figure 4.44 shows three cases from the many sketches done while the witnesses were under the influence of pain medication. To my best estimation, the witness for the top of the three sketches was the most medicated. That witness fell asleep all during the sketching process.[45] The second case represents a witness who was on pain medication and exhibiting signs of being in excruciating pain. This witness had been shot twice and was in intensive care.[46] Because of his particular injuries, he was forced to lie strapped to a board kept at a steep 40 degree incline. The witness for the sketch at the bottom was the most lucid of the three, yet she was shot 15 times and was under the influence of constant intravenous pain medication.[47]

Figure 4.43

A man who knew he was too intoxicated to drive saw the man pictured on the right leave the scene of a crime. This same witness helped create the sketch on the left at a later date when he was sober (courtesy of the Houston Police Deparment).

The deduction here is that witnesses should not be completely discounted as useless if they were under the influence of alcohol when they viewed the suspect to be sketched. Additionally, there are many successful sketches done with witnesses who were overwhelmingly medicated for pain during the sketch interview.

Figure 4.44

All three of these sketches on the left were created from witnesses who were under the influence of pain medication (courtesy of the Houston Police Department).

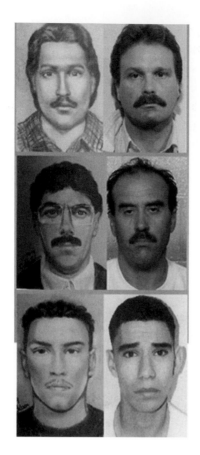

DETERMINING DECEPTION

The majority of witnesses encountered by the forensic artist are innocent victims. Usually the circumstances of the incident make it abundantly obvious the witness for the sketch is absolutely innocent of any crime and deserving of unconditionally caring and congenial treatment. However, on occasion you might encounter a witness who is lying about the incident. Since you usually receive the witness from a detective who is versed in detecting deception, this situation is rare.

The various methods for discerning truthfulness are the focus of much law enforcement training. Any educational seminar for law enforcement personnel who investigate crimes invariably has a segment focused on lie detection when interviewing individuals. Investigators study eye movements when individuals are answering questions (neurolinguistics). They examine micro-expressions of the face, and body language (kinesics). They hold seminars and workshops aimed at determining deception. The reason why detectives give so much of their attention to being able to find out if persons with whom they communicate are lying is their need for this skill during interrogations of suspects. The detective who is able to know when suspects are lying is invaluable to investigations. Some of the methods for determining deception have been studied so extensively there are monthly journals and dozens of textbooks written on the subject. Forensic artists can avail themselves of study in this subject matter from many sources. However, deciding if an interviewee is not being truthful by these methods is meant to be utilized in the context of an interrogation. Even if the interview is conducted in a congenial manner, if the interview is taking place because of a crime that has occurred, all parties are aware the interviewee is a possible suspect.

If you conduct your interview correctly, never engage in an interrogation because the attitude of the witness is of paramount importance. Treating the witness as a suspect will ruin the witness's attitude. Even if you only *think* there is a possibility the person with whom you are doing a sketch is the perpetrator of the crime, those thoughts can ruin a forensic sketch interview. If you are also a sworn officer of a law enforcement agency, you need to play the role of the forensic artist completely. You cannot begin to interrogate an interviewee and then decide to switch to a forensic sketch interview in the middle of the conversation; the mood of the witness already will have been ruined. Individuals working on criminal cases realize it is possible any person might be the perpetrator of a crime. You can still notice when a witness slips up and reveals something that indicates that witness was lying in previous interviews. However, you should not go into the interview completely focused on trying to get the witness to slip up and make a mistake.

Instead, the forensic art interview, with its built-in tendency to comfort the witness, will often produce information that can indicate to the detective if the witness is not telling the truth, if you use the following techniques.

COMFORT LOOSENS THE LIPS

The congenial atmosphere causes witnesses to let down their guard. If these comfortable witnesses describe the event in a vastly different way than they have to the first responders, investigators can be tipped off that at least one version of the story is not true. Said another way, it is natural for a good forensic sketch interviewer to allow witnesses to talk as much as they want and further to speak with enjoyment to a receptive listener. After the interview, you can compare the version told to the detective to what you understood from the witness's ramblings. If there are different versions of the events, one of the versions must be a lie.

The investigator of the case is in charge of deciding between the truth and the lies. You should give the detective on your case any impressions or remarks you have gathered from the witness and let that investigator decide the course of action. Extreme caution should be taken to be certain about the accuracy of any statements repeated to the investigator.

There is another obvious way to determine if a witness is lying during a congenial interview.

TRUTHFUL WITNESSES ARE GLAD TO BE ALIVE

A universal emotion felt by survivors of criminal acts is the joy of having survived. No matter what else has been lost or harmed, if a person is left alive after facing his or her own death, he or she will view life with renewed gratitude and joy.

When a witness is lying about an incident, this joy is absent. This kind of reaction will be quite noticeable after sketching with numerous truthful witnesses. One of the most readily available sources of cheerful conversation with all truthful witnesses is how wonderful it is to be alive. They will all have positive remarks about this subject. Early in my career I noticed that the common trait of witnesses who were lying was their lack of any positive remarks about having survived. This difference is so drastic there is no need to explain it during a seminar. Simply put, liars are depressed and seem like they are performing really hard work that takes a lot of concentration during the entire interview. The work they are doing is trying to keep concentrating on their lie. Truthful witnesses might be enormously sad, but if positive subjects about their lives are brought up, they can be brought to joyful expressions.

REAL CASE SCENARIO OF DECEPTION

A man called authorities to say he had been a victim of armed robbers who also shot his cousin to death. He described being put on the floor of his office face down with his cousin. The cousin was shot in the head and died; the witness was left alive.

A week later, when the witness arrived for the interview, he seemed depressed. All during the sketch he never remarked about how good it was to be alive. Toward the end I finally elicited from the witness that he had a wife and a baby boy who was about 2 years old. This seemed strange since during the interview the witness never mentioned having a family and indeed seemed alone and sad. Sensing something was extremely strange, I asked if the witness had a photo of his baby boy. The witness said yes, but I had to insist before he would pull the photo from his wallet. When this witness pulled out the photo, he looked at the baby in the picture with great sadness, as if the baby was going to die. The witness never once expressed sadness about his cousin's death or happiness about his own life.

Once the sketch was finished and the witness had left (in a depressed, grim mood), the investigator on the case shared the facts of the case as he knew it. The witness's story did not make a lot of sense, and he was the registered owner of the same caliber gun as the one used to kill his cousin. For inexplicable reasons the witness had "lost" the gun; it was nowhere to be found. His wife told the investigator her husband had taken over $20,000 out of the bank to give his cousin to invest. The witness told his wife later the money was likely gone and would never be recouped. The wife suspected the cousin planned to invest the money in a drug deal and it was lost. The investigator concluded the witness had to be lying because his version of the actual robbery could not have occurred. The detective wisely did not tell me any of these facts before the sketch. Since other witnesses who were not being truthful had also not been joyful about being left alive, I was able to indicate to the investigator that I detected deception.

All the other witnesses with whom I have worked who later were found to be lying were universally depressed and seemed as if they were distracted by some great intellectual labor they were performing all during the interview.

ADVOCATE AWAY THE LIE

Figures 1.8 and 4.23 are examples where attempted lies on the part of the witness unique to forensic art interviews were foiled. The unique lie is when a witness attempts *not* to describe the perpetrator of the crime. I am certain several witnesses have described a fictitious person for a sketch, and in that way I have been lied to successfully. Usually there are other indicators to the detective and artist that those kinds of witnesses are being deceptive. A lying witness usually is making an excuse for being gone too long, out too late, or simply wanting attention. However, if the witness truly is a victim of a serious crime such as murder or kidnapping and rape (Figures 1.8 and 4.23, respectively) and out of fear of the attacker is trying to lie about that perpetrator's appearance, there is a technique for pulling an accurate sketch from that witness.

First, the sketch needs to be done out of the witness's sight in a setup similar to that shown in Figure 1.18. Next, you must so ingratiate yourself to the witness and you must advocate and nurture that individual to such an extent that the witness is convinced you are a friend who has his or her best interest in mind. If you are conducting a good forensic art interview, this will naturally occur. However, if you have knowledge the witness is so terrified he or she is afraid to describe the attacker, the interview should be even more nurturing than usual.

REAL CASE SCENARIO WHERE THE WITNESS COULD NOT LIE

Before starting the sketch for Figure 1.8, I was informed the witness was a 16-year-old female who had been drinking heavily and was sitting at the bottom of the steps to her apartment. A man whom she knew as (the following is a pseudonym) "Joe" came by and touched her very inappropriately under her clothing. She was angry and called her boyfriend on a cell phone and related the incident to him. Both she and the boyfriend knew Joe lived in their apartment complex. The 16-year-old female witness then saw her boyfriend walk past her with another man whose name she did not know. Those two males went to Joe's apartment, knocked on the door, and when he answered, the unknown male shot Joe to death.

Before the witness arrived, I knew the girl's family was bound to be irrationally blaming *her* for the murder. The first thing I did when the girl showed up was to tell her it was not her fault Joe was murdered that night. The girl began to cry and say her family was yelling at her. She said her sister wanted to be a police officer and was screaming at her. I vocalized strong indignation about the family's and sister's treatment of the witness. I handed the girl my card and told her the sister should not yell at her anymore and that if she started yelling again, the girl was to hand her sister the card and tell her to call me. I insisted it was no fault of hers that a man she did not know had decided to murder someone that night. I told the girl how beautiful she was and how much fun it would be to go to college and fall in love with a man who would not go to prison (the witness's boyfriend would most likely be convicted of accessory to homicide). I spent a great deal of time saying the witness's sister needed to "shut up" and leave her alone. All during this conversation, I continued to sketch as rapidly as possible, making light of the features the witness chose from the facial identification catalog. Once the image was nearly complete, I acted as if the drawing were an afterthought and told the witness I would show her a rough sketch and would change anything she wanted.

When the witness saw the sketch, she jumped up and cursed angrily. The witness would not say if the sketch looked like the man. I had never seen any witness react to a sketch in this manner. The witness then had me remove the dark shadows below the inner edges of the eyebrows (if you look at Figure 1.8, the suspect has dark areas under the inner edges of the eyebrows). Finally, the witness cursed in anger and frustration and left the room. She immediately joined the detective outside and told him "…I tried to lie to her and I couldn't."

The detective took the sketch to a confidential informant who gave him the name of the murderer.

The reason the witness cursed when she first viewed the sketch was she did not want to sketch a likeness of the man and was startled I had done just that. This young, unwise 16-year-old girl thought she should not describe the killer to detectives, that she would be safer if the murderer was *not* found. She tried to have me make the sketch look dissimilar to the man who killed Joe by making me erase the dark areas under the eyebrows. In the end the girl gave up trying to *not* make a sketch that resembled the murderer because:

- I had advocated for the witness so much she felt as if I were totally on her side.
- The sketch was done out of sight. Like all others in the general population, the witness did not think it was possible to sketch a successful likeness from someone's memory, so she was not worried about what she could not see.
- The sketch was done quickly while the focus of the interview was the witness's issues with her abusive, unsympathetic family. I took the girl's side completely.
- I did not act as if the sketch was important; I simply took the choices made by the girl from the facial identification catalog and sketched as quickly as possible with no fanfare. This allowed the girl to stay focused on her situation and not notice an image was taking shape.

In brief, I wore the girl down with kindness. I had no idea the girl was trying to lie; rather, the standard policy of making the sketch session as congenial as possible, customized for a girl who most certainly was being blamed by her family for a murder she didn't know would happen, changed a witness's mind who was determined to lie about the appearance of a murderer.

ANOTHER SCENARIO WHERE THE WITNESS COULD NOT LIE

A girl in her early 20s who worked as a live-in nanny was kidnapped while she was out with her boyfriend. She was taken to a mobile home where she was sexually assaulted for 2 days and then released alive in the same evening clothes she had on when kidnapped. She stayed up all night with Spanish-speaking homicide detectives who were bilingual; the victim spoke only Spanish.

When I began the interview the next day, I spoke Spanish to the girl, even though my mastery of that language was poor. The act of speaking even poorly in another person's language is an ingratiating gesture, especially if the witness is fatigued and tired of trying to cope in a foreign country.

In the beginning, the girl said the attackers were white males. She seemed extraordinarily sad, not angry or glad to be alive. Soon I learned the witness believed she could not return to her job because the attackers convinced her they would go to her workplace and kill the baby, the family, and her. I realized her job was the most important thing to the assault victim. I forced the witness to call her employer, even though the kidnap victim thought there was no way she could return. As soon as the witness got her employer on the phone, that woman, the mother of the child, assured her she still had a job, that they had gotten an alarm system and two large guard dogs. She further urged the witness to come back and passionately declared that the baby missed its nanny. The call ended with the witness saying, in accented English, "I love you" several times.

Once the witness realized she had her job and former life back, she stated that she should tell the truth and that she believed I was her friend. I limped through "Si, estoy tu amiga!," and soon the girl related the attackers were African-American and the sketch began in earnest. The witness admitted the kidnappers had convinced her to lie about their appearance. The witness had held onto the lie all night with the bilingual homicide detectives. The reason she broke down and told the truth was:

- I found the most important issue that grieved her: that she had lost her job in a strange land.
- Once the witness found out she still had a job and a place to live, the hold of her captors faded away.

After creating the sketch, the girl related there was a check stub in the room where she was held captive. She said no one had listened to her, and she tried to say the name of the business, but her English was too poor for me to understand. I handed her a paper and pencil, a device I used with non-English-speaking interviewees. As soon as the kidnap victim drew a few letters, I realized the name of the fast-food establishment and called the detectives with the clue. The investigators took the sketch to the fast-food restaurant at the address the girl had memorized from the check stub and the manager recognized the man who resembled the sketch as a former employee. A check of the business files gave the investigators an address and soon the suspect was in custody.

In Brief

- Disinterested witnesses can still give descriptions for successful sketches. Remember, the most motivated witnesses say they did not see the face well enough to do a sketch, so the disinterested witness will naturally say that also.
- Logical guidelines can produce a sketch from multiple witnesses that might be even better because of added information and enhanced witness relaxation.
- Sketches can be successfully created from witnesses who were under the influence of alcohol when they saw the suspect, or on pain medication while doing the sketch with the artist.
- Deception can be detected when a witness has no joy at having survived a near-death experience or changes the description of events.
- Use nurturance and help remedy the witness's foremost issues to dissolve his or her determination to lie about the appearance of the attacker when the motive for deception is fear.

FINAL COMMENTS CONCERNING THE INTERVIEW

Many interviews are never completed and sketches not attempted due to fear. You cannot give confidence or bravery to someone. However, it is my goal to create a frame of mind that will sustain you to the end of a sketch, in spite of the almost insurmountable roadblocks that make sketching from a witness appear impossible. Due to a formidable force of will to complete sketches no matter what the obstacle because of my near-death experience, I discovered that almost all reasons shown by the witness, the detectives, the conventional wisdom of colleagues and friends, and even my own could very simply be ignored. These myriad of reasons that apparently prove you cannot sketch from memory are nothing more than inherent perceptions best left ignored. Once you understand that you can sketch no matter what seems to be wrong, the sketches come easily and can result in regular identifications for detectives.

Put another way, you should expect the interview to seem like a wreck. Some of the very best sketches were created during an interview where everything seemed to be going wrong. If you expect these disturbing feelings during the sketch, then the work can proceed smoothly to the end in spite of disruptions. If you know this and try to make the interview the most enjoyable conversation possible, considering the struggle at hand and what the witness has been through, the sketch will always look at least similar to the person being described. If you are a successful forensic artist, you have to believe you can draw an image of something unseen. Every sketch in Figure 4.45 was created during an interview where it seemed like it would be impossible to succeed. I used several of the techniques in this book. The common denominator was that I did whatever it took and finished the sketch no matter what seemed wrong.

If the practicing forensic artist knows sketches were created with witnesses who had all the handicaps mentioned in the previous chapters, then perhaps a soothing courage will take the place of fear. This state of mind will fulfill the goal of this book: to allow the forensic artist, for lack of a more specific expression, to enjoy this work.

It is imperative to mention that a successful forensic artist must care. Just as we cannot quantify how much firefighters care about bringing people out of burning buildings, yet are certain they do care enough to do it all during their career, the successful forensic artist knows the power of caring. If you care about getting an image of the attacker from your victim's memory, you will do whatever it takes to overcome obstacles thrown in front of you by a witness. If you do not care, there will be as many reasons as there are witnesses to simply quit the effort and not ever finish a sketch. On the other hand, caring a great deal will let you finish even the most difficult sketch.

In Brief

Virtually all witnesses will say they don't think they can help create a sketch; you must ignore this and other doubts to be effective. The emotional energy of caring can fuel a successful and enjoyable forensic art career.

Figure 4.45

All the sketches shown here were created during an interview where it seemed impossible to create a successful sketch. The most important lesson for a forensic artist to learn is that good likenesses can be created during unbearably harrowing interviews (all but bottom left courtesy of the Houston Police Department).

REFERENCES

1. Jo Ann Zuniga, "Traffic stop turns tragic for officer/Policeman shot twice, run over," *Houston Chronicle*, January 6, 1991. Eric Hanson, "Suspect in shooting of officer arrested," *Houston Chronicle*, January 10, 1991. "Prison escapee charged with attempted capital murder in attack on officer," Staff, *Houston Chronicle*, January 11, 1991. John Makeig, "'Galleria rapist' gets life in police shooting," *Houston Chronicle*, July 18, 1991. Houston Police Department Incident Number 1449791.

2. "Police seek suspect," *Houston Chronicle*, October 2, 1997. "Indecent exposure charge," *Houston Chronicle*, May 28, 1998. Houston Police Department Incident Number 117495497.

3. S. K. Bardwell, "Robbery attempt turns violent. Firepower reviewed by HPD. Spate of robberies cause for concern," *Houston Chronicle*, March 7, 1997. Eric Hanson, "Suspects in shootout arrested. Tip leads to capture of four in bank robbery attempt," *Houston Chronicle*, March 14, 1997. Steve Brewer, "Serial bank robber sentenced after 2 of his accomplices testify," *Houston Chronicle*, February 3, 1999. Houston Police Department Incident Number 28701497.

4. S. K. Bardwell, "Jewelry heist well planned, officers say," *Houston Chronicle*, January 30, 1996. S. K. Bardwell, "Diamond suspect in sketch," *Houston Chronicle*, January 31, 1996. Jerry Urban and S. K. Bardwell, "Two charged in killing of diamond merchant," *Houston Chronicle*, February 25, 1996. S. K. Bardwell, "Police look for missing jewels in robbery-shooting death case," *Houston Chronicle*, February 27, 1996. S. K. Bardwell, "Three suspects held in connection with jeweler's murder," *Houston Chronicle*, February 24, 1996. Stephanie Asin, "Guard identifies jeweler in murder case," *Houston Chronicle*, August 19, 1997. Stephanie Asin, "Jeweler convicted of killing diamond dealer in robbery," *Houston Chronicle*, August 29, 1997. Stefanie Asin, "Jury sentences jeweler to death/Execution by injection ordered in theft, killing of gem broker death," *Houston Chronicle*, September 5, 1997. Houston Police Department Incident Number 10330996.

5. S. K. Bardwell, "Woman lost bag to thieves at Newark airport on way home," *Houston Chronicle*, October 18, 1997. Houston Police Department Incident Number 128423897.

6. Geoff Davidian, "The Gay Hit Man," *Houston Chronicle*, August 10, 1991. Houston Police Department Incident Number 44008890.

7. James T. Campbell, "Rape victim's plan helps nab suspect," *Houston Chronicle*, July 4, 1990. Houston Police Department Incident Number 57711990.

8. Houston Police Department Incident Number 91136597.

9. Roger Smith "Good Job, Performance with a Plus," *City Savvy Magazine*, April, 2002. Houston Police Department Incident Number 6282694.

10. "Test drive becomes highway robbery," Staff, *Houston Chronicle*, November, 2002. Houston Police Department Incident Number 112093202.

11.   Eric Hanson, "Two families, two tragedies/Parents call for return of stolen baby/
      Abduction occurs at day care center," *Houston Chronicle*, September 24, 1988. Eric
      Hanson, "Stolen baby found safe; 2 arrested," *Houston Chronicle*, September 24,
      1988. Susan Warren, "Motive found in kidnap case," *Houston Chronicle*, September
      25, 1988. Houston Police Department Incident Number 77639488.

12.   Friendswood Police Department Case Number 92-4341.

13.   Paul McKay, "Sketch of witness released/He was last seen with missing motel clerk,"
      Houston Chronicle, January 29, 1999. Harvey Rice, "Man in motel clerk's disappearance
      linked to another case in '91." Harvey Rice, "Searchers find skull of missing desk clerk,"
      Houston Chronicle, February 11, 2000. Harvey Rice, "Slaying victim named 'Sunshine'
      buried/Wanda May Pitts cared for others, family says," *Houston Chronicle*, February 27,
      2000. Montgomery County Sheriff's Case Number 00A003108.

14.   "Pregnant blind woman victim/Man, 25, sought in aggravated rape case," Staff, *The
      Houston Post*, August 4, 1988. Felix Sanchez, "Blind woman identifies rape suspect,"
      The Houston Post, August 5, 1988. Houston Police Department Incident Number
      57430188.

15.   Staff, "Burglar gets life term," *Houston Chronicle*, June 6, 1996. Houston Police Depart-
      ment Incident Number 130467793. Houston Police Department Incident Number
      080656205.

16.   Scott Streater, "Owner of liquor store, customer shot to death," *The Houston Post*,
      August 16, 1994. Scott Streater, "Man faces questions in liquor store killings/Appear-
      ance similar to sketch of suspect," *The Houston Post*, August, 18, 1994. Lisa Teachey,
      "Eatery that turned man away says it wasn't aware of urgency," *Houston Chronicle*,
      August 18, 1994. Staff, "Deputy's hunch solves case/Hobson bears a striking resem-
      blance to a composite of the suspect in the case put together with the help of wit-
      nesses," *Houston Chronicle*, August 19, 1994. Deborah Quinn Hensel, "Deputy's hunch
      yields quick arrest in slayings/Liquor store robbery suspect lived nearby," *The Houston
      Post*, August 19, 1994. Harris County Sheriffs Case Number 9408161797.

17.   Houston Police Department Incident Numbers 66058598 and 62285798.

18.   Eric Hanson, "Woman, 23, is found unharmed," *Houston Chronicle*, February 20, 1991.
      S. K. Bardwell, "Victim's release puzzling/Abductee's release raises questions for inves-
      tigators" *The Houston Post*, February 20, 1991. R. A. Dyer, "Jailed man is linked to 2nd
      abduction," *Houston Chronicle*, February 23, 1991. Staff, "Stalker gets 45-year prison
      term in rape-kidnapping of Mexican woman," *Houston Chronicle*, September 18, 1992.
      Houston Police Department Incident Number 16520491.

19.   Peggy O'Hare, "Girl, 7, raped in brazen abduction/Parents just feet away when child
      kidnapped," *Houston Chronicle*, September 21, 2000. Kelly Pedersen, "East End on
      edge/Parents alarmed over sex assaults in neighborhood," *Houston Chronicle*, Sep-
      tember 23, 2000. Peggy O'Hare, "Police think sex assaults of kids linked," *Houston
      Chronicle*, October 25, 2000. Mike Glenn, "Rape suspect altered looks, police report,"

Houston Chronicle, April 25, 2001. Staff, "Man indicted in cases of sex assaults on girls," *Houston Chronicle*, June 5, 2001. Houston Police Department Incident Number 022782901.

20. Steve Brewer, "Gunman gets life term for invasion of homes," *Houston Chronicle*, December 21, 1999. Houston Police Department Incident Number 153207098.

21. "3 men, 16-year-old boy charged in home invasions, robberies," Staff, *Houston Chronicle*, May 1, 2001. Staff, "Third man convicted in rash of break-ins, rapes," *Houston Chronicle*, June 27, 2002. Houston Police Department Incident Number 021564901 and 042453901.

22. Houston Police Department Incident Number 35987791.

23. Geoff Davidian, "The Gay Hit Man," *Houston Chronicle*, August 10, 1991. Houston Police Department Incident Number 44008890.

24. Houston Police Department Incident Number 28701497.

25. Jennifer Liebrum, "Rape case interests FBI agents/'Lingerie' suspect stirs serial inquiry," *Houston Chronicle*, January 16, 1992. Felix Sanchez, "Picture of stalker emerging/Police guarding details of case against suspect," *The Houston Post*, January 31, 1992. John Makeig, "'Stalker' rapist admits two felonies/Guilty plea may net life term," *Houston Chronicle*, July 7, 1992. John Makeig, "Stalker rapist given life term," *Houston Chronicle*, October 9, 1992. Houston Police Department Incident Number 119325691.

26. Karen Taylor, *Forensic Art and Illustration*, CRC Press, 2001, p. 143.

27. Houston Police Department Incident Numbers from left to right, top to bottom, 4522490, 88542288, 018924701, 122312494, 22782901, and 113921004.

28. Kelly McGuire, "Inmate charged with '94 murder/Chester L. Higginbotham, serving time for a 1995 murder, faces first-degree murder charge for death of Newton woman more than four years ago," *The Hutchinson News*, August 13, 1998. Bill Wilson, "A battle hard won/Police say Krehbiel murder solved," *The Newton Kansan*, August 13, 1998. Laviana Hurst, "Suspect charged in 1994 murder case/Chester Higgenbotham is accused in the beating death of Rhonda Krehbiel of Newton," *The Wichita Eagle*, August 15, 1998. Newton Police Department Case Number 94N1424.

29. Personal conversation in May 1990 with then Harris County Assistant District Attorney and now Honorable Judge Belinda Hill, Harris County Criminal Court No. 230.

30. Ruth Piller, "Suspect, 29, charged in slaying that victim's son couldn't stop," *Houston Chronicle*, March 26, 1989. John Makeig, "Son pleaded with killer to quit stabbing mom," *Houston Chronicle*, May 17, 1990. John Makeig, "Teen identifies defendant as his mother's killer," *Houston Chronicle*, May 16, 1990. Edward Ziegler, "I just want to catch crooks," *Reader's Digest*, May 1990. Houston Police Department Incident Number 24584789.

31.   D. Heimstadt, "Tears," *Archive of Psychohistory*, January 2001.

32.   S. M. Labott, M. E. Wolever, and R. B. Martin, (1990). "The physiological and psychological effects of the expression and inhibition of emotion," *Behavioral Medicine*, 16, 182–189.

33.   B. C. Finney, (1972). "Say it again: An active therapy technique," *Psychotherapy: Theory, Research & Practice*, 9, 157–165.

34.   Staff, "Police search for missing 14-month-old girl," *Houston Chronicle*, October 4, 1987. Staff, "Joyous reunion," *Houston Chronicle*, October 16, 1987. Jo Ann Zuniga, "Liliana's wayward trek comes to end/Kidnapped 14-month-old, mom return to Houston; suspect still being sought," *Houston Chronicle*, October 16, 1987. Lori Rodriguez, "Stories with happy endings," *Houston Chronicle*, October 17, 1987.

35.   Staff, "Police hunt liquor store owner's assailant," *The Houston Post*, August 5, 1989. Staff, "Officers wound suspect wanted in store shooting," *The Houston Post*, August 13, 1989. Houston Police Department Incident Number 70725989.

36.   Lisa Teachey and Stephen Johnson, "Off-duty officer slain at family's store," *Houston Chronicle*, April 7, 1997. S. K. Bardwell, "HPD hopes $21,000 reward helps to solve officer's killing," *Houston Chronicle*, April 8, 1997. S. K. Bardwell, "Help asked in solving murder," *Houston Chronicle*, June 12, 1997. Jerry Urban and Ron Nissimov, "Suspect charged in slaying of HPD officer," *Houston Chronicle*, August 15, 1997. Jo Ann Zuniga, "Vietnam refugee sentenced to die for clerk's killing," *Houston Chronicle*, March 12, 1998. Houston Police Department Incident Number 43386597.

37.   S. K. Bardwell, "Man charged in string of area slayings/Dallas lab found link in suspect's DNA," *Houston Chronicle*, October 28, 2003. Tony Freemantle and Peggy O'Hare, "'I was always scared of him'/Charges shine light on man's dark side, say family, friends," *Houston Chronicle*, October 29, 2003. Ron Nissimov, "DA eyes Shore death penalty/Suspect in string of killings arraigned: judge sets trial date," *Houston Chronicle*, October 30, 2003. Andrew Tilghaman, "Speck of evidence under victim's nail leads to murder trial/Man is accused of killing 4 females beginning in 1986," *Houston Chronicle*, September 24, 2004. Andrew Tilghaman, "Man feared to be serial killer on trial in woman's death/Defense lawyers say he strangled her but deny all else," *Houston Chronicle*, October 20, 2004. Andrew Tilghaman, "Suspect details slaying on tape," *Houston Chronicle*, October 21, 2004. Houston Police Department Incident Number 40587092.

38.   Jennifer Liebrum, "Man charged in assault on fourth child," *Houston Chronicle*, March 8, 1989. "Suspect, 25, arrested," Staff, *Houston Chronicle*, February 16, 1989. Houston Police Department Incident Number 88542288.

39.   Staff, "Duo facing charges in robbery of salon," *The Houston Post*, September 24, 1990. Pasadena Police Case Number 90-43818.

40.   Mike Glenn, "Thief leaves behind wrecked plane, few clues," *Houston Chronicle*, March 1, 2004. Eric Hanson, "Man who stole, crashed plane still sought/'To hit the power lines and walk away unhurt is unbelievable,' Louis Jones, county aviation director," *Houston Chronicle*, March 2, 2004. Richard Stewart, "Police say drunken birthday led to high-flying caper," *Houston Chronicle*, March 3, 2004. Richard Stewart, "Now sober and in jail, flier says he regrets his stunt/'I feel lucky to be here. I feel like I've been given a second chance.'" Richard Stewart, "Pilot's joy ride lands him 6 years in prison/Man celebrated his 21st birthday by stealing a plane, then crashing it," *Houston Chronicle*, August 10, 2004. Brazoria County Sheriffs Case Number 87133204.

41.   Edward Ziegler, "I just want to catch crooks," *Reader's Digest*, May 1990, pp. 139–144.

42.   "Woman who drugged men, stole from them gets 17-year term," Staff, *Houston Chronicle*, September 1, 1993. Houston Police Department Incident Number 75127892.

43.   Harris County Sheriffs Case Number 9206100186.

44.   Staff, "Man sought for questioning in Spring Branch shooting death," *Houston Chronicle*, June 28, 1993. Houston Police Department Incident Number 50453593.

45.   Jo Ann Zuniga, "Traffic stop turns tragic for officer," *Houston Chronicle*, January 6, 1991. Eric Hanson, "Suspect in shooting of officer arrested," *Houston Chronicle*, January 8, 1991. Robert Stanton, " 'Galleria Rapist' receives life sentence in shooting," *The Houston Post*, July 18, 1991. Houston Police Department Incident Number 1449791.

46.   S. K. Bardwell, "Jewelry heist well planned, officers say," *Houston Chronicle*, January 30, 1996. S. K. Bardwell, "Diamond suspect in sketch," *Houston Chronicle*, January 31, 1996. Jerry Urban and S. K. Bardwell, "Two charged in killing of diamond merchant," *Houston Chronicle*, February 25, 1996. S. K. Bardwell, "Police look for missing jewels in robbery-shooting death case," *Houston Chronicle*, February 27, 1996. S. K. Bardwell, "Three suspects held in connection with jeweler's murder," *Houston Chronicle*, February 24, 1996. Stephanie Asin, "Guard identifies jeweler in murder case," *Houston Chronicle*, August 19, 1997. Stephanie Asin, "Jeweler convicted of killing diamond dealer in robbery," *Houston Chronicle*, August 29, 1997. Stefanie Asin, " Jury sentences jeweler to death/Execution by injection ordered in theft, killing of gem broker death," *Houston Chronicle*, September 5, 1997. Houston Police Department Incident Number 10330996.

47.   "Sketch of shooting suspect," Staff, *Houston Chronicle*, December 10, 1999. S. K. Bardwell, "2 arrested in robbery, shooting of woman who was left for dead," *Houston Chronicle*, December 23, 1999. Steve Brewer, " 'I was not going to quit'/Woman refuses to let 15 bullets silence her," *Houston Chronicle*, June 2, 2000. Steve Brewer, "Teen gunman gets life for brutal '99 robbery/Victim shot 15 times, left for dead," *Houston Chronicle*, July 11, 2000. Houston Police Department Incident Number 152410199.

CHAPTER 5

RACES, EXPRESSIONS, TEETH, WOMEN, VEHICLES, TATTOOS, AND JEWELRY

DRAWING RACIAL DIFFERENCES

The forensic artist must convey the proper race with each drawing. Since all artists imbue their portraits with at least a tiny bit of their own appearance, it is difficult for any artist to draw someone of a race other than his or her own in an authentic manner. Put another way, females create feminine portraits, and males render their faces with a masculine appearance. Indian artists will tend to make faces appear Indian and so forth. In the midst of the profoundly difficult forensic sketch situation, the added concentration needed to depict another race can be daunting. In order to perform adequately, a study of the basic differences in shading of the faces of the various races is necessary.

In the broadest manner of speaking regarding the structure of the skull, there are three recognized races. They are termed Negroid, Caucasoid, and Mongoloid. The theory is that all skull structures are either one of these three or a mixture in varying proportions. Figure 5.1 shows skull structures of these three basic races with individuals of that same race directly below. Figure 5.2 shows the same kind of comparison in profile.

These profile views make obvious the most drastic differences. Both the Caucasoid and Mongoloid skulls have a profile with an almost straight line from the bottom of the nose to the bottom of the chin. The Negroid skull shows a marked protrusion or bulging out of the profile from the bottom of the nose to the bottom of the chin. Put another way, the maxillary and mandible bones of the Negroid skull are larger than in the Caucasoid and Mongoloid, in ratio to the skull size.

Two other structures that affect the shading when drawing the face are the bridge of the nose and the zygomatic bones. The Caucasoid will have a taller nasal bone. Put differently, the bridge of a Caucasian individual's nose will protrude further away from the eye socket. In general, the Mongoloid and Negroid will have a flatter nose bridge than the Caucasoid. The zygomatic bone, commonly referred to as the cheekbone, is structured similarly in both Negroid and Caucasoid. Both of these races have retreating zygomatics. This means the bottom of the cheekbone recedes *distally* or *toward the back* of the individual. In

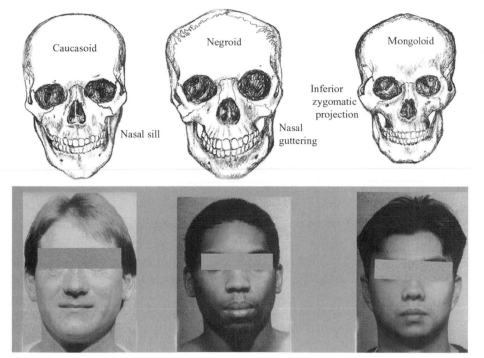

Figure 5.1

From top left to right are frontal images of typical Caucasoid, Negroid, and Mongoloid skulls. Below left to right are individuals somewhat typical of those same types in the same order.

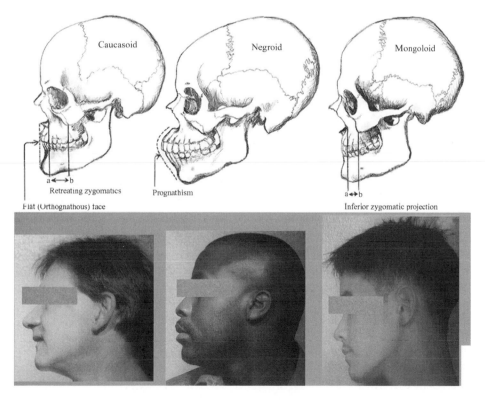

Figure 5.2

From top left to right are profiles of Caucasoid, Negroid, and Mongoloid skulls. Below left to right are individuals somewhat typical of those same types. Notice how the structural differences are more noticeable from this view.

Figure 5.3

Top left to right show a Caucasian male next to an African-American male. The bottom two photos are the same two individuals with the border between the highlight and the shadows of their faces delineated with a dark line.

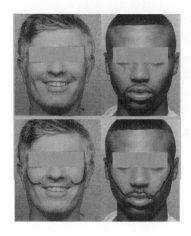

other words, the top of the cheekbone, where the zygomatic and upper maxilla bones suture together, forms the bottom of the eye socket. The bottom part of that same bone protrudes back toward the ear. In the Mongoloid, that bottom part of the cheekbone drops *straight down*. Therefore, when compared to the Negroid and Caucasoid, the bottom of the Mongoloid zygomatic bone projects forward. This is called an inferior zygomatic projection. All these differences in nasal, maxillary, mandibular, and zygomatic bones can be easily viewed in Figure 5.2.

Put simply, the Caucasian face will have highlights on top, and shadows under, the cheeks. The Negroid individual's highlights on the cheeks will continue from the bottom of the eyes to the top of the lips. You don't necessarily need to memorize the names of the facial bones. Rather, you need to know how to depict these differences in your drawing. For purposes of this discussion, the lighting on the faces discussed will be typical portrait lighting. For examples of this see Figures 5.3, 5.4, and 5.5.

Figure 5.4

Top left to right show a Caucasian male next to an African-American male. The bottom two photos are the same two individuals with the border between the highlight and the shadows of their faces delineated with a dark line.

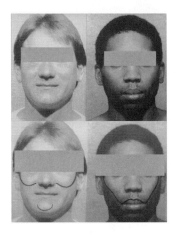

Notice how all the Negroid individuals have the highlighting continue from under their eyes to the top of their lips. The Caucasoid individuals' faces drop off vertically after their cheekbone, so the highlight ends there. The lighting in these photos is not drastic enough to emphasize the shadows cupping under the cheekbone. However, Figure 5.6 is a Caucasian male with drastic lighting.

Notice how the shadows form directly under the cheekbone. Compare that Caucasoid male's shadows with the Negroid examples where the shadows form a triangle, with the smaller part of the triangle starting at the lips and the wider area of the highlight ending under the eyes.

Figure 5.5

Top left to right show an African-American male next to a Caucasian male. The bottom two photos are the same two individuals with the border between the highlight and the shadows of their faces delineated with a dark line.

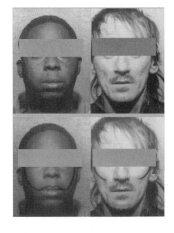

No matter how dark you make the flesh appear on your drawing, the Negroid individual will not appear genuine unless the highlights are indicative of Negroid bone structure. Conversely, a light-skinned Negroid can be indicated when the shadowing is correct, no matter how light the complexion.

Figures 5.7 and 5.8 are other illustrations of the racial differences using skulls with the drawing superimposed and then shown without the skull showing through. Notice how the racial differences are easier to comprehend when subjects are viewed in profile. Understand that those differences are harder to depict in the front view. Drawing these differences in front view should be mastered, since that is the most frequently drawn pose when sketching suspects from a witness's memory.

Figure 5.6

Drastic lighting points out how highlights end at the bottom of the cheeks on the face of a typical Caucasoid (photo by author).

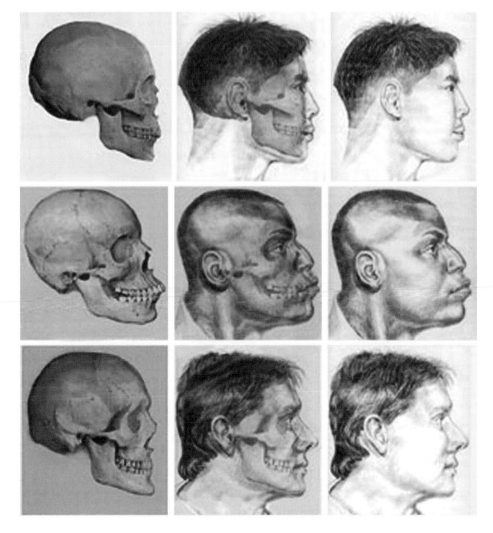

Figure 5.7

From top to bottom on the left are the skulls in profile of a Mongoloid, Negroid, and Caucasoid subjects. To the right of each is a drawing superimposed atop the skull and on the right are the drawings without the skull showing through. See color plate.

Figure 5.8

From top to bottom on the left are skulls of Mongoloid, Negroid, and Caucasoid subjects. To the right of each are first a drawing superimposed upon the skull image and then the drawing without the skull showing through. See color plate.

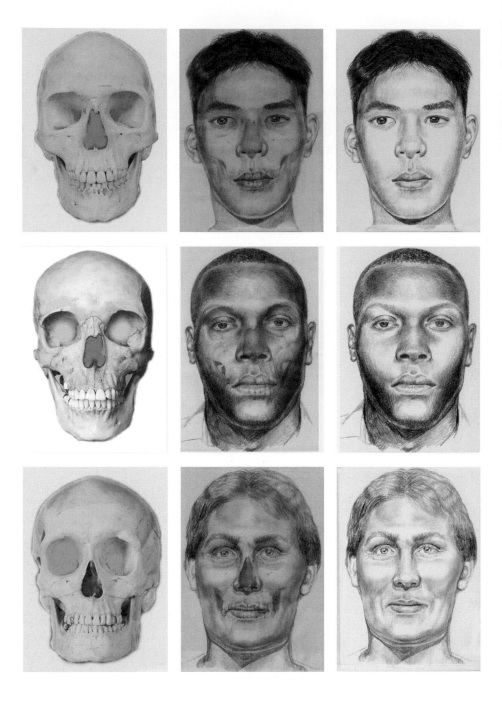

Early in my career, I created a successful sketch of a man who raped and tortured a woman for hours. The sketch next to his mug shot can be seen in Figure 5.9. After this man was caught, a photo of him was obtained for comparison. I practiced self-criticism and realized although the skin of the man in the sketch was rendered in very dark tones, the shadow patterns on the cheeks were those of a Caucasian individual.

In the bottom part of Figure 5.9, I have altered the drawing to show how the minor addition of continuing the highlight from the bottom of the eyes to the top of the lips more closely depicts the correct ethnicity of the subject.

Figures 5.10 and 5.11 are sketches done later in my career, where I had learned to make certain those extended maxillary areas are highlighted.

Since the complete vertical width of the Mongoloid cheekbone is thrust forward, the entire surface of those individuals' faces has an almost equal highlighting. Notice the profile of the Mongoloid example in Figures 5.2 and 5.7 is very flat or straight up and down, compared to the other two types. This is further indication that highlighting for these individuals is uniform over the surface of the face, save only the eyes, lips, and nose.

For examples of sketches of individuals with Mongoloid skull structures done from witness memory, see Figure 5.12.

I adhered to the overall highlighting found on Mongoloid type faces. This imbues the subtle difference that renders these sketches as appearing like the race of the perpetrator being described. Besides this overall facial highlighting and Asian-type eyes, the individuals with Mongoloid skull structures typically have straight dark hair.

Figure 5.9

Top left: A sketch compiled from a witness assaulted by the man on the right. Bottom left: I changed the highlights to more closely resemble those of a typical Negroid individual, bringing the sketch more in alignment with the perpetrator's mug shot[1] (courtesy of the Houston Police Department).

Figure 5.10

Shown on the left are three sketches drawn from the description by witnesses of the perpetrators pictured to the right of all the sketches. The sketches were created later in my career when I more accurately highlighted the face to indicate the forward thrust of the maxilla and mandible bones (courtesy of the Houston Police Department).

SKETCHING FACIAL TYPES IN YOUR AREA

Pondering the different races could seem overwhelming to an artist endeavoring to sketch any and all populations that might be described to him or her by a witness. For instance, the so-called Mongoloid individual could be Chinese, Japanese, Eskimo, American Indian, or Pacific Islander, to name a few. The Caucasoid individual might be Northern European, Middle Eastern, Mediterranean, Latin, or numerous other designations. And lastly the Negroid person could be from any of dozens of countries or areas in Africa and beyond where immigration has mingled their lineage to almost every part of the globe. Further complicating this effort is the fact that the permutations and combinations of racial mixtures are in the millions.

There is a way for you to be able to sketch the various unique populations in your area. Simply gather photos and observe the people who populate the area served. The truth is, each area has its own unique mixture of populations. Obviously there are exceptions to this rule. However, in general, the Negroid, Caucasoid, and Mongoloid individuals will often have typical looks associated with geographical areas. For example, there is a common look among a significant portion of Caucasian people in Kansas. That state was settled early on by Swedish, German, Norwegian, Russian, and other Northern European persons.

There is a somewhat typical look of a "white" person in that area that will differ from, say Chicago, where there are substantial Polish, Italian, and other European population groups. The Hispanic individual in the Miami and Southern Florida area will likely have a Cuban appearance, whereas the Texas Hispanic subject might more often appear Mexican, and the New York Latinos would more commonly be Puerto Rican. An artist in the San Francisco area should try to understand the Asian and Pacific Rim influence in the genetic pool by gathering photos and "people watching" in that area. This discussion speaks to the appearance of persons of differing ethnicities in the broadest terms.

In the most general way, there is a solution to correctly depicting the subtleties of racial appearances in all artists' areas. Instead of attempting the impossible task of determining what mixture of Mongoloid, Caucasoid, and Negroid facial structures is occurring in the peoples of the world, simply become an expert on the appearance of the people your own geographical area. Understanding the mixture of racial traits that influence the look of persons sketched will never be done to perfection. There will always be persons coming in from far away and vastly different from anyone in the local genetic mixtures. However, the best understanding of how the ethnic faces should be sketched as a forensic artist can be accomplished by becoming as familiar as possible with those persons in the surrounding community. This is the method for capturing at least the major looks for people needing to be drawn.

This effort can be two-fold. First, make it your business to be an astute observer of the people in your area. Sporting events, shopping malls, and grocery stores can be treasure troves of people watching. This can also be a great opportunity to discover the latest hairstyles being sported in the area. Second, gather photos of local individuals for the best visual aids. One forensic artist made the ultimate visual aid. Samantha Steinberg of Miami, Florida, created a facial identification catalog with mug shots from her area of the country. Called *Steinberg's Facial Identification Catalog* (Figures 1.23 through 1.26), she defines the racial mixtures in the people she needs to draw. Instead of trying to know the racial lineage of her suspects, she is able to give her witnesses photos of people who reflect the general racial makeup of her community.

Focus drawing practice on any minority which you have trouble sketching. As an example, I found great difficulty drawing Asian individuals. An example of the first Asian sketched is Figure 5.13.

This was one of the first sketches shown on a nationwide television crime-fighting show. The sketch caused a tip to be called into detectives

Figure 5.13

This was the first sketch of an Asian suspect I attempted early in my career. The shadowing under the cheeks is more indicative of a Caucasian structure. The sketch nevertheless helped solve one of the first cases where the television show America's Most Wanted *showed a composite (courtesy of the Houston Police Department).*

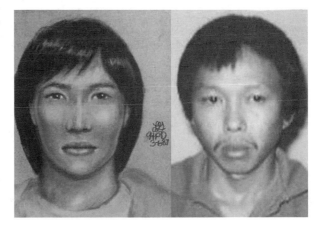

and helped solve the case.[3] However, I practiced self-criticism and realized the drawing had Caucasian cheek structure wherein the shadows fall under the cheeks. Only the eyes and hair are Asian in appearance. Once this deficiency was noticed, many mug shots of Asians were gathered in readiness. The difference in skull structures of Asians compared to other races was acknowledged. I avidly observed Asians in my area grocery stores, shopping malls, public areas, and anywhere possible.

Then in June of 1991 came a home-invasion–robbery case with several formidable handicaps. The witnesses were a Salvadorian family who spoke almost no English. The home invaders were Asian. The Salvadorian family was not familiar with Asian individuals. An added burden was the fact the sketch was done in August and the family had no air conditioning because they had been robbed of nearly $6,000 and could not pay their electric bill. The temperature was in the upper 90s with very high humidity. If I had not brought my stack of photos depicting Asian males from the area, the bottom two sketches in Figure 5.12 would have been nearly impossible to create. The only reason it was possible to construct two distinct individuals with six family members speaking Spanish to my untrained ear was the fact the armed robbers were wearing distinctly different colored tee shirts and had two distinctive hairstyles. The next day a Harris County Sheriff's Deputy was on patrol and saw the two men depicted in the bottom of Figure 5.12 walking down the street.

He thought they looked enough like the sketches to stop and identify them. They became evasive and were eventually identified in the home invasion.[4]

I had practiced drawing eyes from photos I had collected like the examples in Figure 5.14. I also used those photos to practice the overall highlighting seen on the Asian faces in my area. That and my use of visual aids that depicted that population in my area helped create successful likenesses in a tremendously difficult situation.

Those same tactics were used for the sketch at the top of Figure 5.12. The witness for that sketch was completely disinterested. She watched the man in the photo exit a convenience store about 100 feet away from her kitchen window as she was washing dishes. She had resided in that apartment for over 2 years, so viewing a man exiting that store was of little or no interest to her. She was not aware this man had just shot and killed a Houston police officer.[5] The attitude of the witness is mentioned because earlier forensic artists had assumed incorrectly a "disinterested witness" would construct an inferior sketch. However, since the sketch at the top of Figure 5.12 bears a better resemblance than

Figure 5.14

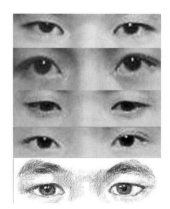

I gathered examples of Asian eye shapes and created many practice sketches like the drawing at the bottom done in graphite pencil on Bristol board with a vellum finish.

the two sketches below created from witnesses who had been home invaded and threatened with their lives, the theory of a disinterested witness being inferior again is proven wrong in these cases.

In Brief

All of the following rules of drawing various races assume conventional portrait lighting.

- Artists find sketching races other than their own difficult and therefore should target drawing practice for those types of faces.
- African faces have highlighting that starts under the eyes and continues in a narrowing area to the top of the lips.
- Anglo faces are highlighted on the top of the cheeks with shadows underneath the cheeks.
- Asians, or individuals with Mongoloid skull types, have flatter nose bridges and cheekbones that protrude at the bottom, allowing highlighting to be evenly distributed over the entire facial area.

The solution for drawing sketches of all races accurately is to observe and collect photos of the populations in your geographical area, with emphasis on races that are difficult to draw.

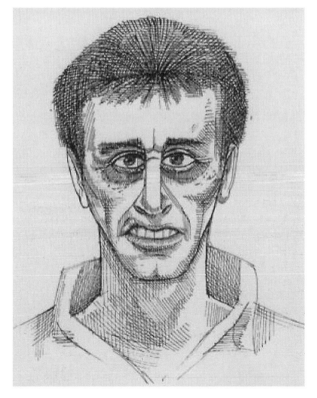

Figure 5.15

Israel's forensic artist Gil Gibli drew this suspected kidnapper in pen and ink from the description of a father who suspected the man described as being the kidnapper of his young daughter. Gil Gibli captured the exceedingly agitated expression of a man who drove by with a kidnapped girl in the trunk of his car (courtesy of Gil Gibli).

EXPRESSION

Figure 5.15 shows the work of Israeli forensic artist Gil Gibli. This uniquely talented illustration artist actually does his composites in pen and ink. Figure 5.15 is the sketch of a kidnapper, taken from the description of the father of the kidnapped girl, who saw the man drive by. The father was unaware that his daughter was in the trunk of the man's car. Fear of being caught caused this drastic expression on the kidnapper's face. Since Gil Gibli is a prominent political cartoonist, his artistic talent for portraying expressions in faces makes the image of this kidnapper jump off the page. Gil's drawing helped identify the suspect and the girl was recovered unharmed.

Figure 5.16 is an amazing forensic sketch from Gil Gibli, done 6 months after his witness had seen this man only briefly. Featured in the multi-award-winning documentary *No. 17*, the sketch

Figure 5.16

Israel's forensic artist Gil Gibli drew this unidentified murder victim in pen and ink. The witness talked briefly to the man shown right months before the sketch interview with Gibli. Because the artist portrayed the amiable expression of the subject, his family was able to recognize him when Gil's sketch was released to the public (courtesy of Gil Gibli).

Gil created helped authorities find the name of an unidentified man murdered in a terrorist bombing. In June of 2002 the man on the right of Figure 5.16 was riding in a bus from Tel Aviv to Tiberius when the vehicle was attacked by a suicide bomber. Seventeen people were killed. Sixteen were identified; number 17 remained unknown. Gil interviewed a girl who had spoken to this man, "No. 17," for only a few moments to gather brief information for a transit survey. This witness got off the bus before the bombing, and subsequently interviewed hundreds of other riders on scores of other buses. Gil therefore had a disinterested witness who had not seen the subject of his drawing for 6 months. Gil created the drawing on the left of Figure 5.16 while being filmed by the documentary crew.

The drawing was released and the family of the man pictured on the right called authorities. They had not heard from their loved one for some time, but since he was an older adult, his family was not alarmed by his absence and had not suspected foul play. Gil's ability to capture not only the general face shape and features but also the contagious smile and personality seen in the photos of the identified man show how adding an expression helped solve this case.

Gil Gibli proves how effective forensic artists can truly be. His drawing, done in the most unforgiving media—pen and ink—and created with so many handicaps, caused the unidentified murder victim to be identified. However, this case involved a congenial man talking to a young girl who was conducting a survey on a bus. Since almost all cases presented to forensic artists involve noncongenial robbers and other felons, the problem of what expression to draw is uncomplicated.

THE MOST COMMON FELON EXPRESSION

Much is made in fine art studies of the various expressions found in human faces. Books on drawing the human face in fine art will show dozens of dramatic poses, with the faces laughing, frowning, crying, and exhibiting other exaggerated expressions.

You need not be overly concerned with the most extreme expressions, since the most common expression displayed by suspects and subsequently asked for in the drawing by witnesses can be viewed in Figures 5.17 and 5.18. This expression is so commonly requested that I find this look in many sketches in every year of cases worked.

Fortunately for the artist, this expression is easy to depict. The corrugator muscle between the eyebrows is flexed, causing vertical lines to form starting at the inner edges of the eyebrows and reaching up toward the center of the forehead. The other part of this typical expression is the slight flexing of the

Figure 5.17

Three examples of the most common expression requested by witnesses to crimes. Notice all have eyebrows flexed together by the corrugator muscle, which causes vertical wrinkles to form leading straight up from the center of the eyebrows. Also the eyes are slightly squinted and a horizontal tightening of the lips can be seen.

Figure 5.18

Here are four more examples of the most common expression requested by witnesses to be drawn on the suspect's face. This expression is so frequently drawn in forensic sketches done with witnesses that any artist who works regularly will most likely have several per year.

orbicularis oculi muscle that, in common terms, would be a slight squinting of the eyes. Usually this expression in the eye area is accompanied by a tight, stern expression in the lips.

You cannot ask leading questions. However, knowing this common expression will allow you to recognize when the witness is trying to explain how it looks in his or her own terms. The moves are easy to make on the sketch. Simply draw some vertical lines that originate from the center edge of the eyebrow. Some individuals have another vertical fold between the eyebrows. Have the witness indicate how plentiful, how dark, and how long these vertical lines are. After drawing the lines, indicate the bulging of the flesh by starting some rounded shading at the line and cupping it under the flesh that protrudes in front of the line.

The squinting of the eyes can be indicated by simply erasing the bottom portion of the iris and lifting up the lower eyelid structures to align with the new iris-bottom contour. Additional bunching up of the flesh under the eyes might be needed to finish the look.

The explanation of the drawing steps shown in Figure 5.19 is as follows. From left to right: First is a sketch depicting an almost pleasant expression. Next is the same sketch with the beginning lines showing the individual flexing his corrugator muscles. Next, shading is added to the bottom of the lines to indicate rounded flesh bulging between the wrinkles. Fourth from the left, the bottom of the iris is erased and the bottom eyelid is elevated slightly with a moderate increase of shading under the bottom eyelid. Lastly, if the witness indicates he or she saw the horizontal wrinkles on the forehead, they can be added. Also, for maximum rage, the lower eyelid is pulled up even further, thus covering more of the lower portion of the iris. This look might also include more intense shading under the bottom lid. I have observed that witnesses rarely ask for as intense an expression as depicted in the far right image. Remember, dark wrinkles should not be added unless the witness remembers seeing them. The drawing involved for these changes took less than 2 minutes.

The witness might have you draw this expression in varying degrees of intensity. Only the immediate areas around the eyes were changed in these drawings,

Figure 5.19

Shown here are drawing moves for one of the most common expressions asked for by witnesses.

yet the face on the far left appears happy and joyful; the one on the far right has an expression of full-blown rage.

If you master this expression and a blank emotionless expression, then the vast majority of expressions requested by witnesses will be doable.

DRAWING TEETH

The other expression requested by witnesses on occasion is that of a typical happy grin. This expression often is seen on pedophiles who are trying to be friendly in order to lure their unsuspecting prey. Other grinning perpetrators will be ones that frequent drinking establishments where an adult might be lured away to become a victim of crime. Some of these situations would be the female who meets a man and feigns romantic desires. Once alone with an unsuspecting male, the woman will surreptitiously slip drugs into his food or drink. Once the male is unconscious, the female can steal his belongings.

Lastly, this expression can be seen in individuals whose teeth and lip structure are such that they almost always show their teeth. This can be an attractive trait if you are a movie star, politician, or beauty-pageant contestant. If you are a perpetrator committing a crime against another person, it is only another way of getting one over on an unsuspecting victim. Figures 5.20 and 5.21 show sketches of cases where these kinds of expressions were seen on the suspect.[6]

Most importantly, there are some individuals whose dentition bears a striking anomaly that must be depicted. This unusual trait in the perpetrator's teeth could be so remarkable as to have him stand out in a way that would help identify him were it included in the sketch. The fact that teeth are relatively permanent and difficult to change enhances the importance of depicting them correctly. Perpetrators might cut, color, or otherwise change their hair easily. Glasses can be worn or not, and clothing can be changed. Teeth,

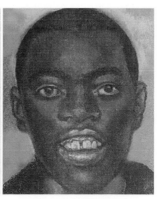

Figure 5.20

Here are three examples sketched from witnesses to crimes where the suspect showed teeth. The forensic artist needs to be capable of drawing teeth realistically for the occasion when this kind of individual is the suspect.

Figure 5.21

Three more examples of sketches from witnesses to crimes where the suspect they saw showed their teeth. The forensic artist must be able to depict teeth accurately for these kinds of suspects since those teeth might be their most recognizable trait.

however, are quite difficult to change. The cost and pain would be prohibitive for most individuals to replace a gold crown with a porcelain-fused-to-metal crown. This would be the only way to change the appearance of gold work noticed by witnesses. Crooked teeth would need more than a year to change by wearing orthodontic devices. Missing teeth would take several visits to the dentist for the construction and cost of prostheses for replacement. The likelihood of the vast majority of criminals spending the time and money to fix their teeth is almost nonexistent. Therefore, you *must* be ready with the ability to draw teeth realistically should the witness see an individual whose teeth are a prominent identifier.

Two such cases can be seen in Figures 5.22 and 5.23. The witness for the sketch in Figure 5.22 was a 13-year-old male who was sexually assaulted. His memory of the solid gold teeth for inclusion in the sketch helped the detective find the perpetrator in less than a day.[7] Figure 5.23 is from an incident where four teenagers saw a man come up to them in the parking lot of a night club and shoot their friend to death for no apparent reason. They gave a description of an average African-American male. However, they described two of his front

Figure 5.22

Below left: At the top is the lower portion of a sketch done from the description of a 13-year-old boy who was sexually assaulted. This sketch included the memorable gold teeth. The photo at the bottom is the lower portion of the suspect's face that was identified quickly from the sketch (courtesy of the Houston Police Department).

Figure 5.23

Far right: Top: The lower portion of a sketch created with three friends who were visiting Houston and were approached by a man in a parking lot who shot their friend to death. The inclusion of various gold additions to the teeth led to a tip that helped detectives solve the case[7] (courtesy of the Houston Police Department).

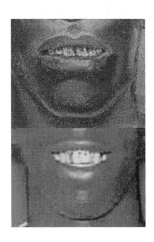

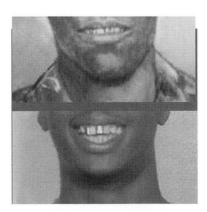

teeth as being gold. Since I was versed in tooth anatomy, I could tell where to place the gold teeth in the smile. Even though the sketch was a pitiful likeness, the inclusion of the unusual dental work led to a tip that identified the suspect to detectives.[8]

Figure 5.24 shows sketches on actual cases for which I had to draw teeth on the suspects due to some unique traits. Figure 5.25 is a sketch with a close-up of the gold star that had to be drawn on this particular suspect to make the best effort to identify him.[8]

Since the majority of these perpetrators were under the stress of trying to commit a crime at the time the witness saw this kind of expression, we can assume those individuals will display this same expression often during their daily life. If they are so prone to showing their teeth even when they are stressed, they most certainly show teeth when they are experiencing relaxation and enjoying their friends' company. Many of the finest artists throughout history have avoided drawing or painting teeth on the subjects of their portraits. As an example, try to picture any face painted by Leonardo daVinci or Michelangelo where the teeth of the subject are seen.

The forensic artist has no such luxury when depiction of unusual dentition could bring in a murderer or other felon. You must learn tooth anatomy *before* you need to sketch such a suspect.

Figure 5.24

Four cases where I had to draw the teeth on the suspect due to unique traits. Suspects are extremely unlikely to take the time, money, and endure the discomfort to change their dentition. Therefore, drawing unusual dentition takes on much greater importance than drawing clothing or even hair.

ANATOMY OF TEETH

The good news is there are only three tooth shapes that need to be seriously studied when sketching from witness memory. The reason for this is that the most teeth you need to draw will be the full-grin expression. The broadest grin, at most, shows the maxillary central incisors, the lateral incisors, and the canines. Each of these three teeth is a mirror image of the same tooth on the opposite side of the mouth. Past the canine, the first and second molars appear as mere vertical oblong oval shapes somewhat in shadow, if they are seen at all. Some individuals show only the maxillary centrals, laterals, and a fraction of the surface of their canines.

Figure 5.25

The top shows a close-up of the mouth of a smiling suspect who had a gold crown with a star configuration; the complete sketch is below.

Some expressions end up as the slack-mouthed expression where only a fraction of the anterior teeth is seen.

I have noticed that most forensic artists, indeed most portrait artists, avoid including teeth in their facial images. After drawing hundreds of portraits before, during, and after attending Dental Laboratory Technology School at the University of Health Science Center at San Antonio, it became apparent that a simple knowledge of those three previously mentioned anterior tooth anatomies rendered the teeth in portraits easy to do and realistic in appearance. Conversely, artists who have not taken a few moments to familiarize themselves with these three unique tooth shapes find grinning expressions difficult and exasperating to draw, and their results can be poor and unrealistic. Since the drawings created in the forensic art field have the potential to identify a wanted felon, and since some witnesses will absolutely need those teeth drawn for the sketch to be right, you should study the following.

Maxillary Central Incisor

The maxillary central incisor could be referred to by the witness as the center front tooth. As shown in the top of Figure 5.26, this tooth is shaped like a chisel. For sake of this discussion, the term "distal" refers to anatomical areas *away* from the centerline, or the center of the teeth, and "mesial" (pronounced **me**-ze-al) refers to anatomical areas that are *toward* the centerline of the dental arch. The vertical mesial edge of the maxillary incisor is rather straight. The distal edge curves out. The incisor on the opposite side is a mirror image of this shape.

Maxillary Lateral Incisor

The maxillary lateral incisor is next to, and distal of, the maxillary central incisor. As shown in Figure 5.27, the lateral incisor is shaped almost identically to

Figure 5.26

Below left: Above are drawings of typical right and left maxillary central incisors. Below are six photos with arrows indicating each individual's maxillary central incisors. Notice how all have similar shapes.

Figure 5.27

Far right: Above are drawings of typical right and left maxillary lateral incisors. Below are six individuals' teeth with arrows pointing out their maxillary lateral incisors. Notice how all these lateral incisors have similar shapes.

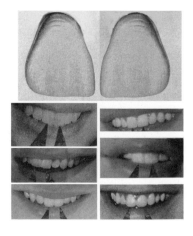

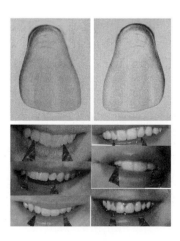

the central. The difference is it is smaller and shorter. The bottom, or incisal edge, is 1 to 1.5 mm shorter than the central incisor. An artist who has not studied tooth anatomy tends to depict the lateral as identical to the central incisor. If you show those two teeth on either side of the centrals to be shorter and a little smaller, the anatomy will seem realistic to the viewer.

Canines

On either side of the maxillary lateral incisors are the canines. Shown in Figure 5.28, each of these upside-down teardrop-shaped teeth is as long or slightly longer than the maxillary central incisors. Most individuals' lips begin to drape down across the teeth at the canines, so often all that needs to be drawn is the bottom half. Similar to the incisors, the vertical mesial edge is the straighter, and the distal edge is curved more.

The next teeth, the maxillary bicuspids, are far enough back in the mouth that they are sometimes not seen. There are two, each distal to each canine, and if they are seen at all, they appear as rounded, vertical columns in shadow.

Figure 5.29 shows why you need to be familiar only with the anatomy of the central and lateral incisors and the canines. This is a photo of a girl with an appliance holding back her lips. Even with this extraordinary stretching back of the lips, those teeth behind the canines are simple vertical columns of tooth. Looking at the grinning mouths in Figures 5.26, 5.27, and 5.28, you can see either none of the bicuspids or only a portion peeking out from the corners of the lips.

Figures 5.20 through 5.25 show sketches on actual cases. These images, generated from witnesses to crimes, show almost no teeth past the lateral incisors. The bicuspids are seen only in a fractional way, if at all. This is more proof that the dentition an artist needs to draw in these situations is limited to the three anterior teeth: the central and lateral incisors and the canines. The point is that

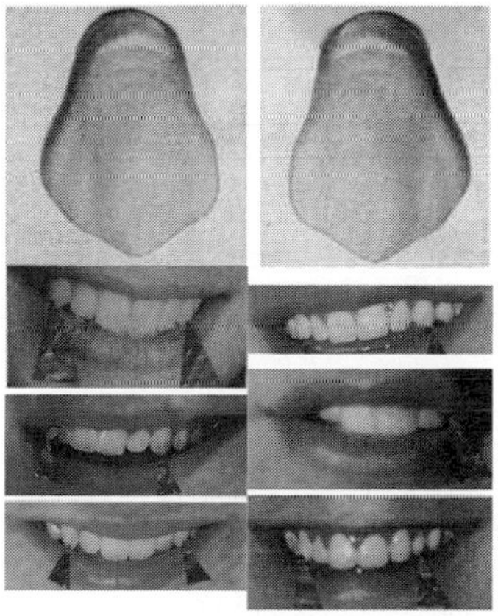

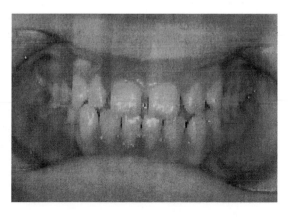

Figure 5.28

Below left: Above are images of the left and right canines. Below are six individuals' teeth with arrows pointing out their maxillary canines. Notice how all the canines have similar shapes

Figure 5.29

This individual has an appliance spreading her lips to maximum width in order to show her teeth. Even with this drastic pose, all the teeth past the canines are seen in only a fractional manner (photo by Dr. Toole, D.D.S.).

you can easily study the aforementioned tooth anatomy and be capable of drawing realistic versions of suspects' grins.

ADDING TEETH TO AN ALREADY FINISHED SKETCH

The witness usually mentions the suspect showing teeth after the sketch is almost finished. It is easier to draw the grin in the portrait as you go along if you know about it in advance. However, Figure 5.30 shows how you can easily draw in teeth to a face that is nearly finished. This female suspect's face was almost drawn to completion when the witness mentioned she showed her teeth, and further that she had a gold maxillary lateral incisor. Since I knew it was imperative to include this in the sketch, I performed the following sketching maneuver and took photographs of the work at several stages.

First the center crease where the lips come together in a dark line is erased. This erasure should approximate the area that will be occupied by the teeth to be drawn. Then lightly draw the teeth, taking care to place them centered under the nose and in the right size, proportional to the size of the face drawn. A visual aid for this can be to ask the witness to show his or her teeth and imbue those approximate proportions to the sketch on the drawing board. Put another way, looking at anyone showing his or her teeth will *approximate* the placement and proportions of the teeth. Notice there is not much drawing to this part since the teeth appear better if they do not have harsh, black lines in between them. Rather, since they are the lightest area on the face, except perhaps the whites of the eyes, normal lighting will cause them to appear as a bright area with almost no shadows in the creases. It is therefore a mistake to draw the kinds of dark shadows in the lines between the teeth as you would with lines in fleshy areas. In fact, accurate tooth depiction will often have the line between the teeth almost disappear from sight, such as the tooth areas in Figure 5.20. Notice the line should be indicated at the top, usually showing the gum area coming down to a point between the teeth. Then very quickly the line can almost disappear and then reappear at the bottom separation of the teeth.

Next the corners of the mouth were darkened where the interior of the mouth could be seen. Lastly, the shiny metal look is added to the tooth the witness indicated had a gold crown. Since teeth look better and

Figure 5.30

A witness wanted to add teeth to the drawing at top left. Shown are the steps for doing this in order of top left, top right, bottom left, bottom right.

more realistic if they are drawn softly with no harsh details, this process, from the first erasure to the last details, took only a few minutes' time.

THE TONGUE

Novice artists have trouble showing the mouth open because they will forget the tongue. Once it is pointed out that everyone has a tongue, it seems obvious. However, there are many artists who try to show dentition and when it somehow does not seem right, they erase their work and draw the mouth shut. One common culprit is the omission of the tongue.

Indicating the tongue is easy, and does not take precise drawing. First, the areas where the viewer is looking into the dark interior of the mouth should be drawn as dark as perhaps the pupils of the eyes or the holes of the nostrils. Then the only way to continue a realistic mouth is to indicate a tongue. If the subject has a diastema (space between the top front, or maxillary central incisors), the top of the gap is dark. However, at the middle of the gap, there should be a tongue indicated behind the teeth. The tongue can be drawn a few shades darker than the lips. To round out this depiction, one might need to indicate the ever-present wetness in the mouth by showing a glistening on the tongue like the bright highlight on the iris of the eye.

Figure 5.31 shows a sketch from a case where the suspect showed lower teeth with a jagged contour. To show these unusual lower teeth, I had to indicate the tongue since the mouth was drawn open. Figure 5.32 shows a perpetrator who had a diastema. The tongue was drawn with wetness indicated by a highlight. This particular sketch helped the detective arrest the man depicted the first day the sketch was distributed to the patrol officers.[9]

SKETCHING FEMALE SUSPECTS

An infant kidnapped by a stranger throws law enforcement and the community into a frenzy trying to find the missing baby. Almost no type of case causes so much all-out effort on the part of authorities. Since almost all perpetrators in these kinds of cases are female, the forensic artist must be able to adeptly sketch women.

You can be lulled into practicing only the skill of sketching masculine features, since males perpetrate 93% of violent crimes. When that rare female perpetrator needs to be drawn, a well-prepared forensic artist should already be

Figure 5.31

The witness for this sketch said the subject showed bottom teeth that were irregular. Inclusion of a tongue in the background was necessary to show the teeth in a realistic way. Notice on the left and right corners where there is no tongue or teeth, the mouth is dark like a cave.

Figure 5.32

Showing teeth was mandatory in this sketch as the perpetrator always showed his teeth. Notice the inclusion of a tongue behind the teeth, highlighted to show wetness, for a realistic depiction of his diastema (a gap between the maxillary central incisors). This sketch helped patrol officers find the perpetrator within 24 hours of release.

skilled in that area. Figures 5.33 and 5.34 show sketches juxtaposed with the women described, both of whom kidnapped babies of strangers.

The pressure to create a successful sketch during both sessions was immense. The sketch in Figure 5.33 was done with the mother of a 10-hour-old baby who had been kidnapped from her hospital bed. The sketch in Figure 5.34 was done with a day-care center owner who had seen a woman kidnap a 6-month-old baby boy from her business. That particular witness was the most hysterical of any I have encountered; she stood during the entire sketch session and screamed all her answers. Pressure was intensified because this business owner insisted she never saw the face of the kidnapper.

I was practiced in depicting feminine features and both babies were returned due in part to the sketches created.[10]

THE OPPOSITE SEX IS NOT SO DIFFERENT

The actual facial structure of women is not much different from that of men. Men generally have squarer, larger chins. Women's chins are more rounded. The problem with this rule is there are abundant examples of women with larger, squarer chins than some men. The only hard and fast rule of anatomical difference is men will have a superciliary arch that bulges out whereas women's will be smooth. Said another way, the bony ridge where the eyebrows lie will stick out on a man's skull. That brow ridge on a woman will be smooth. Men tend to have thicker necks that include an Adam's apple, but this again is not always the case. In fact, the difference in women's and men's faces is slight enough to allow many individuals to pose as the opposite sex.

Therefore, the artist wishing to imbue a sketch with

Figure 5.33

The witness for the sketch on the left had her 10-hour-old baby kidnapped from her hospital bed by the woman on the right. The baby in this case was returned after the sketch appeared on the evening news (courtesy of the Houston Police Department).

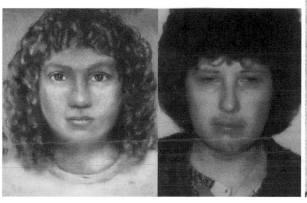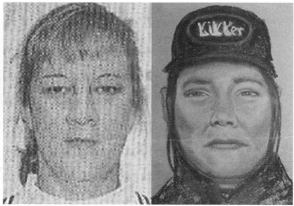

Figure 5.34

The witness for the sketch on the left had just seen the woman on the right kidnap a 3-month-old baby from her day-care center. She was the most hysterical witness encountered during my career (courtesy of the Harris County Sheriffs Department).

Figure 5.35

The sketch, right, was done with a bank teller who was at the drive-thru window when the woman pictured on the left robbed her. Even though the image includes no makeup, almost no hair showing, and a somewhat masculine type of hat, the sketch nevertheless appears feminine (courtesy of the Harris County Sheriffs Department).

feminine qualities must be aware the differences are subtle. Take the sketch in Figure 5.35 as an example. Even though the subject of the sketch is not displaying a feminine hairstyle and has no makeup, the sketch somehow succeeds in looking like a drawing of a woman.[12]

First of all, if you are lucky, the female perpetrator will have on makeup as in Figure 5.36.

Another trait that allows ease in drawing an individual to look like a woman is a feminine hairstyle and earrings. Sketching the right hairstyle on many women can achieve a likeness even if the features are not done as similarly, as in Figure 5.37, where the sketch reminded a detective in another jurisdiction

Figure 5.36

Far left: This sketch shows how easy women are to draw if they are wearing makeup and a distinctly feminine hairstyle.

Figure 5.37

Near left: Even though this sketch has the nose too long, the irises too large, the eyes too close together, the lips too far from the nose, and the chin the wrong shape, the very similar hairstyle and earrings caused a detective in another jurisdiction to recognize this woman (courtesy of the Las Vegas Metropolitan Police Department).

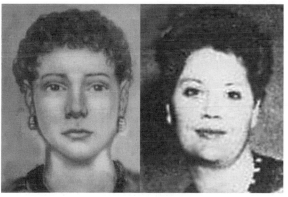

of this perpetrator. Notice the nose is too long, the irises are too large, the eyes and eyebrows are too close together, the mouth is too far away from the nose, and the chin is the wrong shape. The only things really similar are hairstyle and the earrings. These two traits were enough to help solve the case.[13]

Male forensic artists should be warned they will have the most difficulty depicting their sketches as feminine. Just as female artists will have a strong tendency to imbue their drawings with feminine traits, males will tend to draw faces with a masculine look. One vivid example of this tendency of artists to impart qualities of their gender into their drawings can be seen in Figure 5.38. The perpetrator seen at the middle top of that figure was proven to have been the attacker of the witnesses for both sketches on either side of his photo. One scene yielded a fingerprint that matched this individual, the other scene yielded DNA (deoxyribonucleic acid) that matched the individual's. Additionally both witnesses identified the subject as their attacker. The sketch on the left was done by the male artist pictured below on the left. The sketch on the right was drawn by the female artist pictured below on the right. Notice how the sketch on the left has a more masculine appearance; the sketch on the right appears more feminine. We can conclude female artists should concentrate on making their male subjects as masculine as possible. Since I am female and have established a substantial success rate, this is definitely possible. Male artists should have no problem as long as the perpetrator they are drawing is masculine, which is the case during the vast majority of forensic sketches. However, in anticipation of the cases where the perpetrator is female, such as the traumatic cases where a deranged woman kidnaps a child not her own, the male forensic artist should practice making faces look feminine, even when there is no makeup worn.

Figure 5.38

Top center: Photo of a man sketched by two artists from separate incidents. Bottom left is Officer Adrian White, who created the sketch on top left. Bottom right is the artist who drew the sketch at top right. The left sketch is more masculine, like the creator, and the sketch on the right is more feminine, like the artist who drew it (courtesy of Officer Adrian White).

Developing a collection of female photos to use as visual aids is a very good idea. However, I have been able to use the *FBI Facial Identification Catalog* to do many sketches of female perpetrators. The features are simply selected by the witness, then the hair, makeup, and a smooth forehead and rounded chin can combine to make a successful feminine sketch. Figures 5.39 and 5.40 are sketches that were created using the male examples in the *FBI Facial Identification Catalog*.

Figure 5.41 includes two sketches done on different cases. The *FBI Facial Identification Catalog* was used. The addition of a smooth brow ridge, makeup, teeth, some eyebrow tweezing, and feminine hairstyles gave them that womanly look. This is further proof it is possible to use male visual aids to create sketches of female suspects.

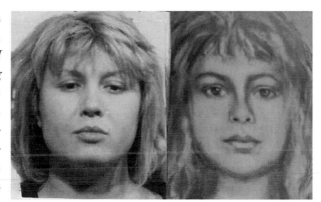

Figure 5.39

The sketch on the left was done using the male examples in the FBI *Facial Identification Catalog from which the witness picked features he thought matched the suspect on the far left. The addition of the feminine hairstyle added a distinctly feminine look (courtesy of the Houston Police Department).*

In Brief

- Be able and willing to draw the most common expressions made by criminals to their victims.
- Become proficient at drawing correct tooth anatomy for the cases when teeth are a major identifier of the suspect.
- Become proficient at drawing female suspects. The need is rare, but women commit one of the most heart-wrenching crimes: infant kidnapping.

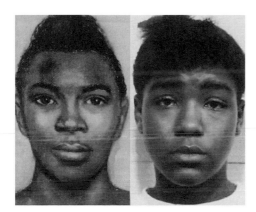

Figure 5.40

The sketch on the left was done using the male examples in the FBI Facial Identification Catalog *from which the witness picked features she thought matched the suspect on the right. A somewhat feminine hairstyle and young, smooth skin helped give the drawing a feminine look (courtesy of the Houston Police Department).*

Figure 5.41

These two sketches of women were also done using the male examples in the FBI Facial Identification Catalog. *Femininity is easily added by keeping the brow ridge smooth and the chin fairly rounded. However, the hair, makeup, and earrings lock in the female appearance.*

VEHICLES USED IN THE COMMISSION OF CRIME

Producing a get-away vehicle image for release to officers and the media can make the difference in capturing a perpetrator on the run. Modern duplication processes allow a forensic artist to produce the image of a known vehicle type quickly and easily. The problem is finding an image of the vehicle used in the crime. Often a get-away vehicle is a few years older than the catalogs of new cars available at the dealership. Greatly compounding the problem are the hundreds of thousands of different makes, years, colors, and models of vehicles that could be used by perpetrators of crimes during a forensic artist's career.

Detectives have been known to cruise parking lots of large shopping areas with a witness in tow, trying to search out just the right color and make of a vehicle used in a crime. They do this in hopes of getting an image of just the right vehicle to help in their search to solve the case.

There is a better, quicker, and easier way to produce an image of the get-away vehicle. A wise forensic artist should develop and maintain a "vehicle identification catalog" so the witness can choose the suspect's mode of transportation in the comfort of an office.

CONSUMER REPORTS *TO THE RESCUE!*

Every April, the nonprofit magazine *Consumer Reports* publishes an automotive edition like the one shown in Figure 5.42. This magazine carries photos of almost every vehicle available for purchase in the United States for that year. If you subscribe to the magazine, after about 3 or 4 years, you will have images of nearly all vehicles on the road. After a few more years, you will have a "vehicle encyclopedia" to find almost any vehicle used in the commission of a crime. The magazine's offices can be contacted to purchase back issues for those artists just starting out who wish to expand quickly into past years.

Figure 5.42

©2006 by Consumers Union of U.S., Inc. Yonkers, NY 10703–1057, a nonprofit organization. Reprinted with permission for educational purposes only. No commercial use permitted. www .ConsumerReports.org.

With these periodicals, the witness can thumb through the approximate year from which the vehicle might be. Once the type of car or truck is identified, the witness almost always can tell if he or she needs to search for an older or newer vehicle, and simply can refer to the earlier or later year's edition of the magazine. Children and some adults might not know the exact name of a manufacturer. However, it is my experience that those types of witnesses will be proficient at *recognizing* the correct vehicle when they see a photo depicting it.

As an example, I had a case where some small children witnessed a kidnapping. They said they thought the car used was a Cadillac. Once those same children viewed the *Consumer Reports* magazine, they all settled on a large older-model Buick. Photos of the vehicles make it much easier on a witness to recall the vehicle. Without vehicle photos, some witnesses would be incapable of helping the artist come up with the correct image. Just as with remembering faces, it is easier for witnesses to recognize an image than it is for them to manufacture the right language to verbally describe the vehicle.

Figure 5.43

A photo of this truck, which closely resembled the get-away vehicle in a homicide, was used to trace a line drawing. Color pastels were then used to fill in details and the unusual graphics on the back window as described by the witness to the crime. See color plate.

This is why the use of a computer scanning various vehicle web sites would be ineffective. The children who saw the Buick would have the computer operator looking through the Cadillac sites for images, and the vehicle would not be found.

Once the witness has settled on the right vehicle photo, simply scan in the image. If the color needs to be changed, there is software available on most computers where the image can be changed to the correct color. Also, the image can be traced the old-fashioned way and bumper damage or special graphics can be added as in Figures 5.43 through 5.46. These hand-drawn images were first traced from photos using an opaque projector and then colored using pastels. That process takes almost 2 hours. Scanning in an image for digital distribution takes less than a few minutes. Changing the color of the image using software takes only a few more minutes.

Figure 5.44

I obtained a photo of this truck that resembled the vehicle used in a homicide. The witness helped me fill in the truck with the correct color and had me add the chrome step and rear bumper damage. This sketch was done with pastels on felt grey Canson Mi-Tientes paper.

A third way to create an image showing alterations on the body without the lengthy hand-drawing process can be seen in Figure 5.47. This technique produces a drawing that is not virtuous, but the information needed is nevertheless conveyed. I took a photocopy of the correct image and drew the features indicated by the witness directly on the photocopy. The medium used was pastels. First a layer of pastels was drawn on, the picture was sprayed with fixative, and other layers were added and sprayed until the witness was satisfied. This particular witness said the truck had worn, oxidized red paint. The surface texture of pastels replicated that oxidized surface very well. This method took an hour less time than the hand-drawn method, and only a few moments longer than the quick scanning method.

Figure 5.45

This truck was done from a photo. The truck was sketched using an opaque projector. The witness helped me fill in the correct color and add rust damage to the rear bumper. The sketch was done with pastels on Canson Mi-Tientes paper.

Figure 5.46

Above right: The detectives of a homicide case had conflicting opinions on the color of a vehicle. They had me draw the vehicle in both colors for media release. This was accomplished by copying the photo of the vehicle using an opaque projector, Canson Mi-Tientes paper, and a pastel pencil. Colors filled in with pastels.

TATTOOS MADE FAST AND EASY

Some tattoos are so elaborate they are almost impossible to remember or describe. Even if the witness can describe an elaborate tattoo, the difficulty and skill needed for drawing the tattoo would be great and time consuming. The problem is that there are some tattoos on suspects that are such a major descriptor of that individual it is obligatory for the artist to render the image with that suspect's sketch. There is a fast and easy way to do almost any tattoo, no matter how elaborate.

GO TO THE SOURCE: YOUR LOCAL TATTOO PARLOR

Figure 5.47

I obtained a photo of this vehicle and simply sketched in the color indicated by the witness onto the surface of the photo. Additionally, I added linear graphics to the rear-side panel as indicated by the witness.

There are patterns available for purchase by commercial tattoo supply manufacturers. These suppliers have catalogs with hundreds of designs from which the tattoo artist and customer can choose. If you obtain a catalog with the same designs the local tattoo artists are using, you will then have a "tattoo encyclopedia" for the witness to peruse.

To obtain these catalogs, I visited one of the better tattoo parlors in my city. There I obtained a tattoo-themed magazine in which catalogs of patterns were advertised. For less than $20 I obtained several books with thousands of tattoo images.

Figure 5.48 shows a sketch done from an elderly woman who was brutally raped. She was feeble and had difficulty talking. The tattoo description would have been nearly impossible if I had not brought a book with tattoo patterns. The elderly woman said the tattoo was a large eagle with a snake

in its talons. I turned to the eagle section in the tattoo pattern catalog and the woman chose an image that closely resembled the tattoo of her attacker. I then enlarged the image on a copy machine and drew a snake in the eagle's talons as indicated by the witness. The finished tattoo image, modified with computer software, can be seen in Figure 5.49. Notice the inclusion of some unintelligible Old English-styled letters the witness saw positioned below the eagle. The tattoo was drawn on a small body to the side of the facial sketch, taking care to make it

Figure 5.48

This sketch was taken from an elderly woman who was brutally assaulted. The use of a tattoo-pattern catalog helped to rapidly find the right tattoo she noticed on his back.

the right size and in the right position on the suspect's body, all at the direction of the witness. The time needed for the woman to pick out the tattoo and create the image for media release was less than 15 minutes. The time to render the sketch of the face would be the same as usual with a little more time for the small tattoo-adorned body to be drawn in on the side.

For most artists, it is advisable to have a person pose to get the right proportions for a human body, even if you are practiced at life drawing. I had the female detective stand, fully clothed, to get an idea of the back, shoulders, and arms of the suspect's body image from behind.

A situation where the tattoo inclusions with the sketch were a determining factor in helping solve the case can be seen in Figures 5.50 and 5.51. The suspect had sexually assaulted a woman he had abducted on New Year's Day. The woman tricked the man into slowing down his car, and she jumped naked from the moving vehicle. She ran to a church and got help.

After creating the sketch of her attacker's face with the artist, she described the many large tattoos she had memorized that were on her attacker's body. As soon as the sketches were released, the suspect's identity was called in to authorities, mainly because the tipster recognized the tattoos.[14]

The sketch was done late at night and both witness and artist were tired. The face of the perpetrator bears a poor resemblance to the sketch. The top of the head is too narrow, the eyebrows are too long and the wrong shape, the eyes are too big, the lips are too thick, the face and the ears are too wide, and the chin is too long. However, the imperfect sketches of the tattoos prompted someone to relate the identity of the perpetrator to the detective working on the case. The face was similar enough; the tipster could not eliminate him as a suspect. Therefore, even though the only thing similar about the face sketch was the sex, race, and the fact that

Figure 5.49

The elderly witness picked out this complicated eagle design from a tattoo-pattern catalog, making the construction of the image for media release fast and easy. The modest expense of purchasing these types of catalogs can save hours of drawing during important cases.

Figure 5.50

The sketch on the left was taken from a woman who was sexually assaulted on New Year's Day. The image prompted a call identifying the man pictured on the right as the perpetrator when combined with his unique tattoos as depicted in Figure 5.51 (courtesy of the Harris County Sheriffs Department).

Figure 5.51

Even though the composite of this rapist was somewhat dissimilar, the unique tattoos taken from the witness's description helped prompt a tip to authorities when these drawings were released. Notice the accuracy of the witness's memory for these tattoos and their location (courtesy of the Harris County Sheriffs Department).

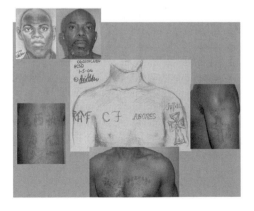

he was bald, the witness's successful efforts at memorizing her attacker's tattoos made the difference in solving the case.

Another case where brief, sketchy drawings of tattoos helped solve a case can be seen in Figure 5.52. A man began a crime spree at 9:35 P.M. Over the next 4 hours he robbed five people, carjacked three vehicles, and, at 1:30 A.M. the next day, killed a man after robbing him. Two days later the artist did a sketch from one of the robbery victims. This witness made a drawing of the type of tattoos he saw covering the entire left arm of the suspect. The artist drew a brief sketch of a left arm and included tattoos with the characteristics indicated by the witness drawing. The witness was not entirely satisfied with the tattoo depictions, but ended the interview saying it was the best that could be done.

Within days a tip came into *Crime Stoppers* from an individual who recognized a man with the same tattoos. After that suspect was interviewed, he admitted to his involvement and the case was solved.[15]

Notice the technique on the previous cases was not to render the tattoos exactly; that was not possible. Rather, the artist was given the approximate shape and nature of the tattoos. Those shapes were drawn on the area of the body indicated by the witness, and of the approximate size per their memory. This kind of identification by broad ranging tattoos must be done by also drawing the body part upon which it appears, in order to show the tattoo's placement and size.

Another case where very vague tattoo depiction helped identify a suspect is shown in Figure 5.53. This sketch was done from three witnesses who were inebriated when they saw a murder at a bar. They all described a suspect with a tattoo. They all knew the placement, which was in a wide half-circle on the upper chest, somewhat in the manner of a necklace. One witness thought there were angular lines crossing each other over the length of the necklace-type design. The artist had the witness draw a schematic of the wavy, crossing lines and determined how wide the "necklace" was, and where it was positioned on the chest.

Once the suspect was identified, detectives discovered the words "These arms of mine" written in cursive letters at about the same position on his chest as the vague tattoo in the sketch. The size and shape of such a tattoo were somewhat unusual, and the man in the photo was identified by a person who frequented the bar where the incident occurred. Even though the resemblance to the face and tattoo are vague, the combination led the detectives to question the suspect and obtain a statement where the suspect placed himself at the bar during the time of the crime. Notice the dark shadow patterns immediately under the bottom lip are the same in sketch and mug shot, and the clothing is also consistent.

Therefore, concerning tattoos, it behooves you to accept imperfection in your efforts to reconstruct the patterns and shapes of them on the suspects being described. Rather, try to get a resemblance of the shape and nature of the tattoo. Then draw the tattoo as close as possible on the correct area of the suspect's body, and in the right size, in proportion to the size of that particular body part.

Figure 5.52

The witness for this drawing made the sketch on the right of the kind of tattoos seen on the suspect. I created the arm with those kinds of tattoos, the size, and at the location indicated by the witness.

SCARS AND OTHER ANOMALIES

A forensic artist should be eager to draw any unusual trait that can help identify the suspect. Figure 5.54 shows the composite sketch of a killer, his mug shot, and the drawing of his permanently crooked finger that helped identify him to detectives.[16] Since hands are one of the most difficult features to draw, even the most practiced artist should have someone pose his or her hand in position and use that for a model from which to sketch. I had one of the witnesses pose her hand for this drawing. This was especially pertinent since the witness saw the suspect's finger and could best replicate the position. The only struggle was to draw the hand with a masculine look from a feminine witness/model.

Scars can be obvious identifiers. Figure 5.55 includes an early sketch done with a witness who was certain her attacker had a scar in his eyebrow. She was able to give a detailed description of the placement, shape, and length of the scar relative to the eyebrow. Even though this primitive sketch has the nose too long, the lips too thin, and is an overall poor rendering, the suspect's scar led officers to question him about the attack when a tipster called in his identity.[17]

The ring described by the same witness and shown in Figure 5.56 was an additional identifier since he was wearing it when authorities contacted him. I included a finger in the ring since the cat's head shape did not appear to be a piece of jewelry when simply sketched alone.

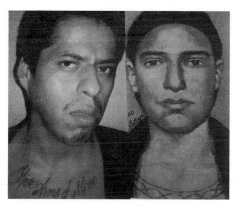

Figure 5.53

The sketch, right, bears only a vague likeness to the face and tattoo of the man on the left; all the witnesses were inebriated when witnessing the crime. The shape and location of the tattoo combined with the somewhat similar face helped detectives find the man on the left (courtesy of the Houston Police Department).

Figure 5.54

Witnesses for these sketches on the left and right said they never observed this man from the front. They claimed they only viewed him from the side. This sketch helped identify the man in the center photo (courtesy of the Montgomery County Sheriffs Department and the Shenandoah Police Department).

Figure 5.55

The sketch in the center done early in my career has many flaws. However, the scar described in the suspect's eyebrow, and the cat's-head ring drawing shown in Figure 5.56, prompted a tip that helped detectives find the perpetrator in the photos (courtesy of the Houston Police Department).

Figure 5.56

I sketched this cat's-head ring on a finger since the image did not appear to be a ring without that body part attached. The ring helped identify the suspect; he was wearing it when apprehended for a traffic infraction in a distant county (courtesy of the Houston Police Department).

JEWELRY

A forensic artist will occasionally be asked to draw unique jewelry taken in a robbery. Pastels lend themselves readily to this subject matter, so for that reason, I recommend having a supply around for just such a need. The pastel medium is easy to blend and indicate shiny, smooth areas quickly. With a little practice you can replicate the look of diamonds, gold, and precious jewels. The concise nature of most jewelry construction makes the images easy and quick to draw.

Figures 5.57 through 5.61 are renderings of jewelry done in pastel on various cases. Drawing is made easier if the jewelry is sketched larger than the actual size. In fact, it would be perfectly valid to draw the jewelry very large. This would also make the items appear in a much more virtuous manner than if you attempt to make them nearly as small as their actual size.

In Figures 5.57 and 5.59, I included an ear to make certain the viewer understood the pieces were earrings. I did not have the constraints of attempting to display the items attractively in a catalog for sale. Were that the case, the inclusion of an ear in the rendering might appear silly. However, since forensic art has a utilitarian purpose, the constraints of making the drawings attractive and tasteful are not involved. For this reason, I included an awkward-looking finger in the drawing of Figure 5.56. The point is not to sell the item of jewelry; instead, the drawing needs to make it clear what kind of item is pictured.

A visual aid for drawing realistic jewelry would be to save those glossy catalogs sent by various retail chains. Ask any male who has purchased an engagement ring to save the catalogs, or buy an item and save the glossy, finely photographed jewelry catalogs that subsequently come in the mail. A small collection of these will aid you in depicting shiny silver, gold, diamonds, and other precious stones. This could also be a springboard for a witness to show how the stolen item resembled or was different from an item shown in the catalog.

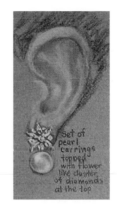

Figure 5.57

This unique earring taken in a robbery was drawn in pastels on felt-gray Canson Mi-Tientes paper. An ear was included to make certain the viewer knew the jewelry item was an earring.

Figure 5.58

This drawing of some unusually colored pearls taken in a large jewelry robbery was done in pastels on felt-gray Canson Mi-Tientes paper. Pastels are ideal for rendering shiny objects.

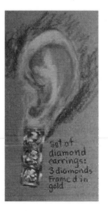

Figure 5.59

This unusual earring was drawn with an ear to make certain the viewer knew the jewelry item was an earring. The medium used was pastels on felt-gray Canson Mi-Tientes paper.

Figure 5.60

These two rings were stolen from a police officer after he was murdered. The medium used, pastels on felt-gray Canson Mi-Tientes paper, is ideal for drawing shiny objects.

Figure 5.61

This unusual watch taken in a robbery/homicide was drawn with pastels on felt-gray Canson Mi-Tientes paper.

In Brief

- Subscribing to the nonprofit magazine *Consumer Reports* is recommended. The April issues contain photos of almost every type of vehicle available for purchase in the country that year. In time (or through ordering back issues), you will have a comprehensive vehicle encyclopedia. The witness can find the right vehicle in moments, and you can copy the image in seconds.
- Obtain catalogs of tattoo patterns to help the witness easily find the right pattern, and to help you quickly replicate the tattoo through electronic copying. For vague tattoos, simulate their shape and size on the correct part of the suspect's body.
- Drawing unusual pieces of jewelry is quick and easy with a little practice and with the aid of catalogs advertising finely photographed pieces. Pastels are the recommended medium.

REFERENCES

1. Harris County Sheriffs Case Number 92031901116.

2. Ed Asher, "Groups uniting in effort to find abductor of boy," *Houston Chronicle*, February 19, 2001. Peggy O'Hare, "Ex-con charged in sexual assault of 6-year-old boy," *Houston Chronicle*, February 27, 2001. Peggy O'Hare, "System didn't stop sex offender/ Assault suspect was on parole but broke rules, records show," *Houston Chronicle*, June 3, 2001. Houston Police Department Incident Number 18924701. Houston Police Department Incident Number 096854503.

3. Staff, "Police seek slaying suspect," *Houston Chronicle*, March 10, 1987. Burke Watson, "Slain woman would have given the shirt off her back, pastor says," *Houston Chronicle*, March 7, 1987. Steven Long, " 'Most Wanted' in Houston/TV crime show turns camera on gang shootout, killing," *Houston Chronicle*, January 15, 1990. Jennifer Liebrum, "Witness helps police crack puzzling 1987 murder case," *Houston Chronicle*, June 4, 1989. Staff, "Slaying solved," *Houston Chronicle*, June 4, 1989. Staff, "Man charged in death of woman who was run over," *Houston Chronicle*, June 11, 1989.

4. Harris County Sheriffs Case Number 9106260314.

5. Lisa Teachey and Stephen Johnson, "Off-duty officer slain at family's store," *Houston Chronicle*, April 7, 1997. S. K. Bardwell, "HPD hopes $21,000 reward helps to solve officer's killing," *Houston Chronicle*, April 8, 1997. Lisa Teachey, "Police chief requests aid in solving officer's slaying," *Houston Chronicle*, June 8, 1997. Jerry Urban and Ron Nissimov, "Suspect charged in slaying of HPD officer," *Houston Chronicle*, August 15, 1997. Jo Ann Zuniga, "Vietnam refugee sentenced to die for clerk's killing," *Houston Chronicle*, March 12, 1998. Houston Police Department Incident Number 43386597.

6. Houston Police Department Photo Lab Number 56195, sketched April 24, 1997. Houston Police Department Incident Number 153207098. Houston Police Department Incident Number 164771505. Houston Police Department Incident Number 156847298. Houston Police Department Photo Lab Number 56195, sketched May 6, 1997. Baytown Police Department Case Number 92-4977.

7. Houston Police Department Incident Number 185536603.

8. Laurie Ledgard, "Police seek suspect in shooting of 2," *The Houston Post*, July 20, 1992. Staff, "Gunfire kills teen-ager," *Houston Chronicle*, July 20, 1992. Staff, "Man handed 60-year term in shootings," *The Houston Post*, July 8, 1994. Houston Police Department Incident Number 77666692.

9. Houston Police Department Incident Number 81470097.

10. Houston Police Department Incident Number 164771505.

11. S. K. Bardwell and Eric Hanson, "A babe in arms/Kidnap suspect may have been delusional," *Houston Chronicle*, October 25, 1995. Houston Police Department Incident Number 12217669512. Jack Douglas, "Abducted tot found unharmed/Alleged kidnapper in custody," *The Houston Post*, November 18, 1987. Harris County Sheriffs Case Number 87215672. Burk Watson, "Officers rescue baby snatched from center," *Houston Chronicle*, November 18, 1987.

12. I.J. Milling, "Female robber was lucky, not skillful, police believe," *Houston Chronicle*, February 9, 1996. Houston Police Department Incident Number 148455095.

13. Houston Police Department Incident Number 123534790.

14. Staff, "Man is sought in abduction, rape," *Houston Chronicle*, January 6, 2006. Staff, "Man is charged in rape, abduction," *Houston Chronicle*, January 10, 2006. Harris County Sheriffs Case Number 060101C680.

15. Mike Glenn, "Victim's family weeps: 'Get these murderers,'" *Houston Chronicle*, July 28, 2003. S. K. Bardwell, "Shooting raises Richmond strip fears," *Houston Chronicle*, July 29, 2003. Peggy O'Hare, "Suspect in crime spree admits role; 2 still sought," *Houston Chronicle*, August 8, 2003. Harris County Sheriffs Case Number 0307270018. Houston Police Department Incident Number 105209303.

16. Paul McKay, "Sketch of witness released/He was last seen with missing motel clerk," *Houston Chronicle*, January 29, 1999. Harvey Rice, "Man in motel clerk's disappearance linked to another case in '91". Harvey Rice, "Searchers find skull of missing desk clerk," *Houston Chronicle*, February 11, 2000. Harvey Rice, "Slaying victim named 'Sunshine' buried/Wanda May Pitts cared for others, family says," *Houston Chronicle*, February 27, 2000. Montgomery County Sheriff's Case Number 00A003108.

17. Staff, "Police question suspect in Astrodome-area rapes/The man, listed as Bobby Morrison in charges filed Sunday, was returned to Houston after Chambers County authorities recognized him from composite drawings released to the media." *Houston Chronicle*, January 26, 1988. Houston Police Department Incident Number 004332188.

CHAPTER 6

AGE PROGRESSION AND POSTMORTEM: PORTRAITS OF UNIDENTIFIED HOMICIDE COMPLAINANTS

Almost every law enforcement agency has a suspect for whom they have a name and photo, but whom they do not have in custody. Many times those suspects escape for years. The trail may go cold, but crime victims and their loved ones still want justice. Investigators will then turn to the forensic artist with the fugitive's photo and ask for a portrait of that individual with the proper number of years added.

Everyone takes particular notice of the age we see on our own faces. The age that takes place on others' faces can be understood and drawn if certain guidelines are understood.

THE SHAPES AND POSITIONS OF THE FACIAL ORIFICES

The openings in the face—the nostrils, eye openings, crease or dark line where the lips meet—stay almost the identical shape even during many years of aging. In other words, age progression portraits can be successful if the right amount of aging is incorporated into the fleshy areas *around* the orifices. These orifices also remain in the same position on the face, relative to the other facial features, after bone growth has ceased. For example, if someone has eyes that are close together and lips that are fairly distant from the nose, these traits will remain the same as the years go by.

Like all rules, there will be small exceptions to the orifices staying the same shape. One exception is the shape of the nostril openings when the individual approaches the elderly years. Because it consists of cartilage, the end of the nose elongates and enlarges slightly during the entirety of an individual's life. For this reason, persons much past their 50s will have a nose tip that extends down toward the nostrils, obscuring them more than in the individual's youth. If the age progression does not go past the mid-50s, this nostril distortion will not be significant.

Another exception would be if the suspect has lost many or all of his or her teeth. This will cause the fleshy areas around the mouth to cave in. Major tooth loss will also cause the mouth to appear closer up toward the nose. However, if the suspect being age progressed has a modicum of funds, in the United States it would be most common for the dentition loss to be replaced by some kind of prosthesis. All areas of the United States have dentists readily available who can provide partial removable appliances, permanent tooth replacements, and even full dentures, to replace lost teeth. Since these replacement teeth mimic the original dentition, the dark line where the lips meet will stay the same shape, and the mouth will appear to be the same distance from the nose.

ADULT WRINKLES AND PLACEMENT ARE PRESENT ON A CHILD'S FACE

The beginnings of adult wrinkles can be seen in a child's face. Careful observation of a subject at a younger age will show the placement of smooth areas of flesh as they dent in under the eyes, around the corners of mouths, and such. These smooth folds of flesh do not change their location, direction, or appreciable difference in shape as the individual grows older. Those same folds simply turn into creases with age and eventually are considered wrinkles. Wrinkles will deepen and thus appear darker as time passes. After much aging those wrinkles might sag a bit lower, but they will be in the same place and follow the same direction as when the subject was young.

These two standards are vividly illustrated by Figure 6.1. At the center top is a Caucasian male aged 24. To the left is the same person at age one. Notice the 1-year-old boy has smooth folds under his eyes and around his mouth. To the right of the male is another photo of him at age six months, where the same folds under the eyes can be clearly seen. The 3-month-old baby photo of him shows the identical folds under the eyes, and even the photo of him at 5 days old at the bottom right shows the beginnings of these under-the-eye folds. If you look closely at the baby photos, the beginnings of the folds outside the corners of the mouth can also be seen. As a man in his 20s, these fleshy folds are the same distance from the eyes and mouth, relative to those features' size, and have the same curvature as when he was a baby. The only difference is his bones have elongated his face from the eyes down and the folds have begun to turn to wrinkles. If an artist needed to create a portrait of this individual at a more advanced age, the wrinkles would simply be made more noticeable by an amount commensurate to the targeted age. The ways the wrinkles become more noticeable are by deepening and developing an actual crease or even an overlapping fold instead of making a smooth undulation.

The nostril holes, eye openings, and crease in the lips also stay the same shape as this male matures from only days to decades old. Even the eyebrows are the same shape; the difference is the darkening of his facial hair as he passes through puberty. Notice the asymmetry of the eyes, eyebrows, and lines under the eyes stays the same. Said differently, if an eyebrow arches up higher and at a different angle above one eye on a child, this pattern will be the same when he is an adult.

The applications of these principles were successfully utilized in the case illustrated by Figure 6.2. This case involves Ora Lott, who murdered a Houston,

Figure 6.1

The beginnings of wrinkles seen in the 24-year-old male at the center top photo can be seen in his younger photos. From top left he was approximately 2 years, top right 6 months, bottom left 3 months, and bottom right 5 days old (photos by author). See color plate.

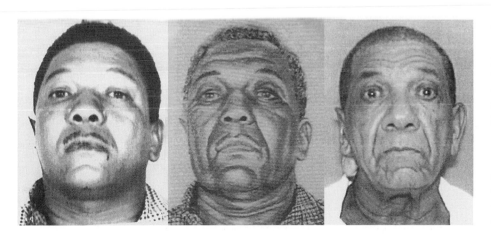

Figure 6.2

The 33-year-old man pictured on the left got away with murder for 30 years. After detectives had me create the age-progression portrait of him at age 63, shown in the center, they were able to track him down within days living in a nearby state (Photo on right courtesy of the Houston Police Department.) See color plate.

Texas, shop owner in front of that man's brother and 11-year-old boy during a robbery of the victim's store in 1964. The police discovered the murderer's identity and the two witnesses positively identified him from a photo-spread line-up. After his positive identification by the brother and son of the victim, detectives were unable to apprehend Lott, and he slipped away. Leads grew cold and other crimes took up the attention of the small group of Houston police detectives working in 1964.

Thirty years later in 1994, the grown son of Lott's murder victim approached the Houston Police Department and asked them to reopen the case. I was given a photo of Ora Lott at age 33 and asked to create a portrait of how he would appear at age 63. The result is the sketch shown in Figure 6.2.

I left the shape of the eye, nostril, and mouth openings the same and aged the fleshy areas around those openings to the level of an African-American male in his mid-60s.

The method used was to gather images of black males in their mid-60s and incorporate that amount of wrinkling and sagging onto the face of the 33-year-old man in the photo. Since Lott was a large, almost overweight person in the earlier photo of him, I assumed he would be average weight, rather than extremely thin in his older age. The hair was kept the same short length since that was the current style for almost all males at the time. A little gray hair was added.

The sketch was completed September 2, 1994, and given to detectives. Investigators from the Gulf Coast Violent Offenders Task Force used the sketch and were able to arrest him in a nearby state on September 30, 1994. Lott answered his door and denied who he was. When he was shown the sketch, he submitted to the arrest with no objection. He told the arresting officers "…he knew he'd done something wrong thirty years ago."[1]

Even though the sketch in Figure 6.1 helped solve the case, there are many mistakes that you can avoid:

- The cartilage of the suspect's nose had grown, making the end longer, bigger, and the nostril holes slightly obscured.
- I failed to add glasses to a man in his 60s. This could have been done easily by drawing them on treated acetate and photographing them on the drawing. Then the detectives could have had an image of the suspect with glasses and without.
- The lips tend to thin during the aging process. Even though the opening stays the same shape, the lips on such an elderly suspect should be drawn thinner. Since I drew the lips as thick as in the photo of Lott at age 33, they were thicker than the suspect's lips at age 63.

Thus, if the glasses had been added, the nose made larger with a tip that droops down more, and the lips made thinner, the sketch would have been very close.

VISUAL AIDS FOR THE SUCCESSFUL AGE-PROGRESSION DRAWING

Besides drawing the nose, eyes, and mouth openings the same shape, the key to successful age-progression drawings is using appropriate visual aids. No artist can possibly have charts for the amount of wrinkling, sagging, and other indications of age you might see on an individual's face. The amount of aging would vary according to race, sex, lifestyle, and the number of years involved, which can vary greatly from one fugitive to another.

Deciding on what amount of aging to draw into the suspect's portrait can be made simple by obtaining two kinds of photos. First, of course, you will have the photo of the known fugitive. Then, you should find a photo of another individual of very similar sex, race, and age as the fugitive's. This other "comparison individual" must be one for whom you have another photo at the age to which the suspect needs to be progressed.

As an example, if the suspect is a Caucasian male aged 21 in the photo and his age now is 36, get photos of a similar Caucasian male at age 21 and age 36. Then the drawing of the suspect should be created, with the photo of the similar individual at ages 21 and 36 placed in view. You can then incorporate the amount of aging shown in the comparison photos into the face of the suspect.

This method makes the age progression customized to the case at hand. This kind of work is infrequent for almost all forensic artists. Also, each case needs to be highly customized. Therefore, you only need to find a comparison individual and a photo of that person at the "target age" for each case as they arise.

HOW TO BECOME PROFICIENT AT AGE PROGRESSION

There is a fail-proof method by which an artist can become quite proficient at age progressions. Obtain photos of individuals when they are young adults. Make certain there are photos of those same individuals at older ages, such as 30s and 40s, but do not look at the older-aged photos. Then draw portraits of the younger individuals age-progressed to the age they are in the unseen photos. Once finished, obtain the photo of the subject at the older age. Compare your age-progression portrait to the photo of the person at the target age and practice self-criticism to understand what mistakes were made. Once you have understood what you did wrong, repeat the process with a set of photos of another individual.

Since the majority of fugitives you will work with are male, it would be best to practice with male subjects. Also, since almost no suspects will be extremely elderly, the older photos would be more representative of work

Figure 6.3

I obtained the photo of a subject at age 18 on the left and created the drawing of him age-progressed to 31 years as shown in the center. Colleagues then produced a photo of the subject at age 31 shown on the right (courtesy of the Houston Police Department). See color plate.

needed if they were in their 30s, 40s, or 50s. Figure 6.3 shows one such practice age-progression I performed. The subject was 18 in the photo used. I attempted to portray him at age 31 since I knew colleagues had a photo of him at that age in their files.

The mechanics of my work on this practice were as follows. First, I traced the image of the man at age 18 as exactly as possible. This "tracing" was done with an overhead opaque projector, specifically an Artograph 1000 K. The sketch was done with a Carb-Othello-Stabillo-Schwann pencil no. 59 (a neutral brown color) on felt gray Canson Mi-tientes paper. The traced drawing was taped to the drawing board on the easel. A photo of a black male in his early 30s was taped next to the drawing as a reference while filling in the details of the face. During the first part of the drawing, attempts were made to create a portrait as much like the photo of the subject at age 18 as possible. Pastel sticks were used for the larger areas such as forehead, cheeks, and chin. Then I emphasized lines that already existed, and caused the cheeks and chin to sag a bit. Notice the lines that barely could be seen on the 18-year-old male were made slightly deeper and longer for his portrait at age 31. The jowl areas were shown to droop slightly. After completing my attempt, I sprayed fixatif on the drawing and photographed it. At that time I obtained the photo of the man at age 31.

Although the age-progression sketch appears quite similar to the photo of the man at the older age, I practiced self-criticism and found the following flaws:

- Even though he was only aged 31, the end of his nose seems slightly larger; the drawing fails to depict this, even though I was aware all nose endings grow throughout an individual's life since they consist of cartilage.
- The drawing included the same lighting, but failed to highlight the filtrum area in the center, thus making it dissimilar at that point with the photo of the subject at the older age.

- At 31, the subject had longer, deeper wrinkles under his eyes than in the age-progression sketch.
- The top of the head in the sketch is wider than in the photo. This is simply due to sloppy tracing technique.
- I failed to replicate the extraordinary thick curly eyelashes seen in the photo at 18 years; at age 31, the subject still had these.

This kind of criticism, where you examine the discrepancies bit by bit, is the only way you can improve and avoid repeating mistakes. If you perform enough of these practices, you will become extremely adept at age-progression portraits.

These practices are an important way to enable you to become proficient at age-progression portraits before you receive a real case. You can also refine the materials and supplies used. Take note of the mistake in Figure 6.2, and use treated acetate to add glasses, mustaches, and/or beards to the basic drawing. Images can be made with all the various scenarios of how the suspect might look. One sketch could even depict the individual as balding or bald if there are indicators that might be the case.

Before starting an age-progression sketch of a fugitive, gather all the information possible about the suspect's lifestyle to aid in the decisions of how to portray fat content (or lack thereof) on the face. These lifestyle tendencies will also influence the amount of skin aging, hair, and clothing style.

Figure 6.4 illustrates a successful age-progression sketch that helped bring in a murderer wanted for 14 years.

This perpetrator posted a large bail after his arrest for a particularly horrifying murder. He shot a man multiple times when the victim tried to stop him from

Figure 6.4

The man pictured left committed a heinous murder and had been a fugitive for 14 years. I created the drawing in the center, age-progressing him to 53 years old. When the drawing was shown on the nationally televised **Unsolved Mysteries** *show he was found. (Photo on right courtesy of the Pasadena Police Department.) See color plate.*

masturbating in front of neighborhood children. When the wounded victim tried to get away, he followed him and shot him again while the victim's mother held his bleeding body. He then retrieved *another* firearm from his vehicle and shot the victim several more times as the victim's sister drove up. In the ensuing chase with police, he tried to shoot a pursuing officer, but his rifle jammed.

After posting bail he was able to liquidate hundreds of thousands of dollars in assets and flee the country.

Since I knew this murderer was a savvy businessman with plentiful assets, I sketched him as if he had maintained his weight. The fugitive was obviously a pedophile since he was naked from the waist down and masturbating in front of neighborhood children at the time the victim approached him. Because I observed many pedophiles to be meticulous about their appearance, I portrayed him as clean-shaven. I also added the popular hairstyle of the time for men in late middle age.

The mechanics for this sketch were first to trace the fugitive's face with an Artograph 1000 K opaque projector, approximately life-size, on Canson Mi-tientes paper using a Carb-Othello-Stabillo-Schwann pencil in color no. 59. After first drawing a portrait duplicating the suspect's photo, the features were aged to resemble a male in his early 50s. Already existent lines were deepened and emphasized. The flesh along the bottom of the mandible was made to sag. The neck was shown to sag more than the subject's had in his 30s. These changes were done with pastels or pastel pencils in neutral shades of warm gray. The most common color used was different shades of raw umber.

The age-progression sketch shown in Figure 6.4 was released on the nationwide television show *Unsolved Mysteries*, where crimes are reenacted dramatically in an effort to bring in fugitives. A man watching the show had just seen this fugitive in Panama and related his location to authorities.[2]

The man was extradited back to Texas, tried, and sentenced to 70 years in prison. Happily this portrait, although it had many flaws, was nevertheless able to help find a murderer who fled far from the scene of his crime and hid for 14 years. Practicing constructive self-criticism, I noted the following:

- The hairstyle was far off; the man wore a wig due to extensive hair loss.
- The end of the nose had gotten larger due to cartilage growth; this was not reflected enough in the sketch.
- Due to ambiguous lighting in the nose-bridge area, that part was drawn too thick.
- The flesh on his neck sagged more toward the front.
- The fat content in the face was accurate and the amount of wrinkling was consistent with the fugitive at his current age.
- The ears were correctly shaped and adequately large, even though they were mostly unseen under hair in the source photo.

Sometimes the artist will not have the ability to accurately guess the changes that might occur in a fugitive's appearance. One such case is illustrated in Figures 6.5 and 6.6. The detective had searched for this homicide suspect for more than a dozen years. He was certain this man, Michael Blane Brashar, had raped and murdered 14-year-old Lisa Dawn Hoag in 1982. The detectives took blood from Brashar that year while he was in custody.

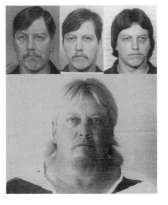

Figure 6.5

At the top left is the age progression of murderer Michael Blane Brashar created from the source photos. The center top photo is Brashar at age 26. The top right photo is Brashar at age 21. The bottom photo is Brashar aged 42 after capture (courtesy of the Houston Police Department).

Brashar disappeared for 20 years. The detective had no cause to obtain a warrant for Brashar's arrest, despite overwhelming suspicion that Brashar was a killer. However, in 2002, DNA advances allowed a match to be made with Brashar's blood and evidence found on Lisa Dawn Hoag's body.

The detective had the artist create an age progression of Brashar, in hopes of finding him. The task involved using photos of Brashar at ages 21 and 26 and creating an image of him at age 42. The artist created the age-progression drawing and the image was released on the television show *America's Most Wanted* on October of 2003. The detectives received a tip from the show and located Brashar in a small town near Birmingham, Alabama.[3]

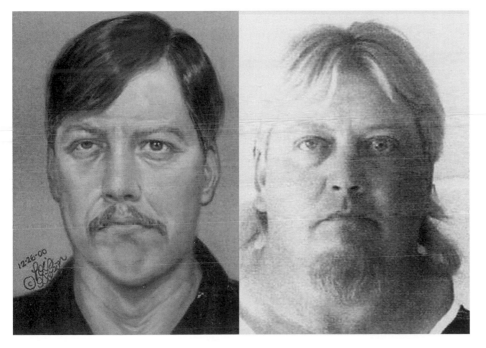

Figure 6.6

The comparison of the age-progression drawing (left) and Brashar after his capture (right) shows that, in spite of the significant weight gain and hair changes, the core features were rendered quite similar (courtesy of the Houston Police Department). See color plate.

As you can see in Figures 6.5 and 6.6, Brashar had gained a great deal of body fat. He had shaved his mustache and grown a goatee. He had bleached his eyebrows, beard, and head hair. Because of these efforts on the fugitive's part to disguise his identity, the age progression drawing appears dissimilar. Nevertheless, the image was accurate enough to prompt a tip to authorities that helped bring the obese, bleached-blond fugitive back to face justice.

Once again I practiced self-criticism and observed the following:

- Despite the altered appearance from weight gain and bleached hair, the features were aged to a good degree of accuracy.

AGE PROGRESSION OF CHILDREN: FACIAL BONE GROWTH

Age progression of adults is mostly a matter of fleshy changes on the surface. The basic frameworks of the features, which are the bones, remain the same after individuals reach adulthood. Age progressing children offers a greater challenge. The pressure to solve this kind of case can be great as it may involve a kidnapping from grieved parents. The fact that the bones of an individual's face grow constantly from birth to adulthood represents a great degree of complexity to the artist attempting such a task. The growth of the facial bones is drastic. Adults' foreheads occupy one-third of their vertical facial length; babies' foreheads occupy one-half. Added to this is the fact that children's eyeballs are almost identical in size to adults, yet their chins are a fraction of the adult chin size. Another vast appearance change occurs when children lose their deciduous teeth in sequence, to be replaced by adult teeth, while their maxillary and mandible bones simultaneously grow larger.

Figure 6.7 gives a basic comparison of a newborn, a 3-year-old, and an adult skull. Notice the drastic change in the ratio of forehead to the eyes-nose-mouth complex. Observing Figure 6.8, you can see the drastic difference in length from the bottom of the eyes to the bottom of the chin when comparing a 6-month-old boy's face to the face of an adult male who is related.

Figures 6.9 through 6.18 show a male and female from a few days old to late teens and early 20s, where the facial bone growth is finished. Notice the continual lengthening of the face from the eyes down. The forehead will stay about the same height compared to the width of the eyes, yet the nose, the distance of the lips from the nose, and the chin will constantly grow longer. Finally, after the chin finishes lengthening, the sides of the mandible, or the jowl area, will thicken or grow wider.

Notice how the shapes that remain constant are the shapes of the eye openings, nostril holes, and mouth openings. Even when the mouth is closed, the dark line where the lips meet stays the same shape from child to adult. Any forensic artist can make these same kinds of comparisons by obtaining family photos of individuals at various successive ages.

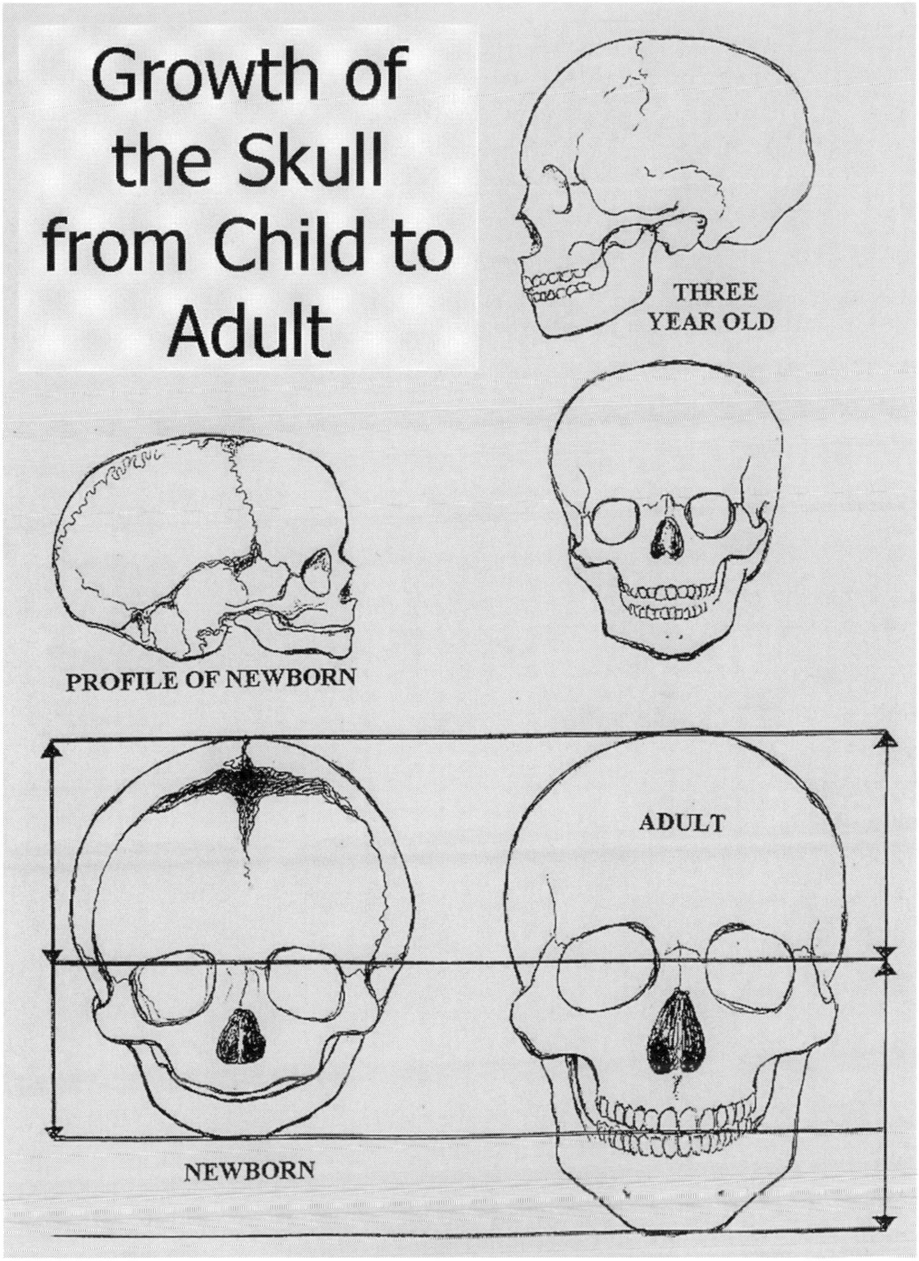

Growth of the Skull from Child to Adult

THREE YEAR OLD

PROFILE OF NEWBORN

ADULT

NEWBORN

Figure 6.7

A child's skull continues to elongate from the bottom of the eyes to the chin as he or she grows toward adulthood. As illustrated here the vertical length of a child's head is one-half eyes to chin, and one-half forehead. The vertical length of an adult's face is one-third forehead, and two-thirds eyes to chin.

Figure 6.8

Portrait of my 6-month-old son with his father shows the proportional differences of the extremes in ages. The adult's forehead takes up one third of his face; the baby's forehead takes up half of the face (pastel on Canson paper, 16" × 20").

Figure 6.9

From left to right are a female Caucasian aged 1½ days, 3 months, 6 months, and 1 year (photos by author).

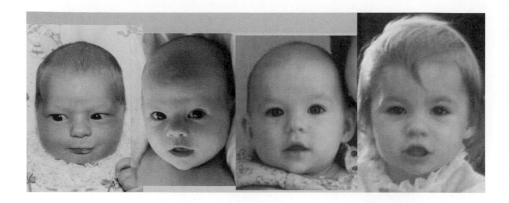

Figure 6.10

From left to right are the same female Caucasian as in Figure 6.9, aged 2, 3, 4, and 5 years (photos by author).

Figure 6.11

From left to right are the same female Caucasian as in Figure 6.9, aged 6, 7, 8, and 9 years (photos by author).

COPING WITH THE DRASTIC CHANGES

There are methods to successfully age-progress children. First of all, the rule "Shapes of the facial orifices stay the same" holds true. Even during all the changes from baby to adult, the openings in the face, the nostrils, eye openings, and crease or dark line where the lips meet, stay the same shape. Therefore, the age progression of a child involves keeping the facial orifices the same, while elongating the bones of the face to the correct length.

The quandary is, how do you gauge the correct amount of bone growth to be depicted in a child age-progression portrait? The answer is somewhat the same as for the adult age-progression drawings. Obtain a photo of a child with

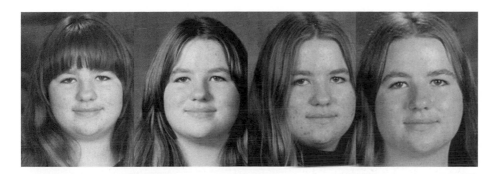

Figure 6.12

From left to right are the same female Caucasian mentioned previously aged 10, 11, 12, and 13 years (photos by author).

Figure 6.13

From left to right are the same female Caucasian mentioned previously aged 14, 15, 16, and 17 years (photos by author).

a similar appearance to the age of the child you are attempting to age-progress. Then obtain another photo of the same child at the age to which the subject needs to be progressed. Even though the comparison photos can be from persons not related to the child, it is preferable to have photos of the child's closest relatives for these comparisons. Family members can tell you whether the child to be sketched looked more like the father, the mother, a brother, and so on, and then provide photos of those similar-looking relatives.

An example of this kind of comparison can be seen in Figures 6.19, 6.20, and 6.21. If you needed to age-progress the 5-year-old boy in the photo on the right of Figure 6.19 to the age of about 16 years, family members might tell you that the boy closely resembled the mother in the photo on the left of that same figure. You could then obtain a photo of the mother near the target age of 16, as shown in Figure 6.20, and sketch the boy with that same amount of bone growth. Another comparison of the mother at age 19 and son at age 17 is shown in Figure 6.21. Notice the eyebrows of both subjects grew much darker and thicker after puberty. If you are attempting an age progression from childhood past pubescent age, you should inquire about such facial-hair changes before doing the sketch. Otherwise, if the very fine, light-brown eyebrow hairs from the child photos in Figure 6.16 were retained, the sketch would be drastically dissimilar to the subject in Figure 6.20 and 6.21.

Figure 6.14

From left to right are a Caucasian male aged 5 days, 3 months, 6 months, 9 months, and 2 years (photos by author).

Figure 6.15

From left to right are the previously shown Caucasian male aged 3, 4, 5, and 6 years (photos by author).

Figure 6.16

From left to right are the previously shown Caucasian male aged 7, 8, 9, and 10 years (photos by author).

Another example of family photos that can be used for a reference is shown in Figure 6.22. The family knows the little girl, shown here on the right at age 3, looks very similar to the father shown on the left at the same age. In order to age progress the little girl to 11 years, a photo of the father at 11 years of age, like the one on the left of Figure 6.23, could be obtained from the family. The amount of that bone growth added to the little girl's face would allow for a sketch similar to the image on the right of Figure 6.23.

However, as seen in Figure 6.24, further complications could arise if the case involves abduction by a noncustodial parent. If the age progression were to be from 2 years to 18 years, the parent might have had enough funds to obtain braces and close the gap in the center top teeth (diastema). Other complications would arise from the fact that, even though most of her features resembled her father's, this particular girl inherited her mother's dark eyelashes. The girl also inherited darker eyebrow hairs as she passed into

Figure 6.17
From left to right are the previously shown Caucasian male aged 12, 14, 16, and 17 years (photos by author).

Figure 6.18
From left to right are the previously shown Caucasian male aged 18, 19, and 20 years (photos by author).

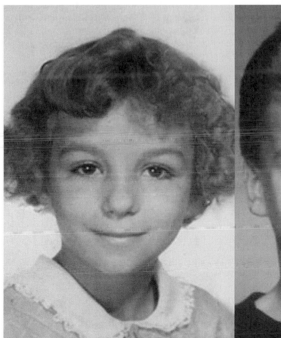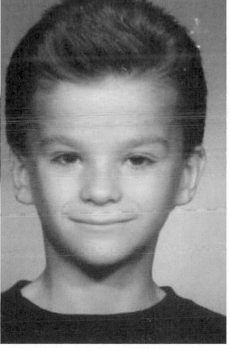

Figure 6.19
From left to right are a mother and son who bear a close family resemblance, both at age 5.

Figure 6.20

A son and his mother both aged 18.

Figure 6.21

The mother aged 19 and her son aged 17. Notice the nearly identical eyebrow shapes.

Figure 6.22
A father and his daughter, both aged 3. Notice the eyebrows are almost identical in their asymmetry. One eyebrow is more arched than the other. The eye shapes are the same. The general shape of the face and coloring are the same. The lips are nearly identical. See color plate.

Figure 6.23
This is the same father and daughter as Figure 6.22 aged 11 and 9, respectively. Notice the dentition is nearly identical, with a diastema and slightly spaced lateral incisors. The father's chin is much longer and the daughter's eyebrows and eyelashes are darker than her father's. See color plate.

Figure 6.24

From left to right are a father aged 11, his daughter, aged 9 then 18, respectively, and her mother at age 19. Notice that braces have closed the diastema in the daughter's teeth. The daughter also inherited her mother's dark eyebrow and eyelash hairs and short chin. See color plate.

puberty (the girl in Figure 6.24 is not wearing eyebrow pencil). It can be seen in the center-right photo the subject has manually tweezed hairs from her brows, significantly changing their shape. And lastly, she never obtained the long vertical growth in her mandible like her father; instead she inherited her mother's smaller chin.

You could quiz the family members to understand the dark eyelash inheritance. This information could also be understood by careful study of the baby photo comparing the daughter to her father. However, the eyebrow darkness could hardly be guessed, and the growth of the chin would be difficult to speculate.

There is only one method available if familial photos are not obtainable. You could procure at least one, and perhaps several, images of similar-appearing children at (1) the age the subject is now and (2) the age to which the subject needs to be progressed. Then lightly trace a drawing depicting the subject of the photo at the current age. From that source, imbue the amount of aging and bone growth seen on the photo(s) of the individual(s) at the "target" age. You could even use photos of children at a younger age and photos of children at the target age with the eyes *the same size* and literally measure the percentage of bone growth from the eyes down. You could then draw the subject with this same percentage of bone growth.

As an example, if you have the photo of a 6-year-old boy who needs to be drawn as he would appear at age 12, simply obtain a photo of a similar boy at ages 6 and 12. First, lightly trace the image of the 6-year-old boy who is to be age-progressed on the drawing paper. Then tape the paper on the drawing board and fasten the photo of the similar-looking boy at age 12 next to the traced drawing. Proceed to draw the same amount of bone growth seen on the 12-year-old onto the subject, making certain to keep the facial orifices the same shape. If you wish, photos of the similar boy from ages 12 and 6 can be measured against each other. Then the subject can be drawn with the same percentage of bone growth, or lengthening from the eyes down as shown in the similar boy's photos.

THE EYE OPENING

The iris occupies more of the eye opening the younger an individual is. The eye opening is almost entirely taken up by iris in the youngest babies. The iris of the eye becomes smaller, relative to the opening, as an individual grows toward adulthood. Finally, an adult has an eye opening whose surface appears to be about one-half iris, and one-half sclera, or white of the eye.

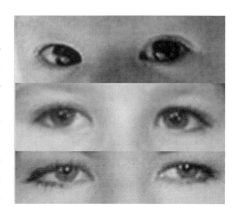

Figure 6.25 shows the same female individual's eyes at 3 months on top, at 6 years in the middle, and at 16 years of age on the bottom. Notice how almost the entire eye opening of the baby consists of iris, the child has far less eye opening taken up by iris, and finally in the adult photo, the iris occupies about half of the surface of the eye opening.

Since the iris tends to push the opening into a rounded shape when the baby makes a typical animated expression, some might think the baby has rounder eye openings. However, Figure 6.26 shows that if a baby relaxes his or her eyelids, the eye opening will be the same shape as when he or she grows to adulthood. The eyes at the top of Figure 6.26 are the same shape (although more closed) as the eyes of the same individual as an adult on the bottom. At the top he is 3 months old, and at the bottom he is an adult.

The decision as to what ratio of iris-to-sclera to draw can be determined by replicating the ratio in the "target" age photo. It would be tedious and overwhelming to make a chart on these ratios. Since most forensic artists will construct age progression portraits on rare occasions, you only need to wait for this kind of work to appear, and gather the appropriate visual aids for that particular case.

Some artists who do age progressions of children exclusively perform the task on computer software. The National Center for Missing and Exploited Children (NCMEC) is a revered nonprofit corporation established in the United States in 1964. The mission of this organization is to find missing children, and to prevent child abduction, molestation, and sexual exploitation. The personnel there who create age progressions of abducted children perform their tasks using computer

Figure 6.25

Top to bottom: Eyes from the same female aged 3 months, 6 years, and 18 years, respectively. Notice how the infant eye opening is almost all iris, more white or sclera showing at 6 years, and at age 18, the iris occupies only half of the eye opening (photos by author). See color plate.

Figure 6.26

The top and bottom photos are eyes from the same male aged 3 months and as an adult, respectively. Notice the eye shape stays the same; the difference is the baby's iris occupies more of the eye opening than the adult's (photos by author).

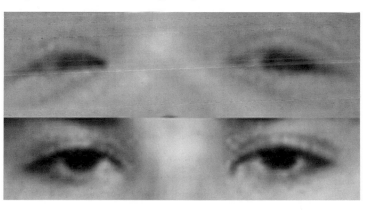

imaging. These professionals of child age progression use the latest image-manipulating software. They combine either photos of family members of the child, or strangers from their database who closely resemble the child, to construct their images. The professionals at NCMEC produce highly accurate images. Their work can be seen nationwide in mailings and national crime fighting television shows.

However, unless you are quite versed at using the software for image manipulation, the hand-drawn method could be quicker. Additionally, if you age progress by hand drawing, you can attempt to customize the older features to resemble the subject in those subtle ways they might differ from their relatives. An example of this would be the darker eyelashes and eyebrows of the girl in Figure 6.24. If a computer operator simply morphed the image of the father's eyes and eyebrows onto the daughter's age progression, this subtle difference would be lost. The "drawing" onto the face of tiny items like eyelashes and eyebrows would be cumbersome and time consuming to do on a computer. The computer-generated age progressions also require a vast array of photos of various races, ages, and sexes, digitally stored, for use when familial photos are not available. If you obtain training at the esteemed NCMEC facility and gain speed using computer-generated images and have access to their database of facial types, this might be the best way to go when performing age progressions. However, if you have only an occasional case of this type during your career, the hand-drawn method might be quicker and easier. Each forensic artist should decide for himself or herself which method to use.

Figures 6.27 and 6.28 show a 30-year age progression of two babies to adulthood. The subjects to be progressed were 1 and 2 years old in the source photos. They needed to be progressed to ages 31 and 32. After the age-progressed portraits were done, they were shown on the nationally televised *Unsolved Mysteries*. A relative who saw the show was able to reunite the men with family members in a distant state after 30 years of separation.[4]

Once again, I practiced self-criticism and found these discrepancies. The age progressions were drawn with average weight. The men who were reunited had stayed thin; therefore, the necks and sides of the cheeks were drawn too thick. The chin of the younger brother was too long in the drawing. The ears in the portrait are not sticking out enough. I had failed to draw two versions of the older subject as an adult: one with short hair, and one with long head and facial

Figure 6.27

On the left is a photo of a 1-year-old boy who had been separated from his sister when she was 4. In the middle is my age-progression portrait of him to age 31. Right is the photo of him as he appeared around the time of the sketch's release (photos courtesy of Christina Shiets).

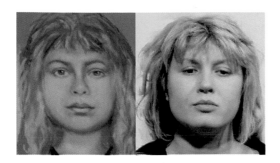

Figure 1.3

The sketch on the left was from a man who was drugged and robbed by the woman on the right. Her fingerprint at a scene and striking resemblance to the sketch identified her to detectives, and the witness picked her out in a line-up (courtesy of the Houston Police Department).

Figure 1.6

The sketch on the left was done in a maternity ward from a mother after her 10-hour-old baby was kidnapped by the woman on the right. The sketch was released and a friend of this kidnapper called authorities. The baby was returned safely that night (courtesy of the Houston Police Department).

Figure 1.9

The sketch on the left was done with an elderly man who saw the man on the right drive past at 45 miles per hour 30 feet away. This witness was under tremendous pressure, and stridently insisted he never saw the driver's face (courtesy of the Ft. Bend County Sheriffs Department).

Figure 2.32

Sketches of various suspects wearing a variety of head gear. All the drawings were done from descriptions by witnesses to actual crimes.

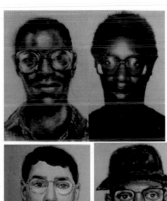

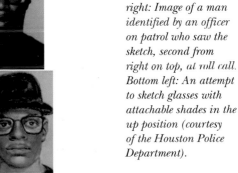

Figure 2.34

Seven sketches and one photo of individuals with glasses. Top right: Image of a man identified by an officer on patrol who saw the sketch, second from right on top, at roll call. Bottom left: An attempt to sketch glasses with attachable shades in the up position (courtesy of the Houston Police Department).

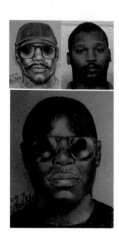

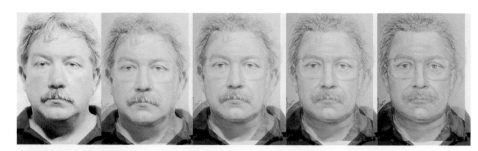

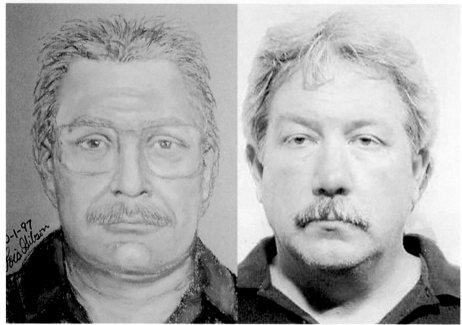

Figure 2.35

Top left: A sketch from a 9-year-old boy who saw his 6-year-old brother kidnapped by the man pictured top right. Another witness gave the description for the bottom sketch of this man with glasses and no hat. Notice that highlights on the dark glasses match highlights on the face (courtesy of the Houston Police Department).

Figure 4.2

From left to right along the top is the photo of the man described, with each image to the right a progressively less transparent overlay of the sketch superimposed atop. The sketch on the bottom left was taken from an 11-year-old girl (courtesy of the Houston Police Department).

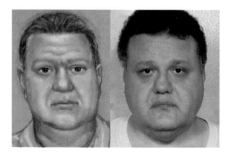

Figure 4.28

The sketch on the left took hours longer than usual and the witness who gave the description considered it a failure. Nevertheless, the sketch helped the detective identify this robber [23] (courtesy of the Houston Police Department).

Figure 4.29

The witness who gave the description for the sketch on the left claimed she never saw the man's face.[24] When the sketch was done, she was ambivalent and expressed doubt it was a good likeness (courtesy of the Houston Police Department).

Figure 4.31

A 10-year old girl who was assaulted by the man on the right gave the description for the sketch on the left. The man on the right called police and turned himself in when he saw the sketch on television news (courtesy of the Houston Police Department).

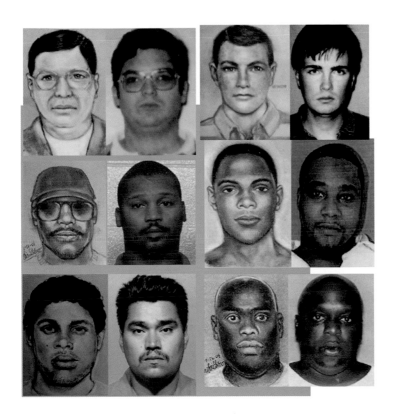

Figure 4.32

All these sketches at left were created from the descriptions of children, and all aided in the identification of the men in the accompanying photos. The witnesses for the sketches, from left to right, top to bottom, were 10, 5, 9, 9, 9, and 11 years of age[27] (courtesy of the Houston Police Department)

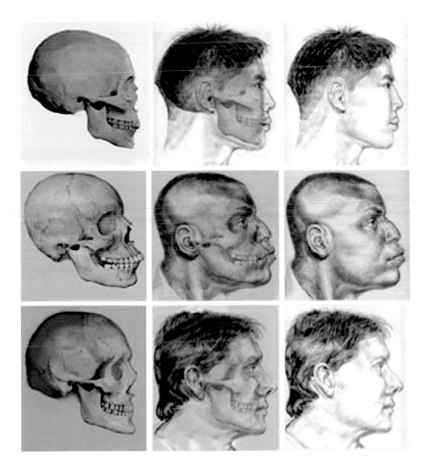

Figure 5.7

From top to bottom on the left are the skulls in profile of a Mongoloid, Negroid, and Caucasoid subjects. To the right of each is a drawing superimposed atop the skull and on the right are the drawings without the skull showing through.

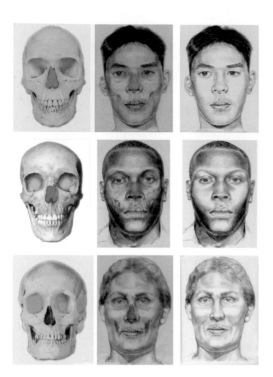

Figure 5.43

A photo of this truck, which closely resembled the get-away vehicle in a homicide, was used to trace a line drawing. Color pastels were then used to fill in details and the unusual graphics on the back window as described by the witness to the crime.

Figure 5.8

From top to bottom on the left are skulls of Mongoloid, Negroid, and Caucasoid subjects. To the right of each are first a drawing superimposed upon the skull image and then the drawing without the skull showing through.

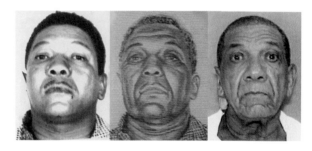

Figure 6.2

The 33-year-old man pictured on the left got away with murder for 30 years. After detectives had me create the age-progression portrait of him at age 63, shown in the center, they were able to track him down within days living in a nearby state (Photo on right courtesy of the Houston Police Department).

Figure 6.3

I obtained the photo of a subject at age 18 on the left and created the drawing of him age-progressed to 31 years as shown in the center. Colleagues then produced a photo of the subject at age 31 shown on the right (courtesy of the Houston Police Department).

Figure 6.1

The beginnings of wrinkles seen in the 24-year-old male at the center top photo can be seen in his younger photos. From top left he was approximately 2 years, top right 6 months, bottom left 3 months, and bottom right 5 days old (photos by author).

Figure 6.4

The man pictured left committed a heinous murder and had been a fugitive for 14 years. I created the drawing in the center, age-progressing him to 53 years old. When the drawing was shown on the nationally televised Unsolved Mysteries *show he was found. (Photo on right courtesy of the Pasadena Police Department).*

Figure 6.6

The comparison of the age-progression drawing (left) and Brashar after his capture (right) shows that, in spite of the significant weight gain and hair changes, the core features were rendered quite similar (courtesy of the Houston Police Department).

Figure 6.22

A father and his daughter, both aged 3. Notice the eyebrows are almost identical in their asymmetry. One eyebrow is more arched than the other. The eye shapes are the same. The general shape of the face and coloring are the same. The lips are nearly identical.

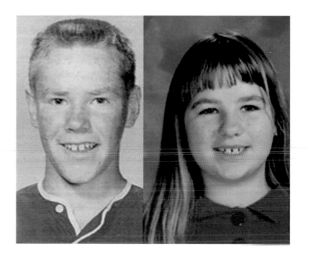

Figure 6.23

This is the same father and daughter as Color Plate 6.22 aged 11 and 9, respectively. Notice the dentition is nearly identical, with a diastema and slightly spaced lateral incisors. The father's chin is much longer and the daughter's eyebrows and eyelashes are darker than her father's.

Figure 6.24

From left to right are a father aged 11, his daughter, aged 9 then 18, respectively, and her mother at age 19. Notice that braces have closed the diastema in the daughter's teeth. The daughter also inherited her mother's dark eyebrow and eyelash hairs and short chin.

Figure 6.25

Top to bottom: Eyes from the same female aged 3 months, 6 years, and 18 years, respectively. Notice how the infant eye opening is almost all iris, more white or sclera showing at 6 years, and at age 18, the iris occupies only half of the eye opening (photos by author).

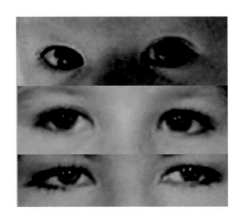

Figure 6.31

This Caucasian female aged 6 years, 3 months, 22 days, shows a beautiful grin with mixed dentition (photo by author).

Figure 6.39

I replicated complicated graphics on the hat and T-shirt of an unidentified deceased man. Family members were able to identify him after viewing these drawings on an Internet web site for unidentified deceased persons. The family told me these clothing articles helped them recognize their relative who had been missing for years.

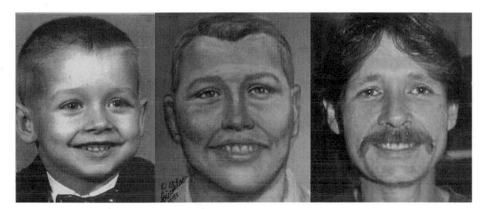

Figure 6.28

Left: The brother of the aforementioned male at age 2 years. Middle: My age-progression sketch of how I thought he would appear at age 32. Right: A photo of his appearance after the sketch was released (photo on left courtesy of Christina Shiets, photo on the right by author).

hair. From this experience, the lesson learned is that an artist should do at least two and possibly more versions of the age progression with various grooming styles. It must be noted that the lips, nose, teeth, forehead, and eye shapes are remarkably similar.

Figure 6.29 is the age progression portrait of the older sibling with the hair and mustache added as they appeared on the long lost brother upon his return. Nothing else on the drawing was changed. This shows how close the portrait could have been had a longer-haired look been included for publication.

The method for these age progressions is as follows. I used felt gray Canson Mi-tientes paper with a Carb-Othello-Stabillo-Schwann pencil no. 59, and traced the image of the two babies with very light strokes. I considered myself quite versed in the look of men in their early 30s since my place of employment offered many individuals of that age group for observation. For this reason, no photo of a comparable individual was used. Instead, I imbued the proper elongation of the face below the eyes, taking the baby straight to adult proportions. I then drew the details of the features, keeping the orifice shapes the same.

I filled in the mouth of the older brother with adult teeth. I retained the upper-lip attitude that exposed the gum tissue to view when the subject grinned. I made certain the iris occupied the amount of space in the eye openings as is usual for adults rather than the larger amount shown in the infant photo of the subject. The eyebrows were given slightly thicker, darker hairs depicting a change that occurs during puberty. The lines under the eyes and the lines running from beside the nose to the outer corners of the mouth were deepened. A slight wrinkling was added to the outer corners of the eyes. All these lines and wrinkles were drawn in the same shape and in the same

Figure 6.29

On the left is the age-progression drawing from Figure 6.28 done with long hair and a mustache added. On the right is the brother as he appeared when the sketch, shown nationwide on the television show Unsolved Mysteries, reunited him with his sister after being separated from her for 30 years.

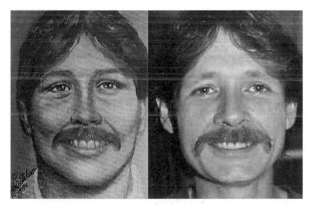

place on the faces of the subjects as a baby's. The biggest mistake was that I did not make the nostril holes *exactly* the same shape as the baby's. Had this been done, the noses on the age progression portraits would have been almost perfect. The mediums used were various pastel and pastel pencils in neutral shades of warm gray from light to dark. The overriding color was raw umber. Mistakes were covered over with pastels that matched the paper, so minimal use of a kneaded eraser was required. The drawing was made on the right side of a doublewide sheet of paper so the left half was able to be folded over the drawing to serve as an attached cover sheet. The drawing was carefully sprayed with fixative when completed.

CHANGING DENTITION FROM CHILD TO ADULT

Individuals will begin losing their deciduous or primary teeth sometime around 6 years of age; adult teeth subsequently erupt in their place. The loss of teeth follows the pattern of their first appearance. The first teeth to show up in a baby's mouth are the lower central incisors, the next are the upper central incisors, then the upper lateral incisors, followed by the lower lateral incisors. The continuing pattern of eruption of primary teeth, the shedding of these, and the eruption of the adult teeth can be charted on Figure 6.30. This chart gives the forensic artist an approximate idea of the stages of dentition at various ages.

The age when the teeth will be missing from a child's smile, and the later date when that gap might be filled in with a permanent tooth, can vary widely. The ability to guess where and when a gap will appear in a child's grin, or when that gap would be filled in, would be beyond even parents who were versed in these dental transitions. An example of this kind of transitional, mixed-dentition mouth can be seen in Figure 6.31. This girl is 6 years, 3 months, and 22 days old. The primary teeth she has lost are beginning to be replaced by adult teeth. Within months the gaps that existed will disappear and other teeth will be shed, causing gaps in other portions of her grin. Other children in her family might lose teeth sooner or later in their life.

Genetic factors can cause a difference in the times of eruption and shedding by more than a year. Because it is so speculative where the gaps in a grin might be, a wise forensic artist should draw children aged 6 to 9 years with a closed-mouth smile. These are the years when the front primary teeth are being shed and replaced by permanent dentition. Even if you guess when a gap might appear and depict that in an age-progression drawing, in less than a year that same gap will be filled with a new permanent tooth, rendering that drawing obsolete. As a personal note, my children's teeth were almost two years apart in the age at which they erupted. Even though they were offspring of the same parents, my son began shedding his teeth at age 6; my daughter did not begin shedding until she was almost 8.

STAGES OF TOOTH ERUPTION

Primary Teeth

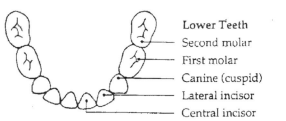

Upper Teeth	Erupt	Shed
Central incisor	8-12 mos.	6-7 yrs.
Lateral incisor	9-13 mos.	7-8 yrs.
Canine (cuspid)	16-22 mos.	10-12 yrs.
First molar	13-19 mos.	9-11 yrs.
Second molar	25-33 mos.	10-12 yrs.

Lower Teeth	Erupt	Shed
Second molar	23-31 mos.	10-12 yrs.
First molar	14-18 mos.	9-11 yrs.
Canine (cuspid)	17-23 mos.	9-12 yrs.
Lateral incisor	10-16 mos.	7-8 yrs.
Central incisor	6-10 mos.	6-7 yrs.

Permanent Teeth

Upper Teeth	Erupt
Central incisor	7-8 yrs.
Lateral incisor	8-9 yrs.
Canine (cuspid)	11-12 yrs.
First premolar (first bicuspid)	10-11 yrs.
Second premolar (second bicuspid)	10-12 yrs.
First molar	6-7 yrs.
Second molar	12-13 yrs.
Third molar (wisdom tooth)	17-21 yrs.

Lower Teeth	Erupt
Third molar (wisdom tooth)	17-21 yrs.
Second molar	11-13 yrs.
First molar	6-7 yrs.
Second premolar (second bicuspid)	11-12 yrs.
First premolar (first bicuspid)	10-12 yrs.
Canine (cuspid)	9-10 yrs.
Lateral incisor	7-8 yrs.
Central incisor	6-7 yrs.

Figure 6.31

This Caucasian female aged 6 years, 3 months, 22 days, shows a beautiful grin with mixed dentition (photo by author). See color plate.

HOW TO BECOME PROFICIENT AT CHILD AGE PROGRESSION

Even though the age progression of children has many more complications than that of adults, there is a method through which you can become quite proficient at this difficult task. Just as was mentioned earlier with adult age progression, you can simulate working on real cases by simply borrowing photos from friends and acquaintances. You should construct an age progression of a child for whom a photo at an older age exists, but do not look at the older-aged photo before creating the age progression portrait. Once the portrait is completed, you can observe the photo of your subject and understand what, if any, mistakes were made. As an example, obtain a photo of a 4-year-old from an acquaintance who also has a photo of that same child at age 12. Draw a portrait of how that young toddler would appear at age 12. Once finished, look at the photo of the child at age 12 and observe the quality of the resemblance. Once the mistakes and successful areas of the drawing are understood, repeat the process with an eye to improving the flaws and repeating the successes. Any artist willing to repeat this process and learn from his or her mistakes can become quite proficient at age progressing children. I highly recommend that you practice in this manner before you work on a real case.

In Brief

- In general, the orifices of the face stay the same shape during the aging process. In adults those orifices also stay in the same position and size, relative to the other features.
- The placement, relative to the other features, and curvature of major wrinkles are present on a person's face at infancy in the form of smooth undulations in the flesh.
- Children experience considerable bone growth in their facial area, with the bones below the eyes elongating until that part of the face grows from being half the vertical length to two-thirds of the face.
- Use photos of individuals from the subject's family, or similar appearing persons, at the age to which the subject is to be progressed, as visual aids.
- The iris occupies almost all the eye opening in a baby. As the individual grows to adulthood, the iris occupies less of the opening, until at the adult stage, the iris occupies about one-half of the eye opening.
- Avoid drawing an age progression of a child from 6 to 9 years with a grin. The shedding of primary teeth and eruption of adult teeth are on a biological timetable that varies too much to predict for a sketch that might be released to the public and shown for more than a year. Draw a closed-mouth smile instead.
- Using friends' and acquaintances' familial photos, you can practice all types of age progressions and become proficient, *if* you are able to learn from your mistakes.

POSTMORTEM PORTRAITS

Murder victims often are found with no identification and in a location that offers no clues as to their identity. Some of the most prolific murderers plan their crimes so their victims are left unidentifiable as part of their method to evade capture. For the purposes of finding the perpetrators of these types of crimes, and to enable loved ones of the victims to discover and deal with their death, you will need to create images of these unidentified murder victims for public release. Additionally, the U.S. media has a practice of *not* showing photos of deceased persons in their regular news releases. Some of the victims, when found, are in such a state of decomposition and/or trauma that not only are their photos distasteful for release to the news, the individuals would be so distorted as to render them unidentifiable.

For these reasons, you will be given the task of coping with the various degrees of distortion seen in unidentified victims from your area. You need only jog someone's memory of a loved one or friend who is missing with your drawing. After a tip is related to authorities, the deceased individual's fingerprints, dentition, scars, and other physical evidence can make the positive identification. Some artists say this is the most difficult work they perform. However, helping bring fallen loved ones home and offering detectives help in solving a murder make this work worthwhile. The following are suggestions for working with the various problems that commonly occur in drawing postmortem portraits.

VICTIMS FOUND SOON AFTER DEATH

Murder victims found soon after their death can be dealt with in a manner not too different from drawing portraits of persons who are alive. Unless the deceased individual has been highly traumatized, the problems are usually no more than changing an awkward angle of photography or leaving off blood or wounds. One common task is drawing a person whose eyes are closed as if they are open. Another necessity is drawing clear images of any clothing unusual enough to help identify the unknown deceased victim. Some subjects will have a loose, half open mouth. You need only draw the muscles surrounding the mouth tightening until the mouth closes. If it seems appropriate for the subject, a slight smile can be added.

If you have a case in your area of an unidentified murder victim, do your best to go to the medical examiner to see, and if possible draw, the victim in person. Photos will not do the deceased person justice.

This in-person type of drawing situation will produce the best portrait with the most accuracy. The proportions, color, hair texture, virtually every item of the image, will be more accurate if you see the deceased in person. Since visiting a medical examiner's facility might prove offensive to some, here are some methods to ease this kind of visit.

Notify the detective that you plan to go to the medical examiner's facility so he or she can clear the way. The staff at the facility should be notified so they might prepare an area and bring the murder victim out to be viewed. I have found staff at these types of facilities to be most gracious and helpful. Make every effort to perform this in-person drawing *before* the autopsy. The staff is proficient at performing the autopsy and then repositioning the features so that if relatives were contacted, they could view and hopefully recognize the individual. However, the procedures do distort the features. For optimum viewing and drawing, reach the side of the victim before these necessary processes are performed.

An easel is a must in this type of situation. The easel can be adjusted so you can stand while drawing. Standing is necessary since bodies are rolled out for view on stainless steel gurneys that are about waist high. In order to view the individual face-to-face for a portrait, you must stand in a hovering position over the subject's face, then quickly turn back to the drawing board. This back and forth needs to be repeated numerous times for the drawing to be constructed. If the board is held high enough to draw standing up, the process goes quickly. Without an easel, the drawing board would need to be leaned against the gurney or some other item in the medical examiner's facility. It would be a long, difficult process if you needed to sit at a table easel or hand-hold the drawing board while sketching.

Some artists feel the most disagreeable part of drawing at the medical examiner's facility is the odor. The singular way to deaden the sense of smell is to smoke a large cigar. Smoking about one-half inch of the cigar is enough to deaden the sense of smell. Float the smoke inside your mouth and allow the smoke to flow out your nostrils. Do not pull the smoke into the lungs. I believe tobacco use is harmful and I don't smoke, but I have found almost complete relief from objectionable odors during work at the medical examiner's by using a strong cigar since the olfactory nerves are rendered almost senseless.

Figure 6.32 shows a sketch done at the Joseph A. Jachimczyk Forensic Center in person with the homicide victim. The victim's relatives were prompted to identify her soon after the sketch was released.[5] The photos taken of the murdered woman at the scene

Figure 6.32

This sketch on the left was done with the murdered woman pictured on the right in person at the morgue. The photos of the woman shown to me made her appear dirty and messy. In person the woman appeared statuesque and smooth-skinned (courtesy of the Harris County Medical Examiners Department).

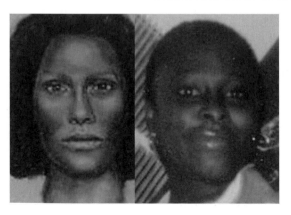

made her appear messy and ugly. Upon viewing the body, it was obvious the individual was tall with an almost perfect build. She also appeared to have flawless skin and hair and was obviously a strikingly attractive African-American female. The entire tone of the sketch was done differently than had it been done only from photos.

Figure 6.33 shows a sketch of a woman whose face was so mutilated that an in-person viewing was the only way possible to make the drawing. The person who murdered her had taken a large metal drawer and repeatedly bashed in her face. Her face was broken into stair steps, with the nose bashed in about one inch below the forehead, the bottom part of the nose bashed in about an inch below the top half, the maxillary bone shoved in one inch below the nose, and so on. With the face in several sections, I had to study the head for a long while and somehow piece it together visually. Since it was during a cold season, the hat found with the body was added to the drawing. I cannot emphasize enough how this drawing would have been impossible to do from two-dimensional photos. Notice the tiny dark mole above the subject's right eyebrow that was observed. Also, the large nose ending, compared to the top of the nose, was depicted correctly. These items would not have been gleaned from photos.

Figure 6.33

The sketch on the left was done in person with the murdered woman at the morgue. The woman's face was bashed into several sections and would have been nearly impossible to decipher from photos (courtesy of the Harris County Medical Examiners Department).

Unfortunately, often you will be given only photos from which to draw portraits of homicide victims. Detectives will follow promising leads for weeks or months before they realize the murdered person cannot be identified. By that time, the body has already been buried. Often these photos were not taken with the idea of an artist creating a life-like portrait from them in mind. They can be quite challenging to use as a visual aid to produce a likeness.

One common problem is a photo with the subject's eyes closed. In order to draw that individual with open eyes, there is an important rule to remember. The eyelid, when open, will curve *around* the eyeball. Therefore, even though the eye opening seems straight when the eyes are mostly closed, when the eyes are opened, that opening will be rounded. One way to practice this is to take a photo of a friend or family member with his or her eyes closed. Then make a quick sketch from that photo source showing the eyes open. A quick comparison of the subject with his or her eyes open will show if it was done right. You will soon become proficient at this task with only a few practices. The exercises should be done before there is an unidentified homicide victim depending on your skills to be returned to his or her family.

Figure 6.34 shows a photo with the eyes almost closed. I drew the eyes open as seen in the sketch on the right. I observed the full, long hair from the scene photo on the far left. Even though the face shot showed almost no hair, the

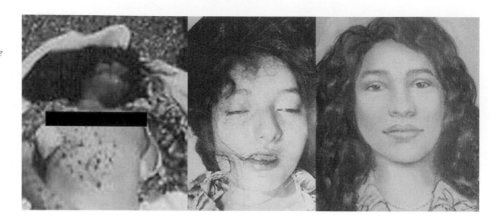

Figure 6.34

I often must draw eyes open from photos where the victim's eyes are closed as in the center photo above. From the photo on the left I ascertained this woman had very thick hair, which was then depicted in the sketch on the right (courtesy of the Houston Police Department).

Figure 6.35

On the left are the only photos available showing this unidentified homicide victim's face for me to use for the portrait on the right. The best pose for an artist would be a front-face shot. However, these oblique angles are often the only poses photographed when the people working the scene do not anticipate the subject's requiring an artist's rendering (courtesy of the Harris County Medical Examiners Department).

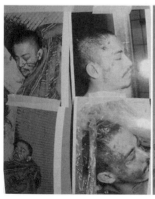 

scene photo gave enough information for me to construct a full hairstyle on the postmortem portrait. This sketch aided in the family's identifying the murdered woman. The sketch was considered accurate enough to be used as her image with the media during the following decade as her murder was linked to four other homicides.[6]

Photos of the murdered person taken from oblique angles offer another challenge to the forensic artist attempting to recreate a recognizable portrait. A straight-on frontal pose would be ideal, but as can be seen in Figure 6.35, sometimes the photographer at the scene captures all kinds of other angles, but no frontal shots. Since this happens with regularity, you need to observe odd angles of faces and be able to create a frontal pose. The best technique for this situation is to tape all the poses to the drawing board surrounding the sketch as it is created. This arrangement lets you view all the poses as needed while composing the drawing.

Figure 6.36 shows the only two face shots available for an unidentified homicide victim taped next to the sketch for simultaneous viewing. Notice I did not alter the pose in the drawing appreciably from the photo on the left. This maximum adherence to the pose in the photo makes for less speculation. One technique for getting as much right as possible with postmortem portraits is to vary as little as possible from the information in the photograph.

You should always obtain photos taken at the scene where the body was found. This will allow the hairstyle to be best understood. After bodies are taken to the medical examiner, they are sometimes not photographed until the individual is washed down. This drenching process usually obliterates the appearance of the murdered person's hairstyle as it would be remembered by acquaintances. Often the correct hairstyle and texture can be seen in the scene photos. Then the photos taken at the medical examiner's facility might offer a more concise view of the face. You need only combine the face with the accurate hairstyle from the various photos.

Figure 6.37 shows the only photos of the face of an unidentified homicide victim. The ruler is placed near the wounds to have a scale next to his features and help identify the size and shape of the object used to bludgeon the victim. The victim's beard was shaved to search for other wounds. I was given the one photo of him *with* the beard to add that to the sketch since it was assumed he was usually bearded. As you can see, the beard was taken from one photo; the eyes, nose, and mouth from another; and the entire head had to be made to appear upright and in a frontal pose for the sketch.

In an effort to enhance the chances of identifying the homicide victim, you should create clear depictions of any unique clothing or possessions found on the body. Figures 6.38 through 6.41 show various portraits that include such items. Often when the clothing is sketched from photos, the graphics on T-shirts are almost totally obscured by blood or other stains. Whether it is a tattoo, an initial on a belt, an unusual wallet, or graphics on a shirt, the effort must be made for the victim who can no longer cry out to be noticed. In the case of Figure 6.39, the family noticed the resemblance of the unusual hat and shirt, along with the facial resemblance. The family was so taken with the resemblance, they asked for a copy of the drawing, which they framed and gave to the victim's mother. The family's remembrance of their loved one wearing the items in the drawing helped prompt them to call in his identity to authorities.[7]

Notice the tattoo in Figure 6.40 was enlarged over the part of the body where it was located. This drawing appears cumbersome, but a tattoo is not much of an identifier unless the location is also shown. The T-shirt seemed to advertise a local, small business, which could be an important clue to the person's identity, so that was depicted. The initials on the back of the subject's belt in Figure 6.41 and a unique wallet in Figure 6.38 seemed to be important identifiers so those also were drawn.

Figure 6.36

A drawing flanked by the only face shots taken of an unidentified homicide victim. Notice I sketched a pose that varied little from one of the poses in the photographs. This lessens the risk of portraying something incorrectly (courtesy of the Harris County Medical Examiners Department).

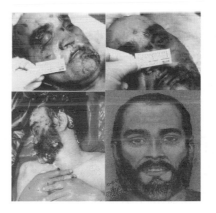

Figure 6.37

At the top are the only photos of the face of an unidentified homicide victim. I was asked to sketch him with a beard since that is how he was found. On the bottom left is the only photo taken of the subject with his beard (courtesy of the Harris County Medical Examiners Department).

Figure 6.38

(Above) I drew an unusual wallet, key fob, and graphics on a T-shirt found on the body of an unidentified homicide victim in an effort to enhance the chances he would be identified.

Figure 6.39

(Above right) I replicated complicated graphics on the hat and T-shirt of an unidentified deceased man. Family members were able to identify him after viewing these drawings on an Internet web site for unidentified deceased persons. The family told me these clothing articles helped them recognize their relative who had been missing for years. See color plate.

Figure 6.40

On the bottom right of this post-mortem sketch of an unidentified homicide victim is a tattoo over the leg showing the exact location of that identifier. Another identifier is the T-shirt graphics from a small business.

DEALING WITH GROSS IMPERFECTION

Many postmortem portraits seem impossible to create. For these cases you must rely on the expertise of the medical examiner and other forensic professionals.

As an example, the process of deterioration can quickly render a subject unrecognizable. In a cold climate, the face of an abandoned homicide victim might remain recognizable for weeks or even months. However, in a hot climate, a murdered body will begin to decompose immediately. One of the first processes to occur is the swelling of the body. If the contours of the face swell up so much as half an inch, it can represent the addition of 60 to 100 pounds to a living individual. Therefore, this postmortem swelling can rapidly change the subject to a person drastically dissimilar to the person acquaintances would recognize. If there is any swelling, input from the medical examiner about the height and weight will help create a portrait with the correct fat content in the face. With that information, you can draw the eyes, lips, and nose as seen, then slim down the outer contours where the swelling is observed.

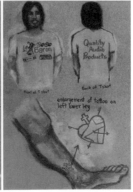

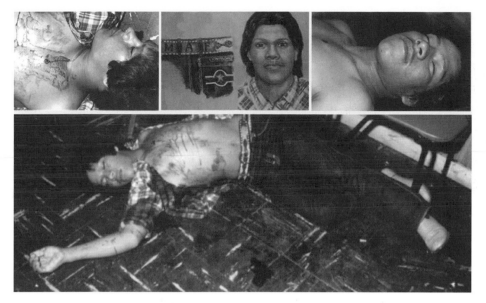

Figure 6.41
I drew the plaid shirt worn by this murder victim (top center). The design on the jeans pocket and initials on the leather belt are included to enhance the chances for identification. Scene photos like the bottom one give information about age and body fat content (courtesy of the Harris County Medical Examiners Department).

These professionals will also be able to tell you if blemishes were present before the person died, or if instead they were the acts of insects or other creatures after the subject's death. All these facts should be related in the medical examiner's report; therefore, you should read this report thoroughly before undertaking this kind of sketch. Jot down any questions to ask the medical examiner before starting the artwork. Since no person or work is perfect, the written report on your subject might not include all information needed to create a life-like portrait. If there is any clarification needed from the professional who did the report, do not fail to ask those questions.

The following are a few terms to help understand those kinds of reports:

- **Antemortem:** Before death
- **Perimortem:** Near or around the time of death
- **Postmortem:** After death

The medical examiner's determination of when the unidentified man in Figure 6.42 was injured helped me create an accurate postmortem sketch. I was told not to include the obvious red marks. At first I thought they were a case of bad acne. However, the medical examiner determined this man was bitten by fire ants, antemortem, perimortem, and postmortem. Because of this determination, the artist knew to draw the man with smooth skin, leaving out the obvious insect bites. Persons in the southern United States know that fire ants will attack in droves if one steps on or near their colony. They leave bite marks that look just like those on the face of the man in Figure 6.42.

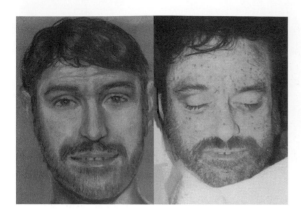

Figure 6.42

I understood the face should be drawn with smooth, unblemished skin after the medical examiner explained the obvious red marks on this unidentified victim's face were caused by fire ant bites (courtesy of the Harris County Medical Examiners Department).

Figure 6.43

Smooth holes with sharp top edges indicate the teeth at the front of this mandible were in place before the subject died (courtesy of the Harris County Medical Examiners Department).

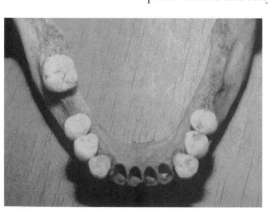

Discovering whether teeth that appear absent were there before the subject died is of paramount importance for the artist's rendering of the mouth area for that case. If the medical examiner's analysis reads that a missing tooth was "absent postmortem," this means the subject had that tooth when he or she was alive and it can be shown in the drawing. Conversely, when teeth are determined to be "absent antemortem," the person was missing that tooth before he or she died. This means the subject should look like he or she is missing that tooth in the drawing.

You can make this determination on your own easily if clear photos are available of the tooth areas. If the hole where the tooth is missing is smooth and the edges sharply defined, this means the person died *with that tooth in place.* If you are alive when a tooth is lost due to trauma or surgery, the bone surrounding the hole begins to grow together *immediately.* In only a matter of weeks the hole will be significantly filled in with bone growth. Said differently, the bones around the edges of a hole where a tooth has been missing while the person was alive will be rippled and growing toward the center of that hole. If the tooth has been missing very long, the hole will be completely filled in with bone.

For bodies murdered and left in the open, the postmortem tooth loss occurs most often in the anterior or front teeth since they have only one root. These single-rooted teeth tend to wash away or be carried away by scavenging creatures. The posterior teeth such as the bicuspids and molars, have multiple roots and thus tend to be difficult to dislodge.

This is illustrated by Figures 6.43, 6.44, and 6.45. Figure 6.44 offers a view of a maxillary bone where on the bottom left teeth were pulled long before death, indicated by the area being completely grown over with bone. The top left smooth hole with sharp edges indicates this maxillary canine was in place before the subject died. The maxillary central incisor to the right of the missing canine has a porcelain-fused-to-metal crown restoration. To the right of the maxillary central incisors still in place is a missing lateral incisor that was in place before death as indicated by the smooth, clean-edged hole at that location. Notice the small hole seen below the canine on the right, above the two molars. This indicates a tooth that was removed before death. Since the bone growth has not completely filled in the hole, it can be safely assumed this tooth was pulled more recently than the missing teeth on the left side of the photo.

Figure 6.45 shows a mandible with teeth pulled long before death on the left of the photo as indicated by bone growth that has completely filled in the holes where the tooth roots once grew. In the top left of the alveolar ridge is a smooth hole where a bicuspid existed during the subject's life. At the top of the alveolar ridge, from left to right, are a badly decayed canine, a mandibular lateral incisor, two central incisors, and another lateral incisor, all showing occlusal edge wear. Two of the teeth on the right side of the photo, a bicuspid and a molar, have amalgam restorations, commonly referred to as "fillings."

Depicting a tooth for a drawing when all that can be seen is an empty hole, you should imitate the nature of the surrounding teeth that *can* be seen. For instance, if the individual has large, white teeth, draw *that* kind of tooth in the place where the subject has lost his or hers postmortem. Likewise, if the surrounding teeth are slender and a yellowed color, construct the postmortem missing tooth as slender and yellowed.

This knowledge of postmortem tooth loss aided in a case so difficult, a sketch should not have been attempted. Practicing forensic artists are known to tell an investigator they refuse to attempt a portrait from remains that are too degraded to imagine an image. Once almost any significant bloating or decomposition has occurred, you would do a better job working from a clean skull.

Figure 6.46 is the photo of an unidentified homicide victim. She was found dumped in a remote area with a bullet in her head. For reasons not understood, the medical examiner's investigator assigned to the case refused to provide me with a cleaned skull. This can occur when various individuals entrusted with the body refuse to disarticulate the skull from the body and remove the tissue from that portion.

In a feeble attempt to identify the murdered woman, I gathered from the medical examiners that she was a white female in her 20s or 30s. They also determined her to be 5' 4" in height, weighing 97 pounds. Although it was certain this weight was less than the victim would have been when alive, the jeans and panties found on the body were a fit for a slender body. This indicated the face would have very little fat content. I could vaguely observe the straight, short hairstyle. I constructed vivid drawings of the unusual denim blouse with lace overlays shown in Figure 6.48. The victim's white woven-leather-strap shoes were recreated artistically in Figure 6.49. Finally, the unusual costume jewelry shown in Figure 6.47 were depicted on a poorly rendered hand covering the

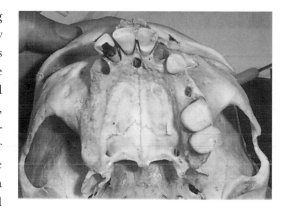

Figure 6.44

This view of the maxillary bone is able to reveal a vast amount of the dental history of the subject to the learned observer (courtesy of the Harris County Medical Examiners Department).

Figure 6.45

This mandible shows a great amount of dental information and history to the learned observer (courtesy of the Harris County Medical Examiners Department)

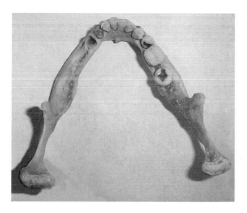

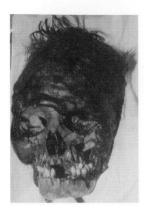

Figure 6.46

This murder victim was not found until her body had reached a mummified state. She was shot in the head and dumped in a remote area. Because of the tissue distortion, I could only discern the short, straight hair and the mandible and lower maxillary areas (courtesy of the Harris County Medical Examiners Department).

Figure 6.47

These are the numerous pieces of jewelry found on the subject in Figure 6.46 (courtesy of the Harris County Medical Examiners Department).

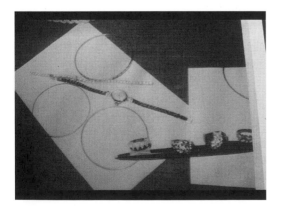

part of the face obliterated by the black, mummified flesh covering the victim's head in the photo. (The hand was drawn poorly because I had little hope my work would identify the murdered victim.)

The mandible and front of the maxillary bones showed clean holes where it was obvious teeth existed before the victim was murdered. Further, the holes seemed regular in size, with even placement. The mandible was somewhat large and square-shaped for a female. These observations allowed me to effectively sketch the lower part of the face. Because of the resemblance of the drawing, the detectives were able to connect their unknown homicide victim to a 32-year-old woman who had been reported missing. The medical examiners had earlier obtained fingerprints from her mummified fingers; those were a match to the 32-year-old pictured on the far right of Figure 6.50.[8]

This case does not present enough information for a drawing to be done. The personnel at the medical examiner's should provide the skull from such a case with the tissue removed. It should be noted the medical examiner now properly prepares such specimens when needed.

Figures 6.51 through 6.54 show another case where the artist should have been given a clean skull with which to reconstruct the face. However, the victim was a small, malnourished child who had been killed by blunt force trauma to her body. She had been murdered, wrapped in a blanket, and dumped in a water-filled ditch near a residential area. Since no adult had come forward searching for a missing child, it was necessary to assume the person or persons entrusted with the unidentified child's care must also be her killer(s). The detectives and the media clamored for an image to solve the heart-wrenching crime.

For the sake of expediting the work, I observed the landmarks on the skull to create a two-dimensional facial resemblance from photos. The work was rather like a skull-reconstruction with some tissue obscuring the view of the bones. Enough forehead flesh and all the hair were left, which let me know the victim was a black female with curly black hair. The photos of the body gave an indication of fat content (or lack thereof) for the face. The medical examiner estimated her age to be 4 or 5 years. However, I noticed adult teeth at the front of the mouth. The forensic dentist was able to inform the artist that all the front teeth on the bottom arch were adult. The maxillary centrals and laterals were adult, all teeth posterior of those on both arches were deciduous teeth. This meant the little girl was probably at least 6 years old. Sadly, the dentist determined the missing maxillary central incisor had been knocked out, probably during the same traumatic incident that caused the other central incisor to be knocked back up into the alveolar ridge from which it had begun to grow.

Figure 6.48

On the right is a detailed color pastel drawing of the stained shirt on the left. The victim in Figure 6.46 was found wearing this shirt (courtesy of the Harris County Medical Examiners Department).

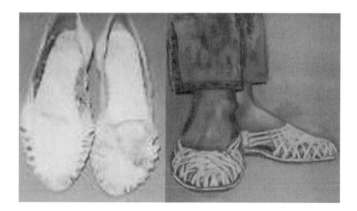

Figure 6.49

I created a pastel of the shoes on the right from the photo on the left of those worn by the unidentified murder victim in Figure 6.46 (courtesy of the Harris County Medical Examiners Department).

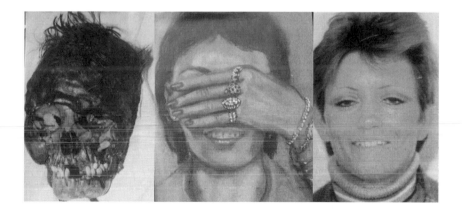

Figure 6.50

Center: A drawing of the top of the head and the mouth and chin, the only parts discernable from the photo shown in Figure 6.46. The rest of the face is covered with a poorly-drawn hand wearing the victim's unusual jewelry. The drawing led to the identification of the woman on the right (courtesy of the Houston Police Department).

Enough tissue was present to actually see where the muscles on each side of the eyes had attached to the inside of the eye opening. Enough of the nose was left to construct the placement and size of the nostril holes. It was obvious the little girl had a large, attractive arch of teeth that would offer a robust grin. I used these landmarks and drew the sketch on the left side of Figure 6.55. After

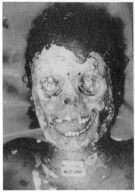
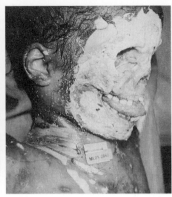
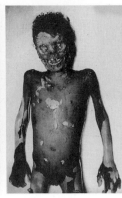
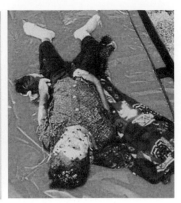

Figure 6.51

This is the best photo of a girl dubbed "Angel Doe" who was beaten to death. She was 3 feet, 11 inches tall, weighed 47 pounds, and her age was estimated at between 4 and 9 years (courtesy of the Harris County Medical Examiners Department).

Figure 6.52

This is a side view of "Angel Doe." A decedent's tongue will protrude out of the mouth in this manner after death. Skin and hair seen in the photo identify the girl as African-American (courtesy of the Harris County Medical Examiners Department).

Figure 6.53

This photo of the body gives some indication of the child's age, state of emaciation, and race (courtesy of the Harris County Medical Examiners Department).

Figure 6.54

This photo of the body soon after discovery lying on the medical examiner's water-proof bag shows the clothing "Angel Doe" was wearing and the blanket in which she was wrapped (courtesy of the Harris County Medical Examiners Department).

only a few days of canvassing the neighborhood, a detective brought the sketch back and asked me to make a change. The detective urged me to make the girl look younger, since all the people in the neighborhood were saying the sketch looked like a girl in her teens.

I decided the easiest way to make the portrait appear to be of a younger girl was to make the chin smaller. Even though the mandible bone in the morgue photo appeared to match the chin in the drawing, I obeyed the wishes of the detective and drew the chin much smaller.

The murdered girl remained unidentified for 6 months. At last the grandmother, who claimed she never watched the news, was flipping through the channels and saw the sketch on TV. She thought the sketch looked like her granddaughter, and called in her identity to authorities.[9] Even though the revised sketch was effective, it should be noted the little girl, who is less than 5 in the photo, had a chin as large as the one in the original drawing. As can be seen in Figure 6.55, I was correct drawing the little girl with a large grin that displayed her lower, as well as upper, teeth.

Neither of the previous two cases had the proper specimen for a forensic artist to do a reconstruction of the unidentified murdered person. Reasonable forensic artists would say to turn these cases down, and/or obtain a cleaned skull for the reconstruction. Ideally, that is what should have been done. However, in the real, imperfect world, sometimes an investigator follows

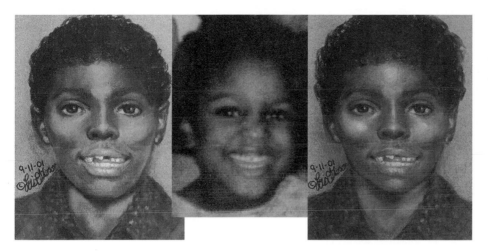

Figure 6.55

Left: The sketch created from the photos in Figures 6.51 through 6.54. Right: A photo with the chin made drastically smaller at the request of a detective who got leads for girls older than "Angel Doe." Center: The little girl who was finally identified (courtesy of the Houston Police Department).

his or her instincts. Artists who can't tell the race of a victim because the skin is discolored because of decomposition can rely on the medical examiner to determine the race. Hair, jewelry, clothing, and other bits of information can sometimes help. In the end, the individual artist must decide his or her actions on a case-by-case basis.

Figure 6.56 offers several views of a child who was starved to death and placed in a trash dumpster.[10] Unlike the previous cases, this body was found quickly so the photos gave a clear idea of the child's face. He was 3 to 6 years old, 31 inches long, and weighed 21 pounds. I first drew the portrait in Figure 6.57 showing a happy child. After several months passed with no leads called in, the detectives had me create another image of the murdered boy. Figure 6.58 was the rendering done at the behest of the detectives, showing the child ravaged by malnourishment. Although this case offered clear features and I was able to create an accurate portrait, the case has little potential to be solved.

In Brief

- Draw postmortem portraits in person at the morgue for the most accurate results.
- Forensic pathologists, dentists, photographers, and other professionals at medical examiner's offices are your source for vital information before starting to draw.
- Deterioration after death can make subjects unrecognizable. Use your instincts and all information surrounding you. It is a must to draw unusual clothing, tattoos, jewelry, or possessions.
- Imbue the postmortem portrait with a life-like expression.

Figure 6.56

Top: A full-length photo of a boy who was starved to death showing the extent of emaciation. Below: Photos of his face that I used to sketch his postmortem portrait in an effort to identify him and find his killers. To date this case remains unsolved (courtesy of the Harris County Medical Examiners Department).

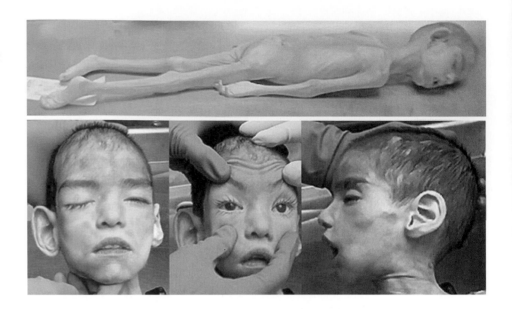

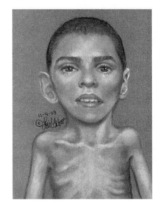

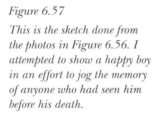

Figure 6.57

This is the sketch done from the photos in Figure 6.56. I attempted to show a happy boy in an effort to jog the memory of anyone who had seen him before his death.

Figure 6.58

At the behest of detectives, I later drew this portrait of the boy pictured in Figure 6.56, showing him in a state of starvation.

REFERENCES

1. S. K. Bardwell, "Thirty-year-long arm of law nabs suspect/Man is arrested in connection with murder," *Houston Chronicle*, October 26, 1994. Alexandra Hardy, "Arrest in 1964 slaying/ Victim's family never gave up," *The Houston Post*, October 26, 1994. Houston Police Department Incident Number 48187194.

2. Jennifer Liebrum, "Fugitive in 1978 slaying apprehended in Panama," *Houston Chronicle*, February 16, 1993. John Makeig, "Jury picked in trial of suspect on 'Unsolved Mysteries' show," *Houston Chronicle*, June 23, 1993. John Makeig, "Exhibitionist arrested in Panama on TV tip is convicted in '78 slaying"; John Makeig, "Exhibitionist-killer gets 70-year sentence in 1978 case," *Houston Chronicle*, June 30, 1993. Stefanie Asin, "TV crime shows take a bite out of crime/Re-enactments help viewers see wanted suspects," *Houston Chronicle*, January 2, 1994.

3. Mike Glenn, "DNA in '82 killing points to suspect," *Houston Chronicle*, March 24, 2001. Dale Lezon, "Man surrenders in 1982 slaying/DNA evidence cracks case," *Houston Chronicle*, October 2, 2003. Staff, "Case on America's Most Wanted," *Houston Chronicle*, October 30, 2003. Houston Police Department Incident Number 39632482.

4. Catherine Self, "National show reunites family after 32 years," *Tomball Potpourri Newspaper*, March 20, 1996.

5. Houston Police Department Incident Number 12929990.

6. Houston Police Department Incident Number 40587092.

7. Harris County Medical Examiner Case Number 87-6186.

8. Houston Police Department Incident Number 110761189. Harris County Medical Examiner Case Number 89-7410.

9. Peggy O'Hare, "Search for a Name/Child's body still unidentified after 3 months," *Houston Chronicle*, December 20, 2001. Bill Murphy, " 'Angel Doe' still a mystery/Months after dead girl found, no one has claimed her," *Houston Chronicle*, March 4, 2002. Mike Glenn, "Grandmother helps ID girl after noticing sketch on TV," *Houston Chronicle*, March 24, 2002. Alan Bernstein, "Family buries 6-year-old known as 'Little Princess,' " *Houston Chronicle*, April 7, 2002. Peggy O'Hare, " 'Angel Doe's' father is held in her death/Dad allegedly beat girl, 6; arrest solves year-old case," *Houston Chronicle*, August 8, 2002. Rad Sallee, "Angel Doe's killer gets life sentence in 2nd trial/Abused girl's body was found in ditch in 2001," *Houston Chronicle*, August 23, 2003. Houston Police Department Incident Number 123629501.

10. Daniel J. Vargas, " 'Beloved little angel'/"Amado Angelito"/Child given name, proper goodbye/Burial: He won't be a number," *Houston Chronicle*, July 31, 2003. Houston Police Department Incident Number 34509303. Harris County Medical Examiner Case Number 030874.

CHAPTER 7

FACIAL RECONSTRUCTION FROM SKELETAL REMAINS

Faces are formed from within by unique facial bones. The basis of our individual appearance is the distinctive skull that lies beneath the surface of skin and muscle. The forensic artist who pays attention to the various undulations of the facial bones can reconstruct an appearance of unidentified murder victims. This talent of bringing to life someone whose appearance seems to be gone can identify a victim and help detectives solve their case. Loved ones can grieve properly when the artistic image tells them the location of their missing person; detectives then know where to begin their canvas of the victim's last known acquaintances.

GERASIMOV

The modern father of facial reconstructions is the legendary Mikhail M. Gerasimov, pictured in Figure 7.1. This Russian professor began facial reconstructions from skulls in 1924. Before Gerasimov, many professionals reconstructed appearances of famous individuals to confirm their identity. Gerasimov was one of the first to perform a facial reconstruction of a murder victim with the goal of solving a crime. In 1941, Gerasimov was asked to reconstruct the face from only the calvarium of an unidentified skeletal remain found in suspicious circumstances. The three-dimensional sculpture he created led to the identification of Valentina Kosova, and solved a murder.[1] Gerasimov explains his work in Figure 7.2 as follows.

> In the case of Valentina Kosova who suddenly disappeared a few days before she was expecting the birth of her first child, a skull lacking the lower jaw.... was submitted as evidence for identification. The reconstruction of the head (upper left and upper right) presented a face with well-marked forehead prominences, rather small eyes, a snub nose with a slightly undulating profile, and a regularly formed mouth. The comparison of the completed reconstruction (below left) with a photograph of Valentina—taken six years before her disappearance—(below right) showed so great a resemblance between them that her remains were identified and her murderer convicted.[2]

Figure 7.1
"Gerasimov at work"
(modified in graphite by
author after photo by Inge
Morath).

The likeness is remarkable, especially considering Gerasimov had to borrow a mandible from a similar individual to accomplish the reconstruction, and he did not use tissue-depth markers. In 1951 he once again performed remarkable work on the case illustrated in Figure 7.3. The reconstruction was made of another unidentified murder victim. Upon seeing Gerasimov's amazing completion of this sculpture, the husband of the victim was compelled to confess to the murder of his wife, Nina Z.

These career efforts culminated in Gerasimov and others founding the Laboratory for Plastic Reconstruction at the Ethnographical Institute of the

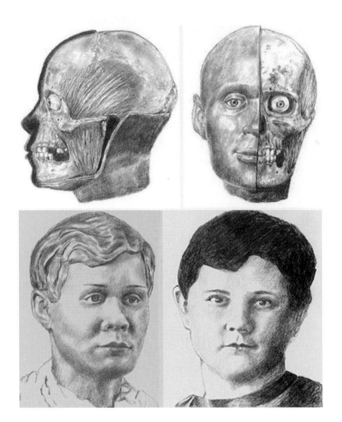

U.S.S.R. Academy of Sciences in 1950, where he worked until his last years. Mikhail M. Gerasimov died at age 62 in July 1970.

After Gerasimov, other facial reconstructionists continued with the important addition of using tissue-depth markers to enhance the technical accuracy of their work. Modern promulgators of the tissue-depth marker method of note are Richard Neave of the United Kingdom and Betty Gatliff of the United States. Neave practices the *anatomical method*, wherein the muscles are sculpted onto the skull before laying on the outer "skin" layer of clay. Betty Gatliff practices the *American method*, where clay of the proper depth is placed on the skull without regard to sculpting the underlying muscles. Gatliff uses tissue depth markers also, and has taught her method in the United States for decades.

Caroline Wilkinson of the United Kingdom continued to perfect the use of the anatomical/

Figure 7.2

Graphite drawing by author of early M. M. Gerasimov facial reconstruction after illustrations from his book, The Face Finder *(Hutchinson & Co., Great Britain, 1971).*

Figure 7.3

Graphite drawing by author after Illustration 4 from M. M. Gerasimov's, The Face Finder *(Hutchison & Co., Great Britain, 1971). "The comparison of the finished reconstitution [sic] (left) with a photograph of the missing dentist Nina Z. (right) showed a surprising likeness which was especially noticeable in the asymmetry of the eyes."[2]*

tissue-depth marker method with her book *Forensic Facial Reconstruction* published in 2004. Wilkinson's book, in addition to her own data, contained landmark data from a large sampling of children and adults gathered using diagnostic ultrasound by the Louisiana State University FACES Laboratory (Forensic Anthropology and Computer Enhancement Services). This group, spearheaded by Mary H. Manhein and including colleagues Ginesse A. Listi, Robert E. Barsley, Robert Mussleman, N. Eileen Barrow, and Douglas H. Ubelaker, collected data from 551 children and 256 adults. This group of researchers created a new set of tissue depth locations (listed and illustrated in the following pages) aimed at bettering reconstruction efforts.

K. T. Taylor of the United States began a method of *drawing* the reconstruction, rather than sculpting. Her two-dimensional method also employs tissue depth markers, based on tables from J. Stanley Rhine and C. Elliot Moore II. Taylor's technique offers great convenience and speed, making it an attractive method for forensic artists working within law enforcement agencies where space and time are limited. Operating in the free-enterprise system of the United States, Gatliff and Taylor were able to attract students who paid to learn their methods for decades, thus spreading these versions of facial reconstructions from skeletal remains to hundreds of individual artists. With the subsequent phenomenal growth of crime-fighting television programs, hundreds of reconstructions are now aired in various electronic media each year with increasingly successful results.

PREFERENCE FOR THE DRAWING METHOD

The first time I was asked to reconstruct the facial appearance from the skull of an unidentified murder victim, I drew the image by looking at a bare skull. This seems the most straightforward method, since an artist, with concentration, can imagine flesh on the bones of a skull. For instance, the reverse frequently is done when various artists look at a living person and observe that one individual has a larger-than-normal chin, another has wide cheekbones, and so on. So in 1983, I was able to do my first postmortem sketch from a bare skull, as shown in Figure 7.4. Soon the medical examiner was able to produce a photo of the girl that had been identified.

Considering that this was a first effort, I was heartened, especially since the hair and white blouse matched. I knew the girl was in her late teens or early 20s and had been murdered in 1972, so I clothed the girl in a blouse commonly worn for school photos at

Figure 7.4

My first facial reconstruction attempt from a skull. The sketch on left was drawn in pastel on Canson Mi-tientes paper observing the skull with no tissue-depth markers. There were no photos or samples of hair (courtesy of the Harris County Medical Examiners Department)

the time. The theory was that family members, when identified, would at least have a school photo of their lost loved one. Since school girls commonly wore white blouses for special occasions in that time period, I picked that garment. Additionally, the hairstyle was chosen because it was a type popular among African-American teenagers and females in their 20s during the early 1970s. The placement of the eyes, lips, and nose could be understood easily by looking at Peck's *Atlas of Human Anatomy for the Artist*, which I purchased for art classes in college. It seemed the anatomy of the face was easily drawn, once the anthropologist determined the race, sex, and age of the subject. As well, the fortunate assumptions about hair and clothing greatly aided in accomplishing a resemblance to the lost girl.

The second reconstruction I created, done the next year, also was drawn by looking at the skull. Shown in Figure 7.5, the case was more unusual, in that the eye sockets were very asymmetrical. Since this male had been murdered in the early 1970s, the hairstyle was chosen as being popular for young teens (the estimated age of the subject). For the same reasons, a common T-shirt was chosen for clothing.

When the boy was identified, it seemed to me that the placement of the features around the bony framework could be done readily, using my anatomy book. The eyebrow on the subject's left does rise up much higher off the eye because of the distinctly larger orbit on that side. The subject was wearing a T-shirt, and the hair was a fortunate choice. The clothing and hair seemed, once again, to be a major factor in accomplishing the resemblance. This boy was several years older than in the photo when he was murdered, so his mandible (chin) grew considerably. Therefore, the chin on the skull matches the drawing whereas the chin in the photo is much smaller.

Figure 7.5

My second attempt to reconstruct a face from skeletal remains. I was told this male was murdered in the early 1970s, that he was Caucasian, aged late teens to early 20s (courtesy of the Harris County Medical Examiners Department).

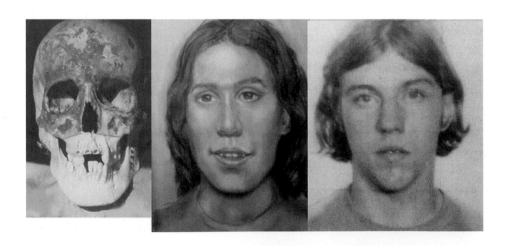

In October 1989, I finished work on the reconstruction in Figure 7.6. In December 1990, I became aware that K. T. Taylor in Austin was using a similar method.[3] Taylor utilizes tissue-depth markers on points conforming to studies made by Stanley Rhine, Ph.D., before drawing her images.

The two-dimensional or drawing method will be examined in detail first since this technique has proven to be successful and is the most economical in effort, time, supplies, and space needed. Forensic artists with a full workload might appreciate the features of this kind of facial reconstruction for the skulls of their unidentified homicide victims.

GETTING STARTED

The following beginning steps, through the discussions surrounding Figure 7.17, will be the same whether you plan to draw the face from a skull or sculpt the appearance.

RECEIVING THE SKULL

The most common scenario wherein you receive a skull for facial reconstruction is when detectives or medical examiners have a case where the subject, who may or may not be a homicide victim, is unidentified and unrecognizable. Sometimes the victim has flesh attached to the skull in various degrees of decomposition. The medical examiner will use unobtrusive methods to remove the tissue from the skull before passing it to you. Other occasions will involve an individual who has lain unnoticed long enough that all tissue has dissolved back to the elements, some to the point where there is no putrid odor left on the bones.

Figure 7.6

Presented with the skull on the left from an unidentified murder victim, I drew the reconstruction in the middle with pastels on Canson Mitientes paper. On the right is the photo of the woman identified (courtesy of the Harris County Medical Examiners Department). See color plate.

The proper transferal of such a specimen involves some paper work you will sign, acknowledging the receipt of the skull and ancillary items. Other paper work included will be a forensic anthropologist's report and an autopsy. Additionally there should be an incident report from the agency handling the case and scene photos. You have the right to request all these items if you are expected to create an image of the decedent. These items will tell you the following information.

Anthropologist Report

This invaluable report gives you necessary information, including the age, sex, and race of the individual. The anthropologist can also give height estimation, type of frame, and other indications about how the individual lived. Indications on the skeleton can reveal if a female had borne offspring, if a male had above average muscle development, the handedness, whether the individual had engaged in persistent hard labor, and much more.

Since the anthropologist ascertains information from a skeleton, the determinations of age can be somewhat vague. The age might be given in a wide range of years, such as "45 to 55 years old." Even for younger victims, the anthropologist determining the age might write something like "6 to 8 years old." Though there are other places on the skeleton that give indications of age to the observant anthropologist, the primary indicator of age on the skull is the teeth.[4] For this reason, many forensic pathologists (persons who perform autopsy) have a forensic dentist (odontologist) available. If a forensic odontologist is not available at your medical examiner's office, you can gather important information by bringing the specimen to a dentist who has been in practice for many years, or contact the American Academy of Forensic Sciences for a local professional. I have consulted as many as three dentists on a single case, since a seasoned dentist can observe the teeth and give a good estimate of the individual's age. Dentists also might have information about any dental work that was done on the subject's teeth. If the skull is from a child, a pediatric dentist can help the artist zero in on the age of that young individual.

Determining the sex is more certain. Later in this chapter indications that can be seen on the skull will be given. However, a forensic anthropologist who can observe the entire skeleton can also confirm sex by looking at the pelvic bone, the ribs, and other items.

> Forensic anthropologists are certified by the American Academy of Forensic Anthropology (AABFA). This organization can help you find a competent professional in your area. The AABFA calls this specialty *Physical Anthropology*. This designation requires a Ph.D. and successful completion of a written practical exam for certification. For your anthropologist to give expert testimony in courts of law, he or she must be certified.

Law Enforcement Report

The photos taken at the scene where your subject was found can yield invaluable information. Look closely and see what personal items are on the body. Combining the size of clothing with the anthropologist's height determination will tell you how much fat content to show on the face. As an example, Figure 7.7 shows items found on a murdered girl's body. When she was found, decomposition had progressed until only a skeleton remained. She was wearing a shirt with knife holes that matched those on her red-lace, size 34 C bra. She was also wearing size 7 denim shorts (all sizes are U.S.). These clothing items indicated the decedent had a nearly ideal figure. I could further surmise there would be scant fat content on her face. Her hair measured 24 to 28 inches long and scene photos showed it to be thick and wavy with curls on the end. All of these pieces of information prompted me to create the portrait in Figure 7.8.

The detective can tell you what kind of people might be found in the area of the skeletal find. The detective on this case mentioned prostitutes frequently strolled the stretch of a major road near where the body was found. Figure 7.9 shows a white, short-heeled, size 6½ (U.S.) shoe found on the body. Next to the shoe is the drawing I created, showing what a slender girl would look like wearing size 7 shorts and the dainty heels. These kinds of information gained from the officer who made the scene of the murder can guide you in the character of the images created to help identify the unknown victim.

FORENSIC PATHOLOGIST

The professionals who perform autopsies are capable of informing the detective as to the cause of death (drowning, blunt trauma to the head, gunshot wound, etc.) and even the manner of death (murder, accidental, suicide, etc.). However, when the decedent's soft tissue is completely absent, leaving nothing but bones, these determinations can be difficult if not impossible. Sometimes the hyoid bone is found to be fractured, which indicates strangulation. Some

Figure 7.7

(Bottom left) Figure drawn on left with clothing found on the body shown at the top and bottom right. T-shirt was size medium, brassiere was size 34C, and the shorts were size 7 (all sizes U.S.). Hair approximately 24 to 28 inches long, dark brown, thick, and curly (courtesy Harris County Medical Examiners). See color plate.

Figure 7.8

Skull of murder victim on left next to drawing of facial reconstruction on right (courtesy Harris County Medical Examiners).

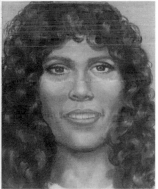

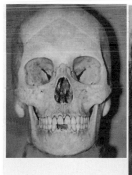

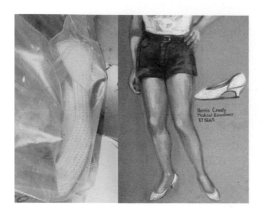

Figure 7.9

Shoe of murder victim on left was U.S. size 6½ and very short cut-off jeans U.S. size 7 led me to draw the girl with an attractive figure shown on right (courtesy Harris County Medical Examiner). See color plate.

forensic pathologists will find knife or other weapon marks on the bone, including bullet holes through the cranium. Figure 7.10 shows both profiles of an unidentified Asian female who was found decomposing in a river. The medical examiner could tell the cause of death was a gunshot wound to the head. The manner was homicide, since the angle of the bullet precludes suicide.

In order to communicate with medical examiners, homicide detectives, and court personnel, you should understand the terms described in the following box.

Cause of death: Injury or disease that leads to a fatal outcome. Causes of death can be knife wound, gunshot wound, a blow to the head, heart attack, or pneumonia.

Manner of death: Defined as circumstances surrounding the death. This term is broken into two categories, *natural* and *unnatural*. Unnatural death is the type almost always involving law enforcement and is further divided into four types: homicide, suicide, accident, and undetermined.

Absent any indications on the bones, the forensic pathologist might not be able to give either the cause or manner of death. When the body of the decedent remains unidentified, the forensic pathologist's office becomes a coordinator between the detective, the forensic anthropologist, the forensic dentist, and the forensic artist. The goal is always to identify the unknown. When no missing person's case matches the unknown decedent, these professionals turn to a forensic artist for an image that might be shown to the public in efforts to discover the identity of the person left in their care.

Figure 7.10

Both profile views show this subject's cause of death to be gunshot wound and manner of death to be homicide (courtesy of the Harris County Medical Examiners Department).

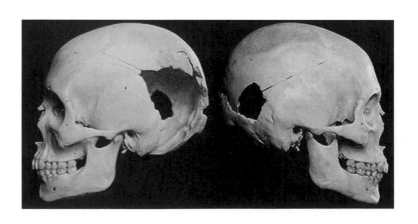

HANDLING THE SKULL

You should understand that the medical examiner's office is assigned the task of identifying the dead, and he or she has protocols that should be observed. Part of the protocol is to maintain respectful custody of the decedents. He or she must store those individuals who are not identified. Whenever receiving a skeletal remain from your medical examiner's office, always treat that specimen with respect. Take great care in storing each case in a locked, secure area, such as a padlocked metal cabinet in a secure police department building.

You should ask if there is a need to wear latex gloves to keep from transferring DNA onto or from the specimen. This is almost never the case for a forensic artist, but if the reconstruction is a rush job, gloves might be necessary. Such an occasion for gloves is shown in Figure 7.11. This is a member of the staff of the medical examiner handling the cranium of a newly discovered male found in an overgrown vacant lot in a downtown area. Obviously the gloves protect from the transfer of undesirable residue. Some artists prefer to wear gloves at all times when handling a skull. However, if the medical examiner has taken all the DNA samples needed, and the skull is cleaned adequately, the specimen can be handled with bare hands.

Never hold a skull by putting your fingers through the eye or nose holes. All these openings have fragile bones just inside that can easily be fractured. Hold the skull carefully with both hands as shown in Figure 7.12. Never allow the skull to lie on a flat surface, like a table, where it might roll off. Instead, use something like a soft ring of Styrofoam cut out so a skull might fit in the rounded out center as seen in Figure 7.13. This item can be purchased economically at a craft shop. Some artists use a cork ring; still others simply place the skull on a large bean bag.

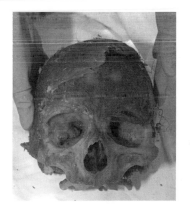

Figure 7.11

(Left) Wearing gloves when handling a skull can be necessary to prevent transfer of DNA (courtesy Harris County Medical Examiner).

Figure 7.12

(Right) One of the correct ways to handle a skull. Never place your fingers into the orbits or nasal aperture as fragile bones within might be damaged (photo by author).

Figure 7.13

A styrofoam circle will allow examination of the skull without risk of damage from rolling off a table. The texture of the circle's surface holds the specimen gently in place (photos by author).

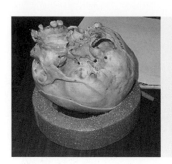
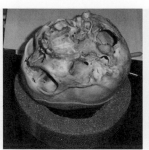
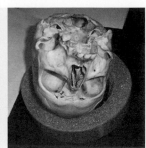

MAINTAIN THE PAPER TRAIL

Never forget that the specimen you have received is evidence. You should sign dated papers saying you have received the item, and the person delivering the specimen to you should sign the same paper indicating his or her delivery of same. If the specimen is delivered in the mail, there will most certainly be paperwork indicating receivership included. No matter how the skull is delivered, if there is no paperwork of this kind, be prepared with your own form. A simple dated document where both deliverer and receiver sign, including the case number from the source agency and your department's case number, will suffice. Your case number can be in sequence and of the same nature as those used when sketching images from witness descriptions. If you are a freelance forensic artist, these same rules apply. This document should say *what* you received, *from whom*, and *when*.

When making the original inventory of receiving the skull, be particularly aware of teeth. After death, an individual's teeth will often fall out. Persons familiar with skulls found outdoors observe that anterior, or front, teeth are most likely to fall out because they have only one root. Additionally, searchers at the scene of discovery often find teeth scattered around. Occasionally teeth will shake out of their proper location during transport. These are an important part of that individual's appearance; therefore, you must guard against losing these small items. Diligently find and make a count of the number of teeth received and include this in your written record. Later, you can place the teeth back in their proper location, if need be with the help of a dental professional.

Figure 7.14 includes a diagram that can guide replacing teeth in their proper place in the skull. Notice all teeth have their own unique shape. All teeth on one side of the arch are a mirror image of the same teeth on the other side of the arch. Even if, say, a second molar looks almost identical to the molar on the opposite side, each molar will be slightly tilted toward the center-front of

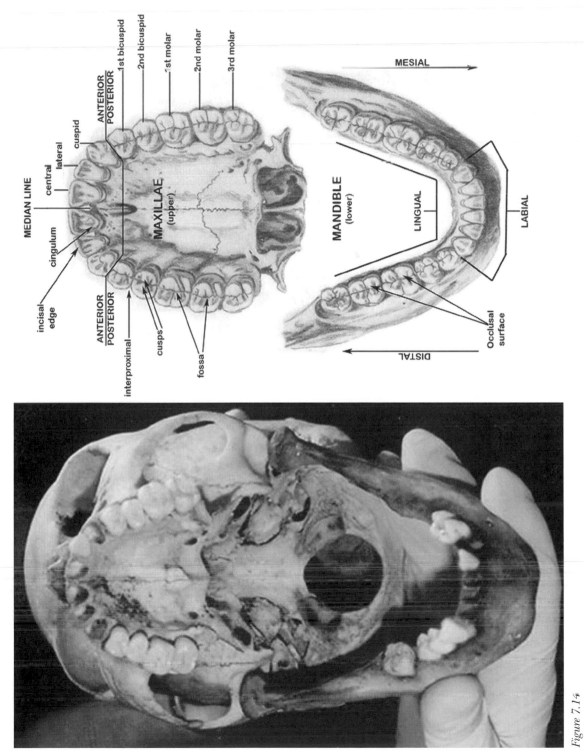

Figure 7.14

At left is a typical specimen with many teeth missing. The chart on the right will aid in replacing loose teeth received with a skull; the dental terms will help understand the medical examiner's and/or forensic anthropologist's reports (courtesy of the Harris County Medical Examiners Department).

the mouth when viewed from the occlusal surface. Because of this tilting of anatomy, seemingly identical teeth can still be restored to their proper position. I have always been able to return loose teeth to their proper place using such a diagram. Fortunately, the teeth fit perfectly snug if the proper position has been found. Conversely, if the tooth just won't fit, that is not its proper location.

Once all the available teeth are in their proper position, glue them in place using glue that can be dissolved with acetone. *Do not* glue the teeth until the proper position has been found for *all* misplaced teeth.

Other items that might be included would be hair in a vial or envelope (to understand color and texture), eyeglasses, dentures or partial-removable dental appliances, and jewelry.

Usually the originating agency will mark its case number on the mandible and calvarium of each skull. Include this number as an adjunct to your agency's case number. Make certain to connect all photos to their proper case by either marking them or keeping them in an envelope or folder with the proper case number.

Figure 7.15

Shown are two views of a mandible. Commonly referred to as a jawbone, this bottom portion of the skull falls away from the calvarium after decomposition of fleshy areas (courtesy Harris County Medical Examiner).

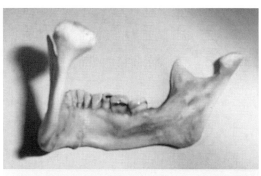
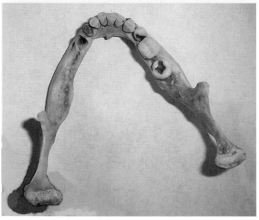

DENTAL ASSESSMENT

Before attaching the mandible to the calvarium, make certain to ascertain all the information needed from observing the occlusal surface of the teeth. Once the mandible has been attached, it will be too late. Since teeth are an important indicator of age, and give some insight as to the lifestyle of the owner, take the opportunity and learn everything possible from observing the dentition before this area is hidden from sight when the mouth is glued shut. Take good photos of the occlusal surface of the teeth.

ATTACH THE MANDIBLE

Skulls come in two pieces: the mandible and the calvarium. Figure 7.15 shows two views of the mandible. This is commonly referred to as a jawbone. This bone supports the bottom teeth on its upper side, and forms the basis for the chin on its lower side. Figure 7.16 shows the calvarium portion of the skull. In order to reconstruct the face, the mandible and calvarium need to be reattached as they were in life.

The location where the condylar process of the mandibular ramus fits into the mandibular fossa is called the temporomandibular joint. This remarkably unique joint has a function that allows the mandible to move up and down, frontward and backward, *and* side to side. Because of its specialized function there are several soft-tissue structures separating the bony areas, such as the synovial membrane, an upper and lower joint cavity separated by an articular disc, and fibro-cartilage on the articular surface. The distance of separation deduced from life-size models is approxi-

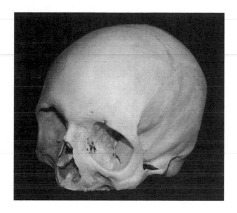

Figure 7.16

Example of a calvarium, which will separate from the mandible after decomposition. The mandible attaches at the temporomandibular joints, which are anterior to the external auditory meatus (ear hole) (photo by author).

mately 4 millimeters.[5] An ideal material for constructing this spacing is picture-mounting adhesive pads. These are sold as small 3-millimeter-thick blocks or strips with adhesive on both sides and are used to attach posters or photos to walls. These can be layered for more spacing. Cut the pad into pieces that will fit into the mandibular fossa, which is actually located on the temporal bone just in front of the external auditory meatus. Figure 7.17 shows a mandible connected to the calvarium at the temporomandibular joint, with a piece of picture mounting adhesive as a spacer. You can also use clay, cotton, cardboard, or other materials for this spacing. Any glue used must be acetone-soluble so glued items can be removed without damaging the bone. A common source of acetone is fingernail polish remover.

Next the skull can be mounted for observation. If you are preparing to use the two-dimensional, or drawing, method of facial reconstruction, the skull can be placed on a platform of plastalina modeling clay. This clay never dries and is easily modeled into any shape. As can be seen in Figure 7.18, Plastalina clay comes in many colors and can be purchased in large 5-pound packages. The clay in the photo has no sulfur content so it will not degrade the skull.

A skull mounted in the proper position is seen in Figure 7.19. The clay can easily be molded to support every skull. The skull can be gently pressed into the clay until it is in the correct position. Pieces of clay can then be added at the base

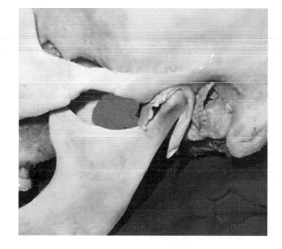

Figure 7.17

The condyle of the mandible attached to the calvarium at the temporomandibular joint with a piece of photo mounting adhesive as a spacer to replicate the structures that exist in that area in a living individual (photo by author).

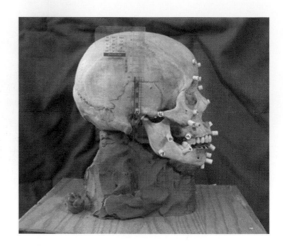

Figure 7.18

(Above left) A calvarium with 5-pound packages of Plastalina clay in several different colors. This clay, by Van Aken, is sulfur-free and oil-based so it never dries. This easily molded clay is ideal for facial reconstructions on skulls (photo by author).

Figure 7.19

(Above right) The skull can be mounted easily on a pedestal of Plastalina clay (courtesy of the Harris County Medical Examiners Department).

of the calvarium or wherever needed to maintain stability. Use a small piece of pressed board on which to place the clay pedestal. Whenever a drawing session is finished, the skull can be effortlessly removed and placed in a box that can be secured in a locked storing area. Since the clay pedestal is on a board, this item can be removed to another area, freeing up that space of the room for other work.

In Brief

Respectfully receive the skull, performing necessary paperwork, and be prepared to store the specimen in a secured location.
Gather all information from the:
- Forensic anthropologist
- Forensic pathologist
- Forensic odontologist or practiced dentist
- Law enforcement investigator

Teeth are most important to appearance and age determination. Diligently gather, correctly reposition, and examine dentition before attaching mandible to calvarium.

Attach the mandible with a spacer of approximately 3 to 6 millimeters between the condylar process of the mandible and the mandibular fossa of the calvarium to replicate structures present there in life.

MECHANICS OF THE DRAWING METHOD

Figure 7.20 is a skull with landmarks identified pertinent to facial reconstructionists.

The first step is to take high-quality photos of the skull. The resulting photos need to be life size. For this purpose, the skull needs to be photographed with a ruler set parallel to the facial plane. When the size of the photo is such that a

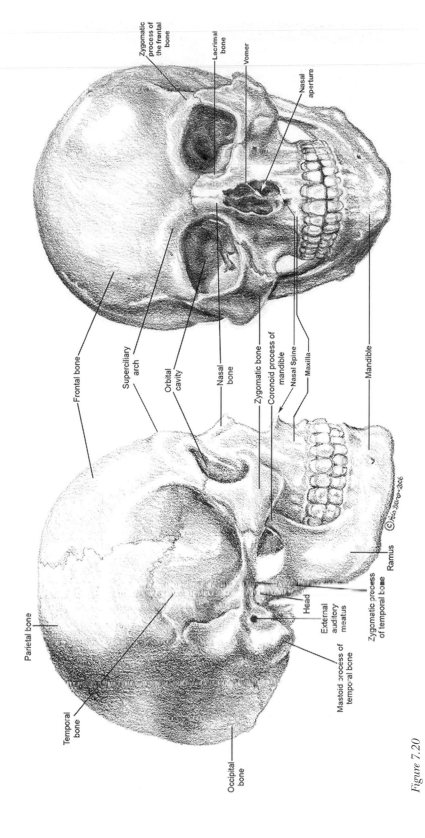

Figure 7.20

Anatomical points of the skull (illustration © author).

Figure 7.21

The above photo is life size. Notice the red ruler in the photo is exactly the same size as a ruler with black lettering placed on top of the picture (courtesy of the Harris County Medical Examiners Department).

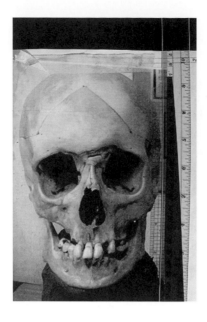

ruler placed atop it is exactly the same size as the ruler in the photo, as in Figure 7.21, the photo is ready to use.

Take photos from the front and profile. For both profile and front views, the skull needs to be positioned in the *Frankfort Horizontal Plane*. This simply replicates the natural head position when someone is alive. In other words, the position of the skull in the Frankfort Horizontal Plane is like someone looking straight ahead, or posed for a common high-school yearbook photo. Using this position will give you a view like commercial photographers would use for their subjects, thus increasing the likelihood that photos of the person when alive would be similar. The technical explanation of positioning the skull this way is to have the lowest point on the lower margin of the orbit align horizontally with the top edge of the external auditory meatus (the ear hole). See Figure 7.22 for an illustration of this position.

Figure 7.22

Skull positioned in the Frankfort Horizontal Plane, the most desirable position for photographing, drawing, and otherwise reconstructing the face on a skull. Proposed by W. M. Krogman in his The Human Skeleton in Forensic Medicine *(Charles C. Thomas, Springfield, IL, 1987), it replicates the natural forward-facing position of a living person (illustration by author).*

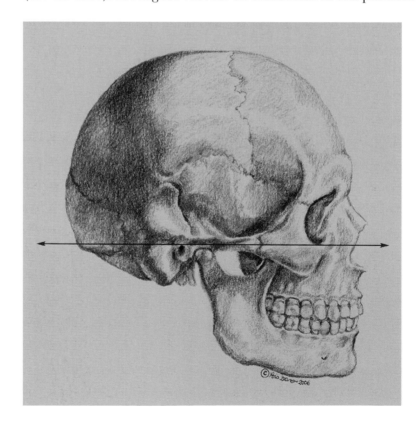

Once the photos of an exact one-on-one ratio are completed, you can trace the images of the skull onto high-quality tracing paper. Some artists prefer to trace the image on high-rag content tracing vellum upon which they create the entire facial-reconstruction drawing. The only problem with this method is the image of the skull becomes obscured as the drawing nears completion. If you employ enough pigment for a full-bodied portrait, the skull's image is completely obscured.

Figures 7.23 through 7.34 illustrate a method where you can continue to check the outlines of the skull even when applying completely opaque pigment. Begin by tracing the skull onto treated acetate. This acetate is almost as clear as a pane of glass. The treatment on the drawing surface allows this otherwise slick surface to accept markings from pencil, pen, and other drawing utensils. Begin this process by taping the acetate firmly above the area upon which the face will be drawn. Make certain the acetate is taped adequately to survive the entire drawing process without moving. Use of masking tape will inhibit destruction of the paper beneath when finally removed.

The tracing is accomplished by placing the skull photo directly under the acetate and drawing the image of that skull on the acetate with a dark graphite pencil. A soft charcoal pencil will also work well. As you can see in Figure 7.23, this tracing should include only the basic elements of the skull, leaving out minute details. Next, take a piece of carbon paper and place it, pigment side down, toward the paper upon which the drawing of the face will be done. If you are annoyed by the blue markings made by carbon paper and the difficulty of erasing these marks, or the incompatibility of the blue color with the medium you plan to use, you can manufacture your own "carbon" paper. As demonstrated in Figure 7.24, simply take the

Figure 7.23

(Below left) Photo of skull covered with treated acetate upon which has been drawn the basic outlines and anatomical points with a soft charcoal pencil (photo by author).

Figure 7.24

(Below right) Apply charcoal densely on a piece of paper, then lay it pigment side down on the paper where the final portrait will be drawn. Lay the life-size copy of the skull photo on top of both pieces of paper and trace the outline, using firm pressure to mark through the three layers (photo by author).

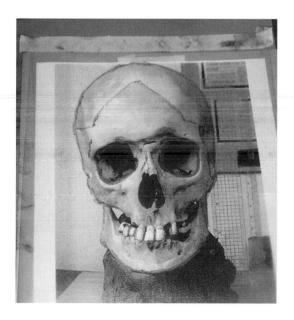

pigment that *will* be compatible and completely cover to saturation the surface of a piece of paper. This works best if the paper used has a surface with "tooth" or roughness. Then use the treated piece of paper as you would the carbon paper.

The papers should be laid one on top of another in the following manner.

- Place the drawing paper upon which the facial reconstruction portrait will be created on the bottom.
- Lay the carbon paper or treated paper with pigment side down on top of the drawing paper. This paper does not need to be taped in place.
- Place the photo of the skull face up. This photo should be taped to the drawing paper, with the carbon or treated paper laying loose under it. Tape in a manner that will allow removal without tearing the surface of the drawing paper.
- Lay the piece of treated acetate treated side up. Make certain this acetate is attached firmly to the drawing paper upon which the portrait will be made.

Once the papers are aligned, draw the basic outline of the skull on the treated acetate. Take time and make the drawing accurate, as this will be your guide to the bony parameters during the creation of the portrait. Next, lift up the acetate and bear down on the photo to make certain the outlines of the skull go through to the drawing paper on the bottom. Obviously the photo used needs to be one for which there is, or can be made, another exact copy. Essentially the high pressure needed to draw on top of this photo so the marks will show up on the bottom piece of paper will abrade the picture's surface, thus causing it to be sacrificed.

When the outlines are done to satisfaction, remove the carbon paper and photo as seen in Figures 7.25, 7.26, and 7.27. Now tape the drawing

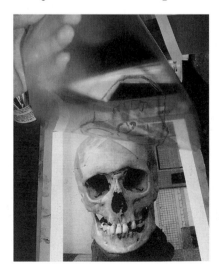

Figure 7.25

This is a view of the acetate pulled away from the surface of the life-size skull photo. Once the acetate is taped firmly in place, a drawing of the skull is made by tracing over the most obvious anatomy points (photo by author).

paper onto a drawing board at the easel, making certain the treated acetate with the skull drawing stays attached. A Stanrite 500 easel is preferable because it has an attachable light. From then to the finish, you can work on the portrait with the skull outline on the treated acetate folded behind the drawing board, as seen in Figures 7.28 through 7.32. You can intermittently drop the acetate back down over the drawing, as in Figure 7.31, to make certain the features are in line with the bony landmarks. Make certain to check often—do

Figure 7.26

(Far left) After an adequate drawing is done, remove the hand-made carbon paper and the photo of the skull, making certain the acetate with the skull drawing is kept firmly in place (photo by author).

Figure 7.27

(Left) With the acetate in place, you can begin the drawing by taping the paper upon which the portrait will be done on the drawing board at the lighted easel (photo by author).

not release the finished drawing unless a few final checks have been performed.

Notice I purposely created hair that was ambiguous. This was because there was no hair to be seen with the body. The anthropologist determined the subject to be Mongoloid/Caucasoid mixed. Since dark hair would be the

Figure 7.28

Begin the drawing with the skull in view at eye level and a profile version at hand (photo by author).

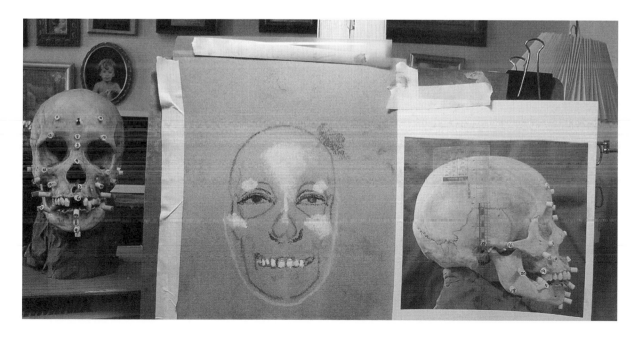

Figure 7.29

Beginning stages of pastel portrait of the front view with the acetate drawing of the skull pulled back behind the drawing board (photo by author).

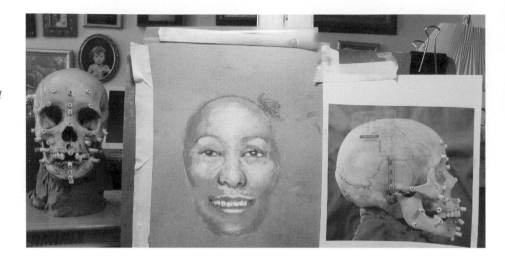

Figure 7.30

Middle stage of pastel portrait of the front view with the acetate drawing of the skull pulled back behind the drawing board (photo by author).

Figure 7.31

The acetate laid on top of the drawing helps make certain the anatomical areas of the skull are still regarded as the drawing nears completion (photo by author).

Figure 7.32

The finished portrait is done with ambiguous hair; it could be curly or straight, very dark, or somewhat light. The volume will be cropped off for media release (photo by author).

dominant trait for this population grouping, the decision was to make the hair dark. Notice that the hair in the finished drawing is so ambiguous that it could be straight, curly, short, or long. The method for producing this intentional ambiguity is simply to create a dark, amorphous area around the face, thus expanding the possibilities for identifying the subject. I also created two looks: one smiling with teeth showing and one without, as seen in Figure 7.33.

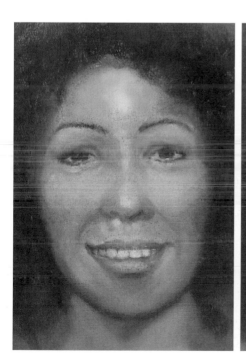

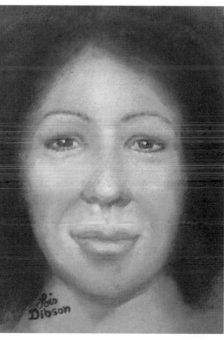

Figure 7.33

For media release, I produced two versions, one grinning and one with a closed mouth smile, to cover the most possible looks.

CASE STUDY: TWO-DIMENSIONAL OR DRAWING METHOD

I received the skull of a murder victim in September of 2006. The investigators asked for a quick completion of the facial reconstruction as they were certain she was a victim of a serial killer working where the body was dumped.

To save time, I drew the version with the teeth showing and took quality photos of that. Then the mouth area of the portrait was reworked and the portrait was photographed again. These two versions are an effort to enhance the chance a loved one might recognize the "look" of the missing person. If the subject was a male, do a short-hair, clean-faced version, and one with longer hair, a mustache, a beard, and such. These versions can be done in many combinations; simply do the drawing, take photos, add changes, and repeat the process.

Figure 7.34 shows the beginning strokes of pastel on the drawing that has been traced from a life-size photo of the skull. At the bottom of Figure 7.34 is the completed drawing still on the easel. Figure 7.35 are photos of the finished drawing with a grinning expression next to a version with a closed mouth expression. Extensive photos were taken of the drawing showing teeth; then the same drawing was converted to the somber expression for photos of that version. This case is an example of the benefits the two-dimensional or drawing method provides. The time taken from attaching the tissue-depth markers to offering the photos for release to the media was a matter of a few days. The family of the missing woman called authorities immediately as they were acutely aware she hadn't called them in months.[6] Figure 7.36 is a comparison of the reconstruction with a photo of the identified woman.

Notice the healing of the facial wound is different than depicted in the drawing. However, the family was aware she had been in an automobile accident and had bones broken in her face. They were also aware she had scars, but they do not show in the snapshot in Figure 7.36. Therefore, the scars shown on the drawing did prompt the family of the woman to connect her to the image released by the media.

Another case with which the drawing method allowed for rapid media release can be seen in Figures 7.37 and 7.38. The forensic anthropologist determined this female was African American, 5′6″ to 5′8″ tall, aged 15 to 19 years. No clothing was found on the body, so I assumed a medium amount of fat content to the face.

Notice the almost clear treated acetate with the drawing of the skull on top of the preliminary drawing. I drew her with an amorphous hairstyle. Figure 7.38 shows the identified girl next to the reconstruction drawing.

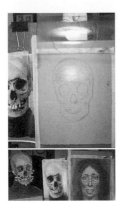

Figure 7.34

The top is the beginning of a case where the skull drawing has already been done and the acetate is placed behind the drawing board. Below is the same case nearly finished with the skull in full view, a life-size photo of the skull juxtaposed to the drawing, and the acetate skull drawing laid atop for a last check of anatomy (photo by author).

Figure 7.35

I created a version with a grin on the left and a closed-mouth version on the right.

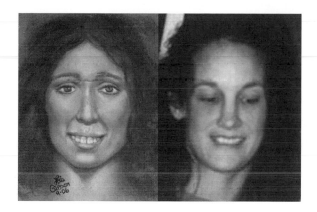

Figure 7.36

(Far left) On the left is the sketch released to the media, to the right is the identified woman (courtesy of the Houston Police Department). See color plate.

Figure 7.37

(Left) The top is the reconstruction of an unknown homicide victim in the beginning stages with the skull drawing on treated acetate lain atop, in view of a photo of the skull at eye level. The bottom is the almost-finished drawing.

Much information for the drawing method of facial reconstruction can be extrapolated from the anthropologist's reports, the clothing found at the scene, the medical examiner's observations, the forensic dentist, and the detective working the case. Skin color, race, hair texture, body fat content from clothing size compared to height all can be estimated by the artist from these information sources. The feature placement, that is to say, the relationship of soft tissue to bone, must be gained from anatomical textbooks or dissections. The masterful facial reconstructionist M. M. Gerasimov did not use tissue depth markers, yet his likenesses were remarkable. Perhaps his early and continued immersion in anatomical studies is the source of his success. Artists beginning to reconstruct a face from a skeletal remain should already be versed at drawing and/or sculpting eyes, noses, and lips.

The only uncertainty is what size and position on the skull should the various features be created. There are three anatomical textbooks that give a thorough understanding of how the features articulate with their corresponding

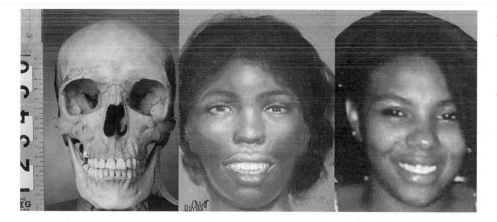

Figure 7.38

From left to right are the skull, drawing, and identified woman (courtesy of the Houston Police Department).

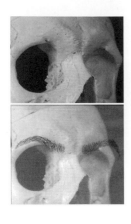

bony framework: *Anatomy, A Regional Atlas of the Human Body*, by Clemente (Urban & Schwarzenberg, Baltimore), *Wolff's Anatomy of the Eye and Orbit*, by Bron, Tripathi, and Tripathi (Chapman & Hall, London), and *Gray's Anatomy for Students*, by Drake, Vogl, and Mitchell (Elsevier, Philadelphia). Careful study of these and similar texts can help you place features in the accurate position.

FEATURE PLACEMENT

EYEBROWS

The eyebrow, beginning at the center of the face, starts under the superciliary ridge. This bony ridge that runs horizontally above the orbits of the eyes is also referred to as the brow ridge. The eyebrow starts at the lower center point of this ridge, the part that tilts downward, toward the top of the nose. From its origin near the center of the face, and from its lowest point, the eyebrow angles upward until it crosses to the upper side of the superciliary ridge. This transition of the line of brow hairs occurs at the point where the iris would be, if the subject were looking straight forward. The line of the remainder of the brow continues slightly above the crest of the brow ridge and follows that contour as it flows into the zygomatic process of the frontal bone. Most eyebrows end slightly above, right at, or slightly below the suture between the zygomatic bone and the zygomatic process of the frontal bone.[7]

Figure 7.39

A subject with distinctive superciliary ridge. The bottom image shows the general direction and placement of the eyebrows on this part of the skull anatomy (courtesy of the Harris County Medical Examiners Department).

Figure 7.39 shows the eye area of a skull with a particularly noticeable brow ridge, below which is a drawing of where the eyebrows would be placed in relation to those underlying bones. Notice toward the center of the face there is an underside of the brow ridge that is tilted downward. Even a female whose skull would be smooth in this same area has a portion just toward the center and slightly above the orbits that also tilts downward where the eyebrows would start their growth from the center of the face outward. Figures 7.40 through 7.42 are examples of skulls with the eyebrows drawn using these parameters. Below each are the corresponding subjects' eyes and brows.

Figure 7.40

Brows drawn on the skull (above) and the identified individual (below). The circles drawn inside the orbits were done using a U.S. quarter as a template to approximate the size and placement of the eyeball (courtesy of the Harris County Medical Examiners Department and the Houston Police Department).

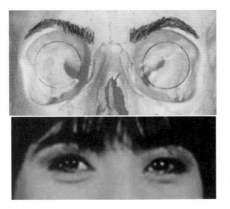

Hair-Growth Direction Is Important

Duplicating the direction of hair growth will lend a more realistic look to your portrait of an unidentified deceased person, just as it would a living person. Figure 7.43 is a sketch with arrows showing the direction the hairs in eye-brows grow at various locations on the eyebrow as they relate to the underlying bone.

The hairs of the brow grow in different directions depending on which portion of the brow they occur. The hairs at the center grow vertically. Hairs along the portion of brow that travel from under to over the superciliary crest grow at

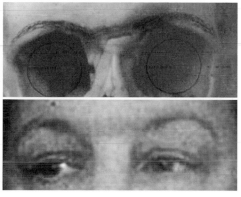

an approximate 45-degree angle tilted toward the outside of the face. The hairs on the outer third of the eyebrow have a growth direction that is horizontal, and the last hairs will aim downward. This downward angle will depend on the angle of the outer superciliar crest as it turns into the zygomatic process of the frontal bone. These "outer" eyebrow hairs will follow the angle of the underlying bone, whether the angle is steep or shallow.

Figure 7.41

Above: Brows drawn on treated acetate laid atop the orbit area of the skull. Below: The identified woman's photo. Notice the shattered and subsequently healed bones above the nasal bone and some healed fractures on the inner corners of the orbits (courtesy of the Harris County Medical Examiners Department and the Houston Police Department).

AN EFFECTIVE AID TO CORRECT FEATURE PLACEMENT

One of the best guides to understanding where soft tissue features are oriented on the skull is as near as your mirror. For the work on Figures 7.4, 7.5, and 7.6, I performed a hands-on study of how my own features were positioned on the skull. Accuracies accomplished on these cases are due, at least in part, to the practice of detailed self-examination of my features as they relate to my skull while looking in the mirror. After each case, it became apparent this self examination of landmarks was an effective tool in facial reconstructions of other individuals' skulls.

SELF-EXAMINATION: UNDERSTANDING SOFT TISSUE RELATIONSHIPS TO THE SKULL

First, wash your hands thoroughly. Then, if looking for eyebrow placement, the procedure is simple. While looking in the mirror, carefully push your fingers into the areas around the orbit. With no noticeable injury, you can find

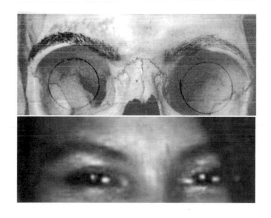

Figure 7.42

Brows drawn on treated acetate laid atop the orbit area of the skull (above). Below: The identified woman's photo. The circles drawn inside the orbits were done using a U.S. quarter as a template to approximate the eyeball's size and placement (courtesy of the Harris County Medical Examiners Department and the Houston Police Department).

Figure 7.43

The arrows above the eyebrow indicate the general direction of hair growth that changes several times along the length of the eyebrow. Replicating these hair-growth directions correctly when drawing eyebrows will give a realistic appearance.

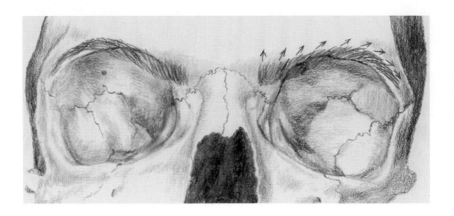

the inner rim of the upper orbit and the rounded protrusion of the superciliary ridge. While feeling these landmarks, observe the path of the eyebrow as it makes its way over this area. Just as all people have the same types of teeth that erupt from the same areas of the skull, so too will individuals' eyebrows occupy the same pathway over the bony areas above the eyes. One caveat is women who have aggressively removed hair from the brows will not provide the most accurate understanding of eyebrow placement. Another enhancement of this practice would be to engage another person who will let you perform the same palpations around the eyes.

Figure 7.6 seems to have very fortunate eyebrow placement. The brows for this case were drawn immediately after I had performed this deep tissue palpation around my own eyebrows while looking in a mirror, and then had done the same to a volunteer down the hall at my office. The volunteer was a male officer who was large-framed (6′4″), with thick eyebrows. Even though this individual had significantly divergent gender, build, and brow thickness to the female subject whose face was being reconstructed, examining his soft-tissue-to-bone relationship still gave me insight as to the female subject's correct eyebrow placement.

The same procedure can be performed around the nose area. You will find a sort of shallow valley or bony groove surrounding the outer edges of the nose where the various muscles align along the nasal aperture. Additionally, the approximate beginning of the outer edges of the nostrils in relation to the nasal aperture can be observed. Since the nasal bone, or bridge of the nose, is separated from the outer skin by only a few millimeters of tissue, and the nasal spine can be located easily, you can observe your profile and see where the end of the nose occurs and its accompanying shape, relative to these two bony landmarks.

The relationship of teeth to lips is most easy to observe, since the lips and jowls are quite rubbery and can be moved away from the teeth and back at will.

Previously, practitioners who reconstructed faces from skulls have relied on charts and diagrams and tables of tissue depths. Some of the best at this work

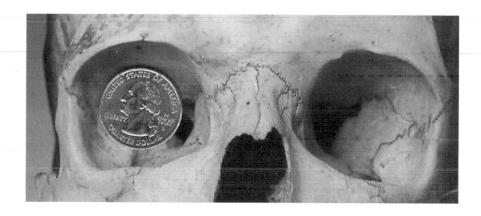

Figure 7.44
The U.S. 25-cent coin replicates the approximate diameter of the eyeball. Make certain to draw the more decisive line about two millimeters inside the original circle drawn with the coin as a template to correct for the pencil line overshooting the edge of the coin (courtesy of the Harris County Medical Examiners Department).

have been privy to professional dissections of individuals. These activities have offered insights, and this text has an abundance of diagrams and tissue depth tables. However, practitioners would miss an opportunity for deep understanding of facial anatomy if they do not examine the specimens nearest them.

EYE SIZE AND PLACEMENT

The human eyeball is between 24.134 and 23.947 millimeters in diameter.[8]

Careful measurement of a U.S. 25-cent coin shows a diameter of about 24 millimeters. This coin therefore makes a convenient template for drawing the eyeball in its orbit-centered position if the drawing is exactly the size of the skull. Figure 7.44 shows this common coin placed in the orbit area of a female approximately 5 foot 7 inches tall. After tracing the circle with the coin in place, remove the coin and draw more decisive lines inside the tracing, since the pencil lead will always make a mark outside the template.

The iris of the eye averages 11 to 12 millimeters in diameter.[9] Construct an iris with this diameter in the middle of the circle representing the eyeball.

Position of the Eye

The inner corner of the eye is attached by the medial palpebral ligament. The place of attachment is across the front of the lacrimal groove, anterior to (in front of) the lacrimal sac, and on top of the anterior lacrimal crest.[10] The outer edge of the eye is attached by the lateral palpebral ligament to a small bump on the inside rim of the orbit called the lateral orbital tubercle.[11] Figure 7.45 at top shows the bony landmarks involved in suspending the eye across the orbit; below is a schematic of how the soft tissue is positioned on the bony framework. The most concise illustrations of the inner corner of the eye show the medial palpebral ligament stretching from the eyeball to across the lacrimal fossa (which contains the lacrimal sac) and continuing across the anterior crest

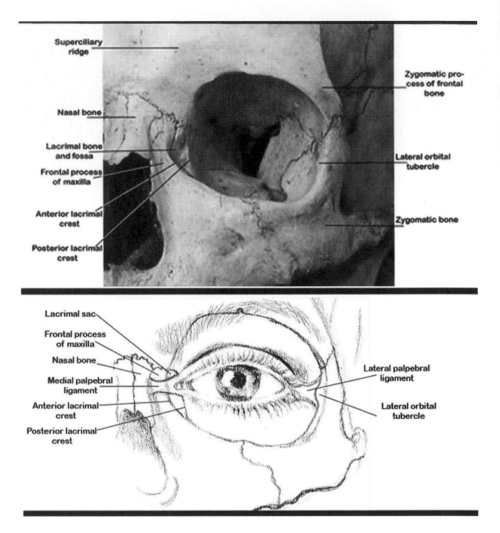

of the lacrimal bone, finally inserting on the frontal process of the maxilla. *Wolff's Anatomy of the Eye and Orbit*, by Bron, Tripathi, and Tripathi (London, 1997), a book dedicated completely to the anatomy of the eye and surrounding anatomy, shows the medial palpebral ligament insertion on the frontal process of the maxilla, ending at the edge of the nasal bone.

The bony attachment for the lateral palpebral ligament is not always an obvious landmark. The most robust lateral orbital tubercle will only be a small, smooth protrusion the size of a small grain of wheat. Often you will find this slight bump on the inside of the lateral edge of the orbit by rubbing lightly along the surface. Figure 7.46 shows three cases with the

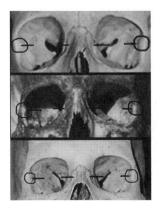

lateral orbital tubercles outlined and pointed out with arrows. Another way to find this landmark is to look just below the suture between the zygomatic bone and the zygomatic process of the frontal bone.

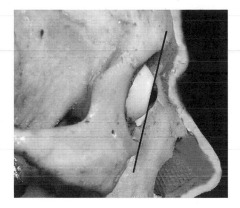

Figure 7.47

The eyeball in profile would be positioned so that a line from the top middle edge to the bottom middle edge of the orbit crosses through the cornea and is touching and parallel to the flat plane of the iris (modified from Wilkinson).

The eye in profile should be set in the horizontal plane of that view so that a line running from the center top of the orbit to the center bottom of the orbit should pass so that it "... touches the iris, rather than the cornea."[12] The cornea is a clear, bloodless structure that covers the iris and pupil; the cornea is the part of the eye upon which you place a contact lens. Figure 7.47 shows a prosthetic eye set in the proper location.

In Brief

Using a life-size photo of the skull you can employ various tracing techniques to create an accurately proportioned portrait while always referring back to the skull.

Eyebrows grow from under the brow ridge at the center near the nose, climb over the ridge above the middle of the eye, and follow the upper contour of the zygomatic process of the frontal bone to their outer end. Replicate eyebrow hair-growth direction for a realistic image.

Thoughtful palpations of skull areas through tissue in living subjects can enlighten you to feature placement.

The human eyeball is approximately 24 millimeters in diameter; the iris is 11 to 12 millimeters in diameter.

The surface of the eye is attached medially at the anterior lacrimal crest; laterally at the lateral orbital tubercle. An eyeball is positioned correctly in profile if a line between the middle of the upper and lower orbital rims passes through the cornea.

PLACEMENT OF THE NOSE

The area of the skull from which you must extrapolate the nose consists of the nasal bone, nasal aperture, and the anterior nasal spine. Just like all parts of the face, these anatomy points will have unique shapes depending on the individual. Figure 7.48 shows the anatomy points with three divergent nasal apertures and anterior nasal spine shapes, with corresponding nose images.

An early formula for placement of the outer edges of the bottom of the nose (ala) outside the aperture is 5 to 8 millimeters on each side outside the widest portion of that opening.[13]

Figure 7.48

To the left are anatomical points important to reconstructing the nose. Top center are three nose types with their corresponding schematic drawing with ala positions marked. Below each are close-ups of nasal areas for specimens with similar aperture shapes (modified after Taylor).

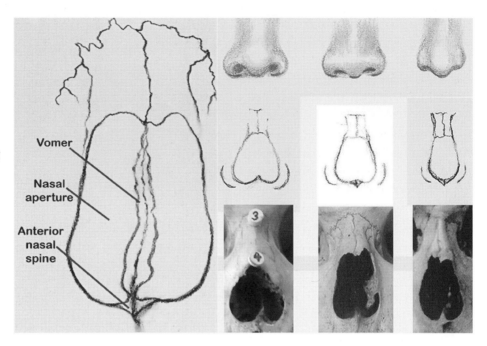

This calculation was set forth by Krogman in his 1968 book, *The Human Skeleton in Forensic Medicine*. Krogman indicated the 5 mm width was for Caucasians and 8 mm was for Negroid. Said another way, Krogman estimated you should add 10 mm of tissue to the width (measured at widest point) of a Caucasian aperture, and 16 mm tissue to the width (measured at widest point) of a Negroid aperture. The two alae, the curvatures surrounding the nostril holes, are estimated to be from 5 mm to 8 mm wide; see Figure 7.50 for a method to measure this area. Since Krogman gave no formula for Mongoloids, some have opined one should average the width for a best guess on those subjects. Perhaps more weight should be given to the overall type of skull with which you are presented. If the individual is wide and thick boned, and the aperture is also wide, a larger number would probably be correct, and a slender individual with a slender aperture would indicate a smaller width. Additionally, the shape of the nasal spine will dictate the shape of the end of the nose. K. T. Taylor expounds thusly:

> "My personal observation is that **a reasonable assumption may be made with regard to the shape of the nasal spine in relation to the shape of the tip of the nose.** Although the nose tip is composed of cartilage, it makes sense that a slight, pointed anterior nasal spine was designed to support a slight, pointed soft tissue nasal tip. On the other hand, a very sturdy, broad nasal tip may have been designed to bear the load of a bulkier soft tissue nasal tip. A bifurcated nasal spine may indicate a more visibly dual-lobed soft tissue nasal tip, with a discernible split in between the lower cartilages. My own identified cases seem to bear this out, although there has been no formal study."[14]

Figure 7.49 illustrates Taylor's statement. One can see the nose **A** has a tiny, pointed nasal spine, whereas the nasal spine at the bottom of the aperture on **B** is five times as wide and shaped more like a shovel than a point. Individual **A** has a slender, delicate skull compared to the thicker, more robust skull of subject **B**. There was no bifurcated nasal spine available, but Taylor's assertion that spine would indicate a bifurcated nose tip seems reasonable.

Figure 7.50 is an example of lines drawn at the widest point of the nasal aperture with a perpendicular line along which you can measure out the distance to the placement of the outer curve of the ala. Make certain the bottom of the alae are just below the aperture.

The change in direction at the edge of the nose opening often indicates the height and contour of the alae. Figure 7.51 at top is an anatomical drawing featuring the cartilage, which is attached to and extends from the nasal aperture, bone, and anterior spine. Below are two views of a nasal aperture with arrows pointing at the change in direction that probably coincides with the area where those various cartilage structures of the ala were attached. Using this landmark, if it has not been damaged, we know where to start the outward curve of the ala, and the shape of that curvature. Figure 7.52 contains three views of the cartilage structures of the nose. Picturing these structures can help visualize the nose width and shape.

Another way to determine the width of the nose in front view is illustrated by Figure 7.53. The slender muscle positioned vertically along the outer contour of the nose bears the long name of *levator labii superioris alaeque nasi*. Not only does this muscle describe the outline of the nose in frontal view, its outer contour is the same as the outer edge of the ala. In other words, if you can envision the placement of this muscle, you can envision the outer edge of the nose. Take note, this muscle originates from the upper part of the frontal process of the maxilla.

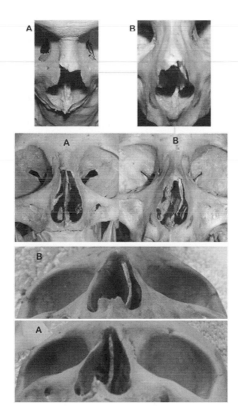

Figure 7.49

The widely divergent nasal spines of subject A and B would suggest a different nose tip. The nasal spine of A is small and pointed, suggesting a smaller, more pointed nose ending; the nasal spine for subject B suggests a wider nose as the nasal spine is wide.

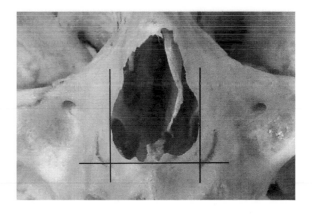

Figure 7.50

To mark the outer edges of the ala, measure the widest point of the nasal aperture and place the markings 5 to 8 millimeters to either side. This approximate distance from the aperture is affected by the sex and race of the subject.

Figure 7.51

Top: cartilage structures of the nose (modified after Clemente). At the bottom are two views of a nasal aperture. Arrows point to the change in direction of the nasal aperture. This indicates the beginning of the outward curve of the ala; notice the lesser alar cartilages nestled there.

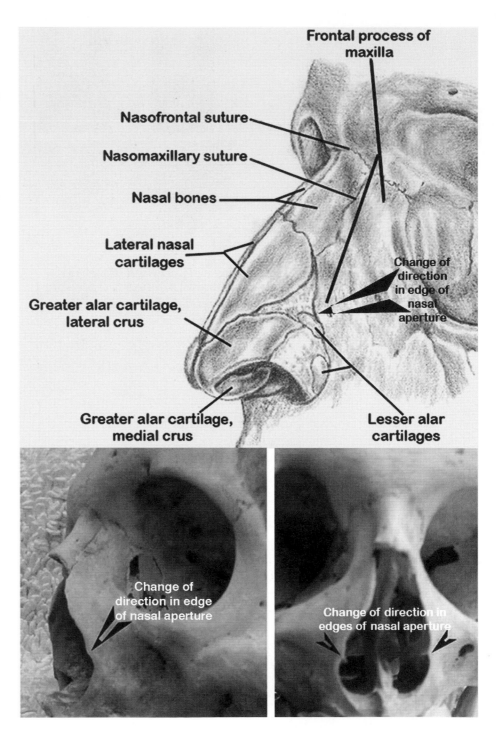

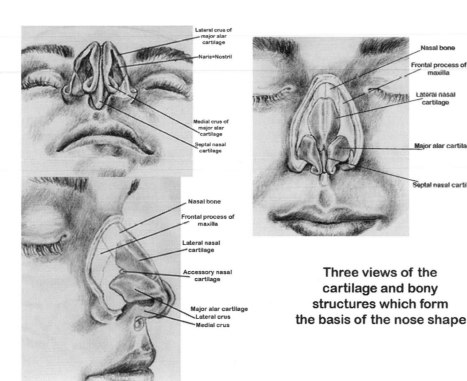

Three views of the cartilage and bony structures which form the basis of the nose shape

Figure 7.52

Three views of the nose with cartilage structures exposed (modified after Clemente).

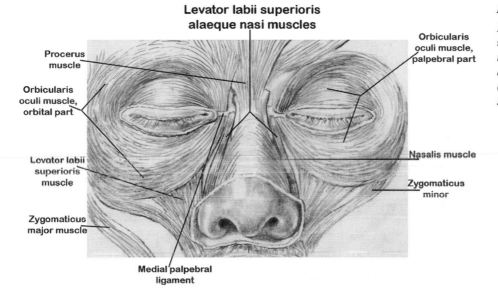

Figure 7.53

Muscles of the upper face with special attention to the levator labii superioris alaeque nasi muscles (modified after Clemente). See color plate.

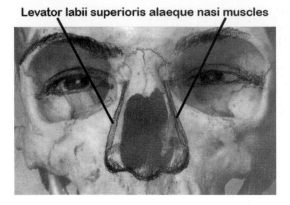

Levator labii superioris alaeque nasi muscles

Figure 7.54

Location of the levator labii superioris alaeque nasi muscles (courtesy of the Harris County Medical Examiners Department).

This origination is immediately beside the medial palpebral ligaments, where the inner corners of the eyes attach, and also parallels the suture between the nasal bone and the frontal process of the maxillary bone. The lower end of the levator labii superioris alaeque nasi splits into two portions: One inserts into the alar cartilage; the other inserts into the upper lip, medial to the levator labii superioris. These landmarks can help you understand how the outer edge of the slender levator labii superioris alaeque nasi defines the outer edge of the nose. Figure 7.54 is a drawing where the levator labii superioris alaeque nasi muscle placement was used to determine the outline of the nose. Figure 7.55 is a four-part comparison of a nose constructed with this method juxtaposed with the identified subject.

Still another method for determining the outer contour of the ala is aligning them directly above the nearest portions of the canine eminence. This method of estimating the width of the nose has been endorsed by both K. Taylor and M. Gerasimov. In 1957, Broadbent and Mathews asserted the "wings" (ala) of the nose extend to the inner canthus of the eyes. That is to say, if you drop a line from the inner corners of the eyes, it will fall at the outer edge of the bottom of the nose.

Some authorities say the nose is twice the length of the nasal bone.[15] In another mode of estimation, Gerasimov concluded that the nasal aperture, at its widest point, was three-fifths of the overall width of the nose.

In Brief

The outer edges of the nose, or ala, will be approximately:

- 5 to 8 millimeters outside the widest point of the nasal aperture.
- In line with the canine eminence.
- In line with the canthi (inner corners) of the eyes.
- Parallel to the outer edge of where the levator labii superioris alaeque nasi muscles would lie.

Calculate the width assuming the widest point of the nasal aperture is three-fifths of the total nose width. Also, the shape of the nasal spine gives indications about the shape of the nose tip.

ESTIMATING THE NOSE SHAPE IN PROFILE

All these methods are best utilized while working on the profile nose image. Tissue-depth markers enable you to more clearly imagine the profile of the nose. Figure 7.56 details the fleshy structures that surround the bony areas of the nose. Making note of the projection of the anatomy from the maxillary bone outward will help make sense of the various formulae set forth for conjuring the nose shape from only a skull.

Krogman offered a method for the length of nose projection in profile when the nasal spine is present. The nasal spine is measured from its originations at the vomer bone to the anterior-most tip. That number, which is usually less than 8 or 9 millimeters, is multiplied by three. That amount should be the distance from the base of the nose to the tip. This projection starts from the surface of the face. Therefore, the distance should project from tissue depth marker no. 5 (from the Rhine tables), which would be attached directly below the nose.

Observe that the curve of the ala begins in front of, and slightly below, the nasal aperture. This ala placement can be seen in Figure 7.58, and in illustrations for textbooks used by medical students during dissections.[16]

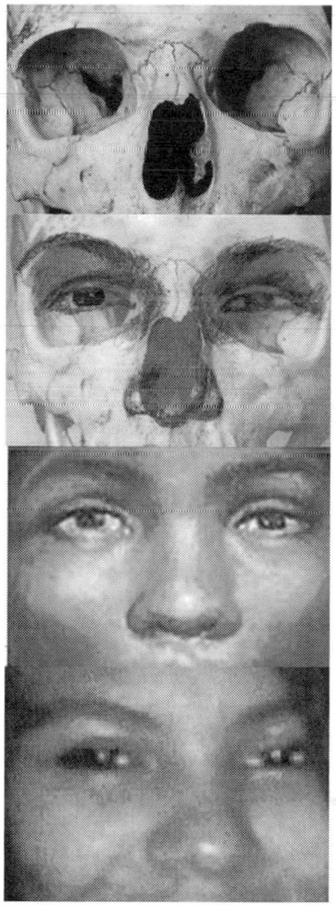

The *direction* of this nose projection is quite

Figure 7.55

Upper skull of unidentified murder victim (top), beginning drawing of feature placement on subject (next to top), finished drawing in pastel of subject (next to bottom), and identified woman (bottom).

important in determining the nose shape. The direction can be ascertained from observation of the direction of the nasal spine. Figure 7.57 offers a close view of four different nasal spines. These various nasal-spine directions will determine the direction of the nose projection.

One established method for constructing the shape of a nose in profile was first practiced by Gerasimov and later employed by John Prag and Richard Neave.[17] This method of nose profile shape calculation estimating the intersection of a line drawn following the last direction of the nasal bone, with a line projected along the angle of the nasal spine, determines the location of the nose tip. A rounded shape would be created at that location, as shown in Figure 7.58.

Another system for estimating the profile of a nose is the Lebedinskaya method. Illustrated in the bottom right of Figure 7.58, this technique is the result of a study by Ubelaker and Prokopec (2002) at the Institute of Ethnology and Anthropology at Moscow. Using a photo of the skull in profile, a line (A) is drawn dissecting the nasion and prosthion. Another line (B) parallels the first line and intersects the most prominent point of the nasal bone. Six parallel lines are drawn perpendicular to lines A and B, and reaching from before the nasal aperture edge, to beyond the tip of the nasal bone. The distance from line B to the edge of the nasal aperture is measured, and a point is marked that same distance, on the opposite side of line B. When these points are connected, the angle and form of the nose are predicted.[18]

Figure 7.56

A cross-section through the midpoint of the anterior portion of the head, showing the fleshy areas as they relate to the skull. This is a fairly realistic view of a cross-section of a cadaver. Notice the cartilage and flesh that overhangs in front and below the nasal spine (modified from Clemente). See color plate.

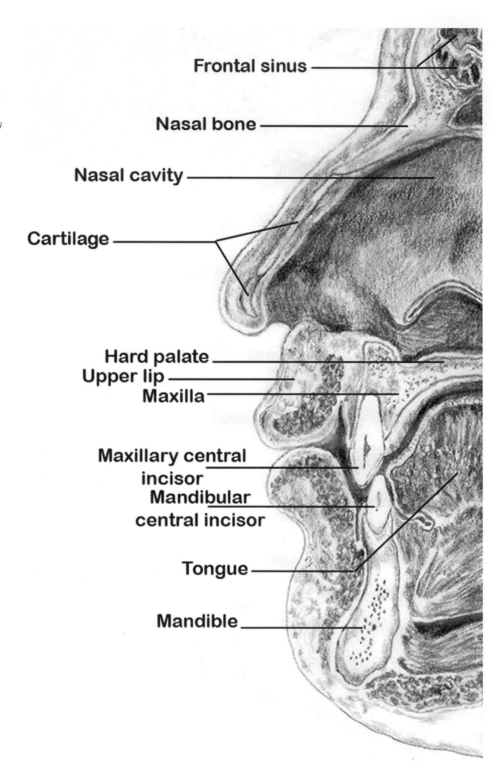

Frontal sinus

Nasal bone

Nasal cavity

Cartilage

Hard palate

Upper lip

Maxilla

Maxillary central incisor

Mandibular central incisor

Tongue

Mandible

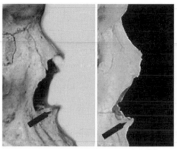

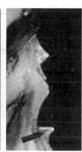
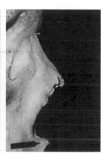

Figure 7.57

Five different nasal spines with an arrow approximating the direction of the nose projection.

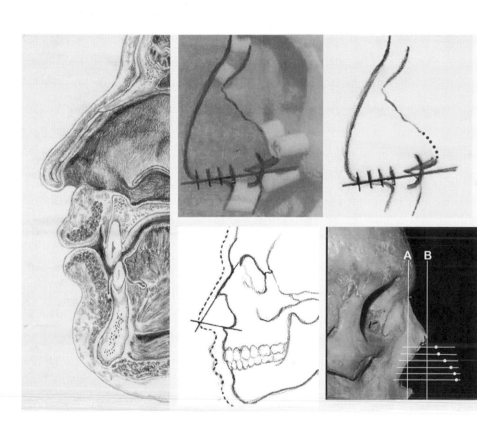

Figure 7.58

Far left: Cross-section view of a cadaver head. Top right: Illustration of Krogman's nose length formula. Center top: The formula superimposed on a skull. Bottom center: After Krogman's diagram of nose-shape approximation. Bottom right: Determination from Prokopec and Ubelaker in a 2002 study at the Institue of Ethnology and Anthropology, Moscow (modified from Wilkinson). See color plate.

Many of these calculations and methods depend on the skull having a nasal spine and nasal bone in place and undamaged. In the world of unidentified murder victims not being found until they are down to the bone, these delicate portions of the anatomy are often missing, having been destroyed during the time the subject lay in remote areas exposed to elements and the local foraging fauna. When these items are missing, you must observe the whole of the subject. The race, age, and sex give hints to nose shapes. Considering the modest amount of tissue covering the bridge of the nose, that shape is readily observed. Only the last half of the nose need be speculative.

In Brief

In profile, the nose is approximately:

■ In the direction and three times the length of the nasal spine, measured from the fleshy surface at the nose base (from tissue-depth marker 5).

■ A shape formed by drawing a line at the angle of and from the nasal bone and spine, the intersection of which lines are the nose tip.

■ The shape indicated by connecting dots formed by points along six parallel lines that are perpendicular to a line touching the farthest edge of the nasal bone, and parallel to a line dissecting the nasion and prosthion. Those points are equidistant yet in the opposite direction of points along the rim of the nasal aperture.

Figure 7.59

Left photo shows teeth with pertinent landmarks. The horizontal line indicates the approximate location and width of the mouth opening. At right are two sets of teeth, with lips superimposed translucently below, and at the bottom the lip drawing without the teeth showing from behind. See color plate.

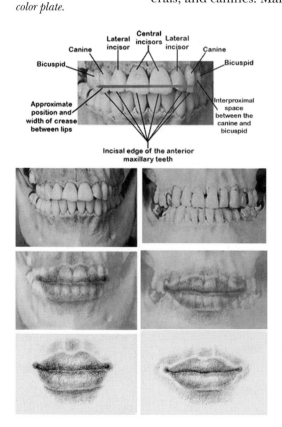

MOUTH AND CHIN RECONSTRUCTION

Speculation of the appearance of the mouth is greatly aided by the teeth, a feature that remains the same after death as before. The general rule is the horizontal lip opening ends at a point between the canine and first bicuspid. Said another way, the mouth opening (and thus the grin) will show the maxillary centrals, laterals, and canines. Many smiles show a side view of the bicuspids and even teeth further back. For the purposes of facial reconstruction, draw a line between the canines on either side, and that will be the span of the mouth opening.

The width of the lips should be approximately the vertical length of the enameled areas of the front central incisors. This means the point where the shiny enamel ends, and the root area (which has a more bone-like surface) begins, to the bottom or incisal edge of the tooth, is equal to the vertical width of the lip. This is the portion of the tooth commonly seen in living individuals. A comprehensive dental laboratory technicians' manual confirms the combined length of the enameled portion of the anterior teeth is about 18 to 22 millimeters.[19]

The horizontal line where the lips meet will occur either at or a few millimeters above or below the incisal edge of the anterior maxillary, or top front teeth.

Figure 7.59 shows these three rules in practice on two cases with quite divergent dentition. On the left is an African-American female with large attractive teeth, and on the right is a Caucasian male with teeth in good proportion and occlusion. When the lips are drawn equal to the vertical length of the front teeth and each end of the mouth opening ends at the interproximal space between the canines and bicuspids, each set of lips seem appropriate to the sex and race of each subject. Notice how both lips meet a millimeter above the incisal edge of the top teeth.

Reconstructing the Grin

Missing teeth can be reconstructed as similar to the surrounding dentition. The average height of the enamel part of the upper center front teeth, or maxillary central incisors, is 10.5 to 11 millimeters. This length refers to the area of the tooth seen in a living person when he or she grins. This exposed portion of the tooth is referred to as the crown. The crown of the tooth is covered with enamel and the length is measured from the incisal (cutting) edge to the cervical line, also referred to as the cementoenamel junction (CEJ). The CEJ is where the root and crown meet. Some dentists call this the "neck" of the tooth. All the other upper teeth will be as long as, or a little shorter than, the central incisors. Therefore, start with the grin 10.5 to 11 millimeters high at its center, and allow the lips to drape over the surrounding teeth until the outer corners of the mouth meet at the junction of the vertical edges of the canine and bicuspid. Give attention to pulling up the corners of the mouth so the grin has a genuine happy look. If the subject has large lower teeth, those will show during the grin. If the teeth seem small and recessive, perhaps the smile will be made with the upper half of the top teeth still covered by the lips as in Figure 7.61. I used this theory, that of small, recessive teeth not being fully displayed during the subject's grinning action, and the photo proves the theory to be correct.

This portion of the reconstruction will benefit from observing yourself and others while in the act of grinning. Notice how other individuals with various kinds of dentition cause their soft tissue to interact with their teeth. Observe the kind of grin that appears on people with teeth like those of the subject you are reconstructing. You might also gather photos of grinning people with dentition similar to the subject to hone in on the correct appearance.

Figure 7.60

Skull of unidentified murder victim on the left, the reconstruction sketch on the right. The teeth were large and bright colored; the clean edge of the holes indicated the missing teeth were present when the subject was alive.

The single-rooted anterior teeth, those most seen during a grin, often are missing. However, Figure 7.60 shows how the missing teeth were drawn as bright and attractive, since the surrounding teeth appeared large and bright. When teeth are lost due to trauma and/or surgery, the bone surrounding the socket immediately begins to grow over the void, creating a rippled socket, which eventually closes. Conversely, smooth edges and inside surfaces indicate the tooth was in place when that person was alive.

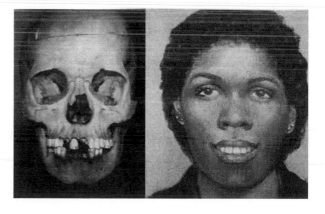

I knew all the front teeth of the subject in Figure 7.60 were present in her grin right up to her death. I observed the surrounding teeth, and reconstructed those teeth known to exist in the subject's smile to match the existing dentition's appearance.

Further, observing the hole left by the tooth root gives an impression of the tooth shape. Figure 7.61 shows how the shape of the missing root aided in replicating the subject's grin. Observation of his teeth (at the top of the illustration) shows the maxillary lateral incisor sockets are much smaller than those of the maxillary central incisors. I was prompted by this understanding to draw the lateral incisors as recessive, and the central incisors (middle top front teeth) as prominent. As can be seen in the identified subject's photo at the bottom right of Figure 7.61, those assumptions facilitated the resemblance of the grin between the drawing and a photo of the subject. In life, he clearly had center front teeth that dominated his grin; the lateral incisors to either side were small enough to seem set back from the center teeth. Take heart when the front teeth are missing. Use photos of real teeth to replicate the anatomy, and observe the hole left by the root to recreate some unique traits.

Another case, shown in Figure 7.62, confirms the successful reconstruction of missing teeth by observing the surrounding dentition. I observed that this murder victim's skull was smaller than my own, yet her teeth were larger. In addition to being large, compared to the skull size, the teeth were a bright

Figure 7.61

The top photo is a close-up of the teeth of this unidentified homicide victim. Close examination shows the root holes for the maxillary lateral incisors are far smaller than those for the central incisors. I then created the sketch, below left, with the teeth showing prominent central incisors and recessive lateral incisors.

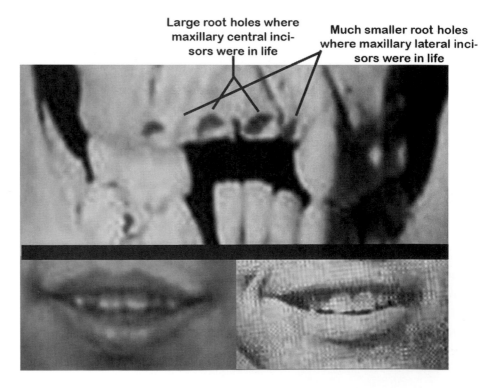

Large root holes where maxillary central incisors were in life

Much smaller root holes where maxillary lateral incisors were in life

color of creamy white, and had no decay or previous dental work. Additionally, the large sockets left by the missing teeth seemed identical in size, comparably speaking, to the teeth still in place. For this reason the drawing showed a pleasant grin. I further assumed this female would wear lipstick since she was in her late teens to early 20s and would probably have a remarkable grin.

Figure 7.63 gives a view to a more troublesome case. The teeth were worn and the subject had an overjet and an overbite. Since the body was found with a wig made of long brown hair, I assumed this individual would take great care to appear attractive, since wearing a wig in the hot, humid climate where the body was found in June meant appearance was far more important than comfort to the wearer. For this reason, even though many of the back teeth were missing or had dental work, a sketch was done with a grin. The missing front teeth (her maxillary right canine and left lateral incisor) were drawn long and slender, matching the teeth still in place. The subject in her photo is not grinning as fully as in the drawing. However, the not-so-accurate drawing was immediately successful since the missing woman's family called authorities and identified her.[20] They remarked that they thought the reconstruction portrait looked like their aunt. Since that aunt was the sister to the subject and thus prompted the call to police, the drawing fulfilled the purpose.

A much more troubling case is illustrated in Figure 7.64. A small toddler was beaten to death, rolled in a blanket, and laid in a water-filled ditch. By the time of discovery, much of the tissue had decomposed, leaving me with photos that were a view of part of the skeleton and decomposed flesh. Using the teeth as a guide to her smile, the drawing was made with a wide grin that showed the lower teeth. The reason for this is the teeth were obviously large compared to the skull size, and the mandibular teeth were large compared to the upper teeth, leading me to surmise this little girl would show her upper and lower teeth during a grin. I called the medical examiner's forensic dentist to consult about what appeared to be a missing front tooth (left maxillary central incisor) next to the other front tooth (right maxillary central incisor), which seemed to be partially erupted. That dentist informed me the girl had experienced trauma during which the left front tooth was knocked out and the right front tooth had been jammed up into the maxillary bone, probably during the same incident. I decided to draw the teeth as they appeared, hoping someone had seen her after the injury. However, the lighting on the portrait was made bright around the mouth area, and the tongue was highlighted in an effort to obscure the appearance of the missing tooth.

An adult relative of the child called authorities with her identity after seeing the forensic portrait on the news.[21]

Just as portraits of beautiful subjects are easy to create, an obviously beautiful grin is easier to reconstruct. Figure 7.65 proves the artist should go ahead and create a vibrant grin if the teeth are large and attractive.

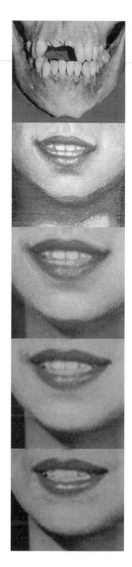

Figure 7.62

Top photo: The maxillary-mandibular area of the skull showing teeth present and clean holes of teeth lost postmortem. Second from top and proceeding down: The drawing from the skull, the photo of the identified individual behind a progressively more translucent drawing. The bottom is the unadorned photo of the individual. See color plate.

Figure 7.63

Left: Photo of maxillary-mandibular area of subject to be facially reconstructed (top). Middle is drawing estimating appearance of that individual's grin; bottom is the grin of the individual identified due to the sketch release to the media.

Figure 7.64

Right: Badly decomposed maxillary-mandibular area of murdered little girl (top). Middle is drawing estimating appearance of little girl's grin; bottom is the grin of the little girl identified due to the sketch release to the media.

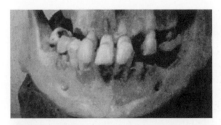
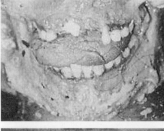
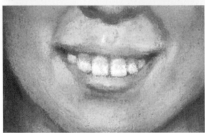
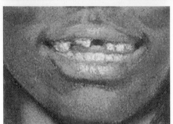
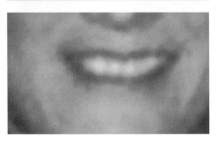
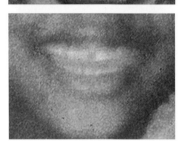

Figure 7.65

Pencil drawing on tracing vellum atop the photo of an unidentified murdered girl's maxillary-mandibular area of skeletal remains (top). Middle is drawing estimating appearance of the individual's grin; bottom is the grin of the identified subject.

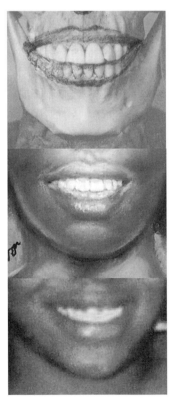

A custom in the United States is to have school photos taken yearly, even among the lowest economic levels. These photos are traditionally posed with a grin or a smile. For this reason, the strategy for identification of an individual with large, bright, well-formed teeth as in this case, would be to show a grin. I could tell this female subject would show an almost solid white area since both her mandibular and maxillary teeth would show. Most individuals have a horizontal indention below the bottom lip. Following the curvature and location of this subject's indention below her lower lip gave that shadow the right shape.

To reconstruct the lips in profile, follow the same rules of the parting line ending at a point around the space between the canine and bicuspid, with that line parallel to and within a few millimeters of the incisal edge of the front teeth. Individuals with teeth that protrude will have a slightly higher lip line. Observe living subjects for understanding the nuances of this lip-line placement.

In Brief

The line where the lips meet runs from the interproximal space of the maxillary canine and bicuspid on one side to the other. Said differently, the mouth opening exposes the top middle six teeth.

Lips are as thick as the enameled portion of the teeth is tall. When teeth are occluded, their combined height is approximately 18 to 22 millimeters.

The height of the enameled portion of maxillary central incisors is approximately 10.5 to 11 millimeters. Show this much tooth height for a full grin.

Replicate surrounding dentition when depicting missing teeth. Observe size and shape of root holes left by missing teeth for clues to the shape and size of those lost teeth.

EAR PLACEMENT AND SIZE

The ear should be placed so that the tragus is atop the ear hole. The top of the ear will be on a parallel line with the brows, and the bottom of the ear will parallel the bottom of the nose. The external auditory meatus offers a distinct landmark for placement. The complicated convolutions of the ear structures need to be replicated for a realistic drawing.

Figure 7.66 has examples of three major races in profile. This view offers the most obvious differences in the facial structures. Anthropologists are able to determine race from other elements, and they should be the final arbiter of any specimen's racial orientation. However, this illustration shows the most obvious and easily observed differences. The Mongoloid skull will have a lower nose bridge. The most striking feature that sets the Mongoloid individual apart from Caucasoid and Negroid is that the bottom portion of the zygomatic, or cheek bone, protrudes forward so the lower half is almost parallel to the upper portion. Said differently, where the zygomatic bone and the maxillary bone come together under the eye orbit, they form the lower rim of the orbit, or the top of the cheek bone. In Caucasoid and Negroid individuals, the bottom of that cheek bone tilts toward the back. That lower portion of the cheekbone in a Mongoloid specimen will be parallel to the top portion. This feature gives the Mongoloid an almost flat-to-the-vertical-axis profile.

The most obvious indication of a Negroid profile is the anterior protrusion of both the maxillary and mandibular alveolar ridges. The alveolar ridges are horseshoe-shaped bony ridges out of which the teeth erupt. The forward protrusion of these bones causes both arches of upper and lower teeth to be thrust forward from the facial plane. The bulging out of the maxillary and mandibular bones from under the nose allows the Negroid

Figure 7.66

Top to bottom are Mongoloid, Negroid, and Caucasoid individuals. From left to right are the skull, a facial drawing on translucent vellum superimposed on the skull, and the drawing with no underlying skull visible (illustration by author).

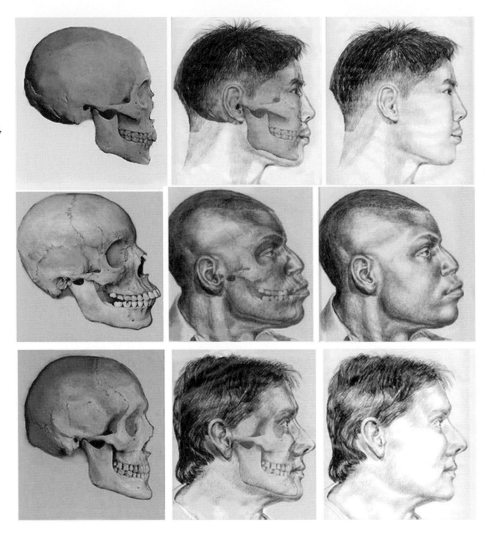

skull to accommodate larger teeth compared to individuals of other races with the same sized skull. This trait will also give the Negroid individual a longer mandible on the horizontal plane. Other, less noticeable traits for the Negroid skull are guttering on the bottom of the nasal aperture and a square shape in that same area.

Caucasoid skulls have nasal openings that are more rounded in their lower contours, compared to Negroid. There will be a sill at the bottom edge of the nasal aperture for Caucasians. The profile from the bottom of the nose to the bottom of the chin will be straight. The nasal bone will be steeper than the Negroid or Mongoloid. The bottom of the cheekbone will tilt toward the back.

SOLUTIONS FOR THE MISSING MANDIBLE

One major portion of the skull, the mandible, will occasionally be found missing from an unidentified skeletal remain. This is especially true since many murderers hide their victims in remote areas where the elements can disturb and misplace portions of the victims' anatomy.

Specimens might have damage in other areas where the artist can reconstruct by duplicating an area on the opposite side that is still present. Also, many cases where portions of the face had been obliterated were reconstructed using the surrounding intact anatomy as a guide. B. P. Gatliff had occasion to reconstruct skulls of several subjects the center of whose faces were obliterated. Using the surrounding bony landmarks as a guide, Gatliff nevertheless recreated the face enough to affect an identification.[22]

Research has proven this technique to be successful in a major 1996 study. Caroline Wilkinson of the University of Manchester writes:

> "Where the missing areas of the skull are from unilateral features, or where both sides of the skull have absent areas; the areas are estimated using the surrounding bones as guides. Research (Colledge, 1996) at the University of Manchester suggested that areas of the skull can be estimated with relative accuracy. Colledge took five skulls and attempted to remodel a different missing area on each skull in a blind study. The missing areas included the mandible, the frontal bone, the zygomatic bones, the maxilla and the occipital bone. The remodeled skull was then compared metrically with the original specimen. Colledge found that the modeled areas were not significantly different from the original parts, except at the mandible. The mandible was remodeled with substantial errors, especially at the jawline and chin height. This would have a significant effect upon the accuracy of any resultant facial reconstruction."[23]

Figure 7.67

Dark portions represent missing areas of the skull as studied by Colledge in 1996. Six specimens were presented for reconstruction attempts with these various areas missing. When the reconstructions were compared to the original intact specimen, it was found all areas were successfully remodeled except for the mandible (modified after Wilkinson).

Figure 7.67 illustrates the various areas of the skull that were absent for facial reconstructions in the Colledge study.

In 1957 Sassouni constructed a method for estimating the size and shape of a missing mandible. Figure 7.68 shows Sassouni's diagrams as they appeared in Krogman's *The Human Skeleton in Forensic Medicine*. The test was to attempt to estimate the size and shape as if the mandible were missing. Once the shape was constructed, the mandible was obtained and a comparison showed minimal errors, as seen in Figure 7.69. This method used the knowledge of how the bottom teeth would occlude with the top teeth, assuming a normal dentition.

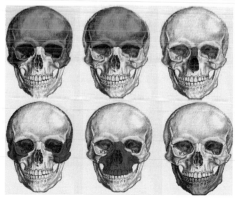

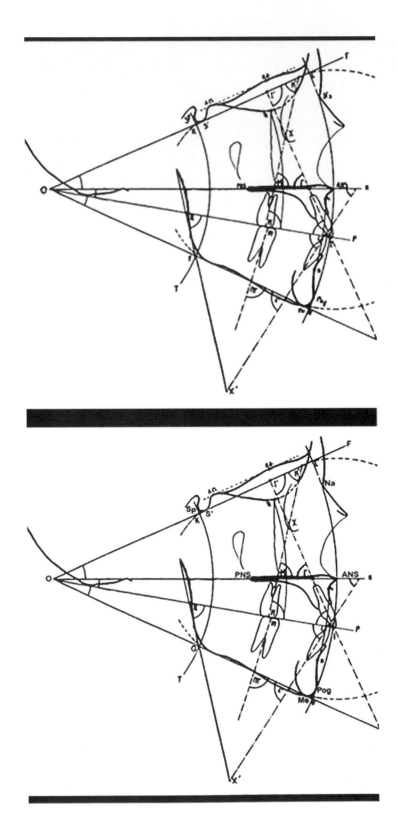

On the top of Figure 7.68 is the diagram, done from a radiograph of the skull, as it originally appeared. On the bottom is the same diagram with the identifying letters and numbers printed more clearly. Krogman explains the diagram as follows.

"Lateral cephalometric radiographs may be used for identification in (this) way. Sassouni ('55) developed an 'analysis' of individuality using four basic planes of reference...; a cranial base plane (OS-F), a palatal plane (ANS-PNS-O), an occlusal (dental) plane (PMO), and a mandibular (base) plane (Me-G-O); two basic arcs, with point O as center: anterior (L-Na-ANS-I-Pog) and posterior (Sp-g). The lateral film may be correlated with the posterioanterior film as in [the top of Figure 7.69] ... Sassouni, '57.

This method can have practical applications. Let us suppose that a skull is found sans maxillary teeth and mandible. How could an entire face be reconstructed? First of all, the part found is x-rayed, in lateral and posterioanterior views, in the Broadbent-Bolton apparatus. Then the tracing is made of the films, in both views, according to the Sassouni "analysis." Assuming that the maxillomandibular dentition and the maxillo-mandibular relationships bear an acceptable relationship to upper face and skull, the occlusal and mandibular planes can be drawn so as to meet at O; similarly, the anterior and posterior arcs can be drawn. Hence, the mandible can be drawn in its presumed vertical and anteroposterior relationships. This procedure is shown in [middle of Figure 7.69]. How well it worked is seen in [bottom of Figure 7.69]. ... Obviously this method is not completely foolproof. It assumes a "normal," well-proportioned face; i.e., all planes meet at or near O, and the anterior and posterior arcs delimit an orthognathous face in good occlusion...."[24]

Gatliff employed this method when presented with a case where the mandible was missing and met with great success. Figure 7.70 is a drawing of the calvarium, the

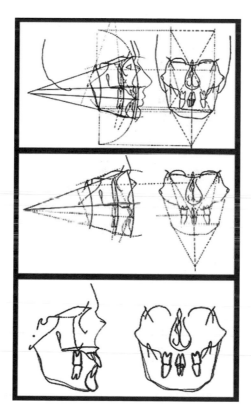

Figure 7.69

Top: Tracings of lateral and frontal x-ray films. Middle: Reconstruction of craniofacial relationships in hypothetical case. Bottom: The results of the experiment (all three images from Sassouni, 1957). From W. M. Krogman and M. Y. Iscan, The Human Skeleton in Forensic Medicine, 1986 (courtesy of Charles C. Thomas Publisher, Ltd., Springfield, Illinois).

Figure 7.70

Successful identification by Betty Pat. Gatliff, using the Sassouni method for approximating a missing mandible. Top left: Profile of skull with missing mandible. Top right: Calvarium with mandible sculpted in clay added. Bottom left: Profile of three-dimensional facial reconstruction by Gatliff. Bottom right: Photo of identified individual (modified in graphite after Gatliff).

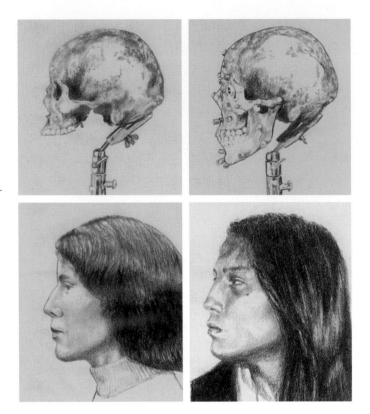

calvarium with a mandible sculpted of clay attached, and below left, her recreation of the unidentified female. As you can see in the photo of the individual who was identified on the lower right, Gatliff's reconstruction was accurate, especially concerning the mandibular area.

The practicing forensic artist should be heartened by the fact that Royal Canadian Mounted Police Sergeant C. J. (Cam) Pye successfully reconstructed an unidentified murder victim for whom he had no mandible, with a method artists everywhere can use. Sergeant Pye contacted a learned dental professional, Dr. David Sweet, who successfully estimated the shape and size of the missing mandible. Figure 7.71 shows all Cam Pye had left of a skull with which to work on the left. Top right shows the x-ray of Cam's specimen taken by David Sweet, D.M.D., Ph.D., DABFO. Dr. Sweet then constructed the diagram on the bottom right, successfully estimating the size and shape of the missing mandible. Dr. Sweet had never seen the Sassouni diagrams,[25] yet his mandibular estimation seems to contain the same elements, in a much less cluttered layout. You can see the highly successful results rendered at the

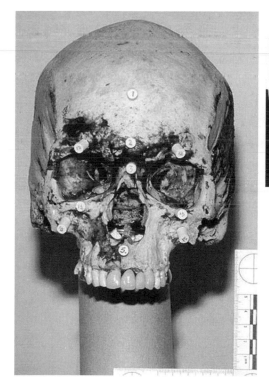

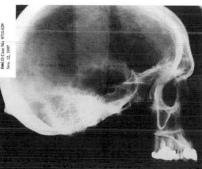

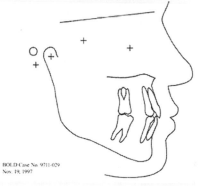

Figure 7.71
Left: Specimen with missing mandible presented to Sergeant Cameron Pye, forensic artist for the Royal Canadian Mounted Police. Upper right: Cephalometric radiograph taken of specimen by Dr. David Sweet. Lower right: Diagram Dr. Sweet produced approximating size and shape of missing mandible for Sgt. Pye (courtesy of Sergeant C. J. Pye and Dr. David Sweet).

hands of Sergeant Cam Pye in Figure 7.72. Dr. David Sweet is a practicing dentist and explained his technique for helping Pye reconstruct his victim with only a calvarium:

> "In this case, I worked from an orthodontic (dental) point of view. I produced a lateral cephalometric radiograph of the found skull and completed an orthodontic measurement analysis of the upper jaw/teeth compared to the base of the skull and various skull landmarks. From this I diagnosed the orthodontic classification of the victim's upper teeth. Then I was able to estimate the contour of the jaw that would support those lower teeth."[25]

Sergeant Pye's work led relatives of the murdered man to identify him even though they had moved far away from the area. The image Pye created reached out to them when publicized and the case was solved. An important feature of the work on this case is that an experienced dentist in the area was able to invent a method for estimating the size and shape of the missing mandible masterfully enough that the sketch on this case shows an almost

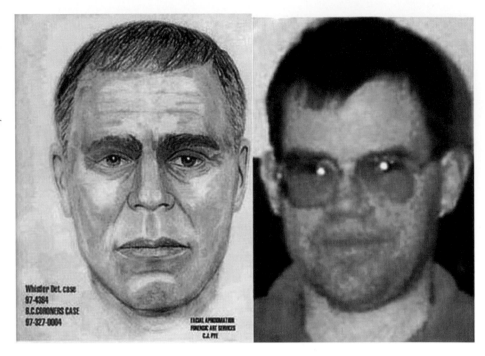

Figure 7.72

Left: An image of Sergeant Cam Pye's facial reconstruction from an unidentified murder victim's skeletal remain that was missing the mandible. Right: Photo of the identified individual (courtesy of Sergeant C. J. Pye and the Royal Canadian Mounted Police).

identical mouth and chin resemblance to the photo of the identified subject. Happily, the practicing forensic artist can deduce that seeking the help of a dentist in his or her area who is so inclined can help create a successful reconstruction, customized to the particular case.

In Brief

- Position the ear with the tragus over the auditory meatus, the top parallel (approximately) to the eye, and the bottom parallel (approximately) to the bottom of the nose, with an approximate 15% tilt of the vertical axis.
- The most consistent Mongoloid skull trait is a low nose bridge and a forward thrusting lower zygomatic process, resulting in a flat profile. The Negroid skull has a square nasal aperture and anterior projection of the maxilla and mandible in the alveolar ridge area. Negroid and Caucasoid skulls exhibit posterior tilting of the lower zygomatic process. The Caucasian profile from the nose to the chin is straight on the vertical plane.
- Forensic artists faced with a facial reconstruction case missing a mandible can contact a local dental expert who is so inclined to take a radiograph and do a version of the Sassouni method for help approximating the size and shape of the chin.

TISSUE-DEPTH DEMARCATION

Several methods for facial reconstruction utilize tissue depth information gathered by various researchers. This information, much of which is gathered in tables in this chapter, can be used as a guide to either drawing or sculpting the features on the bony surface of the skull. Early pioneers of this data gathering were Hiss, who published his data in 1895, and Kollman and Buchly, who produced a table in 1898. This tissue-depth data, collected from cadavers, were used to recreate faces on skulls of famous individuals from history such as Bach and Raphael.

This kind of work was greatly enhanced and expanded by J. Stanley Rhine, Ph.D., and C. Elliot Moore, Ph.D., in their work from the mid-1980s gathering data for American Negroids, Caucasoids, and Southwestern American Indians. These tables list tissue thickness at anatomical points on the skull that coincide with numbers as shown in Figure 7.73. Using these points, gathered from cadavers using slender needles, the practicing artist can glue various markers on the indicated locations for an approximation of the surface of the skin as it once existed on his or her specimen.

The skull with placement of the markers in Figure 7.73 can be studied in conjunction with the explanation of the points that follow. The method proven most effective in this field is to use the flexible cylindrical vinyl eraser sticks that are cut to the proper length determined by the chosen data table, and then glued to the proper location using the skull diagram. Then you can either draw the image using the tissue-depth markers as a guide, or use clay to connect the markers and fill in the unmarked areas.

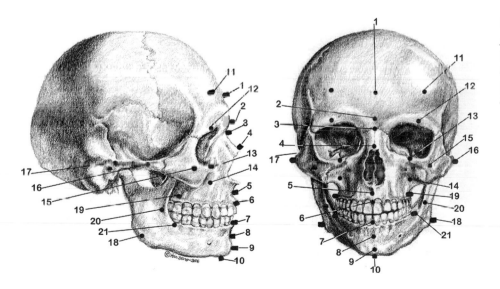

Figure 7.73

Anatomical landmarks for placement of tissue-depth markers (illustration by the author).

TISSUE-DEPTH MARKER LOCATIONS[26]

Numbered anatomical points and names are assigned in the system developed by Dr. Stanley Rhine. Some names also are known by abbreviations as indicated in parentheses.

1 through 10 are located on the midline; cut only one each.

Definitions of Numbered Landmarks

1. **Supraglabella:** Point above the glabella.
2. **Glabella (G):** Most anterior point on the midline above the frontonasal suture.
3. **Nasion (N):** Midline of the suture between the frontal and nasal bones.
4. **End of nasals (Nasals or Na):** Most anterior point of the nasal bone.
5. **Mid-philtrum:** Midline of the maxilla below curvature of anterior nasal spine.
6. **Upper lip margin (Supradentale, i.e., Sd or Alveolare):** Placed midline between maxillary central incisors at the cementoenamel junction (CEJ).
7. **Lower lip margin (Infradentale or Id):** Placed midline between mandibular central incisors at the cementoenamel junction (CEJ).
8. **Chin-lip fold (Supramentale):** Deepest indention midline on mandible between lower teeth and bottom of chin.
9. **Mental eminence (Pogonion or Pog):** Midline on most anterior projecting point of chin.
10. **Under chin (Menton or Me):** Lowest point under center of the mandible.

11 through 21 are cut in pairs as they denote anatomical points on each side of skull.

11. **Frontal eminence:** Most anterior projections of each side of forehead.
12. **Supraorbital:** Centered on the upper border of the orbit.
13. **Suborbital:** Centered on the lower margin of the orbit.
14. **Inferior malar:** Under the cheekbone on the maxilla.
15. **Lateral orbit:** 10 mm below outer margin of orbit.
16. **Zygomatic arch, midway:** Mid point of zygomatic arch or point at which the lateral surface projects farthest away from the calvarium. Does not necessarily correspond with the suture between the zygomatic and temporal bones.
17. **Supraglenoid:** Deepest point above and slightly forward of the ear hole (auditory meatus).
18. **Gonion (Go):** Most prominent point on the angle of the mandible.
19. **Supra 2nd molar (M^2):** Above the maxillary second molar. If missing, above the estimated location.
20. **Occlusal line:** On the anterior ramus of the mandible, below the coronoid process, parallel to where the occlusal (chewing) surfaces of the teeth meet.
21. **Sub 2nd molar:** Below the mandibular second molar. If missing, below the estimated location.

These points are approximations made by dedicated professionals working over the decades. Creating the image that will best approximate a subject's appearance from their skeletal remains takes some artistic imagination. Figure 7.74 shows a profile with the locations indicated and named that might help practitioners visualize how the following data tables can help them create a likeness.

The tables on the following pages represent data collected at the points indicated. Tables 7.1, 7.2, and 7.3 relate directly to points on Figure 7.74 and named on the previous Tissue-Depth Marker Locations list. Tables 7.4 through 7.9 have a different set of tissue-depth points, which are shown on Figures 7.75 and 7.76 and those landmarks are listed in the following Descriptions and Locations of Child Tissue Depths list on the following pages. A good practice would be to understand the names of locations and not depend only on the number of a tissue-depth marker.

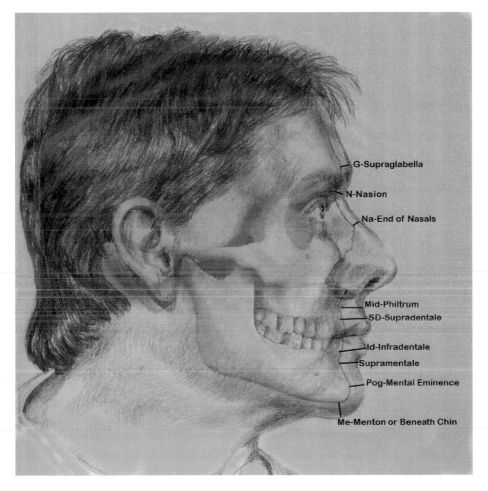

Figure 7.74

Illustration of soft tissue to bone relationship with tissue-depth marker locations named (illustration by the author). See color plate.

Table 7.1.   Tissue Depth of American Negroids (in millimeters)

Measurement	Slender		Normal		Obese	
	Male (24)	Female (5)	Male (27)	Female (10)	Male (1)	Female (2)
Midline						
1. Supraglabella	4.00	5.00	5.00	4.50	5.00	3.50
2. Glabella	5.25	6.00	6.25	6.00	7.50	6.00
3. Nasion	5.25	5.25	6.00	5.25	5.25	4.75
4. End of nasals	3.00	3.25	3.75	3.75	3.25	3.00
5. Mid-philtrum	11.75	10.00	12.25	11.25	11.75	12.00
6. Upper lip margin	12.50	12.00	14.25	12.50	12.50	15.25
7. Lower lip margin	13.75	12.25	15.50	15.00	15.50	12.00
8. Chin-lip fold	11.75	9.50	11.75	12.25	13.00	12.25
9. Mental eminence	11.25	11.00	11.50	12.50	15.25	13.00
10. Beneath chin	8.00	6.50	8.25	8.00	9.50	8.50
Bilateral						
11. Frontal eminence	3.75	3.25	5.00	4.00	5.50	5.00
12. Supraorbital	7.75	7.25	8.50	8.00	11.75	8.50
13. Suborbital	5.75	6.50	7.75	8.25	9.25	9.00
14. Inferior malar	14.00	14.50	16.50	16.75	17.50	18.75
15. Lateral orbit	10.50	12.00	13.25	13.00	20.00	12.75
16. Zygomatic arch, halfway	6.75	8.00	8.25	9.50	13.75	9.25
17. Supraglenoid	9.50	9.75	11.00	11.50	17.50	17.25
18. Gonion	11.50	11.00	13.00	13.50	24.00	17.50
19. Supra 2nd molar	19.00	20.50	23.00	20.25	24.00	23.50
20. Occlusal line	16.75	17.75	19.00	19.25	30.00	20.00
21. Sub 2nd molar	13.50	14.25	16.50	17.00	23.50	20.00

Courtesy of Dr. Stanley Rhine and Dr. H. R. Campbell.

Table 7.2.   Tissue Thickness (mm) of American Caucasoids (European derived) by Rhine and Moore[*]

Measurement	Slender		Normal		Obese	
	Male (3)	**Female (3)**	**Male (37)**	**Female (19)**	**Male (8)**	**Female (3)**
Midline						
1. Supraglabella	2.25	2.50	4.25	3.50	5.50	4.25
2. Glabella	2.50	4.00	5.25	4.75	7.50	7.50
3. Nasion	4.25	5.25	6.50	5.50	7.50	7.00
4. End of nasals	2.50	2.25	3.00	2.75	3.50	4.25
5. Mid-philtrum	6.25	5.00	10.00	8.50	11.00	9.00
6. Upper lip margin	9.75[a]	6.25	9.75	9.00	11.00	11.00
7. Lower lip margin	9.50[a]	8.50	11.00	10.00	12.75	12.25
8. Chin-lip fold	8.75	9.25	10.75	9.50	12.25	13.75
9. Mental eminence	7.00	8.50	11.25	10.00	14.00	14.25
10. Beneath chin	4.50	3.75	7.25	5.75	10.75	9.00
Bilateral						
11. Frontal eminence	3.00	2.75	4.25	3.50	5.50	5.00
12. Supraorbital	6.25	5.25	8.25	7.00	10.25	10.00
13. Suborbital	2.75	4.00	5.75	6.00	8.25	8.50
14. Inferior malar	8.50	7.00	13.25	12.75	15.25	14.00
15. Lateral orbit	5.00	6.00	10.00	10.75	13.75	14.75[a]
16. Zygomatic arch, halfway	3.00	3.50	7.25	7.50	11.75	13.00[a]
17. Supraglenoid	4.25	4.25	8.50	8.00	11.25	10.50[a]
18. Gonion	4.50	5.00	11.50	12.00[a]	17.50	17.50
19. Supra 2nd molar	12.00	12.00	19.50	19.25	25.00	23.75
20. Occlusal line	12.00	11.00	18.25	17.00	23.50	20.25
21. Sub 2nd molar	10.00	9.50[a]	16.00	15.50	19.75	18.75

* Adapted from Rhine and Moore, 1982; revised 1984. Prepared by J. Stanley Rhine, Ph.D., and C. Elliot Moore II, Ph.D., through the cooperation of J. T. Weston, M.D., Office of the Medical Investigator, State of New Mexico.
[a] Given the small samples, these values have been slightly adjusted from observed to values more in accord with trends in the rest of the data. Other adjustments have been made due to a programming error in the original table.

Table 7.3.   Tissue Thickness (mm) of Southwestern American Indians (Asian-derived) by Rhine

Measurement	Slender		Normal		Obese	
	Male (4)	Female (1)	Male (9)	Female (2)	Male (5)	Female (3)
Midline						
1. Supraglabella	5.75	4.00	5.00	4.50	4.50	4.25
2. Glabella	5.75	4.75	5.75	4.50	6.00	4.50
3. Nasion	5.75	6.50	6.86	7.00	6.50	5.00
4. End of nasals	2.75	2.50	3.50	2.50	3.25	3.25
5. Mid-philtrum	7.50	10.00	9.75	10.00	9.25	8.51
6. Upper lip margin	8.25	9.50	9.75	11.00	9.25	10.00
7. Lower lip margin	9.25	12.00	11.00	12.25	8.75	11.25
8. Chin-lip fold	8.50	9.00	11.50	10.00	9.75	11.00
9. Mental eminence	8.00	11.00	12.00	13.00	12.50	13.25
10. Beneath chin	5.25	8.00	8.00	8.00	8.00	7.75
Bilateral						
11. Frontal eminence	4.75	4.75	4.25	4.00	4.50	4.20
12. Supraorbital	6.75	5.00	9.00	8.50	8.50	8.25
13. Suborbital	3.75	3.25	7.50	6.25	7.75	6.75
14. Inferior malar	10.00	9.00	14.00	12.00	15.75	15.00
15. Lateral orbit	8.00	8.25	12.50	11.50	11.75	13.75
16. Zygomatic arch, midway	6.00	5.75	7.50	7.00	8.75	9.00
17. Supraglenoid	5.75	4.50	8.50	6.25	9.75	7.75
18. Gonion	7.75	6.25	13.25	10.50	15.40	12.75
19. Supra 2nd molar	14.25	11.75	21.50	18.00	23.50	19.00
20. Occlusal line	15.50	12.25	20.75	17.50	22.75	19.25
21. Sub 2nd molar	12.50	10.50	19.25	17.00	18.50	15.75

Courtesy of Stanley Rhine, Ph.D., Laboratories of Physical Anthropology, Maxwell Museum of Anthropology, April 1983.

Table 7.4. Ultrasonic Facial Tissue Measurements (mm) from Black North American Children Aged 3–18 Years

Facial points	3–8 years						9–13 years						14–18 years					
	Female (n = 52)			Male (n = 37)			Female (n = 59)			Male (n = 62)			Female (n = 25)			Male (n = 12)		
	Mean	SD	Range	Mean	SD	Range	Mean	SD	Range	Mean	SD	Range	Mean	SD	Range	Mean	SD	Range
1. Glabella	4.0	0.91	2–6	4.1	0.74	3–6	4.3	0.83	3–6	4.5	0.97	3–7	4.7	1.14	3–7	5.3	0.78	4–7
2. Nasion	4.9	0.96	3–8	5.4*	0.96	3–7	5.4	1.00	3–7	5.4	0.98	3–8	5.3	1.11	4–8	6.1*	0.51	5–7
3. Rhinion	1.7	0.61	1–3	1.8	0.48	1–3	1.7	0.56	1–3	1.9	0.46	1–3	1.7	0.54	1–3	2.1*	0.51	1–3
4. Lateral nostril	7.0	1.48	5–11	7.3	1.68	5–11	7.6	1.58	5–12	7.4	1.91	4–13	8.1	2.14	5–12	7.9	1.98	5–10
5. Midphiltrum	8.9	1.57	6–14	9.0	1.18	6–11	9.6	1.56	7–13	10.0*	1.69	7–18	9.9	2.20	7–16	12.1*	1.73	10–15
6. Labiomental	8.2	2.05	3–15	8.6	1.44	6–12	10.3	1.77	7–15	9.8	1.84	6–13	10.1	1.79	7–13	12.6*	1.93	10–16
7. Mental	8.3	2.16	4–14	8.3	1.59	6–11	10.0	2.60	5–16	9.9	3.03	5–18	10.0	2.65	4–15	9.5	2.78	5–13
8. Menton	4.8	1.61	2–10	4.5	1.12	2–6	5.8	2.15	2–12	5.5	2.09	2–11	5.6	1.93	2–10	6.3	1.86	4–10
9. Supraorbital	4.5	1.02	3–7	4.5	0.65	3–6	5.3	1.03	3–8	5.2	1.12	3–9	5.7	1.46	4–10	5.8	0.94	4–7
10. Infraorbital	5.6	1.14	3–9	5.6	1.07	3–8	6.1	1.12	4–10	5.8	1.19	3–9	6.4	1.50	4–11	6.0	0.74	5–7
11. Supracanine	8.8	1.59	5–14	8.9	1.86	6–15	10.0	1.79	7–16	10.7	2.74	7–27	10.6	1.50	8–13	12.3	2.05	9–17
12. Subcanine	9.0	2.20	5–15	8.5	1.24	6–11	10.2	2.16	6–17	11.0	3.02	7–24	11.0	2.25	7–16	12.8	2.67	8–17
13. Upper 2nd molar	23*	3.39	15–32	22.1	2.47	17–27	24.5*	3.72	18–34	23.6	4.35	12–33	27.6*	3.52	22–37	26.0	2.89	21–30
14. Lower 2nd molar	18.0	3.26	10–25	17.4	2.68	10–25	20.0	3.58	10–26	20.1	4.18	11–28	23.2	3.99	18–33	21.9	4.91	12–29
15. Midmandible	9.8	3.16	5–20	8.7	2.03	5–14	10.8	2.99	6–18	10.3	3.86	4–20	12.0	3.16	7–20	11.2	3.93	7–20
16. Lateral orbit	3.9	0.89	2–6	4.1	0.85	2–6	4.4	1.24	2–10	4.4	0.89	3–7	4.6	1.08	3–8	4.4	0.67	3–5
17. Zygomatic attach	8.3*	2.23	4–15	7.8	1.55	5–12	8.9*	2.22	6–14	8.3	2.66	4–15	9.2*	1.58	6–13	7.3	2.05	5–12
18. Gonion	13.5	2.87	8–21	12.8	2.02	10–17	14.6	3.41	3–23	14.7	3.06	9–22	16.2	3.36	10–23	17.9	3.63	1–24
19. Root zygoma	4.7	1.21	3–8	4.2	0.98	3–6	4.8	1.55	3–8	5.0	1.73	2–12	6.2	2.30	3–13	6.0	2.37	3–11

*Significantly thicker by sex.

Note: Modified from Manhein et al. (2000). Reprinted with the permission of Cambridge University Press.

Table 7.5.   *Ultrasonic Facial Tissue Measurements (mm) from White North American Children Aged 3–18 Years*

Facial points	3–8 years						9–13 years						14–18 years					
	Female (n = 43)			Male (n = 36)			Female (n = 51)			Male (n = 45)			Female (n = 35)			Male (n = 27)		
	Mean	SD	Range	Mean	SD	Range	Mean	SD	Range	Mean	SD	Range	Mean	SD	Range	Mean	SD	Range
1. Glabella	3.9	0.98	2–7	4.0	0.84	3–6	4.4	1.08	2–7	4.6	1.04	2–7	4.6	0.98	3–6	5.0	0.73	4–7
2. Nasion	5.0	0.94	3–7	5.7*	0.96	3–8	5.5	1.03	3–8	5.7	1.09	3–8	5.4	0.88	4–8	6.3*	1.07	4–8
3. Rhinion	1.7	0.52	1–3	1.8	0.67	1–4	1.5	0.54	1–3	1.6	0.53	1–3	1.8	0.51	1–3	2.0	0.44	1–3
4. Lateral nostril	7.0	1.86	4–12	7.2	1.75	4–11	7.7	2.00	4–15	7.4	1.71	4–15	7.7	1.78	5–12	7.8	1.96	5–12
5. Midphiltrum	8.3	1.35	6–12	9.0*	1.59	6–12	9.4	1.54	6–13	9.7*	1.50	6–13	9.4	1.46	7–12	11.2*	1.98	7–15
6. Labiomental	7.6	1.51	5–12	8.1*	1.79	6–12	9.0	1.45	6–13	6.9*	1.75	6–13	9.7	1.25	8–13	10.4*	1.28	7–13
7. Mental	7.4	1.81	4–11	8.3	2.14	4–12	8.8	1.98	5–14	8.7	2.93	5–14	8.7	1.75	5–14	9.3	1.90	7–14
8. Menton	4.2	1.19	2–8	4.6	1.13	3–7	5.5	1.64	2–11	5.5	1.44	2–11	5.5	1.36	4–9	6.0	1.57	4–11
9. Supraorbital	4.4	1.15	3–7	4.6	0.84	3–6	5.1	0.92	3–8	5.2	0.82	3–8	5.7	1.47	4–12	5.7	0.83	4–7
10. Infraorbital	5.6	1.12	3–8	5.5	0.94	4–8	5.6	1.08	4–8	5.9	1.14	4–8	6.0	1.25	3–9	5.3	1.23	4–9
11. Supracanine	8.4	1.29	6–11	9.4*	1.98	6–14	9.8	1.68	7–14	10.0	1.77	7–14	10.3	3.22	7–26	11.7*	2.33	8–19
12. Subcanine	7.9	1.44	5–11	8.4	1.40	6–13	9.2	1.61	6–13	9.6	1.70	6–13	9.8	2.40	6–21	10.6	2.32	7–17
13. Upper 2nd molar	22.7	3.48	14–30	23.3	3.73	14–31	24.3	2.88	19–32	24.7	4.30	19–32	26.8	4.96	5–34	27.4	3.38	22–35
14. Lower 2nd molar	18.9	3.59	8–24	20.7	3.64	13–31	20.8	3.63	13–29	21.6	3.71	13–29	23.2	4.58	5–30	23.2	3.48	15–31
15. Midmandible	10.5	3.33	4–18	10.4	2.80	6–15	11.7	3.24	4–18	12.1	3.99	4–18	13.4	2.76	9–19	12.3	4.49	6–24
16. Lateral orbit	4.0	0.89	3–6	4.1	0.91	2–6	4.6	1.09	3–9	4.4	0.87	3–9	4.5	0.85	3–6	4.3	0.86	3–7
17. Zygomatic attach	8.4	2.44	5–15	8.4	2.29	5–15	9.5	2.24	5–14	9.1	2.46	5–14	9.5	1.85	6–16	8.0	1.76	6–13
18. Gonion	13.9	3.27	7–22	13.7	2.89	8–20	14.4	2.90	8–19	15.4	3.63	8–19	17.0	2.67	12–22	18.1	3.04	14–24
19. Root zygoma	4.6	1.51	3–10	4.8	1.02	3–7	5.2	1.58	3–10	5.4	1.79	3–10	6.8	1.88	4–12	6.0	2.07	4–12

*Significantly thicker by sex.
Note: Modified from Manhein et al. (2000). Reprinted with the permission of Cambridge University Press.

Table 7.6.   Ultrasonic Facial Tissue Measurements (mm) from Hispanic North American Children Aged 3–18 Years

| Facial points | 3–8 years | | | | | | 9–13 years | | | | | | 14–18 years | | | | | |
| | Female (n = 6) | | | Male (n = 3) | | | Female (n = 9) | | | Male (n = 8) | | | Female (n = 1) | | | Male (n = 4) | | |
	Mean	SD	Range	Mean	SD	Range	Mean	SD	Range	Mean	SD	Range	Mean	SD	Range	Mean	SD	Range
1. Glabella	4.2	0.75	3–5	4.7	0.58	4–5	3.8	0.83	3–5	4.1	0.83	3–5	7.0			4.5	1.00	4–6
2. Nasion	5.0	1.10	3–6	6.3	1.15	5–7	5.3	0.87	4–6	4.9	1.35	3–7	5.0			4.8	0.50	4–5
3. Rhinion	1.7	0.52	1–2	1.7	0.58	1–2	1.6	0.53	1–2	1.6	0.52	1–2	1.0			1.5	0.58	1–2
4. Lateral nostril	6.3	1.03	5–8	6.3	1.53	5–8	5.7	1.12	5–8	7.9	2.23	5–12	9.0			5.0	0.82	4–6
5. Midphiltrum	8.0	1.55	7–10	7.3	0.58	7–8	9.2	1.20	8–11	9.3	1.75	5–10	8.0			11.5	1.29	10–13
6. Labiomental	8.7	2.07	6–11	7.0	2.00	5–9	9.2	1.48	7–12	10.0	1.85	6–12	11.0			11.3	2.06	9–14
7. Mental	8.0	2.00	5–10	6.0	1.00	5–7	8.4	1.59	6–11	8.4	2.77	5–13	15.0			10.3	0.96	9–1?
8. Menton	4.2	1.72	2–6	4.7	1.53	3–6	5.1	1.36	3–7	5.1	0.99	4–6	9.0			5.8	0.96	5–7
9. Supraorbital	4.2	0.75	3–5	4.3	0.58	4–5	4.9	0.93	3–6	4.9	0.99	4–6	7.0			5.5	1.29	4–7
10. Infraorbital	5.5	1.87	3–8	5.0	2.00	3–7	5.0	1.12	3–6	6.4	1.41	4–9	10.0			5.8	0.96	5–7
11. Supracanine	9.3	2.66	7–14	8.0	1.00	7–9	10.3	1.66	9–13	10.0	2.33	6–13	11.0			12.0	0.82	11–13
12. Subcanine	8.2	2.32	6–11	6.7	0.58	6–7	8.3	1.32	6–10	10.8	2.12	8–14	10.0			10.0	3.16	6–13
13. Upper 2nd molar	24.8	3.37	20–28	19.7	3.51	16–23	24.6	4.13	16–29	24.4	2.33	21–28	32.0			25.3	4.27	19–28
14. Lower 2nd molar	20.8	6.15	10–28	14.7	4.73	11–20	20.0	5.12	9–26	21.8	2.83	18–27	24.0			21.0	1.41	20–23
15. Midmandible	11.5	3.54	5–16	7.3	4.04	5–12	11.3	2.78	6–15	10.8	3.11	5–14	18.0			10.3	4.57	5–15
16. Lateral orbit	4.3	0.82	3–5	3.0	0.00	3–3	3.8	0.44	3–4	4.6	0.52	4–5	5.0			4.3	0.96	3–5
17. Zygomatic attach	8.5	2.66	5–13	6.3	2.10	4–8	7.4	1.13	6–9	8.4	1.69	6–11	14.0			7.8	1.89	5–9
18. Gonion	14.0	3.41	8–18	13.7	5.03	9–19	14.6	3.05	10–19	15.4	4.63	7–21	24.0			15.3	4.86	9–20
19. Root zygoma	4.3	0.82	3–5	4.3	2.31	3–7	4.6	1.33	3–6	6.3	1.28	5–8	8.0			4.8	1.50	3–6

Note: Modified from Manhein et al. (2000). Reprinted with the permission of Cambridge University Press.

Table 7.7.   *Ultrasonic Facial Tissue Measurements (mm) from White British Children Aged 11–18 Years*

| Facial points | 11–12 years | | | | | | 13–14 years | | | | | |
| | Male (n = 30) | | | Female (n = 28) | | | Male (n = 21) | | | Female (n = 23) | | |
	Mean	SD	Range	Mean	SD	Range	Mean	SD	Range	Mean	SD	Range
1. Forehead	4.6	0.97	3–7	4.3	0.83	3–6	5.0	0.89	4–7	5.0	0.88	3–6
2. Glabella	4.9	0.89	4–7	4.5	0.63	3–6	5.2	0.89	4–7	5.2	0.86	4–7
3. Nasion	4.7	0.88	3–7	4.3	0.72	3–6	5.2	0.89	4–7	4.7	0.95	3–7
4. Rhinion	2.7*	0.73	1–4	2.2	0.40	1–3	2.4	0.84	1–4	2.2	0.61	1–4
5. Midphiltrum	11.0	1.60	7–13	9.9	1.91	6–13	10.3	2.20	7–15	9.6	2.14	6–13
6. Upper lip	10.7	1.56	7–13	10.0	1.53	7–13	10.6	1.78	8–17	9.2	1.66	6–12
7. Lower lip	12.1	1.79	9–15	11.4	1.48	8–14	12.2*	2.13	5–12	10.5	1.74	6–13
8. Labiomental	10.2	1.54	7–14	9.8	1.44	7–13	8.9	2.09	7–13	9.4	2.29	5–14
9. Mental	9.8	2.08	6–16	10.2	2.10	7–15	10.1	1.98	5–8	8.9	1.94	6–12
10. Gnathion	6.7	1.23	5–10	6.0	1.08	4–8	6.0	0.94	7–13	6.0	1.22	4–9
11. Lateral forehead	5.7	1.00	4–8	4.7	0.81	3–6	5.4	0.95	4–8	5.4	0.93	4–7
12. Supraorbital	6.1*	0.96	4–8	5.4	0.90	4–8	6.6	0.98	5–8	6.5	0.91	4–8
13. Infraorbital	7.6*	1.12	6–10	7.0	1.04	5–9	8.3	1.30	6–10	7.3	1.20	5–9
14. Lateral nose	6.9	1.37	4–10	6.3	1.33	4–10	6.4*	1.79	4–10	5.9	1.25	4–10
15. Lateral orbit	6.9	1.08	5–9	7.4	1.97	5–15	7.1	1.12	5–8	7.4	1.15	5–10
16. Zygomatic attach	12.3	3.12	8–3	13.0	3.89	7–21	10.7	2.48	7–16	10.2	1.81	8–15
17. Upper 1st molar	16.7	5.46	10–28	17.4	6.76	10–30	14.7	3.31	10–21	16.2	3.15	11–22
18. Lower 1st molar	16.0	4.46	10–27	15.5	4.66	9–27	14.6	2.28	9–20	14.5	2.84	9–20
19. Midmandible	10.2	2.59	7–22	9.8	2.05	7–14	9.1	1.84	7–13	9.1	1.87	6–15
20. Zygomatic arch	8.0	1.53	5–11	8.0	2.05	6–10	8.4	1.63	6–12	7.9	1.87	5–12
21. Midmasseter	18.4	4.73	7–28	17.3	4.85	9–25	17.4	4.94	9–25	16.6	4.97	8–23

Facial points	11–12 years Male (n = 30) Mean	SD	Range	11–12 years Female (n = 28) Mean	SD	Range	13–14 years Male (n = 21) Mean	SD	Range	13–14 years Female (n = 23) Mean	SD	Range
22. Forehead	4.6	0.66	3–6	4.7	0.64	3–6	4.8	0.77	3–6	4.8	1.04	3–7
23. Glabella	5.0	0.89	4–6	4.9	0.66	4–7	5.2	0.74	4–7	5.2	1.20	3–8
24. Nasion	4.9	1.03	3–7	4.8	0.76	3–7	5.3	0.87	2–4	5.0	1.31	2–9
25. Rhinion	2.5	0.66	1–4	2.6	0.62	2–4	2.5	0.61	9–16	2.5	0.82	1–4
26. Midphiltrum	10.9	1.97	6–14	11.2	1.83	7–16	12.5*	1.86	9–18	10.9	1.49	7–13
27. Upper lip	11.6	1.42	8–14	11.2	1.54	8–15	12.1	1.85	9–20	10.8	1.62	8–14
28. Lower lip	12.8	2.19	9–19	13.0	2.03	8–17	13.8*	2.40	9–16	12.0	1.59	9–16
29. Labiomental	10.8	2.12	6–14	11.1	1.65	7–13	11.9	1.30	9–13	11.1	1.02	9–13
30. Mental	10.9	1.40	8–13	10.0	1.84	6–13	10.9	0.97	6–10	11.0	1.92	7–15
31. Gnathion	6.9	1.48	4–11	7.2	1.18	5–9	7.7	1.06	4–8	7.3	1.39	5–10
32. Lateral forehead	5.6	0.76	4–7	5.6	0.95	4–8	5.2	1.23	4–8	5.3	1.34	3–8
33. Supraorbital	6.4	0.73	5–8	6.0	0.90	4–8	5.9	1.23	6–11	6.2	1.16	4–8
34. Infraorbital	7.2	0.59	6–9	7.8	1.61	5–10	7.9	1.17	5–10	7.5	1.21	4–10
35. Lateral nose	6.1	0.96	5–9	6.9	1.51	5–10	6.7	1.52	5–9	6.9	1.35	4–10
36. Lateral orbit	7.2	1.28	5–10	7.5	1.36	5–10	7.4	1.16	7–14	7.8	1.52	4–11
37. Zygomatic attach	11.5	2.27	7–15	13.6	2.71	9–20	11.3	1.79	10–27	13.2	2.33	9–19
38. Upper 1st molar	18.4	4.75	12–25	20.9*	3.41	14–27	18.3	4.83	12–24	19.2*	5.32	9–28
39. Lower 1st molar	16.6	4.33	11–25	18.4	4.26	12–29	16.7	3.36	6–16	17.0	4.41	10–27
40. Midmand ble	9.4	1.90	6–14	10.9	3.06	8–22	9.3	2.38	6–11	9.6	2.19	6–13
41. Zygomatic arch	7.5	1.05	6–10	8.3	3.06	6–10	7.9	1.28	11–24	8.4	2.19	5–12
42. Midmasseter	18.8	4.50	8–24	20.2	4.04	11–25	21.9	3.37	6–11	21.5	3.91	11–31

*Significantly thicker by sex.
Source: Wilkinson (2002).
Reprinted with the permission of Cambridge University Press.

Table 7.8.   *Comparison of Facial Tissue Measurements (mm) between White and Black American Adults and Children*

Facial points	White adults		White children		Black adults		Black children	
	Male (48) Mean	Female (82) Mean	Male (108) Mean	Female (129) Mean	Male (22) Mean	Female (44) Mean	Male (111) Mean	Female (136) Mean
1. Glabella	5.5*	4.9	4.5	4.3	5.3	4.6	4.6	4.3
2. Nasion	6.6*	5.8	5.9	5.3	6.2	5.7	5.6	5.2
3. Rhinion	1.6	1.8	1.8	1.7	2.0	1.7	1.9	1.7
4. Lateral nostril	9.6*	9.3*	7.5	7.5	9.8*	8.4*	7.5	7.6
5. Midphiltrum	10.0	8.1	10.0	9*	12*	8.7	10.2	9.5*
6. Labiomental	12*	10.3*	9.4	8.8	12.7*	11.2*	10.3	9.5
7. Mental	11.2*	10.4*	8.8	8.3	12.2*	10.9*	9.2	9.4
8. Menton	7*	6.5*	5.4	5.1	7.9*	6.8*	5.3	5.4
9. Supraorbital	6.1*	6*	5.2	5.1	6.4	6.0	5.2	5.2
10. Infraorbital	6.0	6.5*	5.6	5.7	6.4	6.3	5.8	6.0
11. Supracanine	10.3	8.2	10.4	9.5*	11.6*	9.5	10.6	9.8
12. Subcanine	10.9*	9.2	9.5	9.0	12.6*	11.6*	10.8	10.1
13. Upper 2nd molar	28.9*	27.1*	25.1	24.6	27.8*	26.7*	23.9	25.0
14. Lower 2nd molar	22.1	23.1*	21.8	21.0	24.1*	21.8*	19.8	20.4
15. Midmandible	14.3*	14.2*	11.6	11.9	13.7*	13*	10.1	7.2
16. Lateral orbit	4.8	4.6	4.3	4.4	4.3	4.9	4.2	4.3
17. Zygomatic attach	7.7	9.8*	8.5*	9.1	7.4	9.9	7.8	8.8
18. Gonion	18.2*	16.1*	15.7	15.1	20.9*	16*	15.1	14.8
19. Root zygoma	6.3*	6.4*	5.4	5.5	6.6*	6.0	5.1	5.2

*Significantly thicker between adults and children.
Modified from Manhein et al. (2000). Reprinted with the permission of Cambridge University Press.

Table 7.9. Adult White and Black American Facial Tissue Measurements

Facial points	Black Americans										White Americans															
	19–34 years				35–45 years				45–55 years		19–34 years				35–45 years				45–55 years				>56 years			
	Male (91)		Female (91)		Male (95)		Female (167)		Female (99)		Male (91)		Female (91)		Male (95)		Female (167)		Male (84)		Female (99)		Male (155)		Female (l0)	
	Mean	SD	Mean	SD	Mean	SD	Mean	SD	Mean	SD	Mean	SD	Mean	SD	Mean	SD	Mean	SD	Mean	SD	Mean	SD	Mean	SD	Mean	SD
1. Glabella	5.2*	1.12	4.6	0.7	5.3*	1.53	4.5	0.93	4.8	0.84	5*		4.8	0.95	5.5*	1.27	4.7	1.03	6*	1.41	4.8	1.17	5.6*	1.52	5.2	0.97
2. Nasion	6.6*	0.84	5	0.91	5.7*	2.08	5.2	1.25	6	1	6*		5.5	1.16	6.4*	1.43	5.3	1.39	7.2*	1.64	6.2	0.75	6.6*	1.52	6	1.22
3. Rhinion	2.2*	0.42	1.7	0.46	1.7	0.58	1.5	0.51	2	0.71	1.9	0.45	1.8	0.63	2.4	0.97	1.6	0.51	1.8	0.45	1.8	0.41	2	0	1.8	0.67
4. Alare	9.2	2.82	8.4	1.98	10.3	2.52	8.4	2.01	8.4	1.52	7.5	1.9	8.6	1.99	9.8	1.81	8	1.73	10.4	2.51	10.8	1.94	10.8	3.03	9.8	2.22
5. Midphiltrum	13*	2.2	9.2	1.82	11*	1.73	8.8	1.92	8.2	2.49	11.9*	2.24	9.1	1.69	10.6*	1.43	7.4	1.3	8*	3	8	1.41	9.4*	.52	8	2.65
6. Labiomental	12.7*	2.05	11.8	2.2	12.7*	1.15	11.7	2.42	10	2.55	11.1*	1.85	10.3	1.55	13.1*	1.52	9.6	1.5	11.6*	1.67	9.8	2.32	12.2*	1.79	11.4	1.42
7. Mental eminence	12.1	2.9	10.8	2.68	12.3	4.51	11.2	2.25	10.8	3.11	10*	2.77	9.2	2.08	12*	3.2	9.2	2.14	11*	1.73	10.7	2.8	11.8	2.05	12.3*	1.58
8. Menton	8.8*	1.89	6.7	2.02	7*	2	6.4	2.65	7.2	1.92	7.2*	1.73	6	1.45	8*	1.05	5.4	1.84	7.2*	1.79	6.7	2.94	5.6	0.89	8*	1.87
9. Supraorbital	6.4	1.3	6.1	0.83	5.3	0.58	6	1.22	5.8	0.84	5.3	1.25	5.7	1.04	5.9	0.88	5.5	1.19	7.7	1.67	6.5	0.84	5.6	1.14	6.3	1
10. Infraorbital	5.8	1.26	5.2	1.17	7	1	6.9	1.96	5.8	1.3	5.8	1.58	6.1	1.05	6.2	1.87	5.7	1.33	6.8	0.84	7.3	4.08	5	2	7*	2.5
11. Supracanine	12.8*	1.86	10	2.28	10.3*	1.53	9.6	2.75	9	2.45	11.9*	2.65	9.3	1.74	10.1*	2.13	7.8	1.37	10*	2	7.7	1.86	9.2	1.1	7*	2
12. Subcanine	14.4	2.89	10.9	2.44	10.7	0.58	11.5*	1.6	12.4	3.91	11.5*	2.17	9.4	1.56	10.2*	1.32	8.7	2.23	10*	2.35	9	2.97	11.8*	2.39	8	2
13. Posterior maxilla	28.2*	3.46	26.6	4.35	27.3*	4.51	26.8	4.47	26.8	4.09	28.5*	4.69	26.3	4.94	24.6*	6.45	25.1	6.74	28.2*	7.53	27.2	6.11	23.6	8.11	29.4	4.82
14. Upper molar	24.5	4.05	21.7	3.99	23.7	4.04	22.5	3.93	21.2	5.89	25.1	4.15	23.4	4.53	21.1	6.69	20.1	5.15	21.4	3.85	21.7	5.32	20.6	6.11	27.2	5.59
15. Lower molar	14.1	4.21	12.6	2.85	13.3	2.31	13.1	4.17	13.4	4.04	14.8	4.48	13.7	3.25	15.6	4.81	12.6	4.21	15.4	4.39	13	4.29	11.4	3.65	17.4	3.28
16. Lateral orbit	4.8	0.76	5	0.84	3.7	0.58	4.9	1.18	4.8	0.84	4.2	0.79	4.7	0.88	4.3	0.82	4.3	0.9	5.4	0.55	4.5	1.87	5.2	0.45	4.9	1.76
17. Zygomatic attach	8.4	2.22	10.2*	2.28	6.3	0.58	9.8*	2.38	9.8	3.27	7.8	2.38	9.3*	1.7	8.2	2.2	8.7*	2.74	8.2	2.05	10.2*	1.6	6.4	1.34	11	2.45
18. Gonion	12.1*	3.24	17	4.23	20.7*	2.89	16.2	3.64	14.8	2.86	20*	4.27	17.4	3.7	19.6*	5.87	15.3	4.5	19*	4.69	14.7	4.68	14	4.95	16.9*	3.59
19. Supraglenoid	7.4	1.77	6.4	2.25	5.7	1.15	5.6	2.22	6	2.24	7.8	2.29	7.4	2.07	6.6	3.86	4.9	1.44	5.4	1.52	6	1.55	5.2	1.1	7.4	2.3

* Significantly thicker by sex.

Source: Modified from Manhein et al., 2000. Reprinted with the permission of Cambridge University Press.

Table 7.10.   Adult Facial Tissue Measurements from Different Ethnic Groups

| Facial points | Koreans | | | | Buryats | | | | Kazakhs | | | | Bashkirs | | | | Uzbeks | | | |
| | Male (91) | | Female (91) | | Male (95) | | Female (167) | | Male (84) | | Female (99) | | Male (155) | | Male (55) | | Female (71) | |
	Mean	SD	Mean	SD	Mean	SD	Mean	SD	Mean	SD	Mean	SD	Mean	SD	Mean	SD	Mean	SD
1. Forehead	4.5	0.98	4.5	0.89	4.5	0.88	4.7	0.95	4.5	0.87	4.9	0.9	5.1	0.85	5.1	0.71	5	0.71
2. Superciliary	5.2	0.81	5.2	0.86	5.4	0.79	5.7	1	5.2	0.82	5.6	0.87	5.6	0.89	5.4	0.76	5.5	0.77
3. Glabella	5.1	0.8	5.4	0.89	5.4	0.75	5.6	0.88	5.3	0.79	5.6	0.86	5.6	0.84	5.4	0.75	5.5	0.77
4. Nasion	4.5	0.79	4.4	0.86	4.8	0.85	4.5	0.89	4.8	0.91	4.6	0.7	5.8	0.85	5.7	0.87	5.3	0.77
5. End of nasal	2.8	0.31	2.9	0.35	2.8	0.43	2.8	0.3	3	0.38	2.9	0.38	3.8	0.56	4.1	0.68	4	0.56
6. Lateral of nasal	2.9	0.31	2.9	0.28	2.9	0.33	2.9	0.33	3	0.36	3	0.33	4	0.75	3.9	0.66	3.9	0.58
7. Maxillary	13.2	1.86	13.9	1.65	14.5	1.96	15.8	1.79	13.2	1.63	14.5	1.9	11.6	2.36	14.1	1.88	15.5	2.14
8. Zygomatic attach	9.8	1.85	12.2	2.02	10.6	1.77	13.6	1.78	9.8	2.02	12.6	2.09	9.3	1.47	9.3	2.04	11.7	1.93
9. Zygomatic arch	4.7	0.8	5.6	0.9	4.5	0.89	5	0.77	4.5	0.78	5.3	0.88	5	0.93	4.5	0.58	5	0.7
10. Supracanine	10.4	1.33	9.3	0.95	10.8	1.21	9.8	1.04	10.7	1.34	9.9	1.01	10.1	1.34	10.2	1.66	9.8	1.04
11. Philtrum	11.1	1.44	9.6	1.13	11.8	1.52	10.2	1.23	11.7	1.4	10.3	1.3	11.6	1.64	11.9	1.63	11	1.27
12. Upper lip	12.6	1.73	10.6	1.57	13.5	1.9	11.7	1.81	12.4	1.7	11.1	1.53	13	1.9	13.1	2.02	12.1	1.51
13. Lower lip	13.8	1.51	12.3	1.49	14.5	1.63	13.1	1.73	13.7	1.61	12.4	1.42	14.5	1.72	14	1.98	13.1	1.52
14. Labiomental	11.3	1.34	11.1	1.16	11.7	1.53	11.2	1.37	11.2	1.07	11.1	1.2	11.3	1.47	11.2	1.46	10.8	1.4
15. Pogonion	10.6	1.85	11.1	1.71	11.4	1.93	11.9	1.82	10.9	1.66	11.4	1.53	10.9	1.88	11.2	1.9	10.6	1.52
16. Gnathion	6.3	1.17	6.5	1.12	6.8	1.18	6.9	12.8	6.4	1.25	6.6	1.21			6.4	0.97	6.3	1
17. Lower 2nd molar	12.8	3.43	14.6	2.83	13.1	3.12	14.8	2.54	12.6	2.8	14.6	2.72	10.1	2.26	11.4	2.94	13.1	2.4
18. Midmandible	6.1	1.62	6.9	1.53	6.2	1.43	7.2	1.57	5.6	1.22	7	1.58			6	1.46	6.5	1.09
19. Midmasseter	17	2.26	17	2.18	17.2	2.02	17.5	1.67	17	2.06	16.9	2.13			16.8	2.02	16.9	1.95
20. Gonion	4.6	0.96	5.4	1.22	4.5	0.94	5.1	1.01	4.6	0.79	5.2	1.24	5.4	1.07	5.1	0.72	5.3	0.99

21. Forehead	4.7	0.81	4.9	0.91	4.5	0.72	4.6	0.77	5.3	5.3	0.86	0.77	4.7	0.83	4.6	0.67
22. Superciliary	5.2	0.83	5.8	1.09	5.2	0.72	5.4	0.63	5.8	5.9	0.98	0.95	5.1	0.72	5.3	0.7
23. Glabella	5.3	0.9	5.7	0.98	5.2	0.74	5.4	0.75	5.8	6	0.79	0.89	5.5	0.75	5.5	0.78
24. Nasion	5.8	0.89	5.7	0.84	5.8	1.15	5.4	0.84	5.6	5.5	0.94	0.9	5.4	0.96	5	0.77
25. End of nasal	3.2	0.47	3.4	0.62	3	0.41	3	0.61	3.8	3.7	0.81	0.7	3.1	0.2	3.1	0.25
26. Lateral of nasal	3.3	0.51	3.5	0.51					3.9	3.8	0.83	0.75	3.1	0.27	3.2	0.22
27. Maxillary	13.2	2.58	15.2	1.84					12.4	14.2	2.36	2.49	12.4	1.83	13.5	1.39
28. Zygomatic attach	9.3	1.31	12.3	2.09					9.8	12.4	1.6	1.97	9.3	1.64	11.7	1.77
29. Zygomatic arch	4.8	0.56	5.3	0.96					5.1	5.4	0.87	0.92	4.7	0.64	4.9	0.65
30. Supracanine	10.5	1.41	9.6	0.93	10.7	1.34	9.7	1.24	10.5	9.7	1.3	1.14	11.2	1.32	9.6	1.15
31. Philtrum	12	1.53	10.1	1.06			9.7	1.04	11.5	10.6	1.59	1.49	12.5	1.45	10.6	1.49
32. Upper lip	12.8	1.75	10.8	1.52	12	1.8	10	1.47	12.4	10.9	1.91	1.77	13.2	1.83	11	1.79
33. Lower lip	14.3	1.51	12.2	1.45	13.3	1.77	11.9	1.51	13.8	12.3	1.75	1.7	14.1	1.6	12.2	1.57
34. Labiomental	11.2	1.19	10.4	1.21	11.7	1.5	11.5	1.78	11.5	11.1	1.4	1.21	11.1	1.26	10.5	1.4
35. Pogonion	11.2	1.89	10.8	1.57	11.7	1.89	11.3	1.87	11.6	11.8	1.83	1.74	11.5	1.76	11.1	1.53
36. Gnathion	6.8	0.88	6.3	0.9									6.7	0.94	6.2	0.98
37. Lower 2nd molar	13.3	2.51	14.3	2.77					12	13.8	3.07	2.65	13.2	3.15	14.6	2.55
38. Midmandible	6.8	1.24	7.1	1.38									6	1.07	6	1.15
39. Midmasseter													18	2.08	17.5	2.1
40. Gonion	5.2	0.82	5.5	1					5.2	5.3	1.05	0.98	4.7	0.76	4.7	0.85

Modified from Lebedinskaya et al., 1993.
Reprinted with the permission of Cambridge University Press.

Table 7.11. Adult White European Facial Tissue Measurements

Facial points	20–29 years				30–39 years				40–49 years				50–59 years				60+ years			
	Male (13)		Female (12)		Male (14)		Female (13)		Male (13)		Female (11)		Male (11)		Female (15)		Male (10)		Female (11)	
	Mean	Range	Mean	Range	Mean	Range	Mean	Range	Mean	Range	Mean	Range	Mean	Range	Mean	Range	Mean	Range	Mean	Range
1. Vertex	5	4–6.5	4.5	4–5.5	5	4–6	5	4.5–5.7	5	3.5–7.5	5	4–5.5	5	4–6.5	5	4–7	4.8	3.5–6.7	5	3.5–6.3
2. Trichion	4.3	3.5–5.5	4.1	3.5–5	4.7	3.3–6	4	3.5–5	4.5	3.5–5.7	3.9	3.3–5.3	4.7	3.7–6.3	4	3–4.7	4.9	3.8–5.8	4	3.7–5.5
3. Metopion	5	4–5.5	4.5	3.5–5.2	5	3.7–6.5	4.5	4–5.7	5	3.2–6.5	4.6	3.5–5.2	5	4–6	4.7	3.5–5.2	4.8	4–6	5.2	4.2–5.5
4. Ophyron	5.5	5–6.7	5	4.2–5.8	5.8	4.5–7.5	5.2	4.5–5.8	5.5	3.8–7	5.3	3.8–6	5.8	5–6.5	5.3	3.8–6.3	5.8	4.5–7.3	5.8	5–7.2
5. Glabella	5.7	5.2–6.7	5.5	4.5–6.3	6.2	5–7.7	5.7	5–6.5	6	4.3–7.5	5.9	4.5–6.7	6	5.5–7	6	4.5–7	6.3	5–7.7	6.5	5.3–7.3
6. Nasion	8.2	6.3–10.2	6.9	4.7–7.3	7.3	6–11.3	6.5	6–7.7	6.8	5.3–8.3	6.2	5.3–7.5	7.3	6.2–8.2	6.5	4.8–7.5	7.1	6–9.2	6.5	5.5–7.7
7. Nasal bone	3	1.5–4.5	2.9	1.7–4.0	3.5	2–4.2	3	1.5–4.5	3.9	2.5–4.5	3	1.5–4.5	3.5	1.5–6.3	3	1.5–4	3.7	2.8–5	3	2.2–3.8
8. End of nasal	2.3	1–3.7	2.3	1.5–4.2	2.5	1.5–4.0	2.5	1–3.8	2.7	1.8–4.5	2.4	1–3.2	2.8	1–4	2.3	1.5–4.3	2.6	1.3–4.3	2.5	1.8–3.5
9. Lateral of nasal	7.5	5.8–9	7	4.8–8.5	7.4	5.2–9.5	6.3	4.7–8	7.3	6–9.5	6.7	4.5–9.8	8.2	6.3–12.8	6.5	5.5–9.7	6.7	5.7–10	7.3	5–10.2
10. Alare	13.3	11.2–14.5	11.6	9.3–13	11.7	10–16.2	11	9.2–13.7	12.2	9.3–14.7	11	9.2–12.3	12.5	10.8–13.7	11.5	10–12.8	11.9	9.7–14.3	11.5	9.5–12.8
11. Subnasale	15.5	12.3–17.2	13.8	11.5–15	14.6	12.5–18.7	12.8	11.5–14.5	15.6	9.5–19	12.6	11.5–14.5	14.3	12.2–19.5	13.2	10–15.7	12.9	8.5–15.3	12.2	9.7–14.2
12. Upper lip	14	11.8–17	11.8	10.2–14.2	12.3	9.5–17.3	10.7	9–12.8	12.6	9–18.2	10.5	8.7–11.7	11.8	9.3–14.8	10	8.2–14.5	9.9	7.7–11.7	9.8	8.7–10.3
13. Lower lip	14.2	10.5–16	12	10.8–15.7	14.9	12.3–17.2	12	10–13.7	14.2	11.5–19.2	12.5	9.5–14	13	11.5–16.8	11.8	9.8–16.2	12.7	11.5–16	11.5	9.7–15.3
14. Labiomental	12	10–14	10.4	9.3–12.5	12.1	10.7–14.3	10.8	8.8–12.7	13.3	10–15.8	12.3	9.5–14.2	13	12–16.3	12.2	10.2–13.2	12.8	11.2–15.3	12.7	10.3–15.3
15. Pogonion	9.7	7.3–13.7	9.6	6.7–11.3	10.3	7.8–13	10	7.3–12.2	11.7	8.3–18.2	9.6	5.5–11.8	13.7	9.7–17.3	11.3	8–13.5	12.3	10.3–14.7	12	8.8–13.8
16. Gnathion	7.5	6.5–10	7.1	5.6–8.7	8.3	6–9.7	7.2	5.3–8.8	9.5	6.5–13.7	6.9	5–11	9.8	7–12.7	8	5.5–11.3	8.9	8–11.7	8.7	6–12.2
17. Lateral fore-head	5.5	4.5–6.7	5.2	4.5–5.7	6	5–7	5	4.5–5.7	5.5	4.2–7.3	5.3	4–6.3	6	4.5–8	5	4–6.3	6.2	4.8–7.5	5.3	4.5–6.5

18. Mid-supraorbital	7.3	6.3–9.2	6.6	5.7–6	7.3	6.0–8.5	6.5	5.8–7.5	7.2	5.3–11.7	7.4	5.3–8.3	7.5	6.2–8.5	6.7	6–7.5	6.7	5.8–8.2	6.8	6.3–8
19. Orbitale	5.2	4.2–5.7	5.5	2.7–6.7	5	4.2–8.2	5.5	3.7–8.5	5.8	3.3–7.5	5.4	3.8–7.3	5.5	4.7–9.7	6	3.5–8	5.8	3.7–11.7	6.3	5.2–10.7
20. Canine fossa	18.8	16–23.7	18.8	15.7–21	19.7	16.3–24.7	20.2	16–27.7	21.5	18.2–25.7	19.1	15–23.3	21.8	17–24.5	20.7	14.7–24.7	21.5	15.7–24	22.3	18.2–28
21. Upper 1st molar	20.2	15.7–25.3	19.2	15.8–1.7	22	16–29	21.5	10–29.3	21.7	17.8–28.7	20.5	16.8–24	22.3	14–28.3	19.3	14.3–23.3	18.8	13.8–23.2	20.5	11.8–26.3
22. Lower 1st molar	19	14.5–24.3	16.6	13.3–20.8	18.5	15.3–23	19	14.8–29	18.3	16–24.3	18	15–22.8	18.3	16.3–21.8	17.7	15–21.7	17.2	14.7–19.8	19	11.3–24
23. Mandibular	9.2	6.2–11.8	9.2	6–11.5	10.1	5.2–15	9	5.3–13	10.2	6.3–14.8	9.1	7.5–12.5	12	8.8–15.7	9	5.6–11.3	10.3	9.5–2.5	10.3	8–13.7
24. Frontotemporale	5	4.3–6.0	5	4.3–5.5	5.3	4–6.7	5	4.3–8.7	5.5	3.8–7	4.8	3.5–6.5	5.5	4–7.8	5	3.5–6.3	5.5	4–6.7	5	4–5.3
25. Lateral orbit	5.3	4.3–5.7	5.2	4.2–5	5.2	4.3–6.2	5	4.3–5	5.8	5–7	5.1	3.5–7.5	5.7	4.8–7	5.3	4–5.8	5.5	4.2–6.7	5.5	4.5–7.2
26. Lateral zygomatic	7.5	5.2–9	8.9	7.5–13	7.6	6–9.5	9	7.2–10.7	6.8	4.8–9.3	9.1	6.5–11.3	8	6.3–12	9	6.2–10.8	7.5	5.3–9.5	10.3	6.7–13
27. Zygomaxillare	9.5	8.3–10.7	10.3	8.8–2.3	9.9	5.5–12	10.3	8.3–12.8	10.1	7.5–12.2	10.6	7.8–14.3	10.7	9.2–13.2	10.7	6.5–12.7	9	6.5–1.2	12	7.5–15
28. Midmandible	12	10.7–14.3	10.7	8.0–13	11.9	6.5–16.7	11.5	9.7–15.7	12.8	8–19	11.8	6.8–16.7	14.2	11.8–20.5	12	9.8–15.5	13.4	11.2–16.3	13.7	11.3–19.3
29. Euryon	6	5–9.5	5	4.5–7	6.7	5–9	5.5	4–6.7	6.5	4.5–8	5	4.5–6.5	7	5.5–8	5.3	4–7.2	6.4	5.3–7.8	5.2	4.5–6
30. Temporalis	15.3	13.2–18	14.2	12–17	16.3	13.7–19.3	14.2	8.7–19.8	16.1	13–19.3	14.3	11–16.2	14.7	14.3–22.3	13.3	4.3–19.2	14.9	8.7–7.2	13.3	11.3–18.5
31. Zygomatic arch	5.3	3.5–6.3	4.8	4.3–3.3	5.3	4–9.7	5.2	4–8.5	5.5	4.3–8	5.4	4.3–7.8	5.5	4.8–10.8	5.3	4.3–7	5	3.8–3.2	5.2	4.5–10
32. Midmasseter	19.2	15–23.3	17.2	13.8–21	21.3	15.5–23	18.3	14.8–22.3	20.4	13.7–29.8	17.8	15.3–22.2	20.5	17.7–23	17.3	13.7–22	20.6	16.3–25.3	19.2	15.8–23.7
33. Gonion	11	6.3–15.8	11.6	9.2–16	13.2	8.5–16.3	11.7	9.7–16.2	13.3	13.5–11.8	11.2	9.5–14.5	11.7	6.7–17.7	10.3	4.3–14.5	14.4	7.5–7.3	14.3	11.2–17.3
34. Opisthocranium	5.5	4.5–6.5	4.5	4–5	5.5	4.5–6.5	5	3.5–5.5	5.5	4.5–7.5	5	3.5–6.5	5.5	4.5–7.5	5	4–7	5.5	4.5–7.7	5	3.5–6.3

Source: Modified from Helmer, 1984. Reprinted with the permission of Cambridge University Press.

Table 7.12. *Facial Tissue Measurements (mm) from White North American Children Aged 8–18 Years*

Facial points	8–10 years		11–12 years		13–14 years		16 years		17–18 years	
	Male (83) Mean	Female (80) Mean	Male (66) Mean	Female (56) Mean	Male (61) Mean	Female (57) Mean	Male (38) Mean	Female (38) Mean	Male (37) Mean	Female (29) Mean
1. Forehead	4.9	4.7	5.1	5.1	5.4	5.5	5.8*	5.4	5.8	5.5
2. Glabella	6.1	5.9	6.2	6.1	6.8	6.3	7.0*	6.1	6.4	6.1
3. Nasion	9.3	8.5	9.6*	8.8	9.5*	8.6	9.7*	8.6	9.1	8.4
4. Midnasal	4.2	3.9	4.3	3.9	4.5*	4	4.8*	4	4.6*	3.7
5. Rhinion	2.5	2.5	2.5	2.4	2.6	2.5	2.7	2.4	2.8	2.2
6. Midphiltrum	13.8*	12.5	14.8*	13.7	16*	14.4	17.8*	14.4	17.2*	15.2
7. Upper lip	12.5*	11.2	12.4*	11.4	13.1*	12	14.4*	11.7	14*	12.6
8. Lower lip	15.6*	13.7	15.6*	14.3	16.9*	15.1	17.9*	15.6	17.9*	15.6
9. Labiomental	10.3	9.8	10.7	9.9	11.6	10.5	12.6*	10.9	12.5*	11.1
10. Mental	11.7	10.8	12.2	11.3	13.1	11.9	13.7	12.2	13.7	11.8
11. Gnathion	7.9	7.6	8.4	8.3	8.9	8.7	9	8.4	9.7	8.2

*Significantly thicker by sex.
Note: Modified from Garlie and Saunders (1999). Reprinted with the permission of Cambridge University Press.

Table 7.13. Comparison of Facial Tissue Measurements (mm) between White European Adults and Children

Facial points	White adults (Helmer, 1984) 30–39 years				White children (Wilkinson, 2002) 11–18 years			
	Male (14)		Female (13)		Male (99)		Female (101)	
	Mean	Range	Mean	Range	Mean	SD	Mean	SD
1. Forehead	5.0	4.5–5.5	4.5	4.3–5	4.7	0.85	4.6	0.88
2. Glabella	6.2*	5.3–6.5	5.7	5.2–6	5.1	0.84	4.9	0.89
3. Nasion	7.3*	7–7.5	6.5*	6–6.8	5.0	0.94	4.7	0.98
4. Rhinion	2.5	2–2.7	2.5	2.2–2.7	2.6	0.71	2.4	0.64
5. Midphiltrum	14.6*	13.5–16	12.8*	12.2–13.5	11.2	2.02	10.4	1.94
6. Upper lip	12.3	10.5–12.7	10.7	9.8–11	11.2	1.74	10.3	1.72
7. Lower lip	14.9	13.7–15.3	12.0	11.3–12.5	12.7	2.20	11.7	1.92
8. Labiomental	12.1	11.5–12.8	10.8	10–12	10.5	2.03	10.3	1.78
9. Mental	10.3	9.2–12	10.0	8.8–10.5	10.4	1.73	10.0	2.07
10. Gnathion	8.3*	7–9	7.2	6.2–8.2	6.9	1.32	6.6	1.34
11. Lateral forehead	6.0	5.5–6.5	5.0	5–5.5	5.5	1.01	5.2	1.05
12. Supraorbital	7.3*	6.5–7.5	6.5	6–6.7	6.2	1.01	6.0	1.05
13. Infraorbital	5.0	4.5–5.5	5.5	4.8–6	7.7*	1.15	7.4*	1.30
14. Lateral nose	7.4	6.7–8.5	6.3	5.2–7.5	6.5	1.44	6.5	1.41
15. Lateral orbit	5.2	5–5.5	5.2	4.5–5.5	7.4*	1.15	7.1*	1.55
16. Zygomatic attach	9.9	8.5–10.5	10.3	9.8–11.7	11.5*	2.53	12.6*	3.10
17. Upper 1st molar	22.0*	19–24	21.5	19.5–23.5	17.1	4.90	18.5	5.20
18. Lower 1st molar	18.5	16.7–21.7	19.0	17–22.8	16.0	3.81	16.3	4.34
19. Midmandible	11.9*	10–14	11.5	10–12.2	9.5	2.25	9.8	2.41
20. Zygomatic arch	5.3	4.5–6.3	5.2	4.5–5.3	8.0*	1.40	8.2*	2.41
21. Midmasseter	21.3	18.7–22.2	18.3	15.8–19.2	19.2	4.65	18.9	4.82

*Significantly thicker between adults and children.
Reprinted with the permission of Cambridge University Press.

CHILD FACIAL RECONSTRUCTION

Mary H. Manhein and her Louisiana State University (LSU) FACES Laboratory (Forensic Anthropology and Computer Enhancement Services) in Baton Rouge and the LSU Medical Center School of Dentistry in New Orleans conducted a study resulting in data crucial to reconstructing the faces of unidentified deceased children.[27] Beginning in 1995 and culminating in results published in the 2000 *Journal of Forensic Sciences* article "In Vivo Facial Tissue Depth Measurements for Children and Adults," ultrasound scans were done on 551 children and 256 adults (all live volunteer subjects) to find tissue depths at 19 points across the face. These data facilitate reconstruction of a face for the unidentified murdered child. Forensic artists who need to perform this difficult kind of task benefit from the advanced ultrasound technology used to gather these data. Previously the only tissue depth data available were for adults who were deceased and lying in a horizontal position when measured. Manhein *et al.* took their measurements from living subjects who were upright when the data were collected.

In 1986, Dumont used radiographic analyses to collect mid-facial tissue depths on approximately 200 Caucasian children 9 to 15 years of age.[28] Rathbun and Williamson utilized orthodontic radiographs to collect mid-facial tissue depths on 200 African-American children.[29]

Williamson's additional studies for his master's thesis gathered data on African-American children in Columbia, South Carolina, and Augusta, Georgia.[30] A study of Canadian children conducted by Garlie and Saunders added to the data on mid-facial tissue depths.[31]

The Manhein *et al.* study codified 19 points across the face that customized the data for children and maximized the advantages of ultrasound imaging. The following quote summarizes their measurement site choices:

> "Of the 19 points we measured, 13 are traditional landmarks while six others (points 4, 11, 12, 15, 16, and 19) are areas not measured in the past or are points for which very little data exist. For example, lateral eye (point16) is an area often cited as problematic and difficult to contour in two-dimensional and three-dimensional facial reconstructions because no modern data exist for this site. Also, while current standards exist for points 18 and 14 (the cheek region), these standards have proven to be ineffective in reconstructions...."[32]

These FACES researchers provided the legend, shown in Table 7.14, describing the location of their newly determined anatomical points from their study. This fortunate data gathering is customized to help the practicing forensic artist who must work the case of an unidentified murdered child.

Figure 7.75 is a child's skull showing the 19 points of tissue-depth measured by the FACES Laboratory study; Figure 7.76 is a 7-year-old girl with the measurement sites indicated.

Table 7.14.   Descriptions and Locations of Tissue Depth Markers*

Louisiana State University FACES Laboratory For numbers 1,2,3,5,6,7, and 8 cut one marker. For numbers 4 and 9–19, cut two markers.	
1. Glabella	Approximately 1 cm above and directly between the subject's eyebrows
2. Nasion	Directly between eyes
3. End of nasals	Palpating to determine where bone ends and cartilage begins
4. Lateral nostril	Approximately 0.5 cm to the right of the nostril
5. Midphiltrum	Centered between nose and mouth
6. Chin-lip fold	Centered in fold of chin, below lips
7. Mental eminence	Centered on forward-most projecting point of chin
8. Beneath chin	Centered on inferior surface of mandible
9. Superior eye orbit	Centered on eye, at level of eyebrow
10. Inferior eye orbit	Centered on eye, where inferior bony margin lies
11. Supracanine	Upper lip, lined up superiorly/inferiorly with lateral edge of nostril
12. Subcanine	Lower lip, lined up superiorly/inferiorly with lateral edge of nostril
13. Supra M2	Cheek region, lateral: lined up with bottom of nose; vertical: center of transducer lined up beneath lateral border of eye, measurement taken 0.5 cm to the left of center mark
14. Lower cheek	Cheek region, lateral: lined up with the mouth; vertical; same as 13
15. Midmandible	Inferior border of mandible, vertically lined up same as 13
16. Lateral eye orbit	Lined up laterally with corner of the eye, on the bone
17. Zygomatic	Lined up with the lateral border of the eye, on the zygomatic process
18. Gonion	Found by palpating
19. Root of zygoma	Anterior to and 0.5 cm superior to tragus
20. Greatest lip height	Measured from superiormost point of the upper lip to the inferiormost part of the lower lip

Courtesy of Mary H. Manhein, M.A.; Ginesse A. Listi, M.A.; Robert E. Barsley, D.D.S., J.D.; Robert Musselman, D.D.S.; N. Eileen Barrow, B.F.A.; and Douglas H. Ubelaker, Ph.D.; "In Vivo Facial Tissue Depth Measurements for Children and Adults," *Journal of Forensic Sciences*, 2000, 45(1):51.
*See Figure 7.75 for location on skull.

Figure 7.75

Data points on skull of child correlated to the study published in a 2000 Journal of Forensic Sciences *authored by Mary H. Manhein, M.A.; Ginesse A. Listi, M.A.; Robert E. Barsley, D.D.S., J.D.; Robert Musselman, D.D.S.; N. Eileen Barrow, B.F.A.; and Douglas H. Ubelaker, Ph.D.*

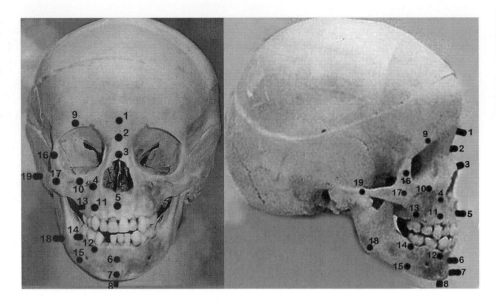

Figure 7.76

Data collection points indicated on face of 7-year-old girl. Modified after the study published in a 2000 Journal of Forensic Sciences *authored by Mary H. Manhein, M.A.; Ginesse A. Listi, M.A.; Robert E. Barsley, D.D.S., J.D.; Robert Musselman, D.D.S.; N. Eileen Barrow, B.F.A.; and Douglas H. Ubelaker, Ph.D.*

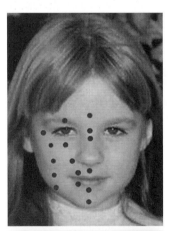

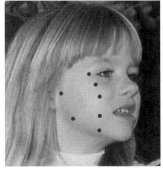

On October 8, 2005, in DuPage County, Illinois, a child was found dumped by a freeway; foul play was suspected and the child was unidentified. I joined DuPage County Sheriffs Forensic Artist Joy Mann in recreating the unknown child's face from the skeletal remains. Figure 7.77 shows the image created during that collaboration.

The child was wearing U.S. size 2T clothing, which usually is worn by children who are aged 2 years and are further in the tall and/or thin demographic segment of that age group. The dentition on this subject, however, was extensive enough to gain a determination by the anthropologist and forensic dentist who examined him to set his age at 3 to 5 years. The experts believed his heritage to be Hispanic/Caucasian. He was 3'2" and weighed approximately 30 lbs. (14 kg). The hair seemed extraordinarily thick and full-bodied, even in his advanced state of decomposition. For this reason, Joy Mann and I developed an image of a boy with thick hair. Additionally, Mann and Gibson observed the boy's teeth to be large, bright colored, and nicely formed. For this reason, a grinning smile was employed.

Figure 7.78 is the image created by the Center for Missing and Exploited Children from the previously mentioned subject; Figure 7.79 shows a version of the same case constructed by the Louisiana State University FACES Laboratory (Forensic Anthropology and Computer Enhancement Services).

The Mann/Gibson collaboration was a two-dimensional drawing. The Center for Missing and Exploited Children performed a computer-generated image utilizing a combination of scanned portions of features. The FACES images are first a clay reconstruction and then a computer enhancement of that clay sculpture.

There are some considerations when performing reconstructions of children's faces. Overall, a child will have a more rounded looking face. Children have the same number of muscles as adults; however, those muscles are attached to much shorter bones. For this reason, children's muscles have rounded profiles, rather than the elongated

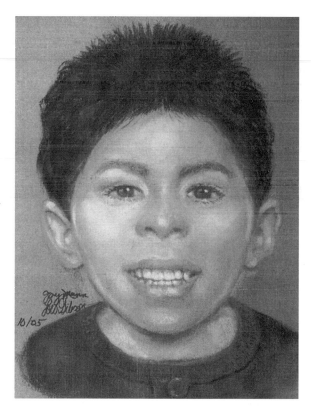

Figure 7.77

Facial reconstruction drawing done by DuPage County (Illinois) Forensic Artist Joy Mann, in collaboration with myself, of an unidentified murdered boy whose body was abandoned near a freeway October 8, 2005 (courtesy of the DuPage County Sheriffs). See color plate.

Figure 7.78

Facial reconstruction done with computer software at the Center for Missing and Exploited Children of an unidentified murdered boy whose body was abandoned near a freeway October 8, 2005 (courtesy of the National Center for Missing and Exploited Children).

John Doe - DuPage County

DOB: Unknown   **Age Now:** 3-5 years
Found: Oct 8th, 2005   **Sex:** Male
Height: 38 inches   **Weight:** 25-35 pounds
Eyes: Unknown   **Hair:** Black
Race: Hispanic/White Hispanic
Found: Un-incorporated Naperville, IL. (DuPage County)

On October 8th, 2005, the body of a young boy was found in un-incorporated DuPage County. The image shown in this flyer is a facial reconstruction as to how he may have appeared in life, but certain details were filled in by the artist to complete the image and should not be used in determining his possible identity. This image is not a photograph. He is a Hispanic or white/Hispanic male, aged between 3-5 years old. He weighed approximately 25-35 pounds, was 38 inches tall and had black hair. The boy was found inside a blue canvass laundry bag with a white drawstring top. He was dressed in a dark blue button down shirt, and dark blue pants, both with the brand name "Faded Glory".

COMPOSITE   MISSING & EXPLOITED

ANYONE HAVING INFORMATION SHOULD CONTACT
National Center for Missing and Exploited Children
1-800-843-5678 (1-800-THE-LOST)
or
DuPage County Sheriff's Office
630-407-2400

Figure 7.79

Facial reconstruction done first as three-dimensional clay sculpture, then as a computer enhancement of that same work; by Forensic Anthropology and Computer Enhancement Services (FACES) Laboratory at Louisiana State University in Baton Rouge, Louisiana, USA. Subject was an unidentified murdered boy, his body abandoned near a freeway October 8, 2005 (courtesy of the FACES Laboratory).

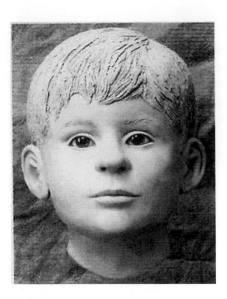

CLAY RECONSTRUCTION

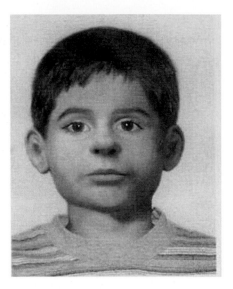

COMPUTER GENERATED PHOTO
FROM CLAY RECONSTRUCTION

contours of adults whose muscles are stretched across longer bones. For instance, the bones below the eyes in an adult face elongate till they occupy two-thirds of the length of the face; those same bones in children occupy only half the face. Figure 7.80 shows the skull of a newborn, a 3-year-old child, and an adult. Next to those specimens is a drawing of the various muscles under

Figure 7.80

From left to right are the front and profile view of: a newborn baby, a 3-year-old, an adult, and the musculature of an adult. Note that the baby and child would have an identical number of muscles placed on what are much shorter facial bones.

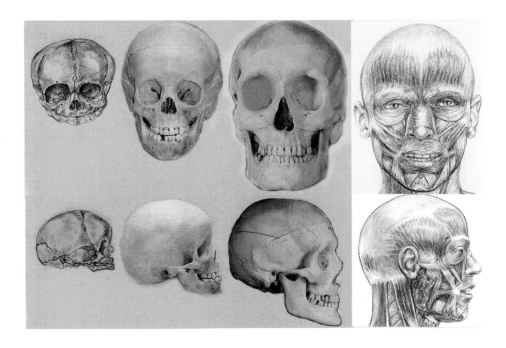

the surface of the face. Children have exactly the same number of muscles, yet those muscles must be jumbled together on shorter facial bones. No wonder the cheeks of children are almost spherical. The insertion of the numerous muscles that attach around the mouth and chin on what are, compared to the adult's, extremely short maxillary and mandibular bones, results in a jumble of muscles that cause the cheeks to be so rounded, that some infants' cheeks appear to protrude out and below the chin. An adult will not have jowls that hang below the chin unless that individual is morbidly obese. Suffice it to say, whatever feature is drawn, unless the child is extremely emaciated, the contours will be more rounded than an adult's.

Another trait that lends a childlike appearance to a facial image is the ratio of iris-to-sclera (white of the eye) in the eye opening. The younger an individual, the larger percentage of the eye opening will be taken up by the iris. In the youngest of infants, nearly the entire eye consists of iris. Figure 7.81 offers a progression of a male subject's eyes from a tiny infant to adulthood. Figure 7.82 is a female subject, showing her eyes from a newborn to adulthood. The ages are listed in the figure captions. However, if the anthropologist gives a certain age, sex, and race determination, the iris-to-sclera ratio can be best understood by obtaining a photo or photos of eyes for an individual of that same age, sex, and race. The artist with such a photo can imbue that same iris-to-sclera ratio in the reconstruction.

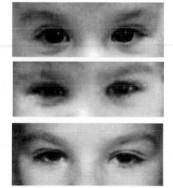

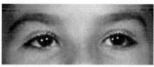

Figure 7.81

Study of how the iris occupies more of the eye opening compared to the white (sclera) portion in younger individuals. From top to bottom, the age of this male is 6 months, 2 years, 5 years, 7 years, 11 years, and 19 years (photos by author). See color plate.

Figure 7.82

Study of how the iris occupies more of the eye opening compared to the white (sclera) portion in younger individuals. From top to bottom, the age of this female is 3 months, 3 years, and 19 years (photos by author).

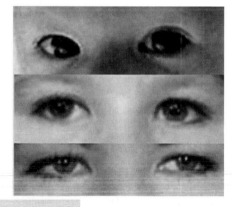

In Brief

- Ever-expanding tissue-depth data studies have greatly enhanced facial reconstruction accuracy. Follow diagrams for proper marker placement and use the appropriate data table for proper thickness on your specimen.
- Modern electronic imaging studies have customized new marker locations and tissue-depth data for child facial reconstructions.
- Children's features are more rounded than adults'. The younger the child, the larger portion of the eye opening is taken up by the iris; use eye photos of children the age of your subject for accurate iris size.

REFERENCES

1.   Mikhail Gerasimov, *The Face Finder*, translated from the German by Alan Houghton Brodrick Hutchinson & Co. Ltd., Great Britain, 1971, p. 36.

2.   Mikhail Gerasimov, *The Face Finder*, translated from the German by Alan Houghton Brodrick, Hutchinson & Co. Ltd., Great Britain, 1971, p. 34.

3.   K. Taylor, Texas Department of Public Safety, personal communication, December 31, 1990.

4.   Caroline Wilkinson, *Forensic Facial Reconstruction*, Cambridge University Press, 2004, p. 70.

5.   R.L. Drake, W. Vogl, A. W. Mitchell, *Gray's Anatomy for Students*, Churchill Livingstone, Elsevier Health Sciences, Philadelphia, p. 874.

6.   Mike Glenn, "Distinctive scar may be key to woman's ID," *Houston Chronicle*, October 7, 2006. Houston Police Department Incident Number 97932606.

7.   Bron Tripathi, and Tripathi, *Wolff's Anatomy of the Eye and Orbit*, Chapman & Hall Medical, London, 8th edition, 1997, p. 17.

8.   William Fisher Norris, and Charles Augustus Oliver, *System of Diseases of the Eye*, J.B. Lippincott & Co., 1900, New York, p. 383.

9.   Op. cit., p. 384.

10.   Carmine D. Clemente, Ph.D., *Anatomy: A Regional Atlas of the Human Body,* 3rd edition, Urban & Schwarzenberg, Baltimore, Maryland, 1987, p. 834.

11.   J. Anthony Bron, B.Sc., F.R.C.S., F.C.O.phth., Ramesh C. Tripathi, M.D., Ph.D., F.A.C.S., M.S. Ophth., D.O.R.C.P&S., F.R.C.Path., F.I.C.S., F.N.A.S(I)., Brenda J. Tripathi, Ph.D., *Wolff's Anatomy of the Eye and Orbit,* 8th edition, Chapman & Hall Medical, London, UK, 1997, pp. 3, 17, 39, 78.

12.   Caroline Wilkinson, *Forensic Facial Reconstruction*, Cambridge University Press, New York 2004, p. 113.

13.   Wilton Krogman, and Mehmet Iscan, *The Human Skeleton in Forensic Medicine*, Charles C. Thomas, Springfield, Illinois, 1986.

14.   K. T. Taylor, *Forensic Art and Illustration,* CRC Press, Boca Raton, Florida, 2001, p. 389.

15.   Caroline Wilkinson, *Forensic Facial Reconstruction*, Cambridge University Press, New York, 2004, pp. 106–107.

16.   R.L. Drake, W. Vogl, A. W. Mitchell, *Gray's Anatomy for Students*, Churchill Livingstone, Elsevier Health Sciences, Philadelphia, p. 1006.

17.   John Prag, and Richard Neave, *Making Faces*, Texas A&M University Press, College Station, Texas, 1997, p. 29.

18.   Caroline Wilkinson, *Forensic Facial Reconstruction*, Cambridge University Press, New York, 2004, pp. 109–110.

19. J. L., Tarr, Colonel, U.S.A.F., T. D., White, Chief of Staff, *Dental Laboratory Technicians' Manual*, U.S. Government Printing Office, Washington, D.C. 1959, pp. 106–107.

20. Glenn, Mike, "Distinctive scar may be key to woman's ID/Body was found in Acres Homes area in June," *Houston Chronicle*, October 7, 2006. Harris County Medical Examiners Case Number 06-1937. Houston Police Department Incident Number 97932606.

21. Peggy O'Hare, "Search for a Name/Child's body still unidentified after 3 months," *Houston Chronicle*, December 20, 2001. Bill Murphy, "'Angel Doe' still a mystery/Months after dead girl found, no one has claimed her," *Houston Chronicle*, March 4, 2002. Mike Glenn, "Grandmother helps ID girl after noticing sketch on TV," *Houston Chronicle*, March 24, 2002. Alan Bernstein, "Family buries 6-year-old known as 'Little Princess,'" *Houston Chronicle*, April 7, 2002. Peggy O'Hare, "'Angel Doe's' father is held in her death/Dad allegedly beat girl, 6; arrest solves year-old case," *Houston Chronicle*, August 8, 2002. Rad Sallee, "Angel Doe's killer gets life sentence in 2nd trial/Abused girl's body was found in ditch in 2001," *Houston Chronicle*, August 23, 2003. Houston Police Department Incident Number 123629501.

22. K. T., Taylor, *Forensic Art and Illustration*, CRC Press, Boca Raton, Florida, 2001, pp. 338–339.

23. Caroline Wilkinson, *Forensic Facial Reconstruction*, Cambridge University Press, New York, 2004, p. 162.

24. Krogman, Wilton, and Iscan, Mehmet, *The Human Skeleton in Forensic Medicine*, Charles C. Thomas, Springfield, Illinois, 1986, p. 465.

25. Personal communication via email from David Sweet, D.M.D., Ph.D., D.A.B.F.O., January 15, 2007.

26. Krogman, Wilton, and Iscan, Mehmet, *The Human Skeleton in Forensic Medicine*, Charles C. Thomas, Springfield, Illinois, 1986, pp. 434–440. Prag, John, and Neave, Richard, *Making Faces*, Texas A&M University Press, College Station, Texas, p. 26. Taylor, K. T. *Forensic Art and Illustration*, CRC Press, Boca Raton, Florida, 2001, pp. 354–355.

27. M. H., Manhein, M.A.; G. A., Listi, M.A.; R. E., Barsley, D.D.S., J.D.; R., Musselman, D.D.S.; N. E., Barrow, B.F.A.; and D. H., Ubelaker, Ph.D.; "In Vivo Facial Tissue Depth Measurements for Children and Adults," *Journal of Forensic Sciences*, 2000, 45(1), pp. 48–60.

28. E. R., Dumont, "Mid-facial tissue depths of white children: An aid in facial feature reconstruction," *Journal of Forensic Sciences*, 1986, (4)31, pp. 1463–1469.

29. M. A., Williamson, "Mid facial tissue depths of African-American children," Program Abstracts of the 45th Annual Meeting of the American Academy of Forensic Science, Boston, MA., 1993.

30. M. A., Williamson, "Mid-facial tissue depths of African-American Children in Columbia, South Carolina and Augusta, Georgia [thesis]," Columbia, University of South Carolina, 1990.

31. T. N., Garlie S. R., Saunders "Midline facial tissue thicknesses of subadults from a longitudinal radiographic study," *Journal of Forensic Sciences*, 1999, 44(a), pp. 61–67.

32. M. H., Manhein, M.A.; G. A., Listi, M.A.; R. E., Barsley, D.D.S., J.D.; R., Musselman, D.D.S.; N. E., Barrow, B.F.A.; and D. H., Ubelaker, Ph.D.; "In Vivo Facial Tissue Depth Measurements for Children and Adults," *Journal of Forensic Sciences*, 2000, 45(1), p. 49.

CHAPTER 8

THREE-DIMENSIONAL FACIAL RECONSTRUCTION OF SKELETAL REMAINS

Artists from ancient times would apply clay to a skull and use shells for the eyes in efforts to revive the appearance of the individual. Hundreds of years later in post-Renaissance Europe, scientific efforts were established to determine tissue depths from cadavers for the purpose of recreating the appearance of famous persons for whom skulls were extant. This urge to place clay upon the underpinnings of a face is common among artists. Indeed, artists versed at portraiture usually are tempted when viewing a skull to imagine the face that once hung there during life. As Harris Hawthorne Wilder, the earliest American pioneer of facial reconstruction, wrote in 1912:

> "...the detailed relationships between the face of the skull and the fleshy face have become more and more definitely known, until it seems now possible, given either one, to reproduce the other with considerable accuracy."[1]

The twentieth century brought burgeoning populations and electronic media, which allowed news of crimes to be known everywhere instantly. This proliferation of crime awareness created a serious purpose for artistic musings over skeletal appearances. Now the artist was needed to bring order to chaos, the kind of chaos that occurs when a detective has a murder, yet does not even know *who* was murdered, the kind of chaos that tortures loved ones when they frantically search for family members who are missing, wondering if they are dead or alive. So now, the work of formulating a face takes on urgency. No longer is the fine artist creating a bust of Bach, Raphael, or Dante; now the artist tries to find the given name of murder victims. The facial reconstruction artist provides a unique professional service, aiding detectives in their hunt for killers, and bringing comfort to loved ones.

The three-dimensional method will take more time and effort, more space and materials, but artists still show the dedication it takes and successes are seen on media regularly where three-dimensional facial reconstructions help identify victims.

THE ANATOMICAL OR MANCHESTER METHOD

Mikhail Gerasimov sculpted the various muscles on skulls for which he wished to reconstruct the face, and used no tissue-depth markers. His work stands as a monument to early successful forensic art, where unidentified murder victims' identities were revealed, resulting in the murderers being prosecuted. Richard Neave of the United Kingdom is a modern practitioner of this anatomical method. Neave combines the use of tissue-depth markers with the practice of sculpting the individual muscles and then adding a layer of clay to represent the skin. Neave has performed reconstructions of several historically significant specimens such as the two Egyptian brothers of Neckht-Ankh and Knum-Nakht, who were mummies housed at the Manchester Museum. Some other Neave reconstructions of note are Philip II of Macedon (Father of Alexander the Great) and King Midas. Soon Neave, using guidelines set up by Gatliff (1984), Krogman and Iscan (1986), and George (1987), began performing forensic investigations where he experienced a 75% success rate for 20 cases worked. Figure 8.1 shows four steps in Neaves's process wherein the muscles are replicated in clay upon the skull and subsequently a layer of clay representing the various layers of tissue and skin are applied on top.

This method, at first glance, seems prohibitively complex to persons who have not studied anatomy. However, constructing a face by replicating each muscle is the best practice possible for successful performance in the simpler American method shown later in this chapter. Following is a brief overview of the Manchester method used on a case.

The subject presented for reconstruction was evaluated by H. Gill-King, Ph.D., D.A.B.F.A., of the University of North Texas Laboratory of Forensic Anthropology. From that report this subject was determined to be an Anglo-Caucasian male with an age range of 50 to 65 years. His height was estimated to be 65.5 inches with a medium frame that displayed an above average muscular development at some time in adult life. The subject further had only one tooth on the upper and lower alveolar ridge, thus indicating it would have been impossible for him to have a denture or a partial removable appliance to replace dentition.

Figure 8.2 shows how the skull was mounted on a stand after gluing the mandible to the calvarium portion of the skull, using acetone-dissolvable glue and proper spacing to replicate the articular disc,

Figure 8.1

The Manchester method of facial reconstruction. Top left: Wooden pegs attached to the plaster skull. Top right: Facial muscles modeled in clay onto the skull copy. Bottom left: Clay skin layer placed over the facial musculature. Bottom right: Finished reconstruction (modified from Neave).

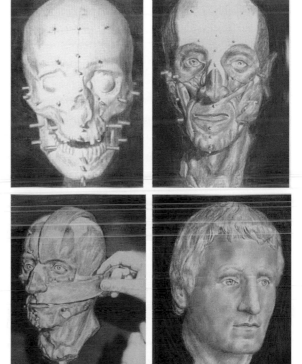

Figure 8.2

Left: The skull with the mandible glued in place using spacers at the temporomandibular joint and slender pieces of balsam wood glued around the dental arch. The spacing between the alveolar ridges of this edentulous subject is approximately 22 mm. Right: The skull with tissue-depth markers made of balsam wood (photos by author).

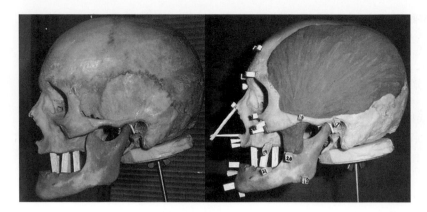

and the synovial and fibrous membranes at the end of the mandibular condyle. The spacing between the alveolar ridges was determined from the *Dental Laboratory Technicians' Manual* to be approximately 22 millimeters.[2]

Tissue depth markers made of balsam wood were then glued in place using data for a slender Caucasian male (see Table 7.2), since the size of clothing compared to the subject's height indicated such a body type. Slender pieces of balsam wood were glued carefully to the ends of the nasal bone and nasal spine, paying close attention to the direction of the last portion of those bony landmarks to define an approximate nose shape. The first muscle sculpted was the temporalis, shown here fanning out on the temporal bone and attaching at the coronoid process of the mandible.

SKULL STAND

Notice this particular skull stand has padding for the underside of the specimen cut from a sheet of commonly used exterior house insulation. On the other side of the wing nut is a 3-inch toggle bolt that has been passed through the large hole at the base of the skull, the foramen magnum. From this toggle-bolt attachment down you can use any sturdy shaft that attaches at the other end to either a heavy-duty tripod head or a Panavise. This kind of apparatus allows the skull to be moved into the Franfort Horizontal Plane for photographing, and other positions convenient to working on the reconstruction. The Panavise or tripod should be firmly mounted on a heavy board large enough to offset the weight of the skull covered in clay while in an upright position. The height of this entire setup should be so that you can work on the skull comfortably.

One adaptation for the skull stand can be seen in Figure 8.3. With this setup, the shaft holding the skull can be removed. This allows the skull to be stored in a box lined with padding to protect the anatomy, and the stand put away in another area. With this feature, the skull is not always left out in an awkward place where the sculpture might be bumped and distorted by other personnel.

Figure 8.3

Left: The base of the skull stand consisting of taking the top of a camera tripod and securing it to a 3/4-inch thick square of plywood cut to 11″ × 11″. A toggle bolt affixed to one coupling is attached inside the foramen magnum of the skull. At the other end a coupling attaches the pipe to the tripod (photos by Tiffany Gibson).

This detachability also allows the work area to be used for other activities where you might not want traumatized witnesses viewing the somewhat shocking sight of a skull in various stages of having its face reconstructed.

The method to construct this skull stand was to attach a one-and-one-quarter-inch poly-vinyl-chloride (PVC) coupling to the base and have another coupling of the same size attached to the skull. The method of attachment is to glue a cap on the end of the coupling and drill a hole through which a toggle bolt for the skull end, or the tripod for the base end, can be bolted together. A pipe that will fit into both couplings is then sawed to the desired length. The schedule 40 PVC pipe employed here commonly is used to construct water lines in housing and can be purchased at any home improvement store. This pipe easily is sawed to any length desired, can be attached with screws, and is strong enough to withstand the weight of the heaviest skull and clay.

Once the skull has been mounted securely on the skull stand and the tissue-depth markers are in place, the muscles are sculpted in their proper shape and size and placed in their proper order.

Figures 8.4 and 8.5 name the muscles of the face and neck. For a detailed understanding of the interior layers of muscles as you might see during a thorough dissection in a gross anatomy class for medical school, an exhaustive volume would be either Clemente's *Anatomy—A Regional Atlas of the Human Body* (Baltimore, MD, 2007) or *Gray's Anatomy for Students* by Drake, Vogl, and Mitchell (Philadelphia, 2005). Figures 8.6 and 8.7 illustrate the various bones of the skull with the demarcation of where one bone ends and another begins. Knowledge of the various bones' locations is necessary since many muscles have an origin at one bone and an insertion location at another bone.

Two kinds of eyes that can be purchased to create a life-like appearance are prosthetic eyes, like those worn by individuals who have lost that part of their anatomy, and specialty eyes sold for special effects in dramatic productions. Figure 8.8 shows both kinds of eyes, front and back view. They are both made of glass; the specialty eyes are like spheres with a cylindrical tube at the back.

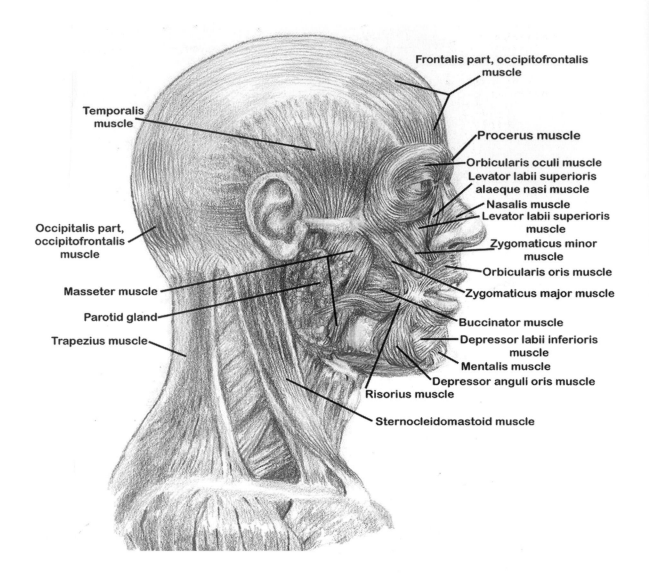

Frontalis part, occipitofrontalis muscle

Temporalis muscle

Procerus muscle

Orbicularis oculi muscle

Levator labii superioris alaeque nasi muscle

Nasalis muscle

Levator labii superioris muscle

Zygomaticus minor muscle

Occipitalis part, occipitofrontalis muscle

Orbicularis oris muscle

Zygomaticus major muscle

Masseter muscle

Buccinator muscle

Parotid gland

Depressor labii inferioris muscle

Trapezius muscle

Mentalis muscle

Depressor anguli oris muscle

Risorius muscle

Sternocleidomastoid muscle

Figure 8.4

Muscles of the head and neck; profile view (illustration by author). See color plate for larger image.

Care must be taken to allow enough room into the padding placed in the eye socket to accommodate the volume of the full sphere and tail end of the specialty eyes. The prosthetic eyes are a rounded, undulated-edged disk shape. The specialty eyes are about $60 a pair, and the prosthetic eyes can be purchased for approximately $150 a pair. Both have the accurate iris size, which is approximately 12 millimeters diameter.

As shown in Figure 8.9, the glass eyes were surrounded with clay before placing them in the orbit that had been padded with tissue. The eyeball is set so a line running from the middle of the top of the orbit to the middle of the bottom intersects what would be the cornea. Clay is added and sculpted around the eyeball to replicate the orbicularis oculi muscles. The cartilage structures on the end of the nose are added.

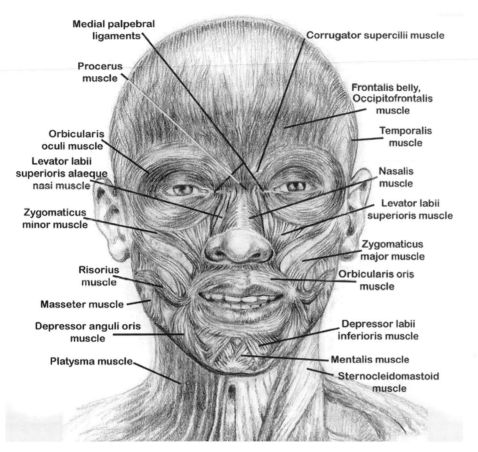

Figure 8.5

Muscles of the head and neck; front view (illustration by author). See color plate for larger image.

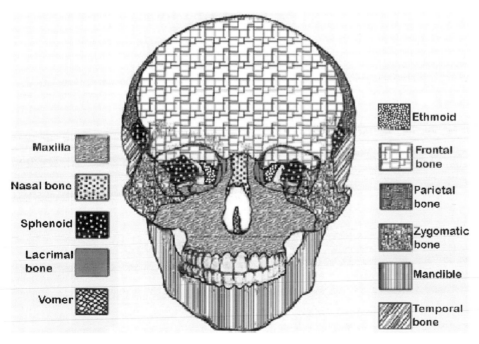

Figure 8.6

Bones of the skull; front view (illustration by Tiffany Gibson).

Figure 8.7

Bones of the skull; profile view (illustration by Tiffany Gibson).

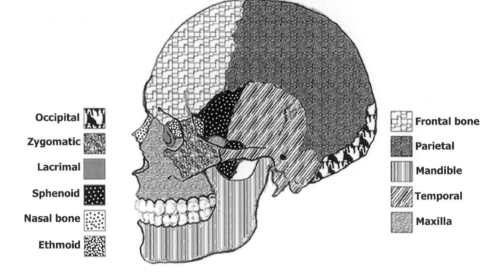

Occipital
Zygomatic
Lacrimal
Sphenoid
Nasal bone
Ethmoid

Frontal bone
Parietal
Mandible
Temporal
Maxilla

Figure 8.8

Back (top) and front (bottom) views of two kinds of artificial eyes. The topmost are specialty eyes used to create theatrical props. The bottom eyes in each photo are real prosthetic eyes made in France. Both types have 12 mm diameter iris (photos by author).

The muscles of the face and scalp are then constructed, making certain to leave several millimeters uncovered at the end of the tissue-depth markers to accommodate the skin layer. Regarding the adherence to the depth indicated by the markers, Richard Neave, the foremost practitioner of the Manchester Method of facial reconstruction, says:

"…Where available the tissue depth pegs can act as guides, and a couple of millimeters of peg should be left visible above the muscle surface … the reconstruction practitioner may wish to deviate from the tissue depths suggested by the pegs. The tissue depth pegs represent average tissue measurements appropriate to the age, sex and racial origin of the skull, but since these are averages, they will not always be accurate for an individual skull. Frequently, the skull morphology will suggest that one or more of the tissue pegs are misleading, and the reconstructor should always

Figure 8.9

Left: top to bottom; eyes from behind with clay, front view, tissue in eye socket, eyes in orbit. Second from left: lateral eye placement. Third from left: nose projection estimated and muscles sculpted on skull. Far right: facial muscles recreated in clay leaving 2 to 8 mm of tissue depth markers showing (photos by author).

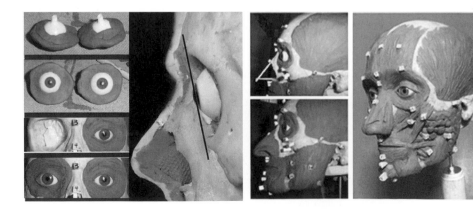

follow the facial contour suggested by the skull. Where the pegs are too projecting or too shallow they can be removed or ignored. The facial musculature will determine the face shape and contours and the tissue depth pegs should only be considered as guides."[3]

FACIAL MUSCLES

Temporalis: (Figure 8.10, B) This muscle originates from the inferior temporal line, passes behind the zygomatic arch, and inserts at the coronoid process and anterior surface of the ramus of the mandible, filling the space behind the zygomatic arch and becoming progressively thinner as it reaches the surface of the skull. When viewed from the front this muscle gives a smooth, rounded contour to the outer edges of the head.

Masseter: (Figure 8.10, M) This bulky, powerful muscle fills out the cheek at the side of the mandible. Rectangular in shape, this muscle originates at the zygomatic surface of the maxilla and the zygomatic arch; it inserts on the lateral surface of the ramus and coronoid process of the mandible.

Buccinator: (Figure 8.10, behind P, Risorius) This quadrilateral muscle originates behind the mandibular ramus at the alveolar processes of the maxillary and mandibular molars and partially fills the space between the masseter and the teeth. The fibers of this muscle then blend with those of the orbicularis oris muscle.

Orbicularis oris: (Figure 8.10, L) This circular muscle covers the teeth and forms the basis for the lips and the mouth opening. The outer edge of this sphincter-like muscle blends with fibers from the buccinator, levators, and depressors of lips and angles, and the zygomatic muscles. A structure called the modiolus at the corners of the mouth cover the intersection of all the muscles and gives this area a smooth appearance.

Mentalis: (Figure 8.10, R) This muscle originates from the incisive fossa of the mandible and inserts into the skin of the chin. This muscle has a conical form and lies beneath the depressor muscles.

Depressor labii inferioris: (Figure 8.10, O) This quadrilateral muscle originates at the inferior border of the mandible and inserts at the skin of the lower lip and overlaps the mentalis fibers at right angles.

Depressor anguli oris: (Figure 8.10, N) This fan-shaped muscle originates at the inferior border of the mandible and inserts at the modialis at the outer corners of the mouth.

Orbicularis oculi: (Figure 8.10, C) This flat circular muscle forms an ellipse inside the orbit and around the eyeball. This muscle derives its outer contours from the shape of the orbit; the inner contours should appear to be an eyelid to the properly set eyeball.

Levator labii superioris alaeque nasi: (Figure 8.10, H) This thin ribbon-type muscle originates at the upper part of the frontal process of the maxilla, level with the inner corner of the eye. As it travels downward, it describes the outer edge of the nose. At the lower end it attaches at two locations: the alar cartilage and into the upper lip with levator labii superioris.

Nasalis: (Figure 8.10, G) This muscle originates from the maxilla lateral to the nasal notch and from above the lateral incisor tooth. It ascends to the bridge of the nose and meshes with the opposite insertion.

Levator anguli oris: (Figure 8.10, Q) This muscle originates from the canine fossa of the maxilla just below the infraorbital foramen. This is a flat muscle that lies under the levator labii superioris and zygomaticus minor muscles.

Levator labii superioris: (Figure 8.10, I) This muscle fans out from the upper lip, between the levators anguli oris and labii superioris alaeque nasi to the lower border of the orbit from maxilla to zygomatic bone.

Corrugator supercilii: (Figure 8.10, underneath Procerus, F) These are small oblong muscles originating at the medial end of the superciliary arch and inserting deep in the surface of the skin above the middle of the supraorbital margin.

Procerus: (Figure 8.10, F) This small triangular-shaped muscle originates from the nasal bone and inserts in the skin on the lower forehead between the eyebrows.

Occipitofrontalis: (Figure 8.10, A) This is the "scalp" muscle. It consists of a frontal belly anteriorly and an occipital belly posteriorly. These are connected by an aponeurotic tendon. The frontal belly covers the forehead and attaches to the skin under the eyebrows. The occipital belly arises from the back of the skull and is smaller than the frontal belly.

Risorius: (Figure 8.10, P) This ribbon-like muscle originates from the parotid fascia and inserts into the skin at the angle of the mouth.

Parotid gland: (Figure 8.10, S) This somewhat amorphous mass occupies the back part of the cheek forward of the ear, below the zygomatic arch and creates

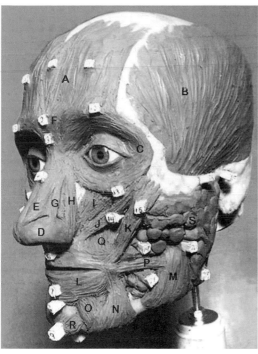

A. Occipitofrontalis
B. Temporalis
C. Orbicularis oculi
D. Greater alar cartilage, lateral crus
E. Lateral nasal cartilage
F. Procerus
G. Nasalis
H. Levator labii superioris alaeque nasi
I. Levator labii superioris
J. Zygomaticus minor
K. Zygomaticus major
L. Orbicularis oris
M. Masseter
N. Depressor anguli oris
O. Depressor labii inferioris
P. Risorius
Q. Levator anguli oris
R. Mentalis
S. Parotid gland

Figure 8.10

Muscles and structures of the face (modified after Neave/Wilkinson).

a padded mass on the edge of the angle of the mandible. This can be depicted with small lumps of clay laid atop the masseter muscle.

Figure 8.11 shows part of the skin layer added with attention to the 50- to 65-year age of the subject. The ear is best sculpted on a lump of clay before attaching it to the head due to the complexity of its form. The ears should be approximately the length of the nose with the top aligned at the eye area and the bottom aligned with the bottom of the nose. The tragus of the ear sits atop the external auditory meatus.

Next the neck was formed from flexible wire mesh like that seen in Figure 8.12. This mesh usually is made of aluminum and bends easily by hand. It is advisable to use heavy gardening gloves when working with this material to avoid tiny cuts to the hands. The muscles of the neck were done and a layer of skin added with the appropriate aged appearance.

Figure 8.11

A layer of clay representing the skin (adhering to the 55–60 year age range) is applied over the muscles. The convoluted ears should be constructed separately on a block of clay, then added when nearly complete. Ears are about the length of the nose and placed with top paralleling the eyes and bottom parallel to the end of the nose (photos by author).

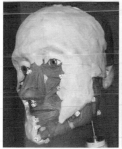

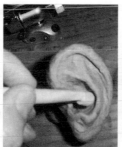

Figure 8.12

Packages of flexible aluminum mesh that can be used to shape the neck and shoulders for the reconstruction (photo by author).

Various colors of clay were used to mix a hue approximating an unshaven cheek and chin area; a stiff brush was used to replicate the texture. Pushing the bristles into the unshaven areas tended to replicate the look of stubble. Grade 40 or 50 sandpaper pressed against the skin elsewhere creates a realistic skin texture. The eyebrows in Figure 8.13 were created by mixing colors of plastiline clay together, much like oil paints, to create hair-like areas that matched the color of that found at the scene of this subject's demise, as shown in Figure 8.16. This mixing of clay colors is easy if you are versed at mixing oil paints. Shown in Figure 8.14, you can use a clay-sculpting tool as a tiny spatula to mix the clay until the right shade is created. Then scrape up tiny slivers of the eyebrow color and apply them to the correct location and in the correct growth direction of the eyebrow hairs. Then stroke the hair-colored clay into the skin-colored clay in the hair-growth direction. As the flesh tone mixes with the hair tones, the natural shadow color seen under eyebrow hairs will form and the result is an almost life-like eyebrow. Mistakes can easily be covered over or scraped off, so there are no ruinous errors. Figure 8.15 shows two phases of clay eyebrow creation.

Figure 8.13

A stiff bristle brush can be used to add texture to the skin. Number 40 to 50 sandpaper can also be torn into small rounded pieces and pressed against the skin for a natural texture. The ears are left smooth.

Figure 8.14

Clay being mixed with a clay-sculpting tool in front of blocks of different colors of clay. Mixing colors from clay is like mixing extra thick oil paints. This is the method I used for mixing the eyelashes and eyebrows.

A close resemblance of the cream-colored jacket the subject is seen wearing in Figure 8.16 was found at a garage sale along with a T-shirt that also resembled that worn by the subject. A wig was purchased and thinned oil paints were used to apply gray to some hair, in the proportion and hue as found at the scene. Since the subject was edentulous (toothless), tissue depth markers nos. 6 and 7 were removed and the mouth was sculpted as if someone had no teeth and was not wearing a denture.

Since this individual probably would have been homeless, due to evidence at the scene where he was found, a sun-damaged skin color was mixed from various clay colors and added to areas of his face that would not be shielded by the ball caps found by his body. Two views of the finished work are seen in Figure 8.17. These are digital photos taken outside with no flash. An assistant held an 18″×24″ open drawing pad behind the photographer so the large area of white paper would reflect some light onto the subject.

Figure 8.15

Top: One eyebrow done using clay mixed to the correct shade. Bottom: Both eyebrows and clay eyelashes applied.

CONSTRUCTING A WORKING COPY OF THE SKULL

The ideal method for reconstructing the face on a skull in three dimensions is to make a copy first. Once the clay is placed on the bones of the face, you become blind to the unique contours and landmarks. Even the smallest layer of clay completely obscures any view of the specimen being reconstructed. As Caroline Wilkinson opines in her work, *Forensic Facial Reconstruction*, "The preferred reconstruction technique is to work directly onto a *copy* of the skull. This decreases the possibility of damage to the specimen, *allows study of the skull throughout the entire reconstructive process*, and leaves a record of the specimen after the reconstruction is disassembled"[4] (emphasis added).

A fragile specimen might not hold the weight of the clay placed atop to sculpt the various features. However, the need to *see* the subtle contours and undulations of the bones as you extrapolate a face from the bony areas is the paramount reason why artists are driven to drawing from the skull, and away from the traditional three-dimensional sculpting method. The problem of viewing the specimen during the entirety of the process is solved by making a copy upon which to work.

Figure 8.16

The top photos show two views of some hair for the elderly subject. The bottom photo shows clearly the cream-colored jacket he wore. I was able to find an almost identical jacket at a garage sale to replicate the clothing for media release. See color plate.

Figure 8.17
Two views of the finished reconstruction. A wig with the appropriate amount of gray hair was added, along with clothing purchased at a garage sale that closely matched that worn by the subject. See color plate.

Gloria Nusse is a premier practitioner of mold making of skulls for the purpose of facial reconstruction. Later in this chapter she will describe her facial reconstruction for a case that prompted the successful identification of her subject. Because of compelling circumstances, Nusse could reconstruct her subject only on a copy of the skull. A further complication was the fact Nusse had only 24 hours during which to finish the cast of the skull. Nusse was successful during this time-pressured mold making, and further, the copy she created led her to create an image that succeeded in identifying her subject. Here, then, are her expert instructions for a proven method of creating a copy of a skull in order to perform a best effort in creating a three-dimensional facial reconstruction.

GLORIA NUSSE: AN INTRODUCTION TO MOLD MAKING OF A SKULL FOR PURPOSES OF RECONSTRUCTING THE FACE IN THREE DIMENSIONS

Making a mold of the skull before beginning a facial reconstruction offers important advantages. Working on a copy allows the sculpture to remain intact, negating the necessity to break down the sculpture after it is photographed. The skull is left available for examination by the artist and other investigators. The sculpture can be used in various press conferences and is available for use in other situations that may arise after the skull is relinquished. Having a casing of a skull can also be helpful for educational purposes, and it may be used in a courtroom exhibit. Often the bones of the skull are damaged, missing, or not always in the most ideal condition. In these instances, a mold may be the best way to proceed with a facial reconstruction.

SKULL PREPARATION

The first step to prepare the skull for molding is to fill in openings and gaps that could be filled in and damaged by the silicone rubber. The openings, foramina, and gaps that are between the sutures lines of the bones are such places. Any gaps or openings that are more than 2 to 3 millimeters wide could be filled in with the silicone. Small bits of silicone could be left behind in the skull and/or break the bones of the skull; therefore, careful preparation must be made at this beginning point of the process. For a skull that is to be used for facial reconstruction, the

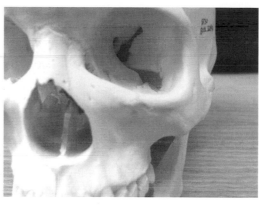

nasal aperture may be partially filled in, making certain the vomer bone and nasal spine are fully exposed. The orbital fossa of the eyes may also be partially filled in, as these bones are very fragile and are likely to break. The posterior margin may be covered, making certain the opening will accommodate the prosthetic eye. Note, if the skull is to be used for a museum display, or if the full orbit and/or nasal aperture must be exposed, then the spaces around the nasal conch and/or the orbital fissures may be lightly covered in clay as seen in Figures 8.18, 8.19, and 8.20.

Figure 8.18

Orbital fissures are lightly bridged with clay for museum-quality specimens.

Normal Skull Preparation

With a normal skull that is not damaged, the pathologist may have opened the cranial vault. Additionally, the maxillae may have been cut to facilitate removal of the teeth for examination. When this happens, the artist will have to reassemble the skull. Placing flat toothpicks along the edges of the cut bone of the cranial vault will fill the space left by the bone saw. The recommended glue for assemblage is model airplane glue since that type can be dissolved with acetone. Under no circumstance should super glue be used, as it is very difficult to remove later. Care must always be taken not to harm the bones of the skull. See Figure 8.21 and 8.22 for glue joints using toothpicks for spacers.

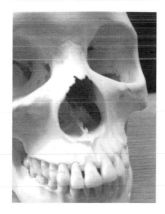

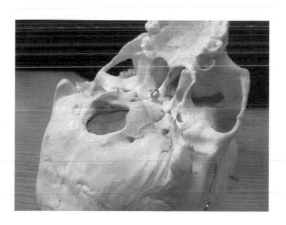

Figure 8.19

Far left: Interior of nasal aperture and nasal concha are lightly covered in clay to add thickness and to protect fragile bones.

Figure 8.20

Left: Foramen magnum and all spaces over 203 mm wide are filled in with clay.

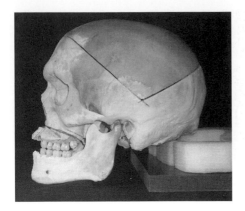

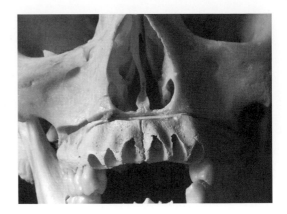

Figure 8.21

A normal skull that has been cut during autopsy, reassembled.

Figure 8.22

Flat toothpicks are inserted and glued in place to accommodate spaces left from saw cuts during autopsy.

Put a small ball of cotton inside the nasal aperture. Then fill in orbital fissures, lacrimal foramina, and nasal aperture with cotton, small pieces of tape, or a light application of clay as in Figure 8.23. Use a small boxwood tool or tongue depressor for an applicator. Be very light-handed, using only enough clay or tape to fill in large openings. Be especially careful not to break the delicate bones inside the nasal aperture and the thin bones of the inner eye. The silicone, which will be applied next, is very thick and sets quite fast. For this reason, it will not seep into very small openings of less than 2 to 3 millimeters. Most important, keep the clay light in application. See Figure 8.24 for proper preparation of the inferior surface of the cranium portion of the skull. Do not smudge the clay into the bone. In order to fill in some of the foramina found on the inferior, or bottom surface, of the skull, you may be able to build up the clay from the interior as in Figure 8.25.

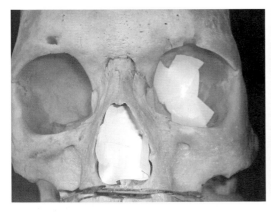

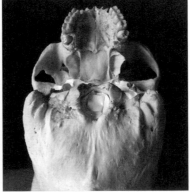

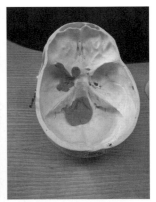

Figure 8.23

For facial reconstruction cases, orbital fissures may be covered with removable tape.

Figure 8.24

Openings in the skull can first be filled with cotton before application of removable tape.

Figure 8.25

Often the best way to fill a foramen or opening in the skull is from the interior.

Working with a Badly Damaged Skull

If the artist is working with a badly damaged or fragmented skull, a mold is often the only way a reconstruction can be started. Consulting with an anthropologist will enable the artist to have a better idea of how the parts fit together. See Figure 8.27 for an example of a badly damaged skull. With careful study and consideration the skull was rejoined using glue and small strips of card stock paper as seen in Figure 8.26. After the skull has been assembled and photographed, the inner cavity of the skull can be loosely filled with plastic saran wrap and cotton balls as shown in Figure 8.28. After this process the cavities can be lightly bridged with clay and finished as with a normal skull.

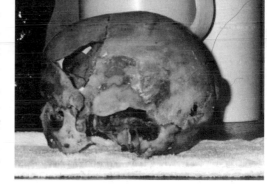

Figure 8.26
Profile of assembled skull.

MOLD PREPARATION

Next the clay must be built up around the skull to form a parting line between the upper and lower parts of the mold. The best placement is one that will not interfere with the facial plane. See Figures 8.29 and 8.30 for the beginning block buildup for this parting line. Figure 8.31 shows the final parting line along the lower edge of the zygomatic bone, following above the external auditory meatus and the superior margin of the teeth. Make certain to fill in the space between the zygomatic bone and the temporal bone. This should form a flat surface so that the opening is bridged between the two halves of the mold. As seen in Figure 8.32, a parting line must also be established for the mandible. Place the parting line between the mental foramen and the inferior margin of the teeth. See Figure 8.33 for the posterior aspect of the mandible. Finally carve a line in the clay completely around the mandible and the skull to form a registration key for the halves of the mold to align.

Figure 8.27

A badly damaged skull that arrived to me in pieces is first put back together.

Figure 8.28

Base of cranium of badly damaged skull with missing parts filled in plastic wrap before clay application.

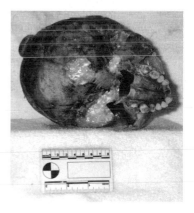

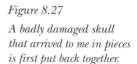

Figure 8.29
Pieces of clay are built up to cradle and block in the parting line on the skull.

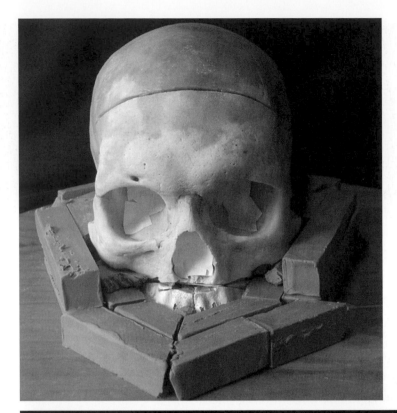

Figure 8.30
Clay blocks are placed to approximate the parting line for the mold.

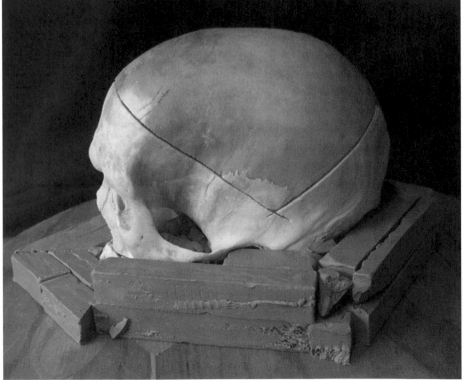

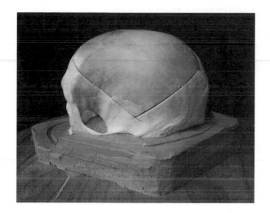

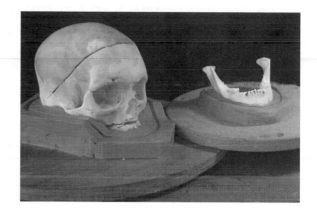

FLEXIBLE MOLD

There are several different formulations of silicone available today for use against human skin; they are used in the medical and prosthetic industry. These are good for our purpose on bone as they are dimensionally stable (meaning they don't have shrinkage), are thick, set up quickly, and will not leave a residue or harm the bone. Silicone is made up of two parts, resin and catalyst. It is referred to as a RTV or Room Temperature Vulcanizing rubber, meaning it cures at room temperature. This type of silicone has platinum cure chemistry as opposed to the tin cure used for most other art or foundry purposes, resulting in an extremely sensitive substance that will not set up if exposed to sulfur. Sulfur is a common material in latex gloves and certain oil base clays, so be careful not to wear latex gloves or use sulfur clay near the mold. In these pictures, a material available from Smooth-on called Body Double was used. Alginate could be used in the same way, although the mold will not be permanent (suppliers are listed at the end of the chapter). I have used a slower catalyst material that is blue in color (the darker substance in Figures 8.36, 8.37, 8.39, and 8.40) for the first coat, in order to minimize air bubbles. For subsequent layers, a faster-set material that is green in color (the lighter substance in Figures 8.36, 8.37, 8.39, and 8.40) was utilized.

Mixing Instructions

Measure the materials into paper cups beforehand, using either a volume or weight standard as per the manufacturer's directions. Mix the two parts together and stir until the color of the mix is uniform. You will have about 5 to 10 minutes before the silicone gets too stiff to use, so mix in small batches, making only what you can comfortably work with during this time frame. It is useful and time saving to premeasure several batches

Figure 8.31

Above right: Final build-up of clay to form parting lines on mandible and cranium of skull. The parting line will create the division for the two-part mold in silicone. Carve a line completely around all the parts to form the registration line.

Figure 8.32

Above left: The opening created by the zygomatic arch must be bridged with clay to accommodate this structure.

Figure 8.33

Parting line on the posterior mandible.

Figure 8.34

Figure 8.34

Starting the silicone layers on the cranium. Notice the silicone is allowed to flow easily over the surface. Brush with a soft brush.

Figure 8.35

The skull is tilted up at an angle to allow the material to flow into the orbits.

before beginning the process. This eliminates halting the process to measure another batch. Be warned—the silicone sticks to itself.

Applying the Silicone

Begin the application over the cranium as seen in Figure 8.34. Try to keep the application as uniform in thickness as possible. You will have only a few minutes of working time to pull drips back up over the skull, so when the material begins to drag, you must stop and let the drips just fall. Be very careful around the orbits and nasal aperture. Tilting the skull back in order to fill in these openings, as seen in Figure 8.35, helps to fill in the orbits and nasal aperture.

When the first coat has set up in about 20 to 30 minutes, begin the second coat. Do not try to add a new layer of silicone until the previous one has set up or you will damage the surface of the mold underneath. Mix each coat as before. Some silicone products have a faster set catalyst, which you can use to make this process faster. I don't recommend you use the faster set on the first layer, as you may trap air bubbles on the surface of the mold.

Figure 8.36

After the first coat has set up, you can place small bits of soft foam into the orbits and nasal aperture to fill in the space. The foam will collapse and not harm the delicate bones of the orbits when the mold is removed.

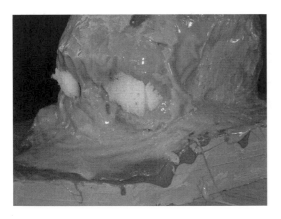

The second coat usually takes less material. Fill in any gaps in the silicone from previous layers. Use two or three coats over the entire skull. Be certain the top of the cranium has a good thickness of material as this will help prevent distortion. For the openings in the orbits, I place small bits of very soft sponge inside to take up the openings, as seen in Figure 8.36. These are placed only after the first layers of silicone have set and there are no gaps. The sponges collapse when the mold is removed, thereby keeping the delicate bones of the orbits safe. Trim the excess silicone from around the base of the cranium and the mandible pieces as shown in Figures 8.37 and 8.38.

MOTHER MOLDS

When making a flexible mold, you must make a hard shell to contain the flexible silicone when it is removed from the skull. Otherwise, the rubber will not hold its shape when it is cast. Most often this is referred to as the *mother mold,* or *mold case.* This is really just a rigid mold that is created over the soft silicone. This can be made from a variety of materials, such as plaster gauze or varaform. Both of these products are made for the medical field and are used for setting broken bones. They are readily available from the suppliers listed at the end of this chapter, or any medical supply house. Any plaster or fiberglass material will also work fine. I have used plaster gauze for the illustrations of this case.

Check for undercuts at this time. An undercut is an area on the surface where there is sufficient negative space to cause the rigid case to catch or get hung up. Most of the negative spaces and undercuts on the skull will be filled in with the silicone. However, because the cranium is round, there will be a natural undercut along either side. Therefore, before you begin, draw a line down the mold, front to back, to divide the skull into two halves. This will allow for any undercuts or places where the rigid mold will get hung up when removing it from the skull and casting. It is better to be safe and just make the mother mold in two halves, as shown in Figure 8.39, if you are not certain about the undercuts.

Cut the plaster gauze into strips that are 4 to 6 inches wide and about 8 to 12 inches long. This is an easy size to handle and can be folded over to make the pieces smaller when needed. I have found that using the gauze four layers at a time works the best and is the strongest. If the pieces are put on too thin, the plaster soaks off in the water. Warm water speeds the setup time. Simply dip bundles of strips into warm water, lightly stroke off the excess moisture, and apply. Make the edges around the rim and across the top along the parting line thicker. The overall thickness of the case should be three to four layers, with the edges four to six layers. It is better to err on the side of too many layers

Figure 8.37

The final layers of silicone are then trimmed.

Figure 8.38

The silicone fills in many of the undercuts of the bone.

Figure 8.39

Above left: Divide the cranium in half and make the mother mold in two parts.

Figure 8.40

Above right: Coat the inner edge of the plaster mother mold with petroleum jelly.

and strong, than too few and weak. You may also want to add a couple of ridges across the top to hold a strap later, and for registration points. After the first side is completed, be certain to coat the top edges with petroleum jelly, so the second side does not bond with the first. You can use a brush for quick overall application as shown in Figure 8.40. Create the second side of the skull case the same as the first, as seen in Figure 8.41.

The mandible mother mold is made the same way, except you will not need to make the mold in two parts. Although you may have to cut along the descending ramus portion later in order to open the mold, this is easily closed later. Let the plaster or case harden before moving on to the next step.

Flip the molds over and carefully remove the clay that was built up, to form the parting line. Gently clean the edge of the mold that is touching the skull as shown in Figure 8.42. However, do not try to trim this edge—just be certain the edge is free from debris and bits of clay.

Figure 8.41

The top of the skull mold is complete. Note the ridges crossing the top of the skull. These help with registration and hold the mold strap.

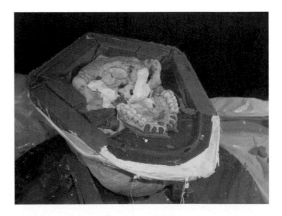

Figure 8.42

Turn the mold over and carefully remove the clay that was used to form the parting line.

The underside of the cranium can be made in one part; the same goes for the mandible base. Check to see that the alveolar sockets, if they are empty, are partially filled with clay. This will prevent the model from getting hung up at that location, or the mandible being broken when it is removed.

Construct two cones from clay, one that is approximately the width of the foramen magnum, and about 1.5 inches tall, and another about half that size for the mandible. Have these ready to use now, or after the first coat of silicone is applied to this side. The pour spout for the cranium can be placed in the foramen magnum now. If you have filled that space with tape or clay, you may wait until the next step. Definitely wait to place the pour spout for the mandible. Be certain to coat the silicone and plaster, or case edges, with petroleum jelly as shown in Figure 8.43. This is necessary to keep the two halves of the silicone and the mother mold from sticking together.

Mix the silicone and apply to the underside in the same manner as with the topside. When the first layer of silicone has almost set, place the cones into the foramen magnum opening and on the inside surface of the mandible as in Figures 8.44 and 8.45. If you already have placed the cone in the foramen magnum, you can just go around it with the silicone as shown in Figure 8.44. Be careful not to let the silicone run inside the skull, because it will be hard to remove later. At this time place several very small straws, wires, or toothpicks along the lower edge of the mandible. These will allow air to escape when you are making the castings.

Build up two or three layers of silicone. I use a slow-setting material for the first coat, which is a bright blue (the darker substance in Figures 8.36, 8.37, 8.39, and 8.40). A fast-setting material, which is green (the lighter substance in Figures 8.36, 8.37, 8.39, and 8.40), is used for the remaining coats. Be sure to check with the manufacturer regarding compatibility between the layers.

Figure 8.43

After cleaning up the mold, coat each side of the silicone and the plaster with petroleum jelly to keep the halves separate.

Figure 8.44

Place a cone for the pour spout in the foramen magnum.

Figure 8.45

Placement for the pour spout on the mandible and placement for the air vents.

When the coats are set up, trim away the excess material. See Figure 8.46 for the finished bottom or underside of the flexible parts.

Make the mother mold or case in the same way as you made the topside. The exception is there is no need to make this mother mold in two parts. Be careful to go around the pour spout and leave the air vents exposed. Make certain the outer edges are very thick as well as the area around the pour spout, as in Figure 8.47, since these areas need added strength.

OPENING THE MOLDS

When the plaster or other material has set up and is hard, the molds are ready to be opened. Insert a small screwdriver or putty knife into the seam and twist slowly and gently to pry the pieces apart. It may be easiest to start with the bottom, as in Figure 8.48. The silicone may try to come along with the hard case. It is better to remove the mother mold or rigid portion first, and then peel the silicone away slowly, so the bones are not accidentally damaged.

Now turn the mold over and gently pull the two halves of the cranial case away from the silicone. After the two parts of the mother mold are removed from the cranium, you will need to carefully cut the silicone in order to remove it from the skull. Since silicone that is cut goes back together better than parts constructed with a built-in parting line, it is better to cut this seam. Slide a tongue depressor underneath the drawn line on the silicone at the back juncture point along the occipital bone. Carefully slice along this line, moving from the back toward the front. Keep the blade against the tongue depressor to avoid nicking the bone. The cut line will need to terminate at the uppermost point on the cranial vault.

Now gently and slowly peel the silicone away from the bone, easing the silicone from the external auditory meatus, various fossae, and other openings where it may get stuck. If the silicone has drips that have worked their way into the skull, they will usually break off as the rubbery form is removed. If not, the drips can be snipped off with a blade or scissors.

Figure 8.46

Below left: The silicone, or flexible mold portion, is complete.

Figure 8.47

Below right: The second half for bottom of the mother mold is complete.

Once the silicone form is removed from the skull, place it back into the mother mold right away so it does not become misshapen. Cut away small openings in the silicone for the pour spouts and check that the air vents are open. Clean up any debris or bits of clay. The finished molds are shown in Figure 8.49.

CLEANING UP THE SKULL

The skull can now be cleaned and restored to its original condition. Use acetone (a common source is fingernail polish remover) to remove bits of glue. Any little bits of silicone that are stuck in the tooth sockets, saw cuts, or other such places can be pried free and pulled out with tweezers. Dental tools work well if you are careful not to scar the bone.

To assemble the parts of the mold and case, hold them in place with a strap or large rubber bands. Balance the mold upside down so that the foramen magnum is upright and the air vent is clear. A bucket usually works well for this.

ASSEMBLE AND CAST THE SKULL

The molds, held together with large rubber bands or mold straps, are seen in Figure 8.50. When casting plaster, acrylic, or urethane, you do not need to use a mold release agent. However, you must always check to make certain your casting will release from the silicone to prevent damage to your mold. The best method of casting is to fill the molds with a small amount of material, and then swirl and rotate the mold to evenly coat the insides. Pour in several layers, allowing each to harden between pours. You may need to experiment with your technique and choice of materials. Practice and experience create the best castings. You may pour the skull solid, but this may cause some shrinkage

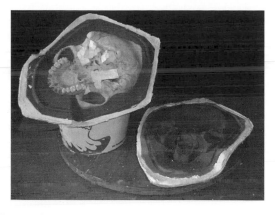

Figure 8.48
Open the mold very carefully and slowly to avoid harming the bones.

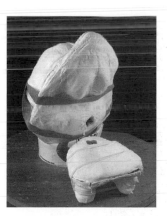

Figure 8.49
Left: The open molds are cleaned and ready to use.

Figure 8.50
Right: The mold straps are in place.

in the casting. This shrinkage may or may not be a problem, depending on how you are using your casting.

After your casting is sufficiently thick, remove the mother mold and then the silicone as you did from the original skull. You can then clean up any "flashing" or marks on the casting left by the mold. Figures 8.51 and 8.52 are examples of a finished casting in urethane resin compared to the original skull.

Two terms used to describe this process that should be emphasized are:

- **Mold**: The negative of the original
- **Cast**: The resulting positive taken from the mold

Often these two terms can get mixed up and cause confusion. As with communicating anatomical terms, the proper word describes placement exactly. Two more useful terms to understand are:

- **Parting line**: The site where the mold separates; this will be the same term for the inner flexible mold and the outer mother mold or case.
- **Undercut**: The negative space below a positive space where a mold can get "hung up" during removal (think of putting your hand on your upper lip and pulling it upward; your finger will get "hung up" on your nose).

There are many ways to make any given mold, almost as many ways as there are mold makers. Presented here is one method that is easy to understand and

Figure 8.51

The final casting with the original skull right side.

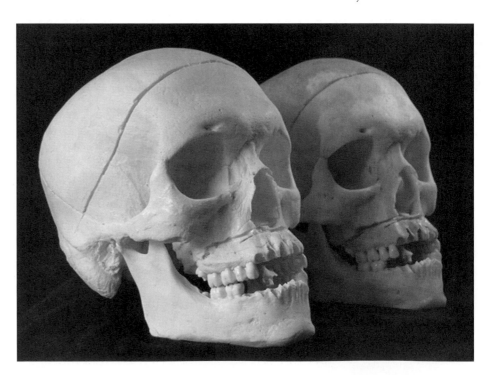

is feasible for most applications. The silicone and plaster gauze utilized here are user-friendly materials and forgiving of mistakes. It would take an entire textbook to describe all the other materials and methods that are available to the mold maker.

As will be described in the case at the end of this chapter, making a mold of the skull may be the only method the artist or investigator has to preserve unique evidence. For this reason, among others, it is worthwhile to learn this technique. Time and experience are the best teachers. You must have the right materials and the willingness to work until you "get it right." However, molding and casting are learned skills that anyone can acquire through patience and practice.

In Brief

Steps to Create a Mold of a Skull

- Prepare the skull.
- Build up the clay for the parting line.
- Mix and apply the silicone.
- Make the case or mother mold.
- Prepare the other side.
- Form the pour spout and air vent.
- Apply separating agents.
- Mix and apply silicone.
- Make case or mother mold.
- Remove skull and cast.

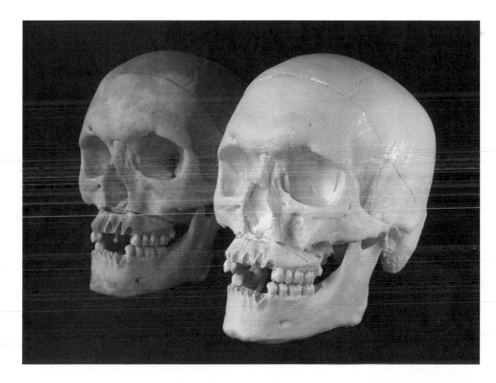

Figure 8.52

The final casting with the original skull left side.

MATERIALS AND SUPPLIES FOR MOLD MAKING

1. Clay (5 pounds)
2. Silicone specially formulated for molding of skin (approximately 2-pint kit)
3. Mother mold material; plaster gauze or other—approximately 15 to 20 sq. feet
4. Clay tools
5. Scissors or blades for cutting
6. Cups and utensils for mixing
7. Water buckets
8. Petroleum jelly
9. Work board—12 to 15 inches square

MATERIAL SOURCES

ART STUF
Douglas and Sturgess, Inc.
730 Bryant Street, San Francisco, California 94107
www.artstuf.com

Smooth-On, Inc.
200 Saint John Street
Easton, Pennsylvania 18042
www.smooth-on.com

THE AMERICAN METHOD OF THREE-DIMENSIONAL FACIAL RECONSTRUCTION

Betty Pat. Gatliff invented a straightforward method of reconstructing the face on unidentified skeletal remains by replicating the tissue depths in clay. Yielding results as successful as Mikhail Gerasimov in Russia and Richard Neave in the United Kingdom, Gatliff's method is much less time consuming. Her first attempt came in 1967 at the behest of Dr. Clyde Snow, who was acting as a consultant for the Oklahoma State Bureau of Investigation and the Oklahoma State Medical Examiner's Office. Snow asked Gatliff to reconstruct the face of an unidentified Native American male. At that time Gatliff was an accomplished medical illustrator. Gatliff read Dr. Krogman's book, *The Human Skeleton in Forensic Medicine*, in preparation for this new work. The successful identification of the subject encouraged Gatliff; she continued the work and developed her method. Gatliff established herself as a world leader in the facial reconstruction field, and since 1983, has offered training to hundreds of individuals, resulting in widespread success of her method. The following is an overview of this proven process.

GETTING STARTED

As with the two-dimensional method described in Chapter 7, there are preliminary steps before the work can begin.

1. Respectfully receive the skull, performing necessary paperwork, and be prepared to store the specimen in a secured location.
2. Gather all information from:
   - Forensic anthropologist
   - Forensic pathologist
   - Forensic odontologist or practiced dentist
   - Law enforcement investigator
3. Teeth are especially important to appearance and age determination. Diligently gather, correctly reposition, and examine dentition before attaching mandible to calvarium.
4. Attach the mandible with a spacer of approximately three to six millimeters between the condyl of the mandible and the mandibular fossa of the cranium to replicate structures present there in life.
5. Secure the skull on a skull stand in the Frankfort Horizontal Plane.
6. Take quality photos from several angles, front and profile.
7. Cut correctly measured tissue-depth markers using proper data (the tissue-depth tables from Chapter 7 have a full range of subject types from which to chose), and affix to correct locations.
8. Set the prosthetic eyes.

This endeavor involves materials and supplies, most of which are available from artist supply sources. Figure 8.53 shows a collection of supplies needed for this kind of reconstruction. Your needs may vary; substitutes of various items are a personal preference. The only specific rule is the glue must be acetone soluble. Never use a "super glue" type product on a skull. The metal miter box will allow you to cut the tiny markers accurately. The clay should be a type that is oil based, thus never dries, and is void of sulfur.

Tools and Supplies
- Precision craft knife
- Clear millimeter ruler, metal millimeter ruler
- Aluminum miter box
- Vinyl eraser sticks
- Clay sculpting tools; whatever you prefer for sculpting faces
- Boley gauge in millimeters
- Roller, pastry size or brayer
- Oil-based modeling clay (commonly referred to as plastalina); if the neck and head are both sculpted; approximately 15 lbs

- Wire form or sculptor's metal-modeling mesh
- Flexible wire or picture-hanging cable
- Wire cutters
- Gardening gloves for working with metal mesh
- Sandpaper, grade 40 or 50
- Cotton balls and swabs

The various sculpting tools tend to gain favor depending on the artist. Many artists eventually find their fingers are the best tools. The author cannot imagine sculpting an ear without the tool, commonly found in sets, that has a rounded knob shape on one end. Feel free to use spoons, butter knives, and any other item that might help sculpt the desired shape.

The clay comes in various colors; consider the subject's race when buying, and also whether you will be using a wig or sculpting the hair. Obviously a darker-skinned race will require one shade of clay, a paler subject a lighter shade. Even though classic Greek statues were originally painted by the artists of those days thousands of years ago, the sculptures that survived have long since lost the paint, and persons in our time accept a sculpture that is entirely one color. However, since the plastilina comes in many shades, it is possible to mix eyebrows, eyelashes, sunburned skin, and other items from clay. The clay can also be tinted easily with regular makeup or even acrylic paint.

The sandpaper and stiff bristle brush are used to give the skin on the face a realistic texture. Old toothbrushes also work just fine for creating texture. The sandpaper must be torn or cut into small, round pieces, so you don't need to buy a large amount. The roller needs to be a miniature version of a rolling pin with a handle. A brayer is a tool used to roll ink out for block printing and works well for this task, as does a small pastry roller.

The metal mesh is used to form the neck and/or shoulders and will make tiny cuts on your hands if you don't use the gardening gloves for protection. The flexible wire or picture-hanging cable is used to attach the neck/shoulder form to the skull stand.

The Boley gauge allows you to measure items that are three-dimensional. Rulers lie flat on two-dimensional surfaces for measuring. However, for the various features sculpted in three dimensions, upon which a ruler cannot conveniently be used as a measure, the Boley gauge works like calipers, but with precise measuring capabilities.

PROSTHETIC EYES

These are not listed in supplies since you can sculpt the eyes. Some sculptors believe the sculpted eyes are the only correct

Figure 8.53

Left to right: Metal sculpting mesh, garden gloves, wire cutters, wire and cable, clay tools, stiff bristle brushes, 50-gauge sandpaper cut into rounded piece, small rolling pin with handle, various colors of oil-based clay, clear millimeter ruler, cotton swabs, X-acto knife atop metal miter box, metal millimeter ruler, acetone-soluble glue, Boley gauge (photo by author).

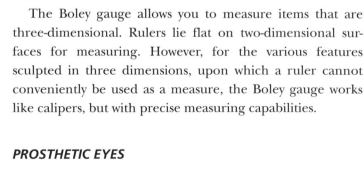

kind to have on a portrait. There are debates among sculptors as to which kinds of sculpted eyes are best. Some sculptors insist simply a deep hole imitative of the pupil is correct; others indicate the iris with gradients of deep circular indentions. However, since this kind of art has a utilitarian purpose, the realistic prosthetic eyes are most commonly used. These are quicker to set into the skull and if made properly, they are automatically the correct size. And though the final sculpt may not satisfy the fine-art aesthetic, if loved ones of the subject are prompted by the sculpture to call in the identity to authorities, the higher purpose is fulfilled. See Figure 8.8 for two kinds of glass eyes, the specialty kind used in models and in movie props, and true prosthetic eyes used by individuals who have lost an eye through trauma or surgery. Other eye types of various cost and quality can be used; the one criterion an eye must fulfill is an iris with about 12 millimeter diameter. The sclera (white portion) needs to be that offered by an eyeball that is approximately 25 millimeters in diameter. Set the eyes with help from Figures 7.44 through 7.47 and the text referring to those illustrations.

After accomplishing the steps mentioned earlier and collecting the listed supplies, the correctly measured tissue-depth markers should be affixed at the appropriate locations. This process is facilitated by Figures 7.73 through 7.76 as well as the surrounding text and tissue-depth charts in Chapter 7.

Most practitioners of the American method do not affix the #6 marker; however, they do use it to gauge the thickness of the lips. Gatliff and others believe markers #14, #19, and #21 (all from the cheek area) give the individual too much of a sunken-cheek look, so those can be left off.

Manhein *et al.* maintain the cheek area data from their study published in 2000 were possibly more accurate. The data were collected from living subjects who were in an upright position as opposed to earlier studies where data were gathered from cadavers who were in a supine position. For this reason the cheek-area markers might be included when reconstructing the face of a child in three dimensions when using data from Manhein *et al.*, Wilkinson, and others who used ultrasonic methods for data gathering.

CLAY APPLICATION

Once the tissue-depth markers are in place, the nasal aperture filled in gently with clay, and the eyes centered and set to the correct depth as in Figure 8.54, the subject is ready for clay application. Roll out ½ inch (approximate) wide strips of clay to the thickness of the tissue depth markers upon which those strips will rest. Keeping the clay at the correct tissue depth insures the best accuracy. Taper the thickness of the strip so it conforms to the thickness of the various markers. Begin with no. 1 and lay the strip down to nos. 2 and 3, adding strips to the no. 12 on each side, as in the far right of Figure 8.54. Next start

Figure 8.54

Left: Tissue-depth markers in place, eyes centered in the orbits. Center: The eye is set into the orbit so a line from top to bottom of the center of the orbit crosses through the cornea. Right: The first clay strips are applied, approximately ½ inch wide and the thickness of the markers they touch. The subject's missing teeth have been filled in with clay approximating the shape of a standard denture he would have worn.

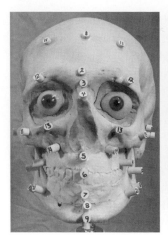
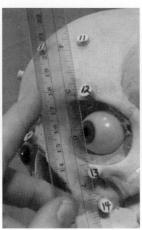
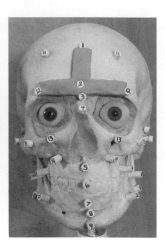

a clay strip at no. 12 and bend it around the outside of the orbit so that there is a small edge of the bony orbit still showing like in Figure 8.55. The tissue covering the outer orbit (frontal process of the zygomatic bone) parallel to the outer corner of the eye is a scant 5 millimeters thick. Use the Boley gauge as in the right side of Figure 8.55 to make certain the clay at this location is not too thick.

Next form a kind of triangle between nos. 17, 16, 15, 20, and 18, as shown on the left of Figure 8.56. After a triangle is constructed with strips, fill in the triangle, being careful to respect the depths indicated by the markers. This area portrays portions of the parotid gland and a posterior part of the masseter muscle.

Figure 8.55

Strips of clay are curved around the outer eye orbit leaving a tiny bit of bone exposed. The tissue parallel to the outer corner of the eye is only about 5 mm thick. Here that area is being measured with a Boley gauge (photos by author).

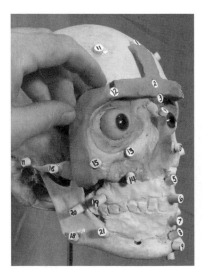
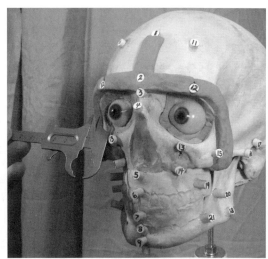

Now the chin is developed by rolling a long strip to the thickness of no. 10, which indicates tissue depth under the chin. Affix this strip evenly under the mandible. Be careful not to distort the thickness, as shown in the middle image of Figure 8.56. At this point, measure an equally long strip to the thickness of no. 9, the marker on the center front of the chin. Apply this strip around the outer edge of the chin to nos. 18 on each side, respecting those thicknesses as on the far right of Figure 8.56. Once the outer and underside of the chin and jaw line are established with these two strips of clay, roll a small cylinder of clay about 7 millimeters thick and place at the junction of the last two strips to fill in the gap. Carefully mold the areas together keeping in mind the shape of the chin. Do not press too hard or the thickness will become distorted.

Fill in the cheek portion between marker no. 13, over to 15, fill in the area above no. 18, and end at the midpoint between nos. 18 and 9 (Figure 8.57) Gatliff advises to leave off nos. 14, 19, and 21 since they make the cheek area too hollow. However, since this subject was almost certainly homeless and his clothing size compared to his height indicated he was emaciated, those markers were respected. Theoretically, more clay can be added when nearly finished if this face appears unreasonably thin.

As in Figure 8.58, add strips of clay to cover the forehead, top, and sides of the head. These strips should be about 15 millimeters or ½ inch wide and as thick as marker no. 1 and laterally as thick as no. 11 to replicate the five layers of tissue that uniformly cover almost the entire cranium. The top of the head from over the eyebrows all the way back to the external occipital protuberance and above the zygomatic arch is covered by the occipitofrontalis muscle. This smooth muscle is covered evenly with two layers of skin and is supported by loose connective tissue and the pericranium. Since all these layers are smooth to the skull, the clay application can also be uniform. After the strips of clay are applied without distortion of their thickness, the spaces in between can be filled in, maintaining that thickness.

Figure 8.56

Left: Fill in from marker nos. 17, 16, to 15; down to no. 18 and along the angle and ramus of the mandible. Center: Attach clay, thickness of marker no. 10, along bottom of mandible. Right: Place clay, thickness of marker no. 9, around outside of lower mandible edge from marker no. 18 to no. 18 on opposite side (photos by author).

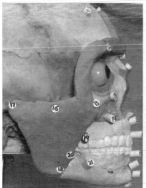
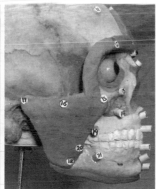
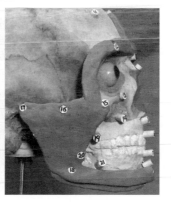

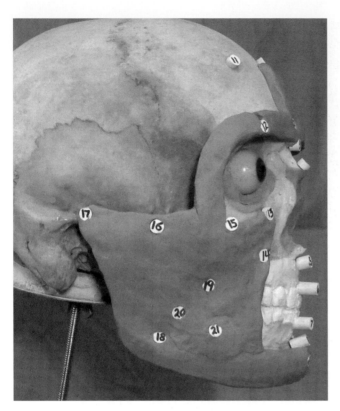

Figure 8.57

Fill in remainder of cheek from marker nos. 13 to 15 and down to the midpoint between marker no. 18 and no. 9 on the mandible. Roll a small cylinder approximately 6 or 7 mm thick and place around the chin between the strips of clay under and around the mandible, and blend strips together (photos by author).

MOUTH CONSTRUCTION

Measure the width of the mouth from the interproximal spaces between the canines and bicuspids on each side. The width of the lips will be equal to the vertical length of the enamel surfaces of the teeth. The subject for this case was edentulous. It appeared as if every tooth had been extracted many years ago since the bones of the alveolar ridge were extremely shrunken. This would be an indication the subject had been fit for dentures at some time in his life. However, no dentures were found, so I loosely sculpted life-size teeth to facilitate reconstruction. The plan was to create a normal mouth first, then construct a look with a sunken oral area last, to broaden the possibilities of identification.

If you are presented with such a case, one way to estimate this space is to add the vertical length of the maxillary central incisors to the length of the mandibular central incisors. The vertical length of the maxillary central incisors is approximately 10.5 to 11 mm and the vertical length for the mandibular incisors is approximately 9.5 mm.[5] A few millimeters should be subtracted from this amount since in a person with normal occlusion, the top teeth overlap the bottom teeth. However, in a relaxed mouth, this overlap would amount to only 2 or 3 millimeters. Therefore, to fill in the space that would replicate dentures, construct an area with clay of about 18 to 22 mm between the alveolar ridges.

Locate the outer corners of the mouth by estimating the location of the missing canines. Find the canine eminence, which is a prominent vertical ridge where the root of the canine was once embedded in the maxilla; this will approximate the location of the canine. The corners of the mouth would be at the lateral or distal edge of the canine. Figure 8.59 has arrows pointing out the canine eminence of the maxilla. Notice how visible this vertical eminence is, even though the tooth was extracted before the subject's demise. The thickness of the lips from the surface of the teeth will be indicated by tissue-depth marker nos. 6 and 7. Figure 8.60 shows the width and height of the mouth being measured against the sculpted teeth with a Boley gauge. A piece of clay rolled to the thickness of marker no. 7 is then cut to a width equal to the combined height of the enameled portion of the upper and lower central incisors.

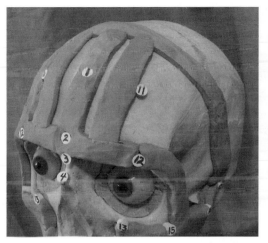

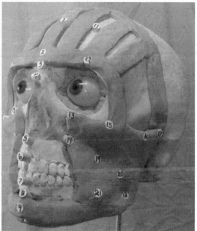

Figure 8.58

Continue to place strips of clay across and on the sides of the head at the thickness of tissue-depth marker no. 1 and laterally as thick as no. 11. The tissue on the cranium is of an almost uniform thickness so is therefore smooth (photos by author).

Figure 8.61 shows the piece of clay cut to the proper length, width, and thickness of the mouth being checked on its edge against no. 6. Those markers are then removed, and the piece of clay approximating the mouth is carefully placed with the outer edges ending at the outer edges of the canines, right before the bicuspids. Carefully carve a line determining the mouth opening parallel to a horizontal line about a millimeter or two above the incisal edges of the maxillary central incisors.

Place two strips of clay the thickness of no. 5 marker at a diagonal from above the mouth, past the nasal aperture to under the eyes at no. 13. Next fill in under the lips, simulating the depressor labii and orbicularis oris muscles. Both additions that add to the representation of the numerous muscles that converge around, above, beside, and below the mouth are illustrated in Figure 8.62.

Now that all the thicknesses in and around the mouth have been established, sculpt the shape of lips keeping in mind the age, sex, and race of your subject (the case pictured here involves a white male 45 to 55 years old). The best sculpting guide would be photos of individuals of the same sex, race, and age of your subject. Place these at an easily observable place and copy the form of

Figure 8.59

Arrows point to the location where the root of the maxillary canine once was in this edentulous subject. Estimate from this canine eminence the outer edge of the canine where the corner of the mouth opening would end (photos by author).

those kinds of lips on your subject. Figure 8.63 illustrates several stages in the development of lips on the previously mentioned case. Notice the finished lips have striations radiating from the inside of the lips to the outer rim. The surrounding skin is textured by impressing small, rounded pieces of grade 50 sandpaper onto the surface (if the paper is left in straight-edged pieces, it will leave straight-edged dents in the clay). For a final touch, very lightly press the textured surface so the marks left by the sandpaper appear more like skin pores. Before media release, a light skin moisturizer applied and then moderately blotted with

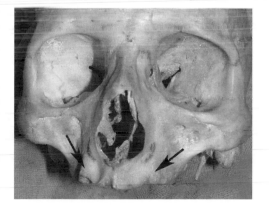

Figure 8.60

Left: The mouth opening measured with a Boley gauge from the interproximal space between the maxillary canine and the bicuspid on each side. Center: Measuring the height of the enamel of both maxillary and mandibular teeth for mouth height. Right: The Boley gauge measures a piece of clay for the mouth (photos by author).

tissue can imbue the surface with a realistic moist skin texture. Petroleum jelly is not recommended for this function as it makes the skin appear far too oily.

The safest way to sculpt lips, if you are not an accomplished sculptor, would be to create some practice lips. Take a photo chosen as most similar to your estimate of the subject considering race, sex, and age. Sculpt just the lips, making them look as much like the photo as possible, as shown in Figure 8.64. The lips in that figure took less than 15 minutes to sculpt. You could perform several such practices before working on the actual subject if needed. An ideal practice would entail using a live model of the proper age, sex, race, and fat content to observe while sculpting the lips. This is because a live person would be three-dimensional,

Figure 8.61

Left: Piece of clay measured to mouth dimensions given, checked for thickness matching marker no. 6 on its edge. Center: Marker removed before placing clay. Right: Horizontal parting line of lips engraved in clay at approximate midpoint.

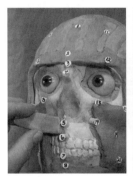 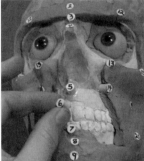 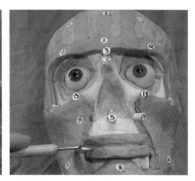

Figure 8.62

Left: Strips of clay the thickness of marker no. 5 placed at the top of the lips, angling past the nasal aperture, and up to marker no. 13 on each side. Center bottom: Fill in the spaces under the lips. Right: An illustration of the various muscles the clay is replicating in these areas (illustration by author).

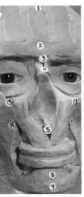 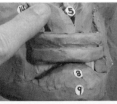 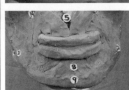 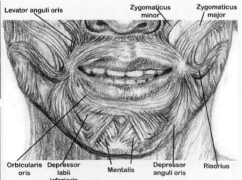

which would give you a more accurate understanding of the shapes you are creating in three dimensions from clay.

If the subject has teeth or a dental prosthesis, an alternate grinning look should be created. This can be easily accomplished by opening the clay lips into an appropriate position. For lip positioning, obtain photos of persons who match the age, race, and gender of your subject in a grinning pose, and copy those lip shapes. Figure 8.65 shows two views of lips sculpted in a grinning pose on an unidentified murder victim who had all of her anterior teeth. If the lip corners end where the canines meet the bicuspid, and those corners are elevated like a real person grinning, the appearance is realistic. I observed photos of Hispanic females aged early 20s grinning as a visual aid for this sculpting since the anthropologist determined she fell into that demographic group.

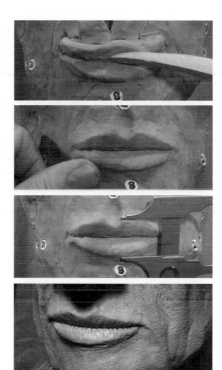

Figure 8.63

Top to bottom: Various stages of sculpting the lips. This subject is a slender, impoverished, Caucasian male aged 45 to 55 years. Next to the bottom: A check of the thickness during the sculpting process to keep the lips within the proper thickness parameters (photos by author).

Figure 8.64

Beneficial practices sculpting the lips can be performed by simply using an image from which to sculpt and sculpting only the lips. This practice set of lips took less than 20 minutes of my time. These kinds of practices can be performed for all features to hone sculpting skills before encountering a genuine case. See color plate.

NOSE CONSTRUCTION

According to Krogman, the nose is 5 millimeters wider on each side of the nasal aperture for Caucasoids, and 8 millimeters wider on each side for Negroids. Mongoloid noses can be estimated as in between these widths. The projection of the nose from the lateral view is three times the length of the nasal spine, measured from the surface of the face, which would be from the surface of marker no. 5. Carefully measure the nasal spine, beginning with its origination at the vomer bone. Figure 8.66 shows three areas being measured: the nasal spine, the width of the nasal aperture, and the demarcation of 5 mm wider than the widest nasal aperture width and 5 mm below the bottom of the nasal aperture.

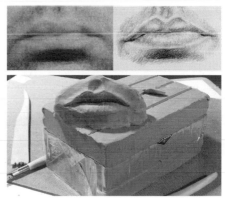

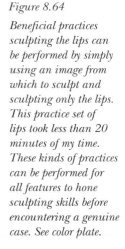

Once the measurements are taken, an easy way to begin the nose is to construct a block of clay as wide as the estimated size of the nose tip, and as long as three times the nasal spine plus the length of marker no. 5. Place that block onto the nasal spine so that the bottom edge attaches approximately 4 or 5 mm below the spine. The clay representing the outer edges of the nose (the ala) will also attach about 4 to 5 mm

Figure 8.65

Two views of lips sculpted on a subject with all the anterior teeth (photo by author).

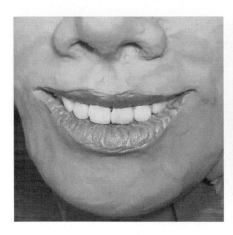

below and outside of the nasal aperture. Use the Boley gauge to measure and mark these points before applying the clay. Figure 8.67 shows a block of clay the approximate width and length of the nose base attached so its bottom edge is about 5 mm below the nasal aperture and spine. Below are the finished nose and an illustration of the various cartilage structures that help make it clear how to shape the end of the nose. In the last stages of sculpting on this case, Taylor's suggestion to construct the nose tip as a reflection of the nasal spine was followed; the subject had a small, thin nasal spine, so the nose tip was likewise made small and thin.

Figure 8.66

Top left: Measuring the widest point of nasal aperture to place marks 5 mm outside that point and 5 mm below nasal aperture (right) for ala placement of this Caucasian male subject. Bottom left: Measuring nasal spine, the nose length in lateral view will be three times this amount plus the depth of marker no. 5.

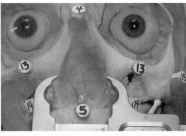

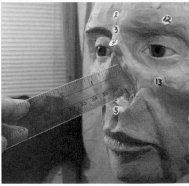

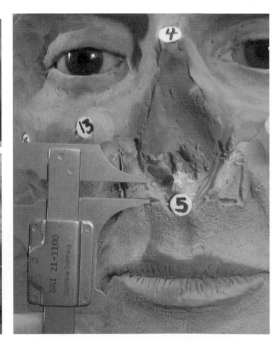

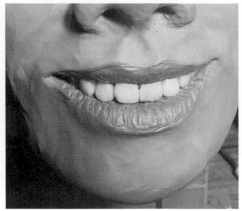

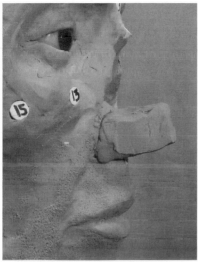

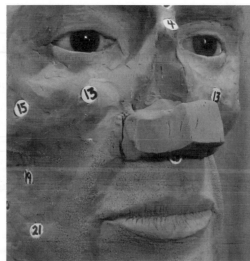

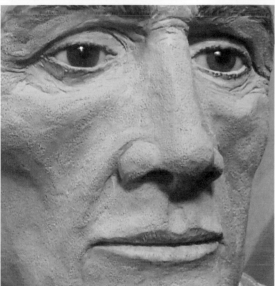

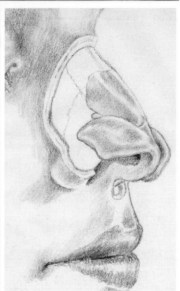

Figure 8.67
Top left: A block of clay is placed about 5 mm below the nasal spine and bottom of the aperture atop marker no. 5. Top right: Another view of this placement. Bottom left: The finished nose. Bottom right: An illustration (by author) of a typical cartilage structure (modified after Clemente).

EYE CONSTRUCTION

Consider the sex, race, and age of the subject for the eye construction. The top of Figure 8.69 shows the orbicularis oculi muscle, which is a flattened doughnut-shaped muscle that encircles the eye from outside the orbit to over the eyeball. This muscle and the accompanying skin layers are what need to be replicated in clay around the prosthetic eye. First construct the lower eyelid shape from clay rolled to a few millimeters' thickness. Cut shapes large enough to reach across the eyeball and past the corner of the eye, as seen in Figure 8.68. This is somewhere between 35 and 45 mm long and shaped in a half-circle. Using clay is a forgiving

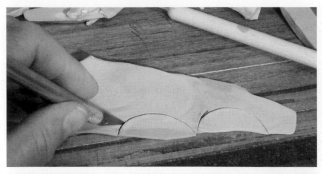

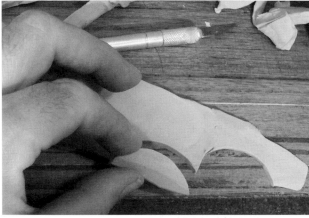

Figure 8.68

Roll clay to about 3 or 4 mm thickness and cut in half-circle shapes, the bottom edge of which are about 35 to 40 mm long for eyelids.

process; if the piece is too small or large, simply cut another until the fit is right. Ease the piece of clay replicating the eyelid under the eyeball until it lies across the bottom of the iris, just under the pupil (Figure 8.69). Place a small ball of clay in the inner corner of the eye to represent the caruncle, the smooth fleshy structure in the medial corners of the eyes. This inner corner of the eye is always a bit lower than the outer corner to facilitate tear drainage.

Next cut a slightly larger half-circle piece of clay for the upper eyelid and ease it into place so it crosses the iris just above the pupil. Shape the eyelids with a light touch, keeping their thickness uniform, just like real eyelids. Now fill in the surrounding areas as seen in the progression of photos in Figure 8.69. Rather than dwell in an academic manner over the various glands, vessels, and other structures that lie under the orbicularis oculi muscles, you should use photo references to guide sculpting the shapes of the eye area. Obtain a good close-up photo of the eyes of an individual who matches the race, sex, and age of your suspect. Have that visual aid in clear view to guide the replication of anatomy in this area of the face. The ideal would be to find a live individual to pose as a model for this sculpting. This would hold true for the entire face, if you could find an individual of the same age, sex, race, and with the proper fat content who would pose to guide the effort.

Once all the shapes have been established, the eyebrows and eyelashes can be indicated. Makeup can be used effectively for this task. Some artists use acrylic paint; still others attach false eyelashes, a particularly effective method if the subject is a female who would probably use mascara. For examples of false-eyelash use, see Gloria Nusse's work in Figures 8.92 through 8.97. For my subject who was a white male 45 to 55 years of age, I used small bits of clay the color of the hair found on the subject in scene photos. The clay is attached using the tip of a sculpting tool for the eyelashes as in Figure 8.70. This is rather like oil painting eyelashes on a canvas. The dark pigmented bits of clay are indicative of where the eyelashes and the shadows of the eyelashes are, instead of having eyelashes actually sticking out from the surface three-dimensionally. For the eyebrows, that same color of clay is stroked on in tiny thin hair-like strips in the direction of eyebrow hair growth as shown in Figure 7.43. Any makeup or paint used should also reflect the proper hair-growth direction.

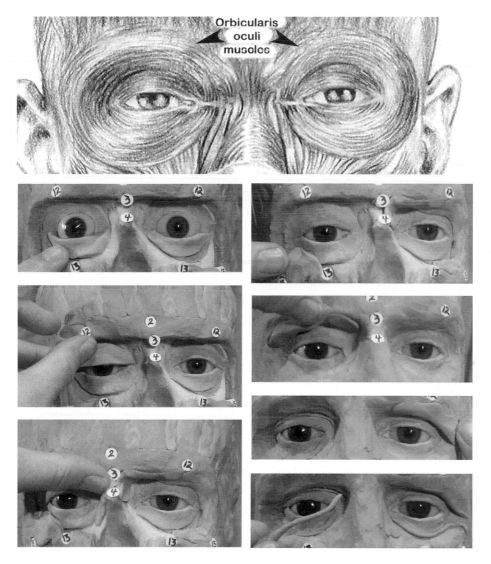

Figure 8.69

Top: Illustration featuring
the orbicularis oculi
muscles. Left, top to
bottom: Sculpting clay
around eyes starting
with bottom lid first.
Right, next to bottom:
Over-hanging upper lids
added to bring subject in
line with his estimated
age of 45 to 55 years.
Bottom right: Tiny rolls
of clay are attached to
simulate wrinkles and
folds on this subject. See
color plate.

CHIN, CHEEKS, AND EAR CONSTRUCTION

The chin and cheeks will be greatly influenced by the age, race, sex, and fat content of the subject. Easiest will be the young, trim individual since the contours of the clay will follow the edge of the mandible and make a slightly curved shape up to the zygomatic arch at the level of marker nos. 13 and 15. If the subject is known to be thin, the clay can curve inward (depending on how thin) below the zygomatic arch as in Figure 8.71. Notice also in that illustration are the age indications for a 45- to 55-year-old male—inclusions of a naso-labial fold. Another indication of age is the sagging of areas along the bottom of the mandible. For the most accurate depiction of chin and cheeks, find a photo of an individual or individuals

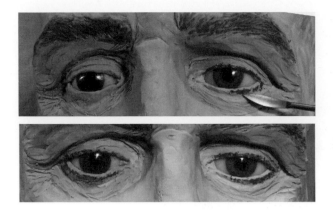

Figure 8.70

Bits of clay mixed to the same color as the hair of the subject as seen in his scene photos are attached to simulate eyelashes and eyebrows.

who match the demographic of your subject and use that for a guide to your sculpting.

The ear is the most complicated feature on the head. A step-by-step method is explained in Figure 8.87. Another method is either to obtain a photo of an ear, or have someone pose, and copy the various folds of that complicated structure. Unlike the cheeks, chin, or lips, the ear is so complicated you must have some kind of visual aid to sculpt all the forms correctly. I will use a photo reference for creating the ear shape at first, and will always have a live model pose for at least the last few minutes of work. Sculpt the ear on a block of clay before attaching it to your subject. As shown in Figure 8.71, the ear should be about as long as the nose. It should be attached so the tragus sits atop the ear hole, with the top parallel to the eye area; the bottom is parallel with the bottom of the nose. The top of the ear should be tilted along its vertical axis toward the back about 15°.

FINISHING TOUCHES

I believe you must take a rest and look at a three-dimensional work anew to see what corrections to make. Some other methods to notice what needs changing and how to change it are the following:

- Look at the work in a mirror.
- Look at the work in drastically different lighting.
- Photograph the work and look at the photos held upside down.

Figure 8.71

The ear should be approximately as long as the nose. Sculpt the complicated ear on a block of clay separately before attaching. You should clear a path through the clay build-up to find the external auditory meatus (ear hole) to ensure correct placement of the ear (photos by author).

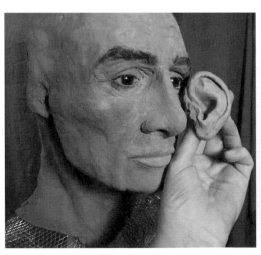
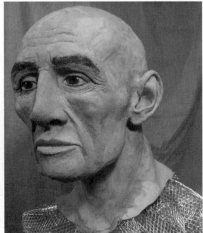

When the basic sculpture is finished, some artists will add hair and clothing. Figure 8.72 shows the last alterations to the nose and ears on the left and center; on the right is a photo taken outside with the addition of clothing similar to that found on the body of the subject. Notice how the outside photo gives the reconstruction a more realistic appearance.

Wigs are a quick and effective method to replicate the subject's hair if it was known to be long or of any considerable volume. Since the scene photos for the subject in Figure 8.72 clearly showed him to have very short, dark, neatly cut hair with a "widow's peak" (a hairline that makes a point above the forehead), I decided to construct the hair out of clay. Since this work of art has a utilitarian purpose, the fact that a wig on a sculpture would not be the best aesthetically doesn't matter. If the image will prompt loved ones to call in the identity of your subject, use the device that will replicate his or her appearance best. Likewise, even though clay does not truly resemble hair, the public is accustomed to seeing portrait sculptures and will recognize the artist is presenting them with an image of someone with hair. Notice in Figure 8.73, even though accomplished artist Dyanne Carpenter simply applied a quick texture with a clay tool, the head of this sculpture appears to be covered with hair.

MEANINGFUL PRACTICE

Practice does make anyone much better at any artistic activity. Many artists make the mistake of creating one or two works of art, expecting great results. Instead artists should accept the fact that virtuous work will come after many tries where the work is not so virtuous. A professional artist should approach his or her art like an athlete. Tennis players who intend to play professionally will play thousands of games of tennis, instead of expecting professional results after only a few games. They will repeat their moves thousands of times. Artists who approach their art in this manner will find success. If they

Figure 8.72

On the left is the finished reconstruction with shoulders formed from metal mesh. The center is with clothing added. The right photo was taken outside, where the lighting gives a more detailed, realistic look (photos by author). See color plate.

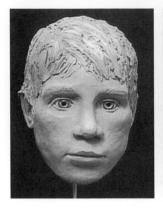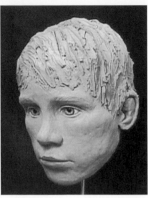

Figure 8.73

Reconstruction by Dyanne Carpenter of a 10-year-old male subject. Carpenter is an accomplished artist who was able to indicate "hair" in clay by simple quick strokes of a clay tool (courtesy of Dyanne Carpenter).

expect to suffer through attempts that are failures and yet keep trying, they eventually will find successful results.

The activity of sculpting clay into facial features need not be a formidable task. Most forensic artists occupy only a fraction of their time reconstructing the faces of skeletal remains. This does not mean that artists cannot engage themselves in meaningful practice aimed at success in this esoteric activity. A dedicated forensic artist can practice sculpting lips, noses, ears, the structures around eyes, and other features, using visual aids such as photos or, ideally, live models. This practice can be comfortably performed by sculpting just one pair of lips at a sitting, or one nose, or even just one eye.

An ideal situation in which to practice would be with good lighting and some entertaining music in the background. Many artists are able to sculpt with an interesting news program on the television while they work. You can glance up now and then to understand the information being given. If you will integrate sculpting practice into your weekly or monthly routine, your work will soon become quite virtuous. If you have trouble self-motivating to practice at home, sculpting classes are available at many colleges and universities. If you have engaged in meaningful practice, when you are faced with a real case where an unidentified individual's identity is in your hands, you will be up to the task. A fortunate by-product will be the ability to create fine art portraits of merit. Another advantage is that practice will allow you to perform the facial reconstruction with some speed when a real case comes your way. The concept is that you should not believe you can magically be successful without practice. If you make practice enjoyable, you will enjoy the "work" when the cases come along.

In Brief

- The Manchester, or anatomical, method of three-dimensional facial reconstruction from a skull is a time-consuming process where the muscles of the head and neck are recreated. Richard Neave of the United Kingdom is the primary purveyor of this method, which uses tissue-depth markers.
- The American or tissue-depth method of three-dimensional facial reconstruction from a skull is a quick process where the face is sculpted using the tissue depth markers as guides. Betty Pat. Gatliff is the primary purveyor of this method.
- The best effort for any three-dimensional facial reconstruction from a skull requires that you make a copy of the skull upon which to work while the real skull is available for observation.
- If you practice sculpting features, you will be prepared on the infrequent occasion when you have a genuine case.

A CASE STUDY: THE CASTRO VALLEY JANE DOE

Gloria Nusse had only 24 hours' access to the skull of an unidentified murder victim. Nusse was able to make two almost-exact copies of the skull with time to spare. The following method she describes for reconstructing the young teenage girl's face led to an identification. The resulting sculpture is almost identical to the girl who was murdered.

Here then, in Nusse's own words, is a detailed description of her methods for this successful facial reconstruction from an unidentified murder victim's skull.

TISSUE-DEPTH METHOD CASE STUDY BY GLORIA NUSSE

I was put into contact with the Alameda County Sheriff's Department, Cold Case Unit and Crimes Against Persons Unit in April of 2005. It was a cold case of a young girl who had been found behind a Castro Valley, California restaurant in 2003. She had remained unidentified despite much effort by the investigators. The local community had adopted her and paid for a cemetery plot and burial, complete with a loving headstone which named her an "Unknown Child of God." The Sheriff, Sergeant Scott Dudek, decided to exhume her in order for a facial reconstruction to be done. Because of the nature of the public's attachment to her and the high public profile of the case, the order for her exhumation was only for one 24-hour period. This meant that we had only 24 hours to remove her body, procure her skull, create a mold, and make any other observations that could help in solving her identity.

Measure Skull and Create Mold

I used the techniques to make the mold outlined in the previous pages and had an exact replica of her skull by the time the sun rose the next day. Figure 8.74 shows the skull ready for mold making, Figure 8.75 shows me working in the middle of the night, and Figure 8.76 is the completed copy of the skull.

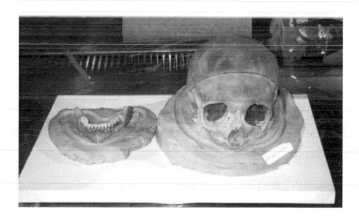

Figure 8.74

Skull of Castro Valley Jane Doe, prepped, set up, and for ready for mold process.

Figure 8.75

Gloria Nusse working through the night making a mold of the Castro Valley Jane Doe skull (photo by David Dellaria). See color plate.

The anthropologist, Dr. Alison Galloway from the University of California at Santa Cruz, had determined the subject's age to be between 14 and 19 years and that her ancestry was most likely a mix of European and Native American. Based on those guidelines from my consultation with Dr. Galloway, I decided to use the tissue-depth studies (the section for 14–18 year olds) from the "Ultrasonic Facial Measurements (mm) from White North American Children Aged 3–18 Years" conducted by Mary Manhein *et al.* (Table 7.5). I supplemented tissue depths for the forehead, occlusal line, and zygomatic bone with the data from "Tissue Thickness (mm) of American Caucasoids (European derived)" by Rhine and Moore (Table 7.2).

Mount Skull and Attach Tissue-Depth Markers

The markers were glued into place after the skull was placed in the Frankfort Horizontal Plane and anchored to a board using a ¾-inch pipe and pipe flange assembly, as seen in Figure 8.77. I used the American method of facial reconstruction, which relied heavily on an in-depth understanding and knowledge of the underlying muscle and tissue anatomy of the face. An understanding of the bones of the skull and their relationship to all those tissues is an absolute must. There are several tricks I have learned over the years as well that I will try to convey to you, but many of the techniques must be learned from experience. The skull on the right of Figure 8.77 is not from the Castro Valley case; it is for marker placement.

The mold making, cutting, and placement of the tissue-depth markers, and mounting the skull on a stand are the technical part and should be performed with as much precision as possible.

Next is the important task of eye placement. It is best to use very good prosthetic eyes, the kinds that are actually used for living people. These can be purchased from a prosthetic eye company such as Monoplex Eye in Massachusetts (USA). The cost is about $150.00 a pair.[6] Sometime doll eyes can be used, but the iris size must be carefully measured. If the size of the iris is off, the quality of the reconstruction may suffer. It is my suggestion to use the best quality materials available so the best quality work will result.

The eye is mounted into the orbit of the skull by means of a small cone of clay stuck to the back of the prosthetic eye. The outer edge of the cornea of the eye should be approximately tangent with the superior and inferior margins of the eye socket. The placement top to bottom and medial to lateral within the socket should be equal and on a 90° axis that is oblique and central in the orbit as seen in Figure 8.78.

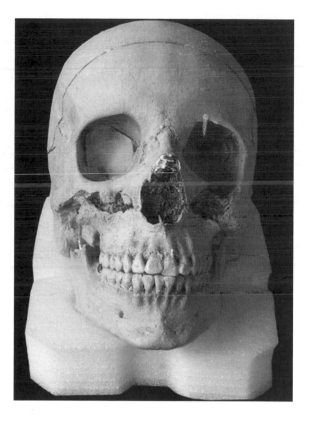

Figure 8.76

Finished casting of the skull. This is the copy Gloria Nusse kept as a reference skull.

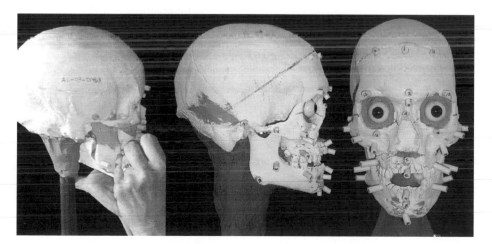

Figure 8.77

Left: Placing tissue-depth markers on the cast of the skull. Middle and right: Profile and front view with eyes set and tissue-depth markers in place (photo by David Dellaria).

The incomparable advantage about having a cast skull is that the real skull is available to study while working on the copy. To craft that situation, I created a second skull copy to use as a guide while I worked on the other copy. I like to keep as much of the skull visible for as long as possible. For this reason I practice a modified lay-up, using some muscle construction as well as laying on clay slabs to create the tissue depth. The best place to begin is the neck. I don't finish the neck in the beginning; rather I create just enough to get the skull stable with some feeling of the underlying structure.

Next I form the great muscles on the side of the face, the temporalis and masseter. These create the general outline of the face when viewed from the front. The temporalis muscle originates from the side of the head on the temporal bone and slips under the zygomatic arch and inserts onto the coronoid process of the mandible. I then place strips of clay rolled out to the depth of the markers over the eye on the brow line and run them up over the forehead. Note here that the numbers of the markers using the Manhein study are slightly different in the region of the zygomatic bones, so it is best to be guided by the names of bones and areas of the face rather than relying just on the numbers of the markers.

Next I place the masseter muscle (Figure 8.79). The clay for this begins at the angled corner, or ramus of the mandible and then passes up to the lower border of the zygomatic arch. Since both the masseter and temporalis muscles are plump, when they are in place, the face has the feeling of fullness. The facial outline is complete now when viewed from the front. In Figure 8.79 you can see these two muscles roughly placed between the markers.

Continuing on, I apply the correct thickness of clay on the front and under the chin. I leave the posterior edge of the mandible uncovered because I want to be able to run my finger along its back side and feel the bone. This mandible edge is a large and important landmark of which I do not want to lose sight. I also leave the outer edge of the eye orbit uncovered as this area is extremely thin. I do not try to make the clay pretty now; I am more concerned with getting the tissues of the face to their correct depth. I am watching all the time for anomalies and asymmetries in the skull.

Figure 8.78

Placement of the eyes centered within an oblique angle (photo by David Dellaria).

Figure 8.79

Application of clay to block out temporalis muscle (photo by David Dellaria).

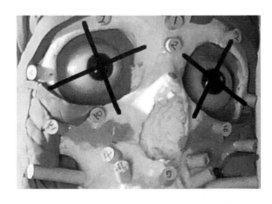

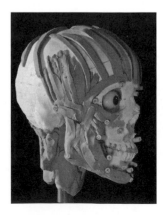

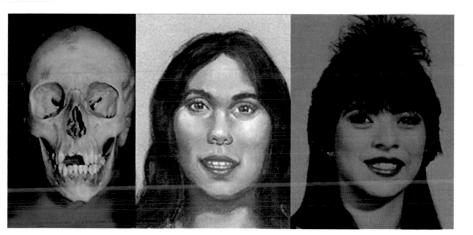

Figure 7.6

Presented with the skull on the left from an unidentified murder victim, I drew the reconstruction in the middle with pastels on Canson Mi-tientes paper. On the right is the photo of the woman identified (courtesy of the Harris County Medical Examiners Department).

Figure 7.7

Figure drawn on left with clothing found on the body shown at the top and bottom right. T-shirt was size medium, brassiere was size 34C, and the shorts were size 7 (all sizes U.S.). Bottom: Hair approximately 24 to 28 inches long, dark brown, thick, and curly (courtesy Harris County Medical Examiners).

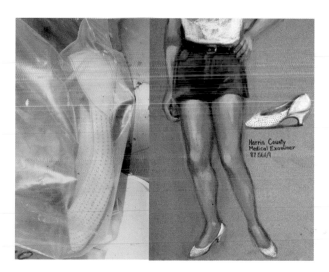

Figure 7.9

Shoe of murder victim on left was U.S. size 6½ and very short cut-off jeans U.S. size 7 led me to draw the girl with an attractive Figure shown on right (courtesy Harris County Medical Examiner).

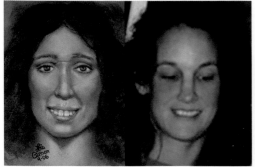

Figure 7.36

On the left is the sketch released to the media, to the right is the identified woman (courtesy of the Houston Police Department).

Figure 7.53

Muscles of the upper face with special attention to the levator labii superioris alaeque nasi muscles (modified after Clemente).

Levator labii superioris alaeque nasi muscles

Procerus muscle

Orbicularis oculi muscle, orbital part

Levator labii superioris muscle

Zygomaticus major muscle

Medial palpebral ligament

Orbicularis oculi muscle, palpebral part

Nasalis muscle

Zygomaticus minor

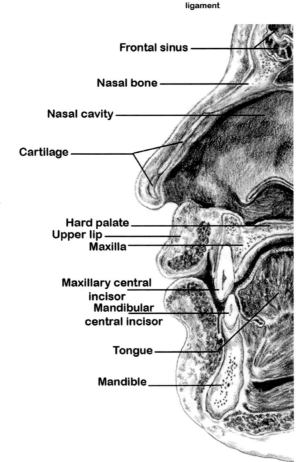

Frontal sinus

Nasal bone

Nasal cavity

Cartilage

Hard palate
Upper lip
Maxilla

Maxillary central incisor
Mandibular central incisor

Tongue

Mandible

Figure 7.56

A cross-section through the midpoint of the anterior portion of the head, showing the fleshy areas as they relate to the skull. This is a fairly realistic view of a cross-section of a cadaver. Notice the cartilage and flesh that overhangs in front and below the nasal spine (modified from Clemente).

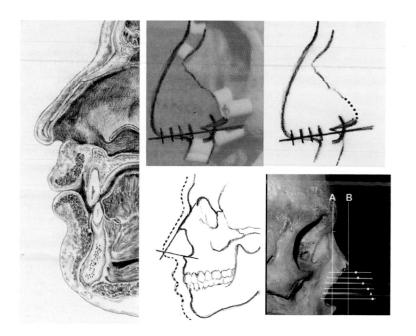

Figure 7.58

Far left: Cross-section view of a cadaver head. Top right. Illustration of Krogman's nose length formula. Center top: The formula superimposed on a skull. Bottom center: After Krogman's diagram of nose-shape approximation. Bottom right: Determination from Prokopec and Ubelaker in a 2002 study at the Institue of Ethnology and Anthropology, Moscow (modified from Wilkinson).

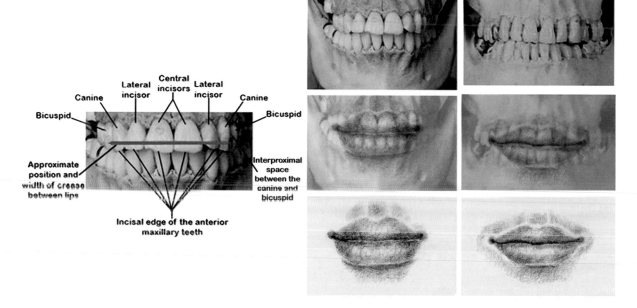

Canine
Lateral incisor
Central incisors
Lateral incisor
Canine
Bicuspid
Bicuspid
Approximate position and width of crease between lips
Interproximal space between the canine and bicuspid
Incisal edge of the anterior maxillary teeth

Figure 7.59

Left photo shows teeth with pertinent landmarks. The horizontal line indicates the approximate location and width of the mouth opening. At right are two sets of teeth, with lips superimposed translucently below, and at the bottom the lip drawing without the teeth showing from behind.

Figure 7.62

Top photo: The maxillary-mandibular area of the skull showing teeth present and clean holes of teeth lost postmortem. Second from top and proceeding down: The drawing from the skull, the photo of the identified individual behind a progressively more translucent drawing. The bottom is the unadorned photo of the individual.

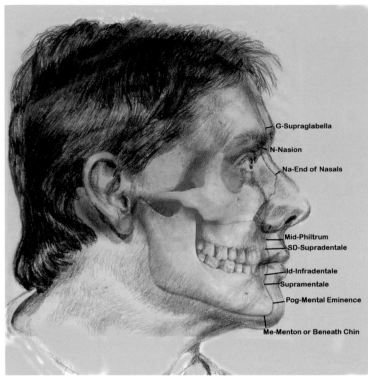

Figure 7.74

Illustration of soft tissue to bone relationship with tissue-depth marker locations named (illustration by the author).

Figure 7.77

Facial reconstruction drawing done by DuPage County (Illinois) Forensic Artist Joy Mann, in collaboration with myself, of an unidentified murdered boy whose body was abandoned near a freeway October 8, 2005 (courtesy of the DuPage County Sheriffs).

Figure 7.81

Study of how the iris occupies more of the eye opening compared to the white (sclera) portion in younger individuals. From top to bottom, the age of this male is 6 months, 2 years, 5 years, 7 years, 11 years, and 19 years (photos by author).

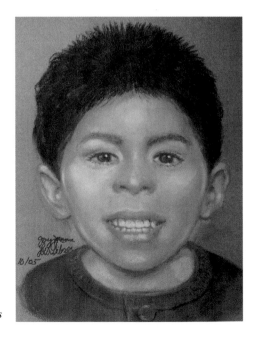

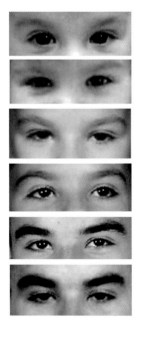

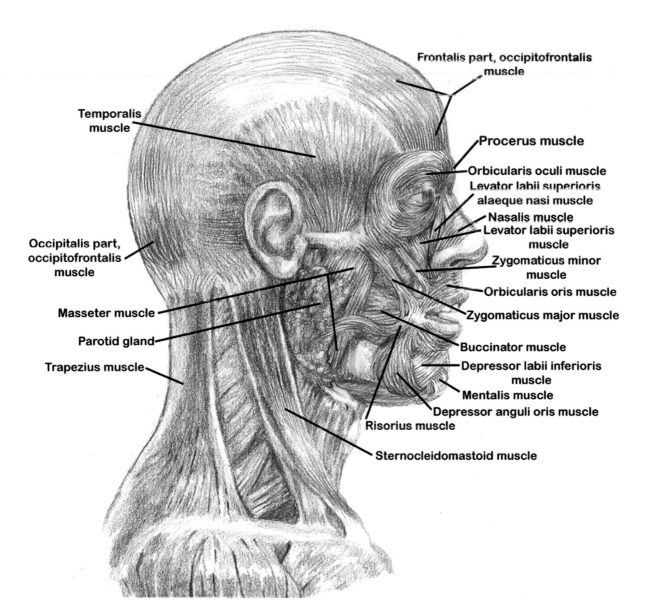

Frontalis part, occipitofrontalis muscle

Temporalis muscle

Procerus muscle

Orbicularis oculi muscle

Levator labii superioris alaeque nasi muscle

Nasalis muscle

Levator labii superioris muscle

Occipitalis part, occipitofrontalis muscle

Zygomaticus minor muscle

Orbicularis oris muscle

Zygomaticus major muscle

Masseter muscle

Buccinator muscle

Parotid gland

Depressor labii inferioris muscle

Mentalis muscle

Trapezius muscle

Depressor anguli oris muscle

Risorius muscle

Sternocleidomastoid muscle

Figure 8.1

Muscles of the head and neck; profile view (illustration by author).

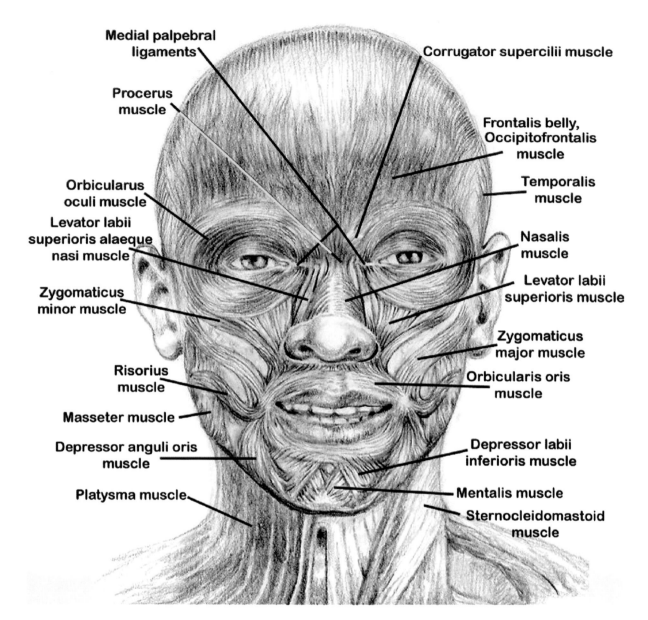

Figure 8.5

Muscles of the head and neck; front view (illustration by author).

Figure 8.16

The top photos show two views of some hair for the elderly subject. The bottom photo shows clearly the cream-colored jacket he wore. I was able to find an almost identical jacket at a garage sale to replicate the clothing for media release.

Figure 8.17

Two views of the finished reconstruction. A wig with the appropriate amount of gray hair was added, along with clothing purchased at a garage sale that closely matched that worn by the subject.

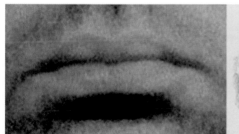

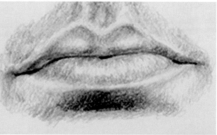

Figure 8.64

Beneficial practices sculpting the lips can be performed by simply using an image from which to sculpt and sculpting only the lips. This practice set of lips took less than 20 minutes of my time. These kinds of practices can be performed for all features to hone sculpting skills before encountering a genuine case.

Figure 8.69

Top: Illustration featuring the orbicularis oculi muscles. Left, top to bottom: Sculpting clay around eyes starting with bottom lid first. Right, next to bottom: Over-hanging upper lids added to bring subject in line with his estimated age of 45 to 55 years. Bottom right: Tiny rolls of clay are attached to simulate wrinkles and folds on this subject.

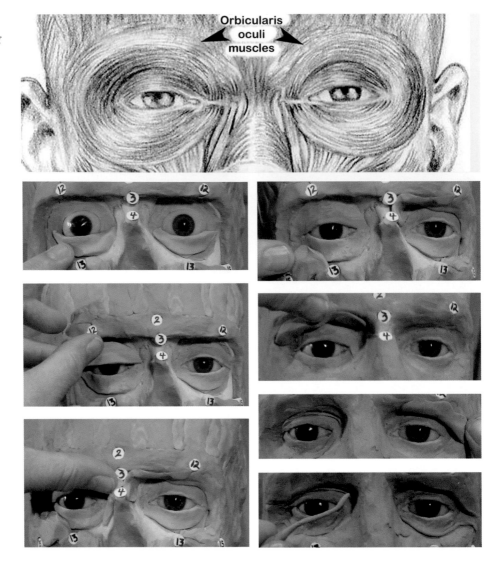

Figure 8.72

On the left is the finished reconstruction with shoulders formed from metal mesh. The center is with clothing added. The right photo was taken outside, where the lighting gives a more detailed, realistic look (photos by author).

Figure 8.75

Gloria Nusse working through the night making a mold of the Castro Valley Jane Doe skull (photo by David Dellaria)

Figure 8.84

Placement of trapezoid-shaped pieces of clay over eyes to create eyelids and filling in of surrounding area.

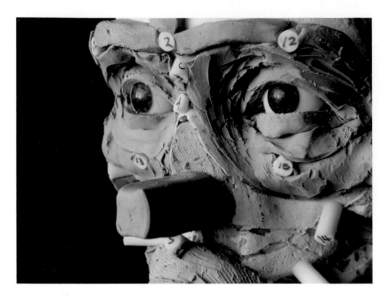

Figure 8.85

Carefully measured block of clay attached for nose projection.

Figure 8.94

Two copies created of the Jane Doe. In front is the plaster copy needed so the Alameda County Sheriffs Investigators could travel with the sculpture to Mexico. In the back is the original clay sculpture. The successful identification of the subject was the result of the image being shown in Mexico (photos by David Dellaria).

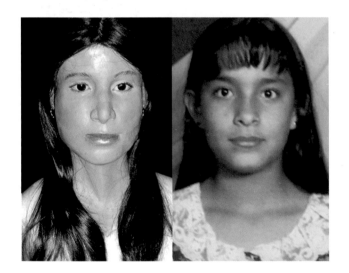

Figure 8.95

On the left is the clay sculpture, on the right a photo of the subject identified at the age of 11 years.

Figure 8.97

On the left is a profile view of the sculpture; on the right is a photo of the subject identified taken a short time before her murder (photo by David Dellaria).

If I see a prominent muscle attachment then I make a note of it and may even then create the muscle there just to highlight this feature. Care must be given not to try to make everything perfect. Remember that this is the time to let the technical aspect rule. It is important to let the tissue markers create the outline. I purposely let the areas be a bit blocky at this point. I keep my hands light. Do not try to press down the clay or work it heavily into the skull (see Figure 8.80).

To create the mouth I measure the distance from the gum line of the teeth top to bottom; this is the height of the mouth barrel. Then I measure the distance across the front six teeth. That is from the distal margins of the canines left to right. This then is the width of a relaxed mouth; if the mouth is to be smiling, it would be wider. I then make a block of clay with those dimensions and the thickness of the marker on the upper lip. This rectangular block is then placed on the mouth so it fits between the gum lines and the canines as seen in Figure 8.81.

The face is like a cylinder, and the mouth wraps around the face. The mouth block should tip down slightly as this will automatically make the lower lip fit under the upper, as in life. After the mouth is correctly positioned, place a long stick, like a bamboo skewer, across the block and rock it along the occlusal line (where the teeth meet). This creates the dividing line between the lips. Take a sharp edge tool to lift the lips apart and to gently shape them.

Adhering to the general feeling of the face being a cylinder, I fill in the rest of the markers toward the mouth. Slanting the strips of clay gives the feeling of the underlying muscles, which also slant toward the mouth. This technique also keeps the face round (Figure 8.82). I try to work on the periphery of the face rather than to just dive into the center straight off and then finish the rest of the head to match. I try to get as much information as I can from the skull first, before beginning the mid-portion of the face. There is a lot of information to be gotten from the shape of the cranium, the jaw line, and the forehead. This initial sculpting is the time as well to finish off the neck. Now the proportions for the mid-face are readily apparent as in Figure 8.83.

Eyes

To shape the eyelids, first find the small protuberance along the inside wall of the socket that is on the lateral margin. This protuberance is usually felt, rather than seen, and is found several millimeters below the zygomatic-frontal suture. Known as the lateral orbital tubercle, this protuberance is where the lateral palpebral ligament attaches. This ligament forms the lower margin of the upper lid. The medial placement for the upper lid is at the anterior lacrimal crest. The upper lid generally passes halfway between the upper iris margin and the pupil. Put two very tiny balls of clay in the medial corners of the eyes at this point to make the small lacrimal caruncle seen in the corner of the eye. To shape the lids, roll out some clay a few millimeters thick and make two isosceles trapezoids for each eye. The long axis should cover the eyeball and reach across the orbit to the points mentioned earlier. Place the lower lid first, then place the upper lid, so its lateral edge covers the lower lid. After the lids are

Figure 8.80
Application of clay to block out shape of masseter muscle (photo by David Dellaria).

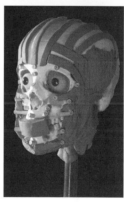

Figure 8.81
Placement of the mouth barrel (photo by David Dellaria).

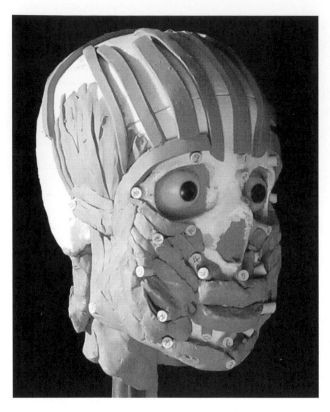

Figure 8.82

Separation of lips and placement of blocks of clay in the mid-face (photo by David Dellaria).

placed, fill in the orbit around the eyelids. There are many clues as to the shape of the eyelid to be found in the orbit (Figure 8.84).

Nose

To form the nose, measure the length of the nasal spine. This is the distance from the vomer to the most anterior point of the nasal spine. Multiply this length by three and add to it the depth of the marker at the mid-philtrum. Make a block of clay to conform to these dimensions in length, and about 15 mm square. Attach this block to the nasal spine below the nasal aperture, which has been filled out with clay (Figure 8.85). To form the ala of the nose, make a ball of clay about 15 mm in diameter and cut it in half. Place each half alongside the nasal aperture so that it is approximately 5 mm outside the lateral edge of the nasal aperture and about 4 mm below (Figure 8.86). The nose can now be finished according to the clues found in the shape of the aperture.

If you have photos taken from the crime scene or morgue, much information about the nose may be visible. For this sculpture, I was able to use such photos to help in the shaping of the nose and ears. Generally, the angle of the nasal spine, the shape of the bridge, and the aperture all give clues to the shape of the nose. Since the nose and eyes are "soft" in that they are open to some interpretation, care must be taken not to override the information found in the skull. You must use only information found in the bones of the face. The tendency is to use elements of the face we are familiar with, such as our own, and this can lead to a misinterpretation.

Ears

There is a great process for creating ears in clay developed by Betty Pat. Gatliff that I like to use. Here are the steps illustrated in Figure 8.87.

1. Roll out two fat cylinders approximately the length of the nose from the nasion to the tip and about 15 mm in diameter. Then roll out two smaller coils of clay about 5 mm in diameter and about 6 inches long (top left Figure 8.87).
2. Hold the fat cylinder in your right hand and with the left, pinch a thumb print shape in the center while pushing the cylinder into a light curve around the indentation. Repeat for the other side, using the other hand, so the cylinders are a mirror image of each other. This shapes the concha and the beginning of the antihelix of the ear (second from top left, Figure 8.87).

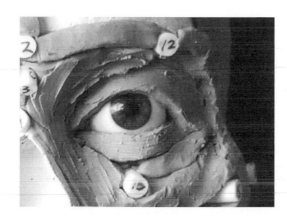

Figure 8.83

Completion of neck with mouth and mid-face. Here you can see the outline of the face and placement of the features (photo by David Dellaria).

Figure 8.84

Placement of trapezoid-shaped pieces of clay over eyes to create eyelids and filling in of surrounding area. See color plate.

3. Using the tip of your pinkie, make a small indentation above the antihelix indentation that is going in the same direction. This is the triangular fossa. Note that these two shapes open up toward the face, in order to capture sound. Again, repeat with the other side and use the other hand; this alternating hands will make it easier to construct the shapes as a mirror image of each other (third from top left, Figure 8.87).

4. Take the small coil and place the tip under the small triangular fossa and roll it around the outside of the ear to form the helix, or snail shape, that forms the outer edge of the ear. Pinch the bottom off to form the lobe of the ear. The rest of the small coil is then placed on the back of the ear to make a small stem that is used to attach the ear to the skull (bottom left of Figure 8.87).[7]

Figure 8.85

Carefully measured block of clay attached for nose projection. See color plate.

Place the ears over the external auditory meatus so the top of the ear tips back about 15 degrees. I use a stick or round tool to make a small hole in the clay ear and line this up with the meatus of the skull. Note that the actual concha of the ear is below the surface of the side of the face. Once the ear is in place, it is possible to then

Figure 8.86

Placement of wings of nose (ala) and filling in of surrounding tissue.

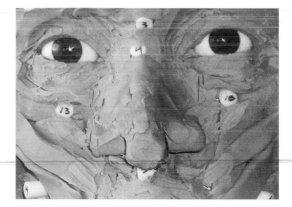

Figure 8.87

Top left: Ear coils. Second from top left: Pinching of coil to make concha. Third from top left: Making triangular fossa. Second from bottom left: Parts of ears, pre-assembly. Bottom left: Assembled ears. Top right: Ear on head. Middle right: Finish work on ear. Bottom right: Almost-finished ear form (modified from Betty Pat. Gatliff).

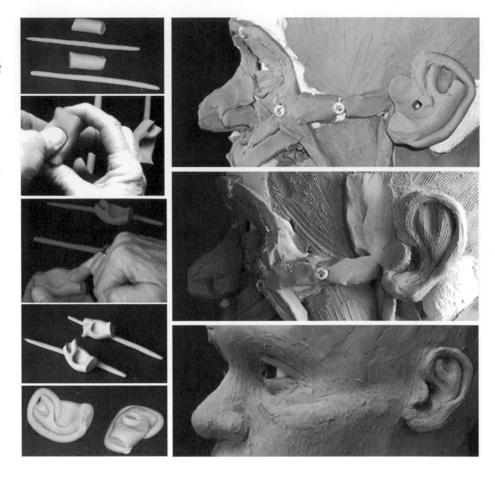

give the ear its special individual characteristics and refine the shape in general (top to bottom right of Figure 8.87). Again, if there are good photos from the morgue or the crime scene that show the ear, these are clues that can be used to sculpt a more exact match.

Now that the technical part of the sculpture is complete, I like to sit back and let the face settle a bit. I like to observe my work and see the natural balance and harmony of the face.

Fine Art Finishing

From this point on, the development of the face depends entirely on the experience of the artist. Since all the information has been laid down so carefully in the previous steps, which were dictated by technical parameters, care must be taken not to mess that up! Keep your hands extremely light and don't press down the clay or smear it. Just slowly and lightly smooth the surface until the blocks and chunks disappear. Keep the real skull or an extra casting nearby and keep referring to it, as you would have been doing all along. Step back often, blur your eyes and look. I like to use a mirror also, because that helps me to see things from a different perspective. I move the sculpture around in my studio to see it in different light. The best information I can give here is to keep things light. I like to keep the markers visible until the last moment, just so I know I am not going overboard (Figure 8.88).

The most amazing thing here is how the face can change in expression with even the slightest movement of the clay. Note that the only clay I add at this point is very small, tiny bits if needed to help round out the face. I do consult here for age appropriate features just to make certain I impart the face with the correct age. Once I am satisfied with the appearance, I cover the markers and do a final smoothing and texture of the skin. This was a very young girl (14 to 18 years), so I did not add much texture to her face (Figures 8.89 and 8.90).

For an older person I might use a bit of clear plastic wrap on top of the clay and press with a tool to make the creases around the eyes and mouth. I use a press mold made from an orange peel and stiff brush to make the skin texture.

I add the eyebrows with small rolls of clay and then use a wire wrapped tool to crease them and make the hair texture.

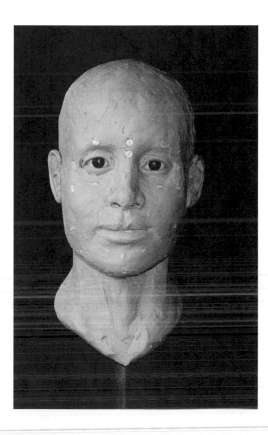

Figure 8.88
*Features of face completed
and ready for finishing.*

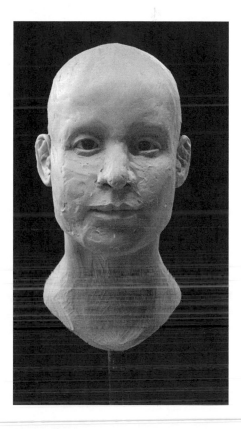

Figure 8.89
*Refinement of face keeping a light touch when
smoothing and finishing.*

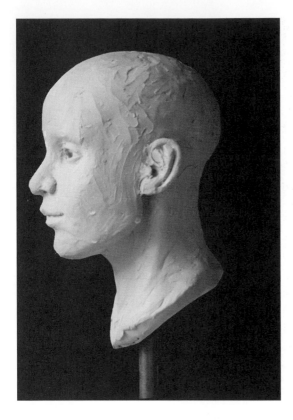

Wigs and Hair

The finishing touches are a bit of a personal preference. Sometimes I put a lot of finish into a piece; sometimes not so much. An example of doing everything possible for the finishing touches such as makeup and wigs can be seen in the comparison of Figures 8.91 and 8.92. In Figure 8.91 I have placed a wig that was not trimmed and tucked to fit down to the skull of the subject. In Figure 8.92 I show the same subject with the same wig that has been customized to the subject. I believe the finishing of the hair and styling of the wig are important. For this case I was able to obtain a sample of her hair for length and color. I took a sample of this with me to purchase a wig to make certain it had the right color and length. The cost was about $250. As with the eyes, I believe it is essential to buy the best wig possible; when you use better materials, you get better results.

After consulting with several hairstylists and theatrical hairdressers, I learned that wigs are made with too much hair. Wigs are made to cover a person's real hair and, in general, are larger than the actual cranium. Because of this I carefully clip out the back and some of the sides in order to make the wig fit tightly to the sculpture. I also anchor the wig to the head with many

Figure 8.90

Profile of nearly finished face. It is not necessary to completely smooth the part under the wig.

Figure 8.91

An unfinished face with an untrimmed wig. The face looks rough and the wig is unacceptable; made for people with hair, it needs thinning and fastening down to the skull contour.

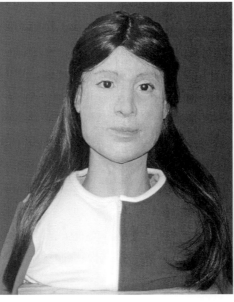

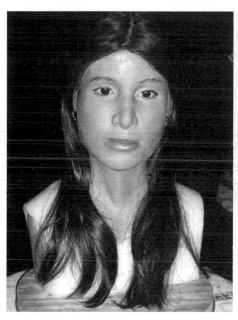 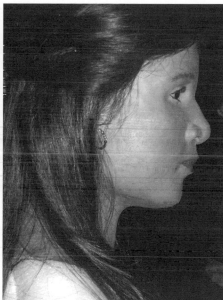

Figure 8.92

Two views with a wig that has been trimmed and tied down to the contour of the subject's head. On the right, the wig has been pulled back with a butterfly clip like one found with the body (photos by David Dellaria).

pins, and sometimes even some glue. On occasion I even use thinning shears to thin the hair. I feel that as I have done the sculptural work to stay true to the cranium and the skull shape, I don't want to obliterate it with a bad wig. I also use care to employ as close to the correct hair color and shape as possible. For this case we could tell the subject had dyed her hair a lighter color, and further that her roots were dark to about 2 inches from the scalp. Because of these observations, I colored her roots dark to that same level; this proved useful to the investigators in the end. Her hair was about 17 inches long, so that is how long I cut the hair on the wig. I took the style from a description of her hair when she was found.

Notice all these are reasons for the artist to have access to all the files, even if only to read them and make notes. If you are creating a facial reconstruction, you need to be considered part of the team and given every resource possible to aid your understanding of the subject's appearance. Sometimes a note about the hair or makeup will be mentioned just briefly in the general description of the body. You need to take all the pieces of information, even the seemingly trivial, and add them up to create a picture of this real person.

Accessories, Clothing, and Jewelry

If there is jewelry, hair accessories, and/or clothing, then try to replicate those. For this case, the subject had a butterfly clip in her hair, gold loop earrings, and a distinctive shirt. The Alameda County Sheriffs had a shirt made that replicated the

Figure 8.93

After the wig has been fitted and trimmed, it is pinned up for further face finishing (photo by David Dellaria).

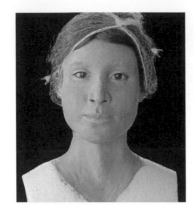

Figure 8.94

Two copies created of the Jane Doe. In front is the plaster copy needed so the Alameda County Sheriffs Investigators could travel with the sculpture to Mexico. In the back is the original clay sculpture. The successful identification of the subject was the result of the image being shown in Mexico (photos by David Dellaria). See color plate.

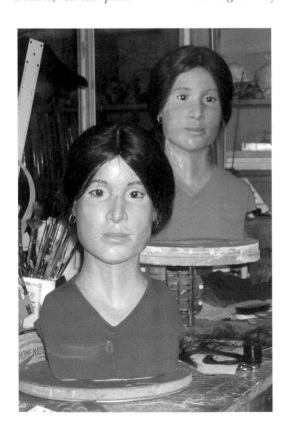

one she was wearing. We used that in the press release photos of her. I purchased earrings and a hair clip similar in size and color to hers and put them on the sculpture as well.

Sometimes when I am working on the face of a reconstruction, it takes on some interesting expressions, with only small, light manipulations of the clay. Figure 8.93 is a snapshot I took because there was something I saw when I had her hair pinned up to finish her face. We later learned she frequently had her hair pinned up, and the snapshot bore a striking resemblance as seen in Figure 8.96.

I applied makeup commonly available at retail stores to the face of this subject. The colors are natural and it seems to stick just fine to the clay. I attached false eyelashes, which I cut down for a natural look. If the final sculpture is going to be in plaster, as was the situation with one copy in this case, I use acrylic paint. One of the extra labors associated with this case was the necessity to make a second plaster copy of the original clay reconstruction so the plaster model could travel with the detectives to Mexico. Figure 8.94 is a photo of the plaster copy in front; the original clay sculpture is in back. Since the clay never dries, the reconstruction could be easily dented and distorted in transit, with no artist around to fix the damage. The plaster copy, though twice the labor, offered a version that was much more impervious to damage.

This case had a satisfactory ending in that the young girl, so brutally murdered, was identified and returned to her family for a proper burial. The Cold Case Unit of the Alameda County Sheriff's Department went to great lengths to get the image of the sculpture out in a wide geographical area. A facial reconstruction works only when the right person(s) sees the image. In this case the investigators worked tirelessly for many months and traveled thousands of miles. They spent hundreds of hours following up every lead in order to achieve their goal. The sculpture reconstructing the murdered girl's face was an important part of their work; it helped generate leads. At the press conference Sergeant Dudek stated the identification would not have happened if not for the sculpture. Figures 8.95, 8.96, and 8.97 are three comparisons of the reconstruction with the identified girl. The first is with a photo of her at age 11, five years before her death. The second is that same photo compared to my snapshot; the last is a comparison with her photo from near the age of her death.

Important Measurements and Relationships (Approximate)

- Size of eyeball: 25 millimeters
- Size of iris: 12 millimeters
- Lateral projection of the nose: Three times the length of nasal spine measured from skin surface (depth of tissue taken at the mid-philtrum)
- Nose width: Caucasoids, 10 mm (5 mm on each side) wider than the widest point of the nasal aperture; Negroids, 16 mm (8 mm on each side) wider than the widest point of the nasal aperture
- Nose bottom: About 5 mm below the nasal aperture
- Width of mouth opening: From the outer edges of top six teeth; from the edge of the maxillary canine where it abuts the bicuspid (interproximal space) to that location on the canine on the opposite side
- Horizontal location of mouth opening: Parallel to a horizontal line a few millimeters above the incisal edge of the maxillary teeth
- Length of maxillary central incisor crown (enameled portion or cervico-incisal length): 10.5 mm
- Length of mandibular central incisor crown (enameled portion or cervico-incisal length): 9.5 mm
- Length of the ears: Same as nose length
- Position of the ears: Top parallel to the eye area, bottom parallel to bottom of the nose

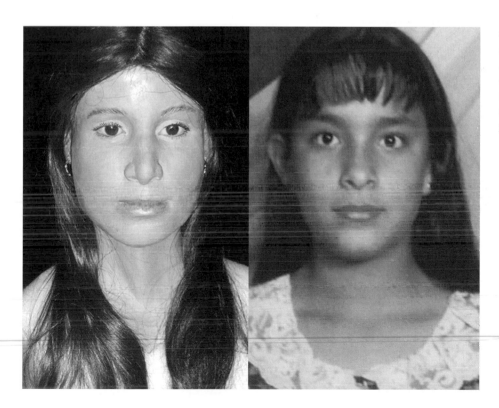

Figure 8.95

On the left is the clay sculpture, on the right a photo of the subject identified at the age of 11 years. See color plate.

Figure 8.96

On the left: An almost-finished version of the clay sculpture with the hair pinned up; on the right is a photo of the subject at age 11. Even at a barely finished state, the features created by Nusse are all consistent with the subject.

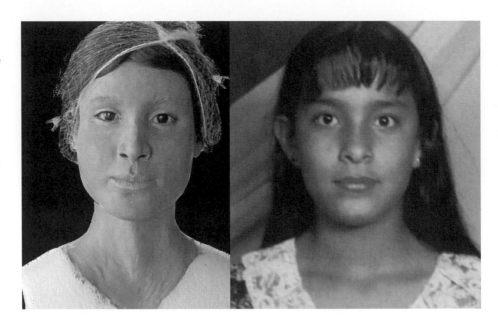

Figure 8.97

On the left is a profile view of the sculpture; on the right is a photo of the subject identified taken a short time before her murder (photo by David Dellaria). See color plate.

REFERENCES

1. Harris Hawthorne Wilder, "The Physiognomy of the Indians of Southern New England," *American Anthropologist*, July-September, 1912, Vol. 14, No. 3, p. 415.

2. J. L. Tarr, Colonel, U.S.A.F. and T. D. White, Chief of Staff, *Dental Laboratory Technicians' Manual*, U.S. Government Printing Office, Washington, D.C. 1959, pp. 106–107.

3. Caroline Wilkinson, *Forensic Facial Reconstruction*, Cambridge University Press, New York, 2004, pp. 187–188.

4. Caroline Wilkinson, *Forensic Facial Reconstruction*, Cambridge University Press, New York, 2004, p. 173.

5. Major M. Ash and Stanley J. Nelson, *Wheeler's Dental Anatomy, Physiology, and Occlusion*, 8th edition, 2003, p. 159.

6. Monoplex Eye Prosthetic LLC, 40 Optical Drive, Unit 11, Southbridge, MA 01550.

7. Betty Pat. Gatliff's Scottsdale School of Art class notes, May 1995.

CHAPTER 9

IMPLEMENTATIONS AND CONCLUSIONS

"When a witness to a crime sees the face of the perpetrator, a forensic artist should be engaged to perform a sketch if detectives are serious about investigating the case."

—Lois Gibson

Forensic art is a relatively new profession. Like anything introduced to the various law enforcement agencies, even the best crime-solving techniques take time to become established. Today no law enforcement agency in the world would think of carrying on investigations without using photography, fingerprint technology, or DNA evidence testing. Yet, each one of these disciplines took years to become accepted as necessary investigative tools.

Consider the use of fingerprints found at the scene of a crime. Fingerprints were used to help solve the first criminal case by Dr. Henry Faulds in Tokyo, Japan in 1880.[1] It was not until 1901, at New Scotland yard of the London Metropolitan Police, that a unit of professionals was formed who used fingerprints systematically to identify criminals. It would be more than four decades later, in 1924, before the United States formalized fingerprint use when an act of Congress formed the Identification Division of the Federal Bureau of Investigation.

Photography was available to the public by 1840, yet the earliest systematic use in the United States by a law enforcement agency of photography for criminal identification did not happen until 1854, in San Francisco. Chicago police did not use photography as part of their official identification system until 1905.[2]

The structure and nature of deoxyribonucleic acid, or DNA, were defined by James Watson and Francis Crick in 1953. At that time, geneticists and chemists knew that each person's genetic material contained unique qualities. However, in 1968 DNA was still not admitted as legitimate evidence during the Robert Chambers "Preppy Murder Case" in New York City. In 1968 there was only one criminal lab in the country to test DNA and the results took 6 months. The Judge in 1968 would not allow DNA evidence admitted in Chambers's trial.[3] By 1998, DNA results for evidence gathered at crime scenes could be returned in days and every court in the land accepted DNA evidence. Today DNA is routinely reported by news organizations as having identified perpetrators of crime.

Because these disciplines proved their success, photography, fingerprint technologies, and DNA evidence, though once scarcely used, are now considered absolutely necessary for serious investigations of crime.

FORENSIC ART: UNTAPPED POTENTIAL

The International Association for Identification officially recognized forensic art as a legitimate discipline in London, England, in 1986. Though strides have been made, the United States, at this writing has fewer than 20 forensic artists who are employed exclusively to perform forensic art duties.

Full-time Forensic Artist: A person employed by a law-enforcement agency whose sole duties are forensic art related.

Thousands of artists, mostly with a strong law enforcement background, have taken training. Yet, even though hundreds of thousands of crimes are committed each year where a witness sees the face of the perpetrator and survives, only the smallest fraction of those cases is worked by a forensic artist. The most perplexing feature of the lack of forensic sketches created is this fact:

If the witness is not lying, 100% of the time when a sketch is done from his or her memory by a reasonably talented, reasonably trained artist, the sketch will at least be *similar* to the person described. Add to that the fact that some sketches with poor resemblances to the perpetrator nevertheless have generated a tip that led to the identification of the perpetrator of the crime, we can deduce forensic sketches always offer the *potential* to help solve the case. If law enforcement officials understood this truth, there would be thousands of full-time forensic artists in this country, not less than 20, as there are at this writing. Commensurately, there would be hundreds of criminals identified from the sketches generated by those professional forensic artists.

Since the concrete advantages of forensic art have not translated into law enforcement universally offering this tool to victims, it must be deduced that forensic art as a profession is in its earliest stages. The effectiveness of forensic sketches has yet to be proven to those who manage law enforcement agencies. Virtually every scene of a crime against a person (robberies, sexual assaults, and some homicides) will have a witness who saw a face; yet the percentage of sketches done, compared to crimes committed, is statistically insignificant (less than 3%). This holds true for all countries, even the United States, which is the leader in forensic art. Only a fraction of scenes yield usable fingerprints, yet fingerprint gathering is considered a mandatory investigative tool. This extremely illogical imbalance should change for the sake of crime victims.

REASONS FOR THE SCARCITY OF FORENSIC ART

First, the forensic artists themselves are fragmented in their attitudes about their own profession. There is even doubt at this early stage that law enforcement agencies are able to allocate funds for forensic artists. The majority of cities and counties in this country make decisions not to allocate funds for forensic artists every year. These decisions are tantamount to early fingerprint technology, or crime-scene and suspect photography, or DNA labs not being funded. Common knowledge says if there are no funds allocated for a function in a bureaucracy (which is what all law enforcement agencies are), then that function does not exist. Considering the fact that some artists have solved the first case for which they have sketched, and all artists who relate their statistics report a 30% (or better) success rate of cases solved versus cases worked, decisions not to fund forensic art are not logical. These decisions are not in the best interest of the victims of crime. Also consider there are thousands of artists who have been trained and are able and willing to perform forensic artwork, and there are hundreds of thousands of crime victims who could use the services of forensic artists. The big question is "Why are there not more forensic artists employed by law enforcement agencies?"

BASIC HUMAN NATURE IS THE ENEMY

It cannot be emphasized enough that every single person *incorrectly* thinks it is not likely an artist can sketch a resemblance of a perpetrator's face from a witness. I have worked more than 3,700 cases at this writing. Almost all witnesses expressed the idea that they did not believe it would be possible to sketch a resemblance of their attacker, or whatever face they had seen, from their description. Every detective doubts this can be done. All commanders of detectives harbor serious doubts that any artist can possibly sketch a resemblance from talking to a witness. This belief is so pervasive that it generates intense media attention when a sketch solves a case. If the conventional wisdom were that a forensic artist can always produce a likeness from a witness, then a sketch helping solve a case would not be news. Yet every forensic artist who has been interviewed by someone in the media will notice how incredulous the reporter is at the artist's ability to sketch a face from the memory of a witness. Forensic artists are overwhelmed by doubt from everyone around them. Forensic artists should stand firm and insist our profession is effective and can help detectives find the suspects for whom they search.

Law enforcement leaders should decide the logical, correct thing to do is fund forensic artists to help their victims of crime find justice. Consider the hundreds of documented cases that are attributed to having been solved by just one artist's sketches, more than 60 of which appear in this text with complete documentation. There are thousands of other cases where forensic artists' sketches prompted the identity of the perpetrator to be discovered by investigators.

Because the vast majority of law enforcement agencies might not understand the function of the forensic artist, a definition of the function will help legitimize the profession:

> The purpose of a forensic artist is to help identify individuals.

The help forensic artists give for identifying individuals takes on several forms:

- Creating an image of the face of a perpetrator from a witness's memory can help the detective find the suspect and solve the case.
- Recreating the faces of unidentified murdered victims from their remains. Should that image help the investigator find the subject's identity, that knowledge can allow the detective to search the subject's background and find the killer, thus solving the case.
- Creating an updated image of a known suspect from earlier photos can help apprehend that fugitive.

By far the largest number of cases for which the forensic artist would be utilized is that of sketching a face from witness memory. This act takes a great deal of courage, because the witness, the detective, the media, and every person surrounding the forensic artist doubt the task can be done. Therefore, established forensic artists have a duty to support forensic art as a tool that solves cases.

TOOLS TO PROPEL THE PROFESSION

QUANTIFY SUCCESSES

No profession performing practical services can advance without quantifying results. Many forensic artists who pioneered the profession did not begin by keeping track of their successes, and so resisted and even refused to start after many years of doing the work. This is understandable, but for the fledgling profession of forensic art to move forward and help thousands more victims and investigators, forensic artists should tally their results.

REASONS TO KEEP TRACK OF SUCCESSES

- **Improvement**: When an artist obtains the photo of the person whom they sketched from a witness's memory, that artist can see what portions of the image were done correctly and incorrectly. The artist can then recall the interview and understand why the mistakes were made and why correct areas were drawn. The artist then is able to make corrections or repeat successful practices. Without this kind of feedback, the artist cannot become better and is doomed to repeat mistakes. This observation of what went wrong with previous sketches is the basis for my success.

- **Basis for increased reimbursement**: Quantifying good results can be the basis for career advancement, including increased pay or a higher pay grade within the organization.
- **Promotion of the profession in the future**: Quantifying results will allow other forensic artists to enter and succeed in the field.
- **Improved witness attitude**: The ever-skeptical witnesses always have a positive upturn in their attitude, thus potentially enhancing their relaxation and memory, when they hear the artist with whom they will be working is successful. Therefore, the successes of the past can bolster successes of the future.
- **Justice**: More quantification will increase utilization of forensic artists. The more forensic artists are utilized, the more victims will find justice as the sketches help identify their attackers. This is the logical, core reason for any law enforcement activity.

According to the forensic artists who report successful results, approximately 30% of their sketches help identify the perpetrator being described. Some artists claim a much higher rate of success.

THE NOT-SO-EXTRA EXTRA JOB

Forensic artists who refuse to quantify results have very good reasons. They claim their city is too spread out, and the detectives are hard to track down in order to ask about their sketch helping solve the case. Searching out results can seem like a frustrating part-time job for no extra pay. I work in the fourth largest city in the United States, and have experienced great difficulty trying to discover the final resolution of cases worked—I believe it is a formidable task that will never be done to perfection. For years the effort to keep after detectives to obtain mug shots of those faces sketched from memories seemed unbearable and annoying. Then I realized that if we accept the act of keeping track of results as another part of the job, the tasks became bearable. The reasons for quantifying results are absolutely too important to dismiss. It is not an extra job; it is an indispensable part of the primary job.

The professional forensic artist must maintain a humble, gracious attitude toward investigators. Never forget, the sketch can only help solve the case by identifying the perpetrator. The investigator might spend hundreds of hours working to solve a case. The tasks might involve interviewing the witness, searching out the suspect, breaking down doors, risking his or her life, holding line-ups, setting up surveillance, and other tasks too numerous to mention. The sketch is only a method to find out the identity of the suspect. I always have had the most cordial professional relationships with detectives because I credit them with solving any case; my work is only for identification purposes. Indeed, there are many cases described in this text where a sketch prompted a tip that instantly led detectives to the suspect and shaved hundreds of hours off the work they would have done on high-profile cases.

But the person in charge of the case is the detective, and he or she is the one responsible for driving the case through the courts to a satisfactory conclusion. Forensic artists should go to great lengths to maintain a congenial relationship with all detectives; this entails never saying one's sketch "solved the case." This good relationship is crucial if a forensic artist is going to be able to effectively quantify successful results from sketches created.

HINTS FOR QUANTIFYING RESULTS

For those who understandably find the gathering of investigative results an onerous task, here are some suggestions that have served me well over the decades.

START AT THE BEGINNING

Artists who do not start from their first sketches to keep track of whether the detective found the perpetrator and further, if their sketch helped that effort, tend to feel overwhelmed later. Instead, if artists keep track from the start, they will find it is a worthwhile and rewarding habit. If you have been a forensic artist for a few years, you should start now, and quantify the results for two or three years. If the successes are about 30% of the cases worked, then you could logically claim a reasonable estimate of about 30% success for the *previous* years.

As the years went by, I kept track of my percentage of successes and the tally varied from 43% one year to 27% another. Recently a compilation of the entire career of 23 years of statistics yielded a 29.4% success rate—very near that often repeated 30%. Cook County Sheriffs Police Detective Luis Santoyo, the forensic artist for the Chicago metropolitan area, reported a 30% success rate during his entire career. Joy Mann, the Forensic Artist for DuPage County Sheriffs, reported a 60% success rate when working juvenile-sex-crime cases on a freelance basis for the Chicago Police Department. Both artists kept records from the very beginning of their careers,[4] even though the areas in which they work are densely populated, making it harder to identify perpetrators.

TRACK YOUR DETECTIVES

Keep the contact information (phone numbers, e-mail addresses) on the outside of the case file for each case. Pull out the case files periodically and make contact to see if the case has been solved. If the answer is affirmative, *humbly* inquire if the image was any aid to the identification of the person sketched. Obtain a photo of the perpetrator whether your sketch was instrumental or not; observing a comparison with the sketch and the mug shot can help improve your techniques.

SEIZE THE MOMENT

The best time to ask the detective for feedback is when you hand over the image to him or her. Detectives are grateful the artist took the time to sketch with their witnesses. This is a good time to request that they let you know when they solve the case! Exhibit a strong desire to see the photo of the perpetrator for a comparison to improve the forensic artwork. When saying goodbye to the witness, enlist his or her help in reminding the detective of the artist's desire to see the results when the case has a satisfactory conclusion. If the sketch session was conducted properly, the witness has grown congenial toward the artist. Therefore, the witness would enjoy sharing the satisfactory conclusion of the case, and since this is a singular event for the witness, he or she will most likely remember the artist when he or she is able to view a line-up and pick out the perpetrator of the crime.

TRACK THE NEWS

Read the crime section of the newspaper covering the area every day. Catch the television news at least once a day. I have discovered dozens of cases that were solved in this manner; subsequent contact with the detective confirmed the results, often finding the sketch played a pivotal role. Some sketches that did not help were nevertheless some of the best likenesses ever produced, so viewing them was quite gratifying.

POSITIVE PRESENTATIONS ARE NECESSARY

Prepare a presentation to be given to various groups meeting in the community explaining how the forensic artist can help solve crimes. These presentations have the potential to:

- Help solve crimes. I can attribute dozens of crimes being solved by persons who saw one of my presentations and then were prompted by their confidence in forensic sketches to call in a beneficial tip to authorities. In one case, a man watering his lawn who had previously seen my presentation saw a man drive by who looked like the sketch of a suspect who had assaulted a woman on his block. He took down the tag number and the driver was found to be the man who molested his neighbor and who had robbed more than a hundred other people.[5]
- Help create better witnesses. As my message about forensic art being an effective tool for the public to identify the criminals got out, more and more witnesses had a predisposition to better remember the face of their attackers. Simply believing that the sketches can be successful on the part of the witness can cut about 30% of time from the sketch interview. These kinds of witnesses with positive attitudes about forensic art seem to help create better likenesses.

■ Spread the word. The majority of forensic artists are the only source of sketches for many surrounding jurisdictions. As the presentations spread the word, more law enforcement agencies will utilize the forensic artist, resulting in more identifications of criminals victimizing persons in the area.

Since the general population, law enforcement personnel included, are not aware of just how successful forensic sketches can be, the forensic artist has an obligation to spread the word about any successes. This kind of communication to groups will only increase the chances that your work will have results.

Most metropolitan police agencies already have programs in place where the general public meets with law enforcement personnel for the purpose of fighting crime. These types of meetings engender unity among neighbors to make the area safer and would gladly welcome a forensic artist presentation. Other civic-minded organizations such as Rotary and Optimist Clubs and numerous professional organizations enjoy meetings where the common good is promoted with thought-provoking speakers. These types of groups would eagerly invite the forensic artist in their area to present.

Prepare comparisons of your work with the proven perpetrator of the crime and create a PowerPoint presentation for these groups of individuals. You will have no trouble remembering the scenarios of what happened before, during, and after the sketch, if and how the sketch aided the investigation, and the outcome for the case in the judicial system. If you can concisely explain these stories of what happened, audiences of all types will be enthralled with the "true crime" stories.

This country regularly elects officials who portray themselves as being "tough on crime." If you can show how you, through sensitivity and artistic talent, have literally gotten "tough on crime" by giving it a face and making criminals find it hard to hide, all persons will greet the presentation enthusiastically.

In Brief

■ Forensic art is in the beginning stages; utilization should vastly increase for the sake of justice.
■ A forensic artist should sketch with any witness to a crime who saw the perpetrator's face if detectives are serious about investigating the case.
■ To propel the forensic art profession, members should quantify results and portray a positive image of the discipline in words and actions.
■ Prepare a presentation and explain how forensic images can help identify criminals to local groups.

THE FORENSIC ARTIST IN COURT

Catching the perpetrator of a crime is of no use if the prosecutor is not able to convict. Getting a subpoena to appear in court often generates uncomfortable feelings. Artists who testify enough soon become skillful and at peace with their role in the proceedings. I have testified in more than 60 trials with a successful prosecution on all but one case. Following are some helpful hints to be prepared for court.

MAINTAIN ACCURATE FILES FOR SKETCHES

All forensic artists should keep a file on every case they work in anticipation of the perpetrator being caught and tried in court. The filing system should allow you to quickly retrieve the file even if the trial is held long after you create the sketch. The best way is to keep a folder with the following:

- The original sketch or a high-quality copy of it
- A case report or notes taken from the detective with details of the case
- Any news clippings concerning the case

For quick retrieval of files no matter how much time has passed, a forensic sketch file ledger should be kept. This ledger would consist of a bound book with a list of the files in chronological order with each file having its own unique number. As an example, the first sketch in 2007 would be 1-07, the next 2-07, and so on. I highlight these numbers down the middle of the ledger in yellow, and that corresponding number on the file jacket is also highlighted in yellow. Each ledger entry and file folder should have:

- Case number
- Date, time, and address of offense
- Name of the detective and agency
- Name of the witness(es)
- Race and gender of suspect(s)
- Date you did the sketch

When this simple filing system is maintained, if a suspect is apprehended after months or years, you can easily look it up by date, detective, agency, or any of the other descriptors included in the ledger. This way you can quickly remind yourself of your part in the case and be prepared to testify.

THE SKETCH AS EVIDENCE

You will be obligated to commit to descriptors about the suspect your witness gives you. However, since you will have to testify in court about the image you create, caution should be used as to what you are willing to commit to paper when you are depending only on witness memory. The remedy to this situation is to avoid writing down unnecessary information, especially if you cannot be certain about some of the descriptors of the suspect.

The beginning of the sketch interview should not consist of an artist filling out a form. Not only does this start the session off with a cold atmosphere, those narrow parameters on the form might cause trouble in the court if the beleaguered witness makes inaccurate guesses about the suspect. Rather, it is safer in court, and begins the interview in a much warmer, cordial manner if the artist intersperses the questions about race, gender, height, age, and body type while engaging in conversation. I like to act as if I am beginning the drawing and the questions are interspersed with pleasant remarks. I find it expedient to print the information about the suspect on the front of the drawing, then drop my hand down a bit and start sketching. The last thing I do is sign and date the sketch with a circled "c" as an artist's copyright.

Since the sketch will be displayed in court, the creator should be prepared to testify to whatever appears on the drawing. I consider the items I write on the face of the sketch very carefully as I only include determinations about which I would feel comfortable testifying in court. Figure 9.1 shows that I leave out many items in order to be safe. As an example, I never have the witness give me a number of pounds for weight. Instead I will write, in whatever words the witness speaks, a body type. These might be "thin, muscular build," "thick, slightly chubby build," or "normal build." Individuals are *always* able to say the kind of build someone has, whereas determining a number of pounds could be difficult. For younger individuals or persons used to the metric system, the number of pounds for their attacker could be impossible to guess correctly.

I always allow as large a range of age in years as possible, such as "late teens to early twenties." I avoid exact numerical ages in writing because once I had a desperate defense attorney try to say his client was innocent because he was 20 and the witness said he appeared 18 or 19. I never ask children younger than early teens to estimate the age in numbers. Children under 12 can tell if the person is elderly or a teenager but might not be that reliable about much else.

I put a wide range for the height if I am unsure. I also would not trust a height estimation from persons who have not reached their final adult growth, or even adults who are very short. The very best estimators of height are single females who are above average height and who are dating, and males who are fairly tall.

As is seen in Figure 9.1, the information I commit to print on the face of the sketch is sparse. With this cautious method, no defense attorney has been able to call into question his client's guilt over anything I put in writing on my drawings in court.

If you are not certain about something, do not put it in writing. If the witness has to guess about the race of the suspect, put all the possibilities he or she mentions and then place question marks in front and at the end of that part. Feel free to put a question mark near any item about which you are unsure. This will confirm it was only a guess in court.

The dress code in court can be understood by looking at most politicians on the campaign trail. Experts on dressing so that one appears credible advise our top politicians; without paying an expert fee, simply copy how politicians dress for a debate. For example, the experts who have researched such things claim that wearing solid navy blue projects the most credibility. You do not need be so restrictive as to wear only a navy blue suit; dressing in a conservative, nonprovocative manner will do. Another example: Women seem more credible if they wear their hair up and carry a briefcase instead of a purse. No woman needs to wear her hair up and carry a briefcase each time she appears in court; however, the hair should be neat and worn conservatively. Makeup and jewelry should be conservative, too.

Have a discussion with the district attorney who is prosecuting the case (a district attorney is a lawyer who is supported by the taxpayers to prosecute criminals who victimize individuals). This discussion is needed so the district attorney will be able to go over the questions you will be asked in court. At this time, the forensic artist can help the district attorney decide how best to ask the questions—these attorneys always want to know the answer they will receive *before* they ask the question.

Figure 9.1

Two examples of sketches with minimum descriptors printed on the sketch. Only those items for which I am willing to testify in court are written down.

> **Warning:** The attorney defending the accused criminal will try to "trick" a witness by asking him or her, in an accusatory manner, if he or she "talked about the case with the district attorney" before the trail. The defense attorney will use a tone of voice that makes it sound as if it is wrong, a sin, to discuss the case before testifying. This is a trick to see if the witness is a novice at testifying. Simply answer with a pleasant "yes." You *must* discuss the case with the district attorney before the trail, so act as if it is obvious that you should discuss the case before testifying. Never act flustered, as if you were caught doing something bad.

There are some questions that are always asked in court that are so easy, you can usually answer without knowing them in advance. For beginners, it might be a good idea to organize in writing and then repeat the answers concisely and pleasantly in the mirror before the trail. After you are sworn in, some of the most common courtroom questions are:

- **What is your name?** (Often you will be asked to say your name slowly and then spell it for the court reporter.)
- **By which agency are you employed?** (If you work freelance, say so; then name agencies that use your services.)
- **What is your title and for how long have you been employed?**
- **What is your education/training, and what are your credentials?**

Be able to answer this last question concisely. Since you do not want to leave out anything important, write this portion down for quick perusal immediately before testifying. Have someone who is versed at identifying good resume builders for job hunters help identify and include all portions of work, education, training, and experience that will put you in a positive light. For instance, I realized after not mentioning this fact during several court appearances that sketching 3,000 realistic fine art portraits on the River Walk in San Antonio was germane to my ability to sketch adeptly with witnesses to crime. I began including that work experience when testifying about my credentials on the stand. This portion of the testimony may motivate you to become a member of the International Association for Identification, which is the professional organization that certifies forensic artists.

- **Did you create this sketch?** (The district attorney will introduce the sketch to the court; get permission to enter it into evidence; give it a number; and show it to the judge, the artist, and the jury, not necessarily in that order.)
- **How did you create this sketch?** (Be able to say this in a *very few* words. All artists know they could talk for hours about how they do the sketch; nevertheless, keep it brief. I say something like, "I relax the witness; show him or her a book from which to pick various features similar to the face he or she saw. I start drawing at the top of the face

and go down to the neck and shoulders." This is almost always *too brief* an answer, but that is desirable. It leaves everyone in the court wanting to hear more and allows the district attorney to ask more questions. Do not bring the *FBI Facial Identification Catalog* or any other visual aid to court. If this is done, the court can force it to be admitted into evidence, causing you to lose the catalog or visual aid. If you are asked if you have the visual aid, simply say "no." Also, a truthful and beneficial remark to make is that it is "standard in the profession" to use such visual aids.)

- **Who gave you the description for the sketch?** (Go over the case file before trial to be reminded of the name and other details about the witness. Cases that get to court are usually so compelling there should be no trouble remembering numerous details about the witness and the incident.)

UNDERSTANDING THE NUANCES

Don't be needlessly angered or hurt when the attorney defending the culprit of the crime questions aggressively when you are testifying. The defense attorney is obligated by the U.S. Constitution to defend the person who is accused of causing all these problems to the department, community, and your witness. It is a great testament to the U.S. judicial system that the guidelines offer a retrial if a defendant has ineffective representation. Therefore, if the defense attorney *does not* put forth a vigorous defense, the taxpayers will have to come up with approximately $10,000 to $80,000 more for a retrial of the case, due to inadequate defense. The defense attorney has an obligation to act distastefully toward all prosecution witnesses.

Most often the prosecution side will win anyway since detectives usually use artists only on the most egregious cases. No matter how nasty the defense attorney may portray the question, if your answer is given in an unruffled and even tone, then the jury and/or judge will consider the witness (you) to be unruffled and without taint, guilt, or impeachable nature. In other words, keep your cool no matter how much the defense turns up the heat of questioning, and you will always seem above reproach.

DIRECTING YOUR ANSWERS

Do not direct your answers to the defense attorney—do not even feel a need to focus all attention on the district attorney. Neither of the attorneys questioning you will decide the case. The people who will decide the guilt or innocence are the jury or the judge, so direct your answers to them. Give expressions, emphasis, and attention toward the jury or judge and look to them for reactions. Look to them to gauge how you should modulate your voice and formulate answers. It does not matter if the defense attorney seems exasperated or disgusted with the artist; if the judge or jury gives the person testifying approving looks, that is what counts in court.

REAL COURT SCENARIO

To illustrate the points made in the previous paragraphs, here is what happened during a trial. The defendant had pushed his way into an apartment by posing as a maintenance man. He then raped two little girls, aged 7 and 9, who were there alone, then stabbed them in their stomachs.

The sketch prompted more than 25 tipsters to call in his name and place of employment when the sketch came out on the television news. The detective got a full confession.

The sketch was done during the month of January of 1988. The sketch was done at the girls' hospital bedside in a stressful situation and I had carelessly put the year as 1987 on the sketch. During the trial the defense attorney had me hold the sketch up next to my face. He asked various questions about how the sketch was done, and then asked what date the sketch was done. I answered with the correct date "in 1988." The defense attorney, with as much scorn in his voice as he could muster, asked me to read the date on the face of the sketch. I smiled and said "Oops, 1987, I made that mistake in my checkbook too all that month," while looking at the jury. The jury all laughed, and the defense attorney objected that the artist's answer was "not responsive." The judge said he would sustain (accept, let stand) the answer. I did not become disturbed or angry in the least, even though it was akin to being the victim of a high school prank. The defense attorney knew full well I had sketched the drawing in 1988 with the little girls. It was his unenviable duty to defend his client in any way he could. The only fault the defense attorney could find was this innocent dumb mistake, commonly made by thousands of persons on thousands of documents in January, of putting the previous year on the date.

The defendant received life in prison.

BECOME AN EXPERT

Become an expert about which portions of your sketches demonstrate the most and least resemblance to the perpetrator described.

Once you have been able to compare a number of your sketches to mug shots of the proven perpetrator of the crime, you will be able to identify the most common variances with the face described. This is a most constructive activity that can prepare you for court.

Find the kinds of differences that are most common between your sketch and the face described. If these facts are known, when a suspect is captured and tried and the artist goes to court, any portions of the sketch that are dissimilar to the accused person's face can be nullified. Conversely, the portions that are similar can be given more weight if the artist has proof from numerous comparisons that when working with a witness, those are the portions of the sketch that are

Figure 9.2

All three sketches compared to mug shots (above) show the most common mistake made by the artist when sketching from witness memory: The outer periphery of the face is out of sync with the facial core.

most commonly similar. If these facts are known, when questioned by the district attorney, the artist can focus attention on the parts of the sketch that are similar, and reasonably explain away the portions that are dissimilar to the accused. This is an ethical, legitimate way to help the jury or judge understand imperfections in the work. No artist can do a perfect portrait of a person even if he or she can see that person. Therefore, any jury will accept that a forensic sketch will have imperfections. If the artist can explain that certain imperfections commonly occur, it will allow the court to understand the witness was remembering just as well as hundreds of other witnesses have when they helped create a drawing. The witness had the same trouble on the same areas of the face as other witnesses to crimes where the proven perpetrator was identified, tried, and convicted.

For example, Figure 9.2 contains pictures I took to court for a trial. I was called by the defense attorney because that attorney thought the sketch was so dissimilar it could help exonerate her client. The attorney was defending a man who was accused of shooting a former athlete and father of two who had a successful business. The shot partially paralyzed him from the waist down.

The defense attorney thought drawing attention to the poor sketch would get her client off since there was much dissimilarity between his face and the drawing.

Although the district attorney promised to provide a photo of the accused before I arrived at the court, due to mistakes in the district attorney's office, I did not have the accused man's photo; I had only a copy of my sketch. Before meeting in a back room and looking at the comparison, I laid the photos in Figure 9.2 on the table in front of the defense attorney and the district attorney. I explained that the most common error in composites after almost 1,000 comparisons was that the peripheral features of the face would be off, whereas the center of the face would be quite similar. I further explained that the eye area was the most likely to be done correctly. I made certain the attorneys noted that I was showing them these facts *before* viewing the comparison of the accused man's mug shot with my sketch. When the district attorney laid the photo of the accused next to the sketch, it was obvious the same mistakes were made in that sketch. The peripheral features of the face were very inaccurate, the facial core was remarkably similar, and the eye area was almost identical.

The defense attorney decided not to call the artist to the stand. The defendant was convicted.

EXPERT WITNESS

Many ways to aid the district attorney with your case necessitate your being designated an expert witness by the judge after an explanation given in open court.

> **Expert Witness**: A person having special training or experience in a specialized field. An expert witness can give opinions concerning areas of his or her expertise, even though this expert was not present at or a witness to the crime. Nonexpert witnesses are permitted to testify only about facts they observed.

There is no mystery about being designated as an expert witness by a judge. The prosecuting attorney will have the forensic artist on the stand, where he or she states his or her name, occupation, place of employment, and such. Then the artist is asked to state his or her credentials/training/education/experience. After the artist has given what should be an impressive array of education and experience in one of the world's most esoteric professions, the defense attorney will say something like, "Judge, I wish to have the witness designated as an expert…." If the Judge says, "I will so allow…" or "I will designate the witness as an expert…," then that witness can give opinions.

Since forensic art is one of the most unusual professions, any experience or training will be highly specialized. After the artist has been designated as an expert witness, the attorney then enters the sketch into evidence. This is done by displaying the sketch in court, after gaining permission by the judge to "publish" the evidence to the court. After the jury, the judge, and the defense attorney and accused have seen the sketch, the prosecutor will ask the artist to comment on the resemblance of the sketch to the accused. The following kinds of comments have worked successfully for years during many successful prosecutions of subjects I sketched.

- Make it abundantly clear the sketch was done only from a description and that you could not see the face.
- Mention that no artist can make a perfect portrait even if the subject sits in front of the artist during the drawing.

Figure 9.3

On the left is a sketch done with a 14-year-old boy who, as was a passenger, saw the man on the right drive by and shoot his brother in the head during a road-rage incident.

Part of the credentials of the artist are that numerous sketches done from witnesses have been compared to photos of the proven perpetrators of the crime over the years, and an understanding of what portions are usually similar and what areas are most often drawn incorrectly has been established. Then compare the features, one at a time, and say they are "consistent" with each other if they are similar, say they are almost exactly alike if that is the case, and say they are dissimilar if they are and the reason why that is the case, such as, "the most common portion of the sketch to be incorrectly drawn is the chin, which I tend to make larger than the person being described, and that is the case here… ."

Figure 9.3 shows a sketch next to a man convicted of shooting a motorist to death in a road-rage incident. The witness for the artist (me) was the 14-year-old brother of the victim. He saw the man in Figure 9.3 make a grinning face as he drove by and then shot his brother in the head. The brother subsequently crashed the vehicle and died.

The sketch generated a lead. That lead, combined with a vehicle with a very unusual bumper sticker, led detectives to the shooter and his passenger/brother.[6] The shooter's brother confessed to being at the scene and many items of ancillary evidence established a very strong case. Since the sketch played a role, I was called in to testify.

After I listed on the stand my 17 years' experience as a forensic artist, my Bachelor of Fine Arts degree, with honors, from the University of Texas at Austin, my graduation from the FBI Academy Forensic Artists' Course, membership in, and certification from, the International Association for Identification, more than 2,500 forensic sketches created from witnesses, and the comparison of more than 700 sketches to photos of proven perpetrators of the crime, the judge designated me as an expert witness.

The prosecutor then asked me to describe what I thought was similar between the sketch and the accused. I stated they were both of a handsome, smooth-faced white male whose age appeared to be early 20s. I pointed out that the accused male's eyebrows were nicely shaped, that were any female to tweeze her eyebrows, the shape of the defendant's eyebrows would be a desirable type to imitate. (Almost all the members of the jury were women and I made these remarks while looking often at the members of the jury.) The accused man maintained an animated demeanor, much like the expression in the sketch, and I made a mention of that fact. I pointed out that the portion of the drawing that was most dissimilar was the chin—it was far too large. I stated that was an error made in almost every forensic drawing I had constructed, when compared to the person described. I noted the ears were almost exactly the same shape.

The sketch was not the most similar in the annals of forensic art; however, the jury knew the witness was a 14-year-old brother who saw the accused for only a fraction of a second as the shooter drove past him and his brother. The case did not stand or fall on my testimony alone. In a simple, truthful manner, I guided the jury as to what was usually most similar (the eye area) and what was usually least similar (the chin area), and that the whole of the look (a good-looking dark-headed white male in his early 20s with an animated expression and nicely shaped eyebrows) was the same. A good term to remember is "consistent." Again, it is wise to assert that no portrait is ever perfect.

During the cross examination, always remain very cordial to the defense attorney. If the defense attorney makes a point, admit in an even tone when he or she is right. When the defense attorney asked, "…isn't the hair completely different?" I answered "yes" in an even tone. Always let the defense attorney win whatever battles he or she can. The prosecution can certainly win the war anyway if the case has merits.

There is no need for a forensic artist to be consumed with dread and fear when compelled to testify at trial. First of all, sketches usually are done on cases where the public, and thus the jury and judge, will be solidly behind law enforcement's case.

Figure 9.4

Right: A photo of the accused without a hat. Center: Witness-memory sketch of her attacker. Left: Once the hat portion of the sketch was added to the photo there was a remarkable resemblance. The prosecutor was able to have me designated as an expert witness and to enter the photo with the cut-out hat during trial.

Figure 9.5

The top left is a man accused of murder. The sketch seemed quite dissimilar until I applied the "hat" to the photo. The prosecutor was able to enter the hat-added image in court, thus aiding the jury in convicting the accused and sentencing him to life.

VISUAL AIDS FOR COURT

The artist can sometimes assist the district attorney on the case. Figure 9.4 is an example of an aid I constructed before testifying. The suspect looked quite dissimilar with his knotted hairstyle. However, I noticed if the exact hat cut out of the drawing was placed over the photo of the accused, the resemblance became very close. Once the prosecutor saw this construction, she decided to use it in court. I was designated an expert witness by the judge, and the prosecutor then requested that the court (the judge) allow the construction in Figure 9.4 be introduced. The judge called the prosecutor and defense attorney to his bench and a discussion ensued. The prosecutor needed only to convince the judge that it would be very common for an individual to put a hat on and/or take a hat off and further that this depiction of the hat was the same as in the sketch and thus the same as described by the witness. The judge allowed this visual aid to be allowed in court and a successful prosecution followed.[7]

Figure 9.5 shows another case where an individual seemed somewhat dissimilar to the sketch. Once the hat in the sketch was attached to the photo of the accused there was a good resemblance between the sketch and the accused. Once again the district attorney had the judge designate me as an expert witness. The prosecutor then convinced the judge to allow the paper hat to be placed on the sketch since it would be common practice for individuals to wear hats, and this matched the hat described by the witness for the sketch. The accused was convicted of the senseless murder of an innocent bystander near a drug deal gone sour and given life in prison.[8]

This kind of evidence is straightforward and can be constructed with a color copier or scanner where size of image can be adjusted. Judges can allow this evidence since it is common for individuals to put on and take off hats. I have also made overlays that gave the accused "haircuts" (obscured long hair on the sketch) to match a short-haired accused man's appearance in court.

In Brief

- Maintain forensic sketch files in anticipation of court testimony.
- Dress appropriately for court.
- Familiarize yourself with the standard questions always asked; give concise answers.
- Since the defense attorney is bound by the U.S. Constitution to vigorously defend the perpetrator you have sketched, do not take aggressive cross-examination personally.
- Your remarks, demeanor, and attention should be focused on the members of the court whom you need to convince—the judge and the jury. No defense attorney ever *decided* a case.
- Build up credentials to become designated as an expert witness in court to further aid the prosecutors by being able to give opinions; join the International Association for Identification and get certified.
- Become versed in common faults and strengths of your forensic art images created from witness descriptions.

REFERENCES

1. Dr. Henry Faulds, British Surgeon-Superintendent of Tsukiji Hospital, Tokyo, Japan, 1880.

2. Chicago Public Library, *Brief History of the Chicago Police Department*, 2007.

3. Linda Fairstein, "Rape and Prosecution," *University of Virginia News*, March 16, 2005.

4. Statistics are from personal conversations with Luis Santoyo and Joy Mann in April, 2007.

5. "Arrest may solve series of sex assaults, robberies, police say," Staff, *Houston Chronicle*, August 31, 1989. "Rapist given 99 years," *Houston Chronicle*, April 9, 1991. Houston Police Department Incident Number 76100989.

6. Lisa Teachey, "Man is charged in road rage slaying/Alleged shooter is also in custody," *Houston Chronicle*, October 19, 1999. Allan Turner, "Two brothers indicted in slaying of teen-ager," *Houston Chronicle*, January 12, 2000. Jerry Urban and Lisa Teachey, "Shooting victim's brother testifies," *Houston Chronicle*, January 23, 2001. "Two brothers are found guilty in shooting death of driver," *Houston Chronicle*, January 25, 2001. Harris County Sheriffs Case Number 9908152364.

7. Houston Police Department Incident Number 90682101.

8. Staff, "Slaying suspect sought," *Houston Chronicle*, February 2, 2000. Lisa Teachey, "Man gets life in drug-related killing," *Houston Chronicle*, September 17, 2002. Harris County Sheriffs Case Number 001301940.

INDEX